RECONCEPTUALIZING FACULTY DEVELOPMENT IN SERVICE-LEARNING/COMMUNITY ENGAGEMENT

RECONCEPTUALIZING FACULTY DEVELOPMENT IN SERVICE-LEARNING/ COMMUNITY ENGAGEMENT

Exploring Intersections, Frameworks, and Models of Practice

Edited by

Becca Berkey, Cara Meixner, Patrick M. Green, and Emily A. Eddins

Foreword by L. Dee Fink

STERLING, VIRGINIA

COPYRIGHT © 2018 BY STYLUS
PUBLISHING, LLC.

Published by Stylus Publishing, LLC 22883 Quicksilver Drive
Sterling, Virginia 20166-2019

All rights reserved. No part of this book may be reprinted or reproduced in any form or by any electronic, mechanical, or other means, now known or hereafter invented, including photocopying, recording, and information storage and retrieval, without permission in writing from the publisher.

Library of Congress Cataloging-in-Publication Data
Names: Berkey, Becca, editor.
Title: Reconceptualizing faculty development in service-learning/community engagement : exploring intersections, frameworks, and models of practice / edited by Becca Berkey, Cara Meixner, Patrick M. Green, and Emily A. Eddins.
Description: Sterling, Virginia : Stylus Publishing, 2018. | Includes bibliographical references and index.
Identifiers: LCCN 2017058347 (print) | LCCN 2018013504 (ebook) | ISBN 9781620366141 (uPDF) | ISBN 9781620366158 (mobi, ePub) | ISBN 9781620366127 (cloth : alk. paper) | ISBN 9781620366134 (pbk. : alk. paper) | ISBN 9781620366141 (library networkable e-edition) | ISBN 9781620366158 (consumer e-edition)
Subjects: LCSH: Community and college--United States. | Community and college--United States--Case studies. | Service learning--United States. | Service learning--United States--Case studies. | College teachers--In-service training--United States. | College teachers--In-service training--United States--Case studies.
Classification: LCC LC238 (ebook) | LCC LC238 .R43 2018 (print) | DDC 378.73--dc23
LC record available at https://lccn.loc.gov/2017058347

13-digit ISBN: 978-1-62036-612-7 (cloth)
13-digit ISBN: 978-1-62036-613-4 (paperback)
13-digit ISBN: 978-1-62036-614-1 (library networkable e-edition)
13-digit ISBN: 978-1-62036-615-8 (consumer e-edition)

Printed in the United States of America

All first editions printed on acid-free paper
that meets the American National Standards Institute
Z39-48 Standard.

Bulk Purchases
Quantity discounts are available for use in workshops and for staff development.
Call 1-800-232-0223

First Edition, 2018

I dedicate this volume to those who have mentored and lifted me up through the years—you have no idea where I would be without you. I draw my inspiration from a vibrant village of scholars, activists, and change-makers I am honored to call my friends. Additionally, I am grateful for my team here at Northeastern, including Lisa, Dave, John, and Hilary, for always supporting and encouraging me. Finally, I am deeply grateful for my loving partner, Jonathan, and stepson, Kaiman, for being my rocks and always believing in me, even when I don't believe in myself.

—Becca Berkey

I dedicate this edited volume to Santa Silverio, whom I met and served in 1992 during my first service-learning experience. Her home had been ravished by Hurricane Andrew, yet her spirit remained unvanquished. The enduring love, compassion, and hope she held for the Homestead community inspired me as much at the age of 16 as it continues to do today. Also, I am grateful for the support of colleagues and loved ones, most especially my dear partner, Dan, and our wonderful children, extended family, and friends. Thank you for being.

—Cara Meixner

Dedicated to my father (who passed while writing this book) and my mother, both of whom made up my first teaching and learning community, for the love letter of their relationship that unfolded before our eyes; to my brothers and sisters, Marty, Tim, Kelli, and Amy, all of whom make up a teaching and learning cohort that I will never leave and never want to, for your love and laughter; for my wife, Colleen, and children, Maura, Sean, and Bridget, who teach me love and learning each day—may you know the love with which you have lifted me up many times over!

—Patrick M. Green

Dedicated to the five most influential people on my trajectory to this life of service-learning and community engagement. First, to my father (who also passed while writing this book) who always pushed me to trust my gut in my life pursuits. To my husband and to my mother, who listened to each step through my first steps into this work as well as the making of this book. And finally, to my graduate adviser, Stu, and my supervisor, Nicole, whose individual footprints on my life and work will always be there and have shaped me into the professional and scholar I am today.

—Emily A. Eddins

CONTENTS

ABBREVIATIONS ... ix

CASE STUDIES ... xiii

FOREWORD ... xvii
L. Dee Fink

PREFACE ... xxiii
Emily A. Eddins and Patrick M. Green

EXPLORING THE BORDERLANDS THROUGH
COLLABORATIVE INQUIRY ... 1
A Narrative Introduction
Patrick M. Green, Emily A. Eddins, Becca Berkey, and Cara Meixner

PART ONE: THE LANDSCAPE OF FACULTY DEVELOPMENT AND COMMUNITY ENGAGEMENT

1 A HOLISTIC FRAMEWORK FOR EDUCATIONAL PROFESSIONAL DEVELOPMENT IN COMMUNITY ENGAGEMENT ... 27
Marshall Welch and Star Plaxton-Moore

2 FACULTY AS COLEARNERS ... 59
Collaborative Engagement and the Power of Story in Faculty Development
Timothy K. Eatman

PART TWO: MODELS OF FACULTY DEVELOPMENT IN SERVICE-LEARNING/COMMUNITY ENGAGEMENT

3 MODELS AND GENRES OF FACULTY DEVELOPMENT ... 85
Emily O. Gravett and Andreas Broscheid

4 SUPPORTING PROFESSIONAL DEVELOPMENT FOR COMMUNITY ENGAGEMENT ... 107
Three Institutional Case Studies
Amy Spring
Case studies contributed by *Caile Spear, Kara Brascia, Mike Stefancic, Anna Bailey, Kristin English, Julia Metzker, Chavonda Mills, Sandra Godwin, Sherril B. Gelmon, Kevin Kecskes, Devorah Lieberman, and Leslie McBride*

5   LEARNING COMMUNITIES AS A CREATIVE CATALYST
    FOR PROFESSIONAL DEVELOPMENT AND INSTITUTIONAL
    CHANGE   137
    Star Plaxton-Moore, Julie Hatcher, Mary Price,
    Carey Borkoski, Vanya Jones, and Mindi Levin

6   MISSION-DRIVEN, LOW-COST CREATIVE PRACTICES   159
    Ann E. Green, Ann Marie Jursca Keffer, Kim Jensen Bohat,
    Melody Bowdon, and Amy Zeh

7   DYNAMICS ON THE EDGE   179
    Exploring Roles and Intersections of Service-Learning and Community
    Engagement and Educational Development
    Cara Meixner, Becca Berkey, and Patrick M. Green

PART THREE: CHALLENGES AND OPPORTUNITIES IN PEDAGOGY AND PARTNERSHIPS

8   SPECIAL PEDAGOGICAL CONSIDERATIONS   203
    Designing Learning in Service-Learning and Community Engagement
    Chirag Variawa

9   THE INTERSECTION OF INSTITUTIONAL CONTEXTS AND
    FACULTY DEVELOPMENT IN SERVICE-LEARNING AND
    COMMUNITY ENGAGEMENT   221
    Stephanie T. Stokamer

10 RECIPROCITY AND PARTNERSHIP   241
    How Do We Know It Is Working?
    Gabriel Ignacio Barreneche, Micki Meyer, and Scott Gross

PART FOUR: ENGENDERING CHANGE IN EDUCATIONAL DEVELOPMENT

11 CONNECTING SERVICE-LEARNING AND COMMUNITY
    ENGAGEMENT FACULTY DEVELOPMENT TO
    COMMUNITY-ENGAGED SCHOLARSHIP   265
    Sherril B. Gelmon and Catherine M. Jordan

12 INNOVATIVE CONSIDERATIONS IN FACULTY DEVELOPMENT
    AND SERVICE-LEARNING AND COMMUNITY ENGAGEMENT   283
    New Perspectives for the Future
    Richard Kiely and Kathleen Sexsmith

    EDITORS AND CONTRIBUTORS   315

    INDEX   327

ABBREVIATIONS

AAC&U	Association of American Colleges & Universities
ADDIE	analyze, design, develop, implement, and evaluate
ARCS Model	attention, relevance, confidence, and satisfaction model
CAS	College of Arts and Sciences at Pacific University
C-bEL	community-based engaged learning
CBL	community-based learning
CBR	community-based research
CCE	Center for Civic Engagement at Pacific University
CCPH	Community Campus Partnerships for Health
CCREC	Center for Collaborative Research for an Equitable California
CE	civic engagement
CEL	community-engaged learning
CEP	community engagement professional
CES	community-engaged scholarship
CES4Health	Community-Engaged Scholarship for Health
CoP	community of practice
CP	community partner
CSL	Center for Service and Learning at Indiana University–Purdue University Indianapolis
CSUSM	California State University San Marcos
CTE	Center for Teaching Excellence at University of San Francisco
ED	educational development
ERIC database	Education Resources Information Center database
ESC	Engagement Scholarship Consortium
ESP (ESP-I and ESP-II)	Engineering Strategies and Practice course at University of Toronto
FEC	Faculty for the Engaged Campus initiative
FLC	faculty learning community
FLO	faculty learning outcomes
FTL	fair trade learning
GA	graduate assistant

GSL	global service-learning
HLLC	Honors Living-Learning Community at Rutgers University-Newark
IA	Imagining America
IARSLCE	International Association for Research on Service-Learning and Community Engagement
KSAB	knowledge, skills, attitudes, behaviors
MERLOT	Multimedia Educational Resource for Learning and Online Teaching
NERCHE	New England Resource Center for Higher Education
OAI	Office of Academic Innovation at Portland State University
P&T	promotion and tenure
P3	A collaboratory for pedagogy, professional development, and publicly engaged scholarship at Rutgers University-Newark
PAEI	Philosophy of Adult Education Inventory
PES	publicly engaged scholarship
POD Network	Professional Organizational Development Network
PQACE	Principles of Quality Academic Civic Engagement at Pacific University
PS	public scholarship
QEP	quality enhancement plan
RFP	request for proposal
SCoP	SOURCE Community of Practice at Johns Hopkins University
S-L and/or SL	service-learning
S-LCE	service-learning and community engagement
SL/CE	service-learning/community engagement
SLP	Service-Learning Program at Marquette University
SoE	Scholarship of Engagement
SOFAR Model	students, organizations, faculty, administrators, and residents model
SoTL	scholarship of teaching and learning
SOURCE	Student Outreach Resource Center at Johns Hopkins University
TA	teaching assistant
UCF	University of Central Florida

UID	universal instructional design
USF	University of San Francisco
VALUE	Valid Assessment of Learning in Undergraduate Education
ZPD	zone of proximal development

CASE STUDIES

Chapter Theme	Institution	Key Takeaways	Transferable Tools and Ideas
Chapter 4: Supporting Professional Development for Community Engagement: Three Institutional Case Studies	Boise State University	Each of the institutions featured in this case study chapter have been engaged in service-learning and community engagement (S-LCE) work for 15 to 20+ years. In the chapter, contributors from each of the institutions explicate the different phases of their programmatic development through "Early," "Midway," and "Advanced" stages, showcasing the program elements regarding faculty development involved and the resources necessary at each stage.	Boise State's case study details how they work with faculty to track them into the most appropriate professional/educational development support opportunities. The information they provide includes the following: • Entry Pathways for New S-L Faculty (Table 4.2) • Faculty Development by Phase (Table 4.3)
	Georgia College & State University (GCSU)		In this case study, GCSU describes the process of making community-based engaged learning (C-bEL) a central component to the undergraduate student experience and the faculty support infrastructure needed for moving that forward in a way that meets community goals, including: • Assessment Toolbox (Figure 4.1) • ENGAGE Learning Outcomes (Figure 4.2)
	Portland State University (PSU)		PSU describes its rich history of development of S-LCE initiatives over time and how faculty development has been central to those efforts. They describe the infrastructure necessary to support this work at a large scale, including: • Center for Academic Excellence Organizational Chart (Figure 4.3)

(Continues)

with the idea of rich learning experiences, a concept that emerged when I wrote my book *Creating Significant Learning Experiences* (Fink, 2003).

A rich learning experience is a single learning activity or experience that is rich because it drives multiple kinds of learning all at the same time, and it does this best when it is different in an important way from much of the learners' previous life experiences. There are several kinds of activities that can provide this new and different experience for students, such as role-playing, simulations, or debates where students are often forced to take a role opposite from their natural inclination or familiarity. But putting students in an authentic social situation, where they work with and contribute to an organization or group of people, many of whom may be different from them, takes the power of a rich learning experience to a whole new level. And this is exactly what having SL/CE experiences in a course does so well.

However, rich learning experiences have one potentially important limitation. Because many kinds of learning are happening simultaneously, learners are often only subconsciously aware that something important has occurred in their knowledge, beliefs, values, or perspectives on life. Hence, they need some way to bring this subconscious awareness up to the conscious level. Learners should periodically step back from the learning experience itself and reflect on what they have learned and how they have learned it.

The contributors mention several times how the professors in their programs engage in this kind of reflection. In chapter 2, "Faculty as Colearners: Collaborative Engagement and the Power of Story in Faculty Development," the contributor notes the "power of story" and the value of allowing previously undisclosed stories to emerge. Reflection is a practice that would support this. The description of the program at Marquette University in chapter 6 mentions the role that faculty learning communities and reflection play in that program. And the chapter 10 contributors state that faculty should reflect on their agency regarding the privilege and power in their roles.

Since this book is about faculty development, the contributors have an obvious reason to mention that they have faculty reflecting on their learning experiences. But the same is also true at the next level in the process. It is important for these professors to have their students reflect on their experiences with SL/CE. Students, like their professors, need some way to bring their subconscious awareness of what they have learned up to the conscious level. Only then will they be fully aware of what they have learned from the special experience they had and be able to ascertain the significance of that learning. This reflection is usually done initially in writing but may be

Chapter Theme	Institution	Key Takeaways	Transferable Tools and Ideas
Chapter 5: Learning Communities as a Creative Catalyst for Professional Development and Institutional Change	University of San Francisco (USF)	At the three institutions featured in this chapter, contributors explore ways of utilizing faculty learning communities (FLCs) not only as a professional development program for S-LCE engaged faculty but also as groups that can influence broader institutional culture and policies related to community engagement. The contributors offer their lessons learned and recommendations for effectively implementing and understanding outcomes of learning communities for both participants and institutions, including a detailed outline of challenges and strengths of each institutional approach (Table 5.2).	USF's Faculty Learning Community on Community-Engaged Learning (FLC-CEL) is discussed in the context of the following goals: • Engage faculty with current critical scholarship in the community engagement field and inform their individual purpose and practice • Develop a cross-disciplinary learning community to support each other and departmental peers to engage in reflective and innovative community-engaged teaching
	Indiana University–Purdue University Indianapolis (IUPUI)		In this case study, IUPUI's Faculty Learning Community on Public Scholarship (FLC-PS) is discussed in the context of the following goals: • Define *public scholarship* in the context of campus-level promotion and tenure (P&T) guidelines, and identify criteria to assist faculty in documenting and evaluating public scholarship • Provide resources to deans and department chairs for adapting these criteria into school-level P&T materials and guidelines
	Johns Hopkins University		The Student Outreach Resource Center at Johns Hopkins University (SOURCE) Online Community of Practice Fellows Program (SoCP) at Johns Hopkins is discussed in the context of the following goals: • Build an online network of faculty and community leaders • Share resources and offer course development support • Leverage the knowledge, experience, and skills of the SL Fellows cohorts

(Continues)

Chapter Theme	Institution	Key Takeaways	Transferable Tools and Ideas
Chapter 6: Mission Driven, Low-Cost Creative Practices	Saint Joseph's University (SJU)	These three case studies present innovative approaches to faculty development for service-learning and community engagement (S-LCE). Creative practices use original ideas in mission-driven contexts and adapt limited resources in innovative ways. While the schools range from a medium-sized, comprehensive university to a large, research institution, the approaches to faculty development at all three institutions have arisen organically from their particular contexts. Each uses evidence-based practices to encourage the pedagogical development of their faculty and enhance overall teaching quality. While each program has developed to reflect local circumstances (e.g., institutional mission), the practices described can be adapted with limited resources.	SJU's case study features a one-to-one faculty mentor program where those experienced with S-LCE are paired with a new faculty member. In this reciprocal relationship, among other commitments these faculty pairs are asked to do the following: • Coordinate and debrief a class visit for a new service-learning faculty member to witness service-learning pedagogy in action • Perform routine in-person visits, e-mail communication, and a review of the syllabus as mutually agreed upon • Visit new faculty member's classroom during her or his first semester of teaching, offering constructive and developmental feedback
	Marquette University		Marquette's contributors detail three successful approaches to faculty development: • FLC on integrated course design (see Table 6.1 for an outline of learning outcomes and Table 6.2 for a rubric used to do peer assessment of S-L syllabi). • Online modules designed to assist with the incorporation of meaningful reflection into S-LCE courses (see Figure 6.1) • Partnership with the Teaching & Learning Center.
	University of Central Florida (UCF)		This case details the service-learning track of UCF's annual Summer Faculty Development Conference, including the following considerations: • Faculty-driven and led programming • Compensation for faculty members' time • Competitive application process • Connections to scholarship of teaching and learning initiatives • Sustainability as promoted through connections with university initiatives and values

FOREWORD

One of the few benefits of being a senior citizen is that one has "historical perspective." As someone who has worked in faculty development for over four decades now, it is clear to me that this book offers a new approach to faculty development.

For the past several decades, faculty developers in North America have focused on helping professors incorporate specific ideas into their teaching in order to increase the impact of their teaching or meet specific challenges. Hence, we offered workshops or individual consultations on pedagogical ideas such as active learning, learning-centered course design, small groups, and educative assessment, as well as on how to teach large classes, incorporate instructional technology, or deal with a class of diverse students. And we have done this with professors from all disciplines.

The approach taken by the contributors in this book is different. They work with teachers on putting together courses with a particular kind of course experience for students, that of service-learning/community engagement (SL/CE). Their argument is that working on this task for an extended period presses teachers to step back from their traditional habits and perspectives on teaching and learning, and rethink macro-issues such as the following:

- What is the purpose of this course (or any course)? Is it primarily to disseminate disciplinary knowledge? Or to create the kind of learning that will add value to students' lives after college?
- What is my identity as a teacher? Am I primarily a subject matter expert? Or am I a designer of valuable learning experiences?
- Who is or should be involved in this course? Is it only me and the students? Or do I also need to recognize the value of involving representatives of community organizations, campus coordinators of community engagement, people from student affairs, and so on?

In my view, the contributors have made a convincing argument that something special can happen when you focus a teacher's attention on getting students involved in SL/CE. This connects in a straightforward way followed by dialogue with other students. Both concurrent and concluding reflections can be valuable.

Teachers can use concurrent reflections by having students keep a journal about their experiences while they are engaged in SL/CE. Here they record or discuss such questions as the following: What did you do or observe? What were your reactions to those experiences; for example, how did it make you feel, what new insights did it prompt about people, different cultures, the behavior of organizational leaders and followers?

After the SL/CE experience has ended, students can do a concluding reflection, perhaps in the form of a learning portfolio (i.e., an extended essay, based on insights achieved from doing the concurrent writing). Learning portfolios can be structured around any set of questions the teacher prefers; I have enjoyed the results when reading student comments on the following questions:

- WHAT Did You Learn from your community engagement experience?

In SL/CE courses, one might ask: What did you learn about . . .
  - Knowledge from Previous Courses: The meaning of the conceptual or theoretical ideas encountered in your previous courses?
  - Yourself: What values, beliefs, capabilities, or life aspirations did you become more conscious of, or want to change?
  - Others: What were the values and beliefs that prompt the variety of behaviors in other people you encountered?
  - Organizations: What makes them effective or ineffective?
  - Society at large: What does society need from individuals as well as from private and public-sector organizations, to be a good and strong society?
- HOW did you learn all this?
  - What experiences were especially powerful for you in terms of prompting the previously mentioned kinds of learning, such as observations of people and events, conversations with individuals or groups, doing things yourself, and so on?
- WHAT VALUE might all of this have for you in the future?
  - How might the kinds of learning you described have an impact on your life in the future, such as on . . .

  a. Your personal life?
  b. Your social interactions with other individuals or groups?
  c. The level and kind of civic involvement and engagement you may choose to have?

d. Your professional life?
- WHAT ELSE has this experience made you want to learn or do?
  - Given these recent experiences, what else do you want to learn about or do later in life?
  - How would you learn about or be able to do that?

One other practice mentioned in chapter 4 caught my attention. Two of the programs describe created levels of faculty accomplishment based on learning about teaching. The program at Boise State University identifies four levels of faculty development: entry phase, practice phase, advanced phase, and mentoring phase. The program at Georgia College & State University also identifies four levels: apprentice, journeyman, master, and fellow. In both programs, the fourth level refers to professors who develop to the point of being able to mentor teachers just beginning to learn how to use SL/CE practices in their courses. One of the things that faculty development programs have long needed, in my view, is a career-encompassing structure that recognizes increased accomplishment based on teaching capabilities, and that parallels the structure that has long been in place for research accomplishments (i.e., the assistant professor, associate professor, and full professor sequence that is widely used in higher education). These two programs have set up a structure that, to a good degree, does that.

In conclusion, I simply want to lay out my own awareness of the benefits of helping professors create learning experiences that effectively incorporate SL/CE. Participating students are the obvious direct beneficiary as they will have a more significant learning experience, one that is broader, deeper, and more life-enriching than they could ever get in a traditional lecture-based, knowledge-focused course. But professors also benefit. They get to see students learning the value of their discipline and/or a particular kind of knowledge, and, through reading the reflections, get to see how that learning is enriching students' lives—at the moment and potentially in the future. (Speaking again as someone who has "been around the block" a few times, this is not currently the norm in higher education.)

In addition to benefiting individuals like the teachers and students, these educational changes can also impact institutions and society. The particular college or university where a strong effort is made to implement SL/CE can benefit both internally and externally. When a sufficient number of professors buy into these ideas, it can lead to a cultural change affecting the way faculty think about such things as the curriculum, the kind of teaching and learning the institution does and should value, promotion and tenure, and so on. And when a critical mass of teachers learn how to use SL/CE experiences effectively in their courses, the institution will gain a reputation within the community and with prospective students that "this is a college or university where something special happens in their educational program"!

And finally, society at large becomes stronger in so many ways when there are more people taking responsible positions in social institutions, people who have the social, professional, civic, and individual life skills that are being generated by the programs described in this book.

However, for any of these wonderful things to happen, faculty members need to learn about the educational value of SL/CE and how to put together an effective set of learning experiences for students. This means faculty developers and service-learning professionals need to learn how to put together an effective program. The chapters in this book offer invaluable guidance on how to do this.

Let's hope that the ideas and suggestions offered by the contributors gain wide circulation and use in our colleges and universities. It would be wonderful to see these many, possible benefits come to widespread fruition!

L. Dee Fink
University of Oklahoma (Retired)
Norman, Oklahoma
June 2018

Reference

Fink, L. D. (2003). *Creating Significant Learning Experiences: An Integrated Approach to Designing College Courses*. San Francisco, CA: Jossey-Bass.

PREFACE

Emily A. Eddins and Patrick M. Green

The fields of service-learning and community engagement (S-LCE) and educational development have become increasingly professionalized in higher education in the past few decades. As these fields have developed, the roles of professionals serving in these areas often intersect with common goals toward learning and teaching. To this point, the role of educational development to foster the pedagogy, instructional design, and curriculum development of S-LCE is multidimensional. Professionals who work in these spaces between S-LCE and educational development have to be attentive to the design of learning, given the potentially transformative nature of S-LCE experiences and courses, for students, faculty, and our communities. Such design requires an emphasis on student learning, an equal focus on faculty preparation and pedagogical training, and a distinct responsibility to the communities and organizations served by these initiatives. In essence, the professionals serve in hybrid roles, as practitioners and scholars, as educators and trainers, as faculty and administrators; they are often positioned in the *in-between spaces*. How do professionals foster such design of faculty educational development that prioritizes student learning, faculty pedagogical training, and community priorities within the complexity of S-LCE? This is the exploratory question at the heart of this text, calling for a reconceptualization of faculty development in S-LCE.

This edited volume aims to provide educational developers and S-LCE practitioner-scholars an analysis of approaches to faculty development around S-LCE. Because this volume is built on a collaborative ethnographic approach, there are numerous chapter and case study contributors who added to the content and discussion of the intersection of S-LCE and faculty development. Using an openly self-reflective approach, the contributors to this volume offer an array of frameworks and models, as well as realistic strategies, to empower readers to build on and enhance their faculty development efforts in S-LCE on their respective campuses. Because the contributors integrate the language and terminology that best fit their particular campus and community contexts, structures, and cultures, there is some variation throughout the book.

As editors of this volume, we provided limited guidance about terminology we prefer to use in our own work, while urging our contributors to use their own words and frameworks that best fit their own institutions, contexts, and everyday professional lives. For example, a faith-based institution may use the language of social justice related to S-LCE whereas a state institution may leverage the term *civic engagement*. Terms like *community-engaged learning, civic engagement, civic scholarship,* and others are woven throughout the text and bring to light the varying application of each in our scholarship and practice. We recognize variance in defining each chosen term in both scholarly literature and in practice, and we strive to have similarly woven concepts and terms throughout the text while allowing for the variation of terms, frameworks, and language that populate our respective professional fields and work. Numerous references and citations drawing from the scholarly literature provide definitions and context within each chapter. In fact, allowing our contributors to frame their discussions with their own terminology also allows this edited volume to demonstrate the breadth of how we speak about and employ these terms in our work. Amid the varied contexts, an overview of terms can help the reader as a general guide to nomenclature in this edited volume.

S-LCE professional is the most prevalent name for practitioners used throughout the text, although other terms drawn from the scholarly literature, for example, include *community engagement professional* (CEP) and *S-LCE scholar-practitioner*. The S-LCE professional role, a multifaceted position whose primary responsibility includes fostering and facilitating S-LCE on campus, is explored thoroughly in this volume.

Similarly, throughout the text, more often than not the term *faculty development* is used much more frequently than *educational development*; however, the term *educational development* has become the more accepted terminology within the Professional Organizational Development (POD) Network of scholars who specialize in this field. In fact, we chose to keep the term *faculty development* in the title of this book, as *educational development* has not yet thoroughly seeped into the S-LCE academic vernacular and might be overlooked. As this text offers scholarly approaches exploring the intersections of S-LCE and faculty development, models and frameworks provided address the evolution toward educational development in S-LCE.

The community partners, stakeholders, organizations, and external constituencies with whom we work are also approached with varying language and framed differently depending on context. For example, one contributing author, a faculty member in engineering, refers fluidly to the external constituents with whom his students work as *client, community partner*, and *stakeholder*. An entire body of work has emerged surrounding *community partnership*, and we recognize that this term is used with great variation in practice. In this volume, *community partners* consist of the external community representatives with which faculty and students are working on behalf of the S-LCE efforts at an institution of higher education.

This edited volume not only provides models and frameworks through case studies and chapter explorations but also establishes an ongoing call to action. It is clear that the practice of S-LCE requires the practice of educational development, and this symbiotic relationship is not only explored but also connected, intersected, negotiated, and liberated. The book further addresses the intersection of S-LCE and educational development, focusing its potential contributions to not only practice but also scholarship, such as the *scholarship of teaching and learning* (SoTL), *publicly engaged scholarship* (PES), and *collaborative inquiry*, among others. These terms are scattered throughout the text and defined in context by the contributors with multiple citations and references.

The overall edited volume is structured with four themes emerging into the sections of the text: the landscape of faculty development and community engagement, models of faculty development in S-LCE, challenges and opportunities in pedagogy and partnerships, and change in educational development. To frame the collaborative construction of this volume and position the reflexive approach of the coediting team, we authored the introduction as our narrative invitation to you, the reader, to reflect on your own experiences, values, and identity within the context of your own professional narrative. As a coediting team, we reflected, read, collaboratively wrote, and dialogued throughout the process of compiling and writing this volume. The introduction reveals in narrative form our collaborative, reflexive journey, exploring our professional identities and detailing the methodological approach to constructing this edited volume. We invite you to take a similar journey through your own reflection, both in reading the chapter and writing your thoughts in response to our critical reflection questions posed throughout the introduction.

The exploration continues in part one with an expedition through the landscape of faculty development and community engagement in chapters 1 and 2, in which the reader will begin to explore different scholarly approaches to various faculty development frameworks. Chapter 1 interrogates the background and essential resources for S-LCE practitioner-scholars to provide and coordinate effective and quality educational development for faculty, students, and community partners. Chapter 2 advances this line of questioning by engaging in a discussion of the frameworks of collaborative engagement and publicly engaged scholarship as essential scaffolding for our work in scholarly, practice-based community endeavors.

Part two leads explores various approaches to the implementation of faculty development in the context of S-LCE. Chapter 3 introduces models of faculty development in S-LCE and discusses the opportunities and challenges of each, particularly considering varying contexts, stages of program development, staffing, resource availability, institutional culture, and other important considerations. In chapters 4, 5, and 6, the reader will review nine case studies of S-LCE and faculty development programs from varied institutional contexts to see how such programs are implemented and understand the lessons learned. The case studies provide an outline of program models and promising practices, including an authentic analysis of the institutional context within which they operate, the positionality of the practitioner-scholars overseeing them, the resources required, and the evidence related to both the successes and challenges of these approaches.

Chapter 4 details integrative, tiered faculty development programs at Boise State University, Georgia State College and University, and Portland State University through institutional contexts, structures, and frameworks. Chapter 5 dives into faculty learning community (FLC) models implemented at the University of San Francisco, Indiana University–Purdue University Indianapolis, and Johns Hopkins University, and the different approaches, structures, and lessons learned from implementing FLCs at these respective institutions. Chapter 6 discusses three cases of creative faculty mentoring programs, including the benefits and program structures of mission-driven, low-cost faculty development initiatives at Saint Joseph's University, Marquette University, and the University of Central Florida. For each case study chapter, we aimed to include universities of varying sizes, geographic locations, institutional structures and missions, and other factors to provide a wide range of approaches, perspectives, and initiatives at each institution. A more in-depth discussion of our processes in crafting the structure of the case studies and other chapters can be found in the Introduction. Closing out part two, chapter 7 further explores the evolution of the educational development field at the intersection of S-LCE and applications in their own institutional contexts, urging the necessity of deeper collaboration between these two fields.

Part three presents the challenges and opportunities in pedagogy and partnerships at the intersection of educational development and S-LCE. In chapter 8, special pedagogical considerations around designing learning environments are explored from the unique perspective of a faculty member implementing service-learning projects in a high-enrollment engineering course, along with the author's reflections on implementing varying instructional development approaches. Chapter 9 then discusses the impact of institutional contexts, structures, values, and missions on decision making in S-LCE for faculty development initiatives. Chapter 10 looks at community partnership through the lens of reciprocity and the metaphorical dance of partnerships, especially through facilitating S-LCE among faculty, community members, and students.

Part four draws the reader toward a call to action, expressing the need for engendering change in educational development and S-LCE. Chapter 11 draws the links among S-LCE, faculty development, and community-engaged scholarship, inviting readers to engage in scholarly efforts, linking theory to practice and enhancing our field in praxis. Part of the intersection examined throughout this volume indicates unexplored territory, a rich opportunity for scholarship and research. Finally, chapter 12 presents a theory of change by proposing an integrative approach to educational development and S-LCE as we envision the future of higher education, introducing innovative considerations to craft our intersected fields through practice and scholarship.

Given the reflexive and collaborative construction of this edited volume, the overall text serves as an invitation for the reader to reconceptualize our work in educational development and S-LCE. The multidimensional nature of our positions are rooted in the complexity of our work. Our professional identities have blurred boundaries and unnamed spaces—which is also the professional location in which we reside. As we reflected on the intersections of faculty development and S-LCE, we kept returning to a key question: are we at an intersection or are we paving new pathways—creating new spaces? The pages that follow invite you, as the reader, to engage this question, exploring the intersections, frameworks, and models delineated throughout these chapters. Ultimately, through the journey of this edited volume, we invite you to explore with us and to identify the landscape or intersection at which you stand—to name the spaces in which you work.

EXPLORING THE BORDERLANDS THROUGH COLLABORATIVE INQUIRY

A Narrative Introduction

Patrick M. Green, Emily A. Eddins, Becca Berkey, and Cara Meixner

Exploring the intersection of faculty development and service-learning and community engagement (S-LCE) is how this edited volume began for our team of four coeditors. From the ongoing pedagogical workshops we provide faculty colleagues to the book groups, cohort programs, and faculty learning communities (FLCs) we coordinate, intriguing interconnections between the two fields have become more and more evident. Faculty development, also known or referred to as educational development, has evolved into a core function of the work of S-LCE professionals. Moreover, educational developers within university centers for teaching and learning often find themselves working with faculty interested in incorporating S-LCE into their work.

As a coediting team of S-LCE practitioner-scholars, faculty, and educational developers, we found ourselves mulling over the following poignant questions, among others: Is the intersection of faculty development and S-LCE nascent, or is it established? Are we seeking to connect these two fields more intentionally, or have we encountered the need to pave new pathways? In contemplation of these questions, we began the process of conceptualizing this edited volume, simultaneously positioning ourselves relative to the book's content, approach, and audience.

This narrative introduction may read unlike those governing edited volumes with which you, as the reader, are familiar. As one might anticipate, we will glance cursorily at the arc of the book, peering into the focus and intent of its subsections and chapters. More integrally, however, we wish to make transparent the very processes, biases, positions, and methods used to frame the volume. By doing so, we pull back the metaphorical curtain, making visible what might otherwise be obscured at the intersection of faculty development and S-LCE. Thus, this narrative introduction reveals the reflexive methodological processes framing the book, with considerable effort given to explicating our positions relative to the content. Therein, we identify themes inherent in our own experiences as educators, inviting the reader to engage in the same reflexive process. From there, we describe the nuanced procedures used to identify chapter contributors, concluding with an overview of the edited volume's arc and contents.

Navigating Intersections, Exploring Borderlands

We are educators facilitating community engagement and faculty development, among many other courses and initiatives, in varied higher education settings. Within this work, some pathways are clearly paved whereas others are disconnected or unchartered. Regardless, what is inherent to each of our positions in academe is the core work of *facilitating connections*—we link faculty to teaching and learning strategies and community partners, we connect students to community engagement opportunities, and we facilitate partnerships between the university and its multiple communities. In many ways, we reside at the intersection of S-LCE and faculty development in order *to* connect.

Indeed, serving in professional roles in higher education with multiple responsibilities, audiences, and functions initially brought us to approaching the milieux of S-LCE and faculty development as intersectional. Yet the metaphor of *intersection* is not fully apt in describing the connection between these fields.

As we critically interrogated our work in S-LCE and faculty development, we found the construct of *borderland* more edifying. We built on the feminist philosopher and cultural theorist Gloria Anzaldúa's (1987) conception of "borderland." In her landmark book *Borderlands/La Frontera: New Mestiza*, she describes the Mexican-American woman's (Mestiza) experience of crossing cultural borders and crafts the image of crossing borders and borderlands. Anzaldúa (1987) explains, "A borderland is a vague and undetermined place created by the emotional residue of an unnatural boundary. It is in a constant state of transition" (p. 3). Tyler (2009) builds on Anzaldua's conception of borderland, explaining that it

> both creates and is created by space and consciousness, culture and people, history, the present, and the future, by fact and folklore, tradition, and experimentation. . . . The borderlands span the boundary and include it, blurring it until there is no this side and that side. (p. 528)

From this idea of borderlands, we colocated a foundational concept that reflects our multidimensional personal and professional identities in this work.

This concept of borderlands connects to Whitchurch's (2013) framing of third spaces and third-space professionals. Whitchurch describes third-space professionals as individuals who hold both academic and professional credentials and exist in a paradoxical, ambiguous, and uncertain space in contemporary education. As educators and learners engaged through our roles in S-LCE and faculty development, we find ourselves at the edges where S-LCE and faculty development touch: curricular and cocurricular, faculty and administrator, theory-driven and practice-based, program manager and program facilitator, each of these roles contributing to our identities as practitioner-scholar and scholar-practitioner. Inhabiting multiple roles at once, we find ourselves navigating the borderlands of learning spaces in and out of the classroom—and the borderlands of our own identities, personal and professional. We find ourselves existing in third spaces as third-space professionals.

As has been noted (Stryker & Burke, 2000), "the greater the number of related identities, the greater the difficulty of dealing simultaneously with relationships among them" (p. 292). Through this chapter's reflection and dialogue—anchored by exploration of our identities, values, and passions—we aim to empower you, and all readers of this text, to reflect and explore your own identities, values, and passions as you read this volume. By sharing our inquiry and methodology, we invite you to practice this reflexive approach, situating yourself in relation to the model and themes developed here. Specifically, we call you to explore and engage through the Reader Reflections featured in this introduction. These are the very questions we asked ourselves and worked through with one another as we embarked on this project and throughout its compilation. In addition, our answers to these questions evolved, and continue to evolve, through the very learning taking place throughout the process; we hope they will for you as well.

Reader Reflections
- Who are you as an educator? What roles do you occupy and how do those roles intersect with one another and with your own identities (e.g., sociocultural, educational)?
- What do you do in S-LCE and educational development spaces, what do you know about these fields, and how does that inform how you approach your work? Where are there gaps in knowledge, understanding, synthesis, and application?

- How are you reflected in the narratives and positions showcased in this book?
- How is your work reflected in the frameworks, case studies, and theories that emerge in this book?
- Which of your borderlands still need to be identified, named, and explored?

Methodological Approaches

To understand the metaphor of *borderlands* is to interrogate the rich tapestry of our own life experiences. Such examination requires a methodological process. We approached this process through a variety of qualitative forms of inquiry, including emergent design (Creswell, 2012), collaborative inquiry (Donohoo, 2013), scholarly personal narrative (Nash, 2004), and transpersonal and heuristic research (Rendón, 2009). Qualitative inquiry focuses on understanding, making meaning of, and explaining social phenomena. This multifaceted approach to inquiry serves as an opportunity to exercise the methodological and reflective practices woven throughout the professions represented in this volume, the rhetoric of the fields, and shared efforts to cocreate knowledge.

Scholarly Personal Narrative, Collaborative Inquiry, and Collaborative Ethnography

Under the auspices of scholarly personal narrative, collaborative inquiry (Donohoo, 2013), and collaborative ethnography (Lassiter, 2005), the coediting team interwove various methodological approaches to make meaning of our distinct and shared positionalities. A narrative is a representation of an individual story, from a particular voice or perspective, and "involves the reconstruction of a person's experience in relationship both to the other and to a social milieu" (Clandinin & Connelly, 2000, p. 5). We began by writing our individual narratives, reflecting on questions similar to the ones we have invited you to ponder. To do so, we utilized scholarly personal narrative (Nash, 2004) as a general framework, relying heavily on the inquiry approach of Rendón's (2014) *Sentipensante (Sensing/Thinking) Pedagogy*. This inquiry approach, which deepens the narrative process and mirrors the pedagogical and epistemological context of our work, highlights transpersonal research, a methodological approach that positions each of us as coresearcher and partner in the process. Rendón explains in transpersonal research how we serve "as partners and co-researchers who turned to one another in truth while we attempt to open the interhuman nature of the experience" (pp. 52–53).

We shared our personal narratives with each other and began to individually identify themes and questions from reading each other's works. Such inquiry evolved into collaborative ethnography, wherein we together studied our shared narratives as artifacts of human culture. Lassiter (2005) explains:

> We might sum up collaborative ethnography as an approach to ethnography that *deliberately* and *explicitly* emphasizes collaboration at every point in the ethnographic process, without veiling it—from project conceptualization, to fieldwork, and, especially, through the writing process. Collaborative ethnography invites commentary from our consultants and seeks to make that commentary overtly part of the ethnographic text as it develops. In turn, this negotiation is reintegrated back into the fieldwork process itself. Importantly, the process yields texts that are co-conceived or cowritten with local communities of collaborators and consider multiple audiences outside the confines of academic discourse, including local constituencies. These texts can—and often do—include multiple authors; but not exclusively so. Collaborative ethnography, then, is both a theoretical and a methodological approach for doing *and* writing ethnography. (p. 15)

The iterative process of cocreation and coauthorship is inherent in the shared narratives detailed later in this chapter. This edited volume rests on the collaborative ethnography design process, as we both coconceived the volume structure and cowrote chapters while working with multiple contributors throughout the text.

Emergent Design: Constructing the Book

Engaging in a literature review of published work in the two distinct fields of S-LCE and educational development, we explored the intersections of the two areas, intentionally attempting to bridge them. Through multiple courses of deliberative dialogue among the coeditor team, we established the explicit purpose of this edited volume. The construction of the book followed the iterative, emergent process generated by the coediting team described in this section.

This edited volume aims to provide scholar-practitioners and S-LCE professionals with an analysis of approaches to faculty development at the intersection of the two fields of educational development and S-LCE. Within these contexts, we decided contributions to the book would include the following:

- An overview of faculty development approaches along with theoretical frameworks to support educational development in the area of S-LCE

- Case studies that provide an outline of program models and promising practices, including an authentic analysis of the institutional context within which they operate, the positionality of the practitioner-scholars overseeing them, the resources required, and the evidence related to both successes and challenges of these approaches
- Potential contributions to scholarship, such as the scholarship of teaching and learning (SoTL) and to institutional change that innovative approaches may produce

Given the emergent design process that ensued, coupled with the goals previously identified, this edited volume's structure is organized in four parts with guidance for the reader written by the editors.

- Part One: The Landscape of Faculty Development and Community Engagement
- Part Two: Models of Faculty Development in Service-Learning/Community Engagement
- Part Three: Challenges and Opportunities in Pedagogy and Partnerships
- Part Four: Engendering Change in Educational Development

The intended audience for this volume is broad, and our aims for this book approach the goals from a twofold perspective: (a) to situate faculty development in S-LCE within the higher education context to demonstrate its necessity to institutionalize and improve practice of S-LCE and (b) to provide the diverse audience of faculty, scholar-practitioners, educational developers, and community engagement professionals with an array of examples and models, as well as realistic strategies, to evolve their faculty development efforts in S-LCE on their respective campuses. To achieve a volume that contributes to and engages audiences across S-LCE, educational development, and beyond, we sought contributors for the first, third, and fourth parts of the volume who represent diverse perspectives within both fields and who are well versed in the topics and areas we identified as important to include. As a coediting team, we had initial ideas for chapter themes but allowed contributors to take these themes in the directions they so desired. In the process, we helped by providing other chapter drafts as requested for author consideration and also offered feedback through reflective conversations with them, creating an iterative process of collaborative narrative which we sought to achieve throughout the text.

In addition to the iterative process for the chapters in parts one, three, and four, we allowed an emergent design approach to inquiry guide our decision-making processes as we set the structure of part two. This design approach included constructing a request for proposal (RFP) protocol for the second section of the book, eliciting case studies with models that demonstrate the connections between S-LCE and faculty development. Sharing the RFP broadly across professional organization networks, our coediting team received 45 case study proposals. After reviewing these proposals with a rubric and specific criteria including content, innovation, integration of faculty development programs and practices, and organization of ideas, along with the writing samples provided by submitters, we narrowed the list down to nine final case studies. Then we thematically analyzed these case studies to determine content focus, establishing clear themes.

This emergent design process contributed to the development of case study themes, chapter topics, order, and organization. Originally we structured the edited volume in three sections, but as the text evolved through emergent design, we restructured and reorganized chapters into the four sections published here. In addition, several case study models determined chapter content and organization for the case study chapters and contributed to the overall layout of the text. The quality and substance of proposals we received encouraged us to invite several contributors who submitted case study proposals to write entire chapters for the text. Again, this iterative approach runs throughout our book construction from beginning to end, and we believe it to be reflective of ourselves as practitioner-scholars—in a constant state of transition, making decisions and then reflecting and evaluating, adjusting, and refining those decisions.

Our Shared Narrative Inquiry

To inspire and ignite the narrative process, we read excerpts on scholarly personal narrative from *Our Stories Matter: Liberating the Voices of Marginalized Students Through Scholarly Personal Narrative Writing* (Nash & Viray, 2013) and inquiry through transpersonal and heuristic research from *Sentipensante (Sensing/Thinking) Pedagogy: Educating for Wholeness, Social Justice and Liberation* (Rendón, 2009). We reflected on the texts and individually wrote five pages reflecting on prompts such as how we came into our role, professionally; what identities and experiences inform our work; and what passions we find in this work. Then we collected our narratives, synthesizing them into raw data to be analyzed with support from NVivo, a qualitative software tool.

We conducted a heuristic analysis to code for themes, building on the methodological approaches previously described. Themes were coded utilizing heuristic and phenomenological techniques, with a consensus coding approach employed by all four coeditors to credential the data. Four main themes emerged: *transformative experiences, values, community-focused*, and *consciousness of identity*. The themes emerging from the narratives each consisted of subthemes that intersected and supported the other themes. Further, there were subthemes extant across each main theme: reflective scholar-practitioner, intersectionality of identities, interdisciplinary approaches to social change, and boundary-crosser. The subthemes and themes are interconnected, as demonstrated by Figure I.1, a heuristic that emerged from analysis of the data of raw narratives.

The four themes outlined in the following sections highlight the inward and outward spaces we inhabit and traverse in our roles, as well as the blurred spaces—the borderlands. We reflect inward and analyze our *values*, seeing those outwardly realized in the layered and multidimensional communities we inhabit. We locate *consciousness of identity* through critical reflection and awareness of our roles and responsibilities in and throughout those spaces, hinged together through *transformative* experiences we encounter as individuals and enact through our *community-focused* work. This inward-outward reflection is not, of course, a linear process, but rather an iterative one. We

Figure I.1. Conceptual map of themes from collaborative inquiry process.

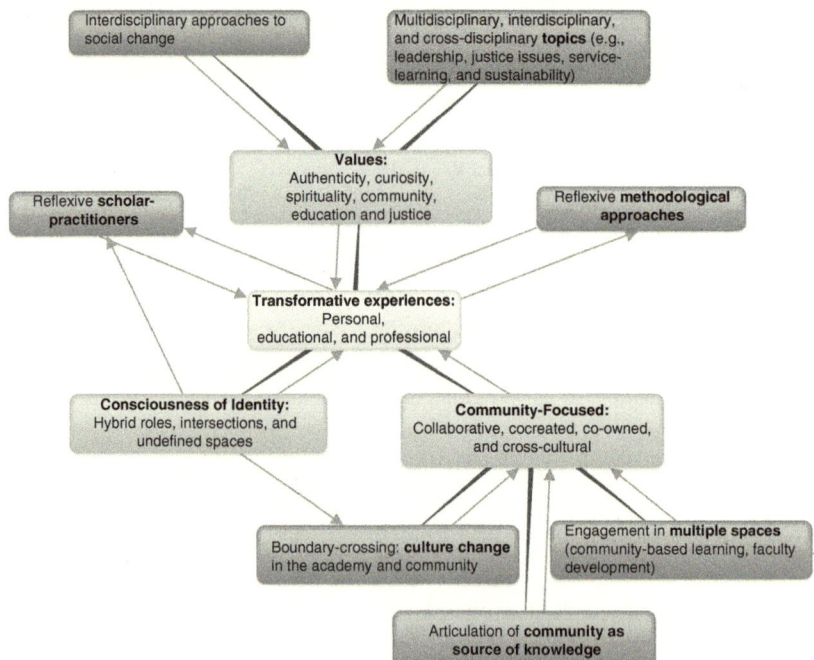

hope that in reviewing our collective narrative, you may traverse both inward and outward.

Reader Reflections
- Which of these themes resonate with you and why?
- Are there other themes essential to your narrative that you would add?

Transformative Experiences

We each came to and are carried through our work by transformational experiences. Drawing from Mezirow and associates' (1990) theory of transformative learning, reflection on critical incidences within our lives has shaped our identities. Articulating personal, professional, and educational experiences that significantly changed our lives and influenced our paths upon reflection support transformative experiences as a foundational theme. Transformational experiences that we have personally experienced, as well as ones we have facilitated and fostered for others, define the ever-evolving nature of our work. Similarly, we recognize transformational experiences as catalysts for reinvention, examination of our identities and values, and a source for contemplation of how we situate our personal-professional selves and navigate our multiple roles, as blended professionals (Whitchurch, 2009) serving in professional and academic spaces. As the central, foundational theme, it informs and is informed by others.

Transformative Experiences as Catalysts

Each of the narratives addressed experiences that were critical to us, personally and professionally. These were transformational in that they allowed us to pivot, change, or progress in new directions. Whitchurch (2013) suggests that third-space professionals are often working in multidisciplinary teams engaged directly with learning, research, and engagement activities, as one of our narratives describes:

> I began to see intersections between community organizations at which I worked and institutions of higher education. I experienced college students volunteering with my education programs (tutoring, GED preparation, literacy skill development). I was signing hour logs for students at state institutions, and saw the capacity of college students and higher education institutions juxtaposed with the assets of community organizations. The potential at these intersections was fascinating, but seemingly underdeveloped.

Situating ourselves in transformational experiences allowed us to see more fully the connections between faculty development and S-LCE—and what brought us to this work. Understanding the third-space professional role and being drawn to it was central:

> This constellation of identities drives, sustains, and nourishes the work that I do in higher education.

Each of our narratives describes transformational experiences as pivotal and defining moments in our lives, which have served as points of reference and a persistent guide as we continue in our personal and professional lives. Although each of our transformational experiences was set in different contexts, the outcome proved similar. We are now able to look back on these experiences that changed us, and therefore how we interact in the world around us. Moving forward from these experiences, the following quotation speaks to how one of us carries that transformation through her professional work:

> Rather than building, I am for the first time in my career in a role focused on evolving and fostering. Also in this place and time I am more convinced than ever of how essential this work is, and how important it is for all learners and humans to cultivate their disciplinary, cross-disciplinary, and/or interdisciplinary civic voices so we can stand in community, face our inherent complexity, propose and enact impassioned and sympathetic solution-oriented approaches, and embrace our interconnectivity with one another and our natural world and its systems.

Such transformational experiences are foundational to our narratives, and as such, this theme serves to undergird the other themes of values, community-focus, and consciousness of identity that emerged from our collaborative ethnography.

Values

In the collaborative analysis of our scholarly personal narratives, the theme of values arose as central, multifaceted, and connected to other identified themes. Values are the integral, and often intractable, phenomenological pillars that guide our thoughts, beliefs, and behaviors—both implicitly and explicitly. Values also constitute core facets of our "inner landscape," which is conceptualized by Parker Palmer, founder of the Center for Courage and Renewal, as tripartite: cognitive and intellectual, emotional and psychological, and spiritual. This inner landscape is informed by *and* interacts with the world around us. In an interview with *Yes! Magazine*, Palmer explores this intersection (van Gelder, 2009):

Engaging the inner life also makes for a more ethical professional practice. . . . When you develop an awareness of your inner life, you became aware of the disparity between your integrity and the way the institutions around you operate. . . . At that point, you have to reach deep and ask yourself, "Am I going to continue to live a divided life? Am I going to tuck this under the rug and pretend that I don't know what's going on? Or am I going to become a moral change agent within my institution and rally like-minded people around me, coalescing our power to bring about institutional change?"

Palmer's deft insights into change agency connect indelibly to our team's conceptualization of values. Together, we explored values beyond the stereotypic confines of individualism; our values are contextualized within these qualities or arenas:

- Communal in orientation (e.g., Nelson Mandela—*ubuntu*)
- Professional anchors
- Relational connectors
- Cultural arbiters and peacemakers
- Compass points—directional, particularly when issues are thorny (often the case in S-LCE)

More specifically, an analysis of subthemes across our narratives revealed five cohering values, encompassing a constellation around which we, the coeditors of this narrative, orbit and interconnect: authenticity, curiosity, education, community, and justice. These subthemes, drawn from the *values* theme, are further defined and explained in the following sections, with examples from our shared narratives provided in Table I.1.

Authenticity
The narratives revealed authenticity as a value tethered to our awareness of self, others, and place in the world. Drawing from Nash's (2004) scholarly personal narrative framework, the very act of creating and sharing our personal narratives was an exercise in authenticity. These musings suggest that authenticity, as a guidepost, is as existential as it is practical. Being "real" entails turning into one's inner truth while exercising transparency in interactions with others.

Curiosity
Though curiosity may be menacing for the feline species, our shared value of curiosity speaks to a scaffolded, lifelong quest to investigate, discover, experiment, understand, and uncover. It is the link between inquiry (our

TABLE I.1
Examples of Themes From Written Reflection as Part of the Collaborative Inquiry Process

Values Subthemes	Examples From Narratives
Authenticity	"I can't help being an open book, I don't know any other way." "I am . . . an instructor who values a classroom-community environment premised upon colearning, authenticity, and vulnerability."
Curiosity	"My desire to learn more generated a new journey." "I am an insatiably curious person, a feminist, an educator, a critical scholar, an activist researcher." "I found myself so engaged in intellectual questions—and from a very young age—that it would later surprise me to learn that not all others had similar curiosities."
Education	"Education was always a foundation in my family. . . . Having parents who worked their way through college, the value of education was readily apparent for my two brothers and two sisters and I. . . . Education and work ethic were synonymous—you worked really hard to go to school, you worked really hard in school, and then you work really hard after school at your job." "I have always viewed myself as an educator, so whether in teaching or administrative roles (or both, as the case has often been), this is a central identity in my work." "The act of writing something different, doing research in a different way, changed the course of how I encounter academic spaces and my purpose in and throughout those spaces."
Community	"There is [in my community] real poverty, real injustice, and real community need, real sea level rise and impacts of climate change, and an incredible amount of hard working people striving to address and rectify those challenges." "Though I had abandoned my religious inclinations, a spirituality of caring and compassion emerged; I found 'church' in my work with communities."
Justice	"To finally have environmental justice brought to my attention as a scholarly field and to see the multitude of justice issues impacting the 2.7 million+ people who are farmworkers in the United States, I finally found the thing I cared so much about that I could spend my life trying to explore, understand, and act on it." "Those spaces allow me to challenge normative structures of society and our institutions in order to seek more just spaces. Thus, my passions for faith and justice, for equity and equality, for human rights, for peace, for the common good, all drive my work in education."

shared reverence for research) and practice (our shared commitment for well-developed program implementation). The narratives were punctuated as much with musings on curiosity as they were with curious musings. Tethered to the value of curiosity is a desired outcome to pursue curious quests not for scruples, but for justice. As children, it would appear that our curiosities led us to question the answers. As adults, our curiosities mobilize change.

Education
Unsurprisingly, valuing education was central to each of our personal narratives. This value, however, is about not only *being educated* but also *educating others and communities* for the betterment of society. And although each of us recognizes our extraordinary privilege in holding advanced degrees, our pathways varied extensively, with at least one of us enduring struggles along the way. Learning is central here, and education is the mechanism to foster this value. Even on the front page of the website of one of our primary professional associations, the International Association for Research on Service-Learning and Community Engagement, a quote from Nelson Mandela proudly proclaims that education "is the most powerful weapon which you can use to change the world."

Community
In *Teaching Community: A Pedagogy of Hope*, bell hooks (2003) seeks to "illuminate the space of the possible where we can work to sustain our hope and create community with justice as the core foundation" (p. xvi). Our editorial team expressed community as a signature value that entails bringing people together *in* community and caring together *for* community. Emblematic of this value are several excerpts wherein we denote connection to community or communities. Intriguingly, our values pointed less to engagement (e.g., community engagement) and more to the role of community as haven and point of connection.

Justice
The value of justice is indelibly integral to our work as educational developers and S-LCE professionals. Both curiosity and education, tied to our experiences within diverse communities, have cultivated within each of us a profound awareness of using privilege to effect change. To do this in *just* ways is also evident in our writings.

This theme and its subthemes make transparent the values that drive our coeditorship of this book. We strive for *authenticity*, writing in ways that are as earnest as they may also be uncomfortable. We value *curiosity*, urging upon ourselves, the contributors, and readers to maintain a playful, inquisitive spirit of learning and engagement. We endear ourselves to *education*—informal and formal—and uphold the notion that each and every one of us, regardless of experience or academic degree, has something powerful to add to the narrative. We situate ourselves in a discursive *community* in hope and expectation of ongoing dialogue leading to small- and large-scale transformations. Most pivotally, we do this work for *justice*, without which there is little toward which to channel hope and action. As we identified these subthemes to further clarify our collective values, we similarly expressed how those values are more outwardly expressed and exercised in the various communities and in our work toward justice and social change.

Community-Focused

A central organizing principle emerged around the community-focused nature of our own identities as individuals, scholars, and practitioners. During the analysis of our personal stories, it became apparent that we each have been influenced by, and seek to influence, our communities in our lives through the creation of collaborative spaces, fostering of cooperative relationships, and truthful recognition of the cocreation and co-ownership of our own work and identities in the communities of which we are part. It is (perhaps) unsurprising that this emerged as a central theme within our personal narratives, given that central to or at least part of all of our professional roles relate to S-LCE.

In the first chapter of their edited volume titled *The Unheard Voices: Community Organizations and Service Learning*, Randy Stoecker and Elizabeth A. Tryon (2009) discuss a "dialectical process" (p. 7) through which university educators and administrators work with, for, and as part of the community(ies) they serve and where they are located. This theme encapsulates that process, as we each live it daily. In chapter 8 of that same volume, author Amy S. Mondloch (2009) discusses the potential role of service-learning in bridging alignment (and potential misalignment) between university and community organizations' missions as a double-edged sword, stating, "Service learning can be fuel for the fire or it can be more sticks thrown helter-skelter into the woods. It's up to us to be conscious of where we put our efforts and to what ends" (p. 140). This tension emerged in both the major theme and subthemes covered in this section as we navigate the often choppy waters of being S-LCE and faculty development professionals.

In consideration of the theme of community-focus: collaborative, cocreated, co-owned, and cross-cultural exemplars emerged that illustrate its centrality:

Creating spaces for students to explore these topics through a variety of disciplinary lenses in different community settings, while also addressing the community's priorities, is the essence of community-based learning.

I examined the collaborative processes among residents of a rural Panamanian community, a locally based ecotourism group, a Panamanian nongovernmental organization, a university Alternative Break Program in the United States, and faculty and student leaders of the groups.

I bring these identities, values, and beliefs to my work with faculty, community partner organizations and residents, my colleagues, and our students. In this work, I strive to live in community and understanding, by principles of cocreation and co-ownership, . . . and to seek to cultivate that understanding in others through meaningful partnership.

These excerpts from our narratives demonstrate our shared focus on community. Three subthemes emerged under this main theme: boundary crossing, community as a source of knowledge, and engagement in multiple spaces. Table I.2 provides examples from our shared narratives to support each of the subthemes.

Boundary Crossing

The subtheme of boundary crossing (culture change in the academy and community) hearkens back to Anzaldúa's (1987) conception of the borderlands. This theme is characterized by the ways in which we each articulate and reflect on how we cultivate change. In addition, this subtheme involves how we cultivate relationships inherent in the overarching community-focused nature of our multiple identities. Doing this means recognizing the pressured and competing commitments at the intersection of the university and community. Similarly, it suggests developing the skills and temperament to see things from multiple perspectives and represent the intentions of all stakeholders. Navigating the centrality of the community and justice in our roles became an organizing subtheme. We traverse and navigate our institutions' broader community-based work with the values and multiple identities involved, seeking to bring together knowledge, action, and connection through building relationships and shared understanding of common goals.

Community as Source of Knowledge

The subtheme of articulation of community as a source of knowledge emerged across our narratives as a way to get at the overarching theme of community-focused, cross-cultural, and coidentified and co-owned work. Essential to our shared identity is the goal to articulate—both to ourselves as well as to our institutions—how crucial it is to facilitate space for community perspectives and community expertise in our planning, implementation, assessment, and

TABLE I.2
**Examples of Community Subthemes Emerging
From the Collaborative Narrative Process**

Community Subthemes	Examples From Narratives
Boundary Crossing	"The institution had procured a reputation for its extraordinary work in leadership and community engagement, but this status lacked vigor, authenticity, and substance. Were we cycling students through altruistic, institution-centric, 'feel good' experiences—or were we excavating the terrain of hegemony, privilege, and status in an attempt to dismantle, disrupt, emancipate, and restore?"
Community as a Source of Knowledge	"I would use my nascent Spanish skills to communicate and connect with the residents, among them a rambunctious, affable mother named Santa Silverio. . . . Santa and I would chat back and forth as we worked side-by-side installing new flooring; I learned that she and her family had emigrated from Cuba, as had most of her neighbors. I learned of her effervescent love for Miami— its energy, diversity, opportunities, and people. I learned from Santa that things were *solo cosas*—just things; what mattered most were the safety of her family and the preservation of her heritage and culture." "I partnered with the Farmworker Association of Florida as a service-learning partner in my own teaching. It was in this collaboration that I first learned about farmworker issues, and a lightbulb went off for me. . . . My doctoral research is at the intersection of environmental justice (EJ), farmworker justice, and social change and coalition building and my research has mostly been community-based participatory in its approach, and qualitative and constructivist in its methods."
Engagement in Multiple Spaces	"Professionally, I am: an action researcher and community-based scholar deeply engaged in advocacy initiatives that improve the lives of persons with brain injury and other disabilities; an instructor who values a classroom-community environment premised upon colearning, authenticity, and vulnerability; and a faculty developer dedicated to cultivating brave spaces where faculty enhance their intersectional identities as teachers, scholars, and servant-leaders. I love the hybrid nature of my position— that of associate professor and administrator." "My professional work in different spaces has undoubtedly informed my role as a scholar-practitioner."

ongoing efforts. Essentially, the community is a source of knowledge, and we aim to integrate this in our work. Identifying the community as a source of knowledge, full of assets that contribute through individual skills, associations, and institutions, presents a fundamental asset-based community development approach that is inherent in our work (Kretzmann & McKnight, 1996).

Engagement in Multiple Spaces
In the final subtheme, engagement in multiple spaces (community-based learning and faculty development), we can see the connection of the previous two subthemes and the overall theme as they relate specifically to our professional roles as S-LCE and/or faculty development professionals. Drawing on Anzaldúa's (1987) conception of borderlands, we engage in multiple settings as well as through multiple roles. In our roles, we wear many hats: administrators, faculty, staff, academics, and so on. Each role that we occupy is informed by and through our community focus. Engagement in multiple spaces connects to other themes and subthemes in this heuristic analysis from boundary crossing to community focus, as we move in and out of the community and academic settings. References to moving in multiple spaces is both literal and geographic for us.

Consciousness of Identity

Across our narratives emerged a significant theme of the consciousness of identity as a distinct characteristic as an educator. Rendón (2014) challenges us, as educators, to reimagine our role in higher education—to fashion an integrative, consonant pedagogy rooted in social justice. To address the social change agency inherent in this role, she draws from Freire's (1971) *critical consciousness* "to become change agents for a better society" (Rendón, 2014, p. 100). This critical consciousness, including the identity of a boundary-crossing change agent and hybrid roles as scholar-practitioner, was woven throughout our narratives.

Throughout the coding process in the analysis of the unstructured data (narratives), there were several subthemes that emerged from the consciousness of identity theme, including awareness of positionality, description of multiple roles, articulation of hybrid roles, and intersection of identities working toward social change. Examples from our shared narratives are featured in Table I.3 to support the subthemes.

TABLE I.3
Examples of Consciousness of Identity Subthemes Emerging
From the Coeditors' Collaborative Narrative Process

Consciousness of Identity Subthemes	Example From Narratives
Awareness of Positionality	"I located myself as a qualitative researcher, exploring the educator's inner experiences of engaging in deep learning experiences with students." "I situate myself as an academic and a practitioner by pushing to explore always the intersection of theory and practice."
Description of Multiple Roles	"I assume the multiple positions and roles required of a service-learning practitioner scholar." "It is curricular and cocurricular; faculty and administrator; theory-driven and practice-based; program manager and program facilitator; and, most of all, practitioner-scholar and scholar-practitioner." "My hybrid role was essential due to the need for developing curriculum around civic engagement and leadership courses."
Articulation of Hybrid Roles	"In this space that I was first exposed to theories of social change I realized that I had a passion for the space between what is traditionally labeled as 'student affairs' and 'academic affairs.'" "Concepts of leadership, social change, and this space of making more engaging the curricular aspects of a student's experience propelled me during the first steps of my professional journey." "At this intersection, the undefined spaces where I find my identity as a practitioner-scholar/scholar-practitioner is where I stand."
Intersection of Identities as Agents of Change	"I have worked at four very different institutions and in roles that, on paper, may look unrelated. However, the common thread among them is that they have all been at the crossroads of the 'curricular' and 'extracurricular' experiences of students. At their core, they were all about the purpose and responsibility of institutions of higher education as centers of social and civic change." "It was a professional step that also participated in educational justice—providing educational access to students, challenging social structures of oppression, and empowering individuals through education."

Awareness of Positionality
The narratives revealed a distinct awareness of positionality, as each of us located ourselves in a distinct but less clearly defined professional identity. References in the narratives to the "conscious, lived experience" and "locating myself" rooted our understanding through self-awareness. Clear evidence of reflection on our location professionally surfaced in the narratives. This self-awareness led to further exploration of our professional roles.

Description of Multiple Roles
The emphasis on multiple roles was a common notion in each of the narratives. The narratives provided insight into professional roles that carried multiple functions, such as administration and teaching or program development and faculty development. Often describing roles as "multidimensional," the narratives provided myriad descriptions. The description of multiple roles also led to a clear articulation of hybrid roles, in which each of us serve in a "both/and" role. For example, responsibilities may include both administration and teaching. Yet the articulation of hybrid roles goes beyond dual roles into roles that bridge and cross boundaries.

Articulation of Hybrid Roles
The narratives demonstrated a shared understanding of our professional roles that were hybrid in nature. In fact, the hybrid nature was often described not as the combination of roles but rather as a distinct "space" across roles. In one narrative, it is stated as "I do not wear different hats; I am different roles at the same time." In other words, our roles cross boundaries. The emphasis on "spaces between" and "undefined spaces" supports the description of boundary crossing associated with these hybrid roles.

Intersection of Identities as Agents of Change
The intersection of our hybrid professional identities are interwoven in these spaces working as agents of change. As one narrative states: "I am the intersection of learning spaces in and out of the classroom." The hybrid role supporting boundary crossing speaks to not only crossing definitive roles to foster learning but also crossing the boundaries and spaces of normative structures to facilitate, and contribute to, change (institutional or social). As agents of change, our roles shift and our professional identity is framed less around function and more explicitly around the boundary crossing in both defined (e.g., institutional) and undefined spaces (e.g., community, hybrid roles).

Articulating Identities In-Between Faculty Development and S-LCE
As the theme and subthemes associated with consciousness of identity indicate, a distinct understanding of our unique role in higher education informs our approach to S-LCE, as well as how we connect faculty through educational development programs. Cognizance of our role allows us to have two feet in each world—community and classroom, academic learning and student development, faculty and administration.

Such identities are informed by the emerging literature around community engagement professionals (CEPs). Dostilio (2017) provides an extensive framework for CEPs, including the role "characterized by sitting betwixt and between boundaries" (p. 5). The variance of these positions encompasses hybrid roles by definition, as Dostilio (2017) explains:

> The conceptions of tempered radicals, transformational leaders, and social entrepreneurs . . . may provide us with templates and vocabularies to explain the ways in which CEPs function as leaders on their campuses and within larger associations of civic workers. (p. 5)

The central tenets established for the conceptual framework of CEPs are clearly stated as tempered radicalism, transformational leadership, and social entrepreneurship. This framework suggests the second generation of engagement professionals are in a unique position to shift toward a new frontier of community engagement.

That new frontier surfaces in the expressed role of CEPs with faculty development. Rarely do we claim an identity of curriculum developers, instructional designers, and learning-space creators. Yet each time we support faculty in the construction of a service-learning course through syllabus development, community partner connections, experiential learning project development, and reflection assignment development, we, in fact, serve in these faculty development roles. As our shared narratives express, and the thematic analysis confirms, claiming our identity as faculty developers is an expression of this new frontier.

In the opening chapter of *The Community Engagement Professional in Higher Education*, contributors Lina D. Dostilio and Lane Perry (2017) state that CEPs—which we refer to in this edited volume as S-LCE professionals—are change-oriented leaders "using their positions within the middle spaces of their organizations to catalyze change and greater realization of postsecondary education's civic purpose" (p. 2). In addition, they reference broader work in the field around S-LCE professionals as border-crossing democratic civic professionals (Dostilio & Perry, 2017; Keith, 2015). As they point out, many times the work and identities of S-LCE professionals focus on "effecting increasingly deeper civic commitments through our administrative labor" (Dostilio & Perry, 2017, p. 8), which is mirrored in the themes and subthemes that emerged around the values and community-focused nature of our personal narratives. Although there are some overlaps between our work and what Dostilio and Perry put forth in their chapter, their focus is more on ethical, civic, and social commitments and how we utilize our professional roles to move toward that (rather than placing them at the center of our work, as we suggest). In doing so, they talk about S-LCE professionals as doing *change-oriented work*, but indicate less directly what that means in relationship with our community(ies). That said, there are many areas of overlap, particularly with boundary crossing and engagement in multiple spaces.

Conclusion: Reflecting Together and Moving Forward

Through collaborative inquiry, thematic analysis of our shared narratives, and exploration of emerging themes, the analysis of our narratives confirms an expressed identity around CEPs as faculty developers that is essential to articulate inversely. In other words, as CEPs, we are educational developers in S-LCE, and, as educational developers in S-LCE, we are also CEPs. The narrative heuristic emerging from our shared narratives provided rich reflexive space for us, as a coediting team, to explore this relationship more fully.

In the chapters that follow, the exploration of these borderlands will continue in dialogue with the reader, with an ongoing invitation to reflect, as the preface indicates (giving a more detailed overview of the text). To provide a brief guide here, in part one, the reader will begin to explore different scholarly approaches introducing new faculty development frameworks. In part two, the reader will engage in models of S-LCE and faculty development programs, including case studies from varied institutional contexts, to see how faculty development programs are implemented in the context of S-LCE, as well as lessons learned. In part three, further exploration of the intersection of S-LCE and faculty development will be highlighted through pedagogical considerations, institutional contexts, and dialogue around community partnership. In part four, the reader will be challenged to engage in change in the space between faculty development and S-LCE, with practical strategies to foster scholarship as well as a theory of change. In effect, this edited volume invites you, as the reader, to consider your own professional identity in this borderland space.

Reader Reflections
- Do you identify as an educational developer, S-LCE professional, or as a third-space professional? Why?
- How do you express your professional identity(ies) in your faculty development and S-LCE work?
- As you reflect on your professional identity(ies), how do you articulate the in-between spaces of your work?
- What frameworks, models, and theories support your work in this space?
- What frameworks, models, and theories do you think need to be developed to support your work more fully?

References

Anzaldúa, G. (1987). *Borderlands/la frontera: The new mestiza*. San Francisco, CA: Spinsters/Aunt Lute.

Clandinin, D. J., & Connelly, F. M. (2000). *Narrative inquiry: Experience and story in qualitative research*. San Francisco, CA: Jossey-Bass.

Creswell, J. W. (2012). *Qualitative inquiry and research design: Choosing among five approaches*. Thousand Oaks, CA: Sage.

Donohoo, J. (2013). *Collaborative inquiry for educators: A facilitator's guide to school improvement*. Thousand Oaks, CA: Corwin.

Dostilio, L. D. (Ed.). (2017). *The community engagement professional in higher education: A competency model for an emerging field*. Boston, MA: Campus Compact.

Dostilio, L. D., & Perry, L. G. (2017). An explanation of the community engagement professionals as professionals and leaders. In L. D. Dostilio (Ed.), *The community engagement professional in higher education: A competency model for an emerging field* (pp. 1–26). Boston, MA: Campus Compact.

Freire, P. (1971). *Pedagogy of the oppressed*. New York, NY: Continuum.

hooks, b. (2003). *Teaching community: A pedagogy of hope*. New York, NY: Routledge.

Keith, N. Z. (2015). *Engaging in social partnerships: Democratic practices for campus-community partnerships*. New York, NY: Routledge.

Kretzmann, J., & McKnight, J. P. (1996). Asset-based community development. *National Civic Review, 85*(4), 23–29.

Lassiter, L. E. (2005). *The Chicago guide to collaborative ethnography*. Chicago, IL: University of Chicago Press.

Mezirow, J., & Associates. (1990). *Fostering critical reflection in adulthood*. San Francisco, CA: Jossey Bass.

Mondloch, A. S. (2009). One director's voice. In R. Stoeker and E. A. Tryon (Eds.), *The unheard voices: Community organizations and service-learning* (pp. 136–146). Philadelphia, PA: Temple University Press.

Nash, R. J. (2004). *Liberating scholarly writing: The power of personal narrative*. New York, NY: Teachers College Press.

Nash, R. J., & Viray, S. (2013). *Our stories matter: Liberating the voices of marginalized students through scholarly personal narrative writing*. New York, NY: Peter Lang.

Rendón, L. I. (2009). *Sentipensante (sensing/thinking) pedagogy: Educating for wholeness, social justice and liberation*. Sterling, VA: Stylus.

Rendón, L. I. (2014). *Sentipensante (sensing/thinking) pedagogy* (2nd ed.). Sterling, VA: Stylus.

Stoecker, R., & Tryon, E. A. (2009). *The unheard voices: Community organizations and service learning*. Philadelphia, PA: Temple University Press.

Stryker, S., & Burke, P. J. (2000). The past, present, and future of an identity theory. *Social Psychology Quarterly, 63*, 284–297.

Tyler, J. A. (2009). Moving beyond scholar-practitioner binaries: Exploring the liminal possibilities of the borderlands. *Advances in Developing Human Resources, 11*(4), 525–535.

van Gelder, S. (2009). Parker Palmer: Know yourself, change your world. *Yes! Magazine*. Retrieved from http://psychm2.pbworks.com/f/Parker+Palmer.pdf

Whitchurch, C. (2009). The rise of the *blended professional* in higher education: A comparison between the United Kingdom, Australia, and the United States. *Higher Education, 58*(3), 407–418.

Whitchurch, C. (2013). *Reconstructing identities in higher education: The rise of Third Space professionals*. London, UK: Routledge.

PART ONE

THE LANDSCAPE OF FACULTY DEVELOPMENT AND COMMUNITY ENGAGEMENT

I

A HOLISTIC FRAMEWORK FOR EDUCATIONAL PROFESSIONAL DEVELOPMENT IN COMMUNITY ENGAGEMENT

Marshall Welch and Star Plaxton-Moore

Community engagement in higher education emerged as a movement a generation ago and has evolved into its own professional field over time (Welch, 2016). Early on, the main role and responsibility of directors of campus centers for community service was to mentor student leaders as what Boyte and Fretz (2011) characterized as "civic professionals" (p. 84) and help to facilitate volunteer service projects. That emphasis on voluntary service gradually transitioned into academically based service delivered through credit-bearing courses commonly known as service-learning. These courses involve a number of stakeholders and have implications for both student civic learning and community impact. Engaged faculty, as the fulcrums on which service-learning courses pivot, have an ethical responsibility to develop the skills, knowledge, and dispositions necessary to do this work with integrity. Because most doctoral programs do not teach competencies specific to community-engaged scholarship (CES), faculty and institutions must rely on service-learning staff for support.

Based on this need, the center administrator has evolved to become what is referred to throughout this book as a service-learning community engagement (S-LCE) professional, interacting with faculty and community partners in addition to working with students. This interaction has primarily entailed providing technical support to instructors as they develop and implement service-learning courses. It is, however, important to note that some institutions may not have a center solely dedicated to service-learning or other forms of community engagement. Instead, these activities may be coordinated by staff from other offices or programs responsible for various aspects of community engagement programming. Related to this is the fact that the diverse backgrounds and professional preparation of these individuals create additional challenges and further complicate the already complex coordination of community engagement. Finally, many of these professionals have an array of roles and responsibilities for related programming in affiliated offices. For example, staff in campus ministry or internship programs at smaller campuses may also be responsible for coordinating service-learning or other cocurricular programs focused on community engagement. The question is what background and resources these professionals need to provide professional development to faculty, students, and community partners.

Faculty development in the context of community engagement has traditionally focused on providing continued technical support to instructors or small groups of faculty members as they conceptualize and implement service-learning courses. In fact, facilitation of this process has become a key role and responsibility for S-LCE professionals. A recent national study revealed that 90% of the respondents reported providing one-on-one technical support to faculty and that nearly 70% of those same responding centers provided some form of faculty development (Welch & Saltmarsh, 2013). In the 2015 survey of its members, Campus Compact reported that just over 75% of the respondents claimed to provide (a) faculty development workshops/fellowships, (b) materials to assist faculty with reflection and assessment, and (c) curriculum models and sample syllabi (Campus Compact, 2014).

Focusing solely on teaching is no longer enough as tenure-track faculty members are expected to disseminate new knowledge in the form of publications and presentations within their discipline(s). As a result, effective S-LCE professionals assist faculty who seek to integrate their engaged teaching with scholarship that makes a significant contribution to their disciplinary field(s), all while meeting promotion and tenure expectations. Likewise, over the past 25 years, the exponential growth of engaged teaching and learning as evidenced by the Carnegie Classification for Community Engagement has generated a concomitant growth of additional administrative coordination at the institutional level (Welch, 2016). This, in turn, has implications for the institution. As such, the S-LCE professional must wear many hats and know how to navigate the culture and political system of higher education to work effectively not only with faculty but also with administrators at various levels. Adding to this complexity is the need for S-LCE professionals to effectively work with community agencies and the constituencies they serve. These collaborations not only involve building trust and relationships but also include educating executive directors and staff of community agencies serving as educational partners on what this work involves and how to work with faculty and students.

Given the array of stakeholders, this chapter presents a shift from the traditional approach and perspective of *faculty* development to a broader and more comprehensive conceptualization of *professional educational* development for multiple stakeholders and contexts. By modifying McKee and Tew's (2013) definition of *faculty development*, we can arrive at a broader understanding that the fundamental purpose of professional development as a whole is to provide educational activities designed to help professionals grow in their professional practice. This semantic shift is also consistent with the Professional and Organizational Network (POD) preference and use of the term *educational development*, as it reflects the breadth of continued educational growth at multiple levels ranging from the individual to programs to the institution to reach a variety of audiences such as graduate students, faculty, and administrators (Little, 2014).

We continue by exploring the emerging role of the S-LCE professional as a developer, followed by defining and describing traditional faculty development designed to advance community engagement that includes a review of current trends and practice. This chapter also presents the pedagogical, political, and philosophical foundations of community engagement to serve as a holistic framework for professional development that can be visualized as a multidirectional wheel. The S-LCE professional serves as a hub to provide continued professional educational support to multiple stakeholders in multiple contexts or settings, each with their own set of factors to consider (see Figure 1.1), described in more detail later in this chapter. The chapter continues by illustrating how this broader perspective reflects an emerging role of the S-LCE professional that goes beyond being a competent workshop facilitator to being a transformative leader who provides professional education to faculty, administrators, and community partners about the nature of this work that will influence the trajectory of the institution to embed and advance community engagement within its mission.

The word *development* implies change as it is defined as "the act or process of growing or causing something to grow or become larger or more advanced" (Development, n.d.). However, there are several factors to consider, each requiring the S-LCE professional to take on different roles and responsibilities throughout the development process. Beyond being a consultant to faculty, the S-LCE professional must be an advocate, counselor, cultural anthropologist and diplomat, matchmaker, navigator, policy wonk,

Figure 1.1. Holistic framework of professional educational development for community engagement.

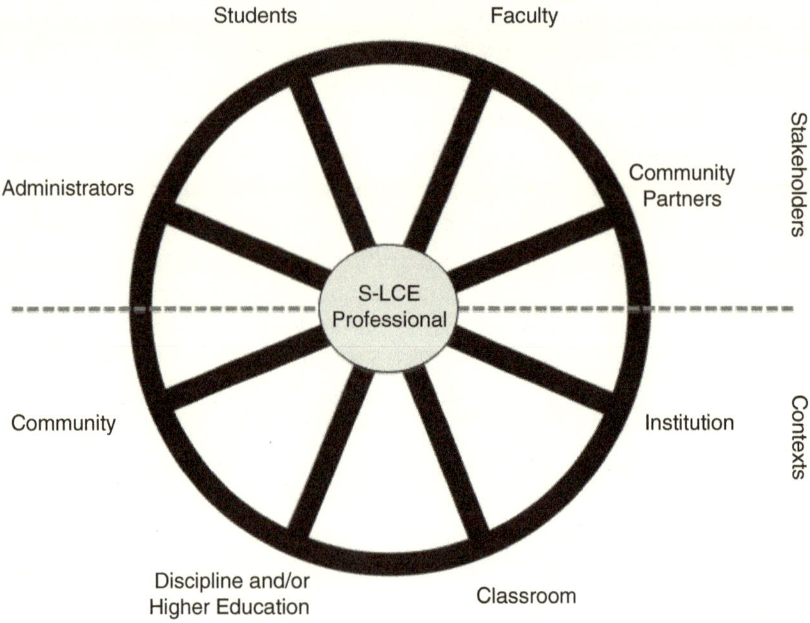

```
                    Students            Faculty

                                                        Stakeholders
    Administrators                    Community
                                      Partners

                          S-LCE
    - - - - - - - - - - Professional - - - - - - - - - - - -

                                                        Contexts
    Community                         Institution


                 Discipline and/or    Classroom
                 Higher Education
```

and scholar. Each of these roles, its function, and related citations are summarized in Table 1.1.

Defining and Describing Traditional Faculty Development for Community-Engaged Learning

As a prerequisite to introducing a holistic framework of professional educational development, we begin by returning to and reviewing the historical focus and terminology of faculty development as a foundation from which to build. *Faculty development* is broadly defined as educational activities designed to help faculty grow in their professional practice (McKee & Tew, 2013). Lawler (2003) characterized effective professional development for a community of adult learners as incorporating the following components: (a) creating a climate of respect, (b) encouraging active participation, (c) building on experience, (d) employing collaborative inquiry, (e) learning for action, and (f) empowering the participants.

In the context of promoting engaged teaching and scholarship, Welch (2016) proposed a basic scope and sequence of faculty development comprising three components or characteristics: knowledge, skills, and application.

TABLE 1.1
Roles and Functions of the S-LCE Professional

Role	Function	Citation
Advocate	Making the case for engaged teaching and scholarship with faculty and administrators Leveraging support and resources to advance engaged teaching and scholarship Identifying and utilizing faculty champions Assuring that community partners have a voice as coeducators	Beere, Votruba, & Wells, 2011; Green et al., 2016; Holland & Langseth, 2010; Sandmann & Plater, 2009
Counselor	Addressing existential unease experienced by faculty as they develop and implement engaged teaching and scholarship	Dostilio et al., 2016
Cultural Anthropologist and Diplomat	Understanding and demonstrating cultural competency and intercultural humility to nurture community partnerships Promoting cultural competency with faculty and students as they work with various groups and settings Knowing and working with key academic cultural factors (e.g., academic freedom) Articulating academic culture to community partners	Saviki, 2008; Welch, 2015, 2016
Matchmaker	Aligning faculty and students with community agencies Connecting novice engaged faculty members with experienced colleagues for mentoring Connecting community partners with resources on campus Assisting faculty in finding dissemination venues for their scholarship	Jones & Palmerton, 2010

(*Continues*)

TABLE 1.1 (Continued)

Role	Function	Citation
Navigator	Understanding and working with the organizational geography and culture of the institution, departments, disciplines, and community Portaging the neoliberal structure of academia	Orphan & O'Meara, 2016; Welch, 2010, 2015, 2016
Policy Wonk	Understanding, utilizing, and influencing institutional policy and procedures (e.g., promotion and tenure, risk management, faculty recruitment/hiring)	Dostilio et al., 2016; Welch, 2010, 2016
Scholar	Understanding and promoting engaged pedagogy and scholarship with various stakeholders and constituencies Facilitating faculty dissemination of new knowledge in publications and presentations Contributing new knowledge to the field by the S-LCE Becoming an informed consumer of the professional literature and best practice	Dostilio et al., 2016; Green et al., 2016

These, in turn, were embedded within a chronology or sequence of activities and steps for developing service-learning courses and/or community-based research projects: *before, during, and after.* The first and second steps comprise familiar and traditional activities associated with developing and implementing community engagement courses. The third chronological step of *after* is somewhat unique and noteworthy as it includes key activities for faculty completing their initial faculty development process not typically considered or implemented. These include (a) assessing the impact of the teaching and scholarship in multiple contexts and settings, (b) mentoring colleagues now entering a new faculty development cohort, (c) serving on advisory committees for the community engagement center on campus, (d) disseminating new knowledge that emerges from their engaged teaching and scholarship, and (e) preparing their portfolio for promotion and tenure review. Gelmon and Agre-Kippenhan (2002) detailed a continuum of seven levels of expertise ranging from an entry level of explorer to a master level. Within their model, they enumerated specific skill sets to include throughout faculty development that include reviewing course implementation logistics, developing community partnerships, and conducting reflection, as well as foundational knowledge of engaged pedagogy and scholarship that pursue multiple viewpoints of students, faculty, community, the institution, and community partnerships. Similarly, Blanchard and colleagues (2009) outlined a hierarchy of skill level attainment for faculty development beginning with novice, moving to intermediate, and finally to advanced levels.

Current Trends and Approaches of Faculty Development to Advance Community Engagement

To provide further context regarding the evolution of faculty development practices in the field, a recent study conducted by the authors combined a review of the literature since 2000 and a survey of S-LCE professionals to provide a thumbnail sketch of current trends and approaches (Welch & Plaxton-Moore, 2017). This study can act as a guidepost for S-LCE professionals, giving them a sense of where the community-engaged faculty development field came from, where it stands now, and where it needs to go to enhance its impact.

Literature Review

An analysis of 28 peer-reviewed articles on S-LCE faculty development illuminated the state of extant literature on this topic and, by extension, the state of S-LCE faculty development across higher education. Each author conducted a separate search of the ERIC database to identify peer-reviewed journal articles from 2000 to 2015 using key terms including *faculty development, faculty training, professional development, service-learning, community engagement, higher education, college,* or *university*. The authors reviewed articles and identified emergent themes to develop a worksheet for analyzing and classifying all articles and allowed for interrater discussion and agreement. The analysis worksheets and discussion resulted in 100% interrater reliability in regard to how the articles were classified (see Table 1.2).

Over half of the articles published since 2000 were program descriptions. Another six were structured as technical guides. Only six articles described original research, with three integrating a quasi-experimental design, two using qualitative methods, and one combining a factor analysis and pre/post measure. Out of the entire body of articles, there were only 13 explicitly articulated theoretical frameworks for adult learning, with Kolb's experiential learning model, Mezirow's transformative learning model, and Rogers's diffusion of innovation model each named in two articles. Two articles proposed competency-based models for S-LCE faculty development (Blanchard et al., 2009; Jordan et al., 2012), providing useful frameworks for subsequent scholars to integrate and adapt to inform their own program curricula and assessment. However, it is important to note that the vast majority of these articles did not include or describe assessment procedures to determine the direct impact the faculty development programming had on participating faculty or the indirect impact it had on other stakeholders.

One promising finding from the literature review was the constellation of six scholarly articles that came out in 2012 related to the Faculty for the Engaged Campus initiative sponsored by Community Campus Partnerships for Health (CCPH). Five of the articles were published in the *Journal of Higher Education Outreach and Engagement*, including one program description that highlighted the broader initiative's challenges, interventions, and lessons learned relating to assessment of faculty development (Seifer, Blanchard, Jordan, Gelmon, & McGinley, 2012) and four research articles that described faculty and institutional outcomes relating to the implementation of faculty development programs sponsored by CCPH (Blanchard, Strauss, & Webb, 2012; Gelmon, Blanchard, Ryan, & Seifer, 2012; Jaeger, Jameson, & Clayton, 2012; Jordan et al., 2012). An additional article (Jameson, Clayton, Jaeger, & Bringle, 2012), published in the *Michigan Journal of Community Service-Learning*, described a mixed methods approach to measuring faculty learning from their faculty development program. Furco and Moely (2012) assessed faculty knowledge and confidence in using new knowledge related to teaching service-learning using a pre/post measure. These articles seemed to set a new and promising standard for rigorous assessment of faculty development programs and legitimate research on the effectiveness of such interventions.

TABLE 1.2
Summary of Literature Review

Author and Year	Type	Design Method	Outcome Measure	Theory
Becket, Refaei, & Skutar (2012)	DP	None	PR	None
Blanchard et al. (2009)	TG	None	None	None
Blanchard, Strauss, & Webb (2012)	DP	None	P/P, GA, O	None
Bowen & Kiser (2009)	DP	CS, Q	PE, SR, I, O	None
Bradshaw (2013)	DP	None	PE, PR, CD	None
Bringle et al. (2000)	DP	None	AR, CD, O	Yes
Browne & Roll (2015)	DP	None	AR	Yes
Butler (2002)	DP	None	AR, CD, Q	None
Carracelas-Juncal et al. (2009)	DP	None	CD, PR	None
DeLugan, Roussos, & Skram (2014)	DP	None	AR	Yes
Dorfman & Murty (2005)	DP	None	CD, O	Yes
Furco & Moely (2012)	EX	COR	P/P, PE	Yes
Gelmon et al. (2012)	EX	DD, QE, Q	P/P, CD, O	Yes
Hamel-Lambert et al. (2012)	DP	None	PE, CD, O	Yes
Hansen (2012)	TG	None	None	None
Harwood et al. (2005)	EX	DD, Q	AR, PE, FG, PR	None
Hughes, Huston, & Stein (2011)	TG	None	AR, PE	Yes
Jaeger, Jameson, & Clayton (2012)	DP	CS	CD, PR, I, O	Yes
Jameson et al. (2012)	EX	QE, Q	P/P, PE, PR	Yes
Jordan et al. (2012)	EX	DD, QE, Q	P/P, PE, CD, PR, I, O	Yes
Leh (2005)	DP	None	PE, PD, I	Yes
Litzky et al. (2010)	TG	None	AR	None
Ryan (2000)	DP	None	PR	None
Seifer et al. (2012)	DP	None	AR, PE, FG, CD	None

(Continues)

TABLE 1.2 (*Continued*)

Author and Year	Type	Design Method	Outcome Measure	Theory
Welch (2002)	DP	None	PE, CD, PD, O	None
Welch (2010)	TG	None	None	None
Whitley & Walsh (2014)	TG	None	None	Yes
Zlotkowski (2001)	TG	None	None	None

Key:
AR = Anecdotal Report
CD = Course Development
COR = Correlational Factor Analysis
CS = Case Study
DP = Descriptive Program
DD = Descriptive Data
EX = Experimental Design
FG = Focus Group/Debriefing
GA = Community Partner Goal Achievement
I = Interview
O = Other
PD = Product Development
PE = Participant Evaluation Survey
P/P = Pre/Post Measure
PR = Personal Reflection
Q = Qualitative Analysis
QE = Quasi-Experimental Design
SR = Syllabus Review
TG = Technical Guide

Source: From "Faculty Development for Advancing Community Engagement in Higher Education: Current Trends and Future Directions," by M. Welch and S. Plaxton-Moore (2017), *Journal of Higher Education Outreach and Engagement 21*(2), 131–165. Reprinted with permission from the *Journal of Higher Education Outreach and Engagement.*

Survey

In addition to the literature review, the authors designed a 22-question survey for S-LCE professionals based on themes from the literature review and field tested it with three peers from diverse institutions before disseminating it by e-mail to a list of 534 S-LCE professionals generated by the New England Resource Center for Higher Education (NERCHE). A total of 83 S-LCE professionals responded to the survey (a 15.5% response rate), providing a snapshot of current faculty development practices emerging from the data that warrants consideration. Of particular note is that just over half (55%) of respondents named S-LCE directors as the persons primarily responsible for providing faculty development for service-learning and community engagement.

The most common formats for faculty support and development were overwhelmingly one-on-one consultations and workshops, with 90% and 86% of respondents claiming to use these approaches, respectively. Interestingly, arguably more cohort-based faculty development models like learning communities and faculty fellow seminars were implemented by less than half of the responding institutions. Of those using a faculty fellows or cohort model, 75% report that each faculty participant participates in over 11 hours of development activities. Eighty-seven percent of institutions that do not implement a cohort model reported that faculty commit to 6 hours or less of formalized faculty development. Cohort models tend to draw one to five faculty participants from each of the following ranks, including full-time tenure track, full-time adjunct, and part-time adjunct instructors. Other forms of faculty development draw from the same demographics, but tenure-track faculty appear to participate in greater numbers, and campus staff and community partners are generally included. The authors surmise that the differences in faculty development formats are influenced by a number of factors, most notably the competency and capacity of S-LCE professionals to design and deliver faculty development, resources and funding for development initiatives, faculty commitments and constraints, and the institutional culture in regard to value placed on CES (Welch & Plaxton-Moore, 2017). Subsequent chapters will describe a range of faculty development models in more detail, including three case studies of faculty learning communities (chapter 5). These case studies present distinctive models and the benefits and challenges of each approach, while also illuminating outcomes that extend beyond faculty learning to influence institutional practices and culture.

In regard to faculty development curriculum, five common topics emerged from a list of 21 provided in the survey, including reflection (90%), course development (89%), principles of community engagement (86%), syllabus development (82%), and assessment (81%). Around half of the respondents stated that they develop their own faculty development curricula, whereas 45% combine existing curricular elements from the broader field with their own unique materials, and a handful exclusively rely on existing curricular resources in the field. Though a large number of S-LCE professionals are creating at least some of the curriculum for their faculty development programs, less than 20% indicated that their program content and structure were informed by a theoretical framework. This finding aligns with the results from the conceptual literature review, as previously reported. It is possible that the lack of theoretical underpinnings for faculty development programs is an indicator that S-LCE professionals are unaware of adult learning theories and how to apply them when designing such programs. One is left to wonder at the effectiveness of faculty development interventions that are not shaped by learning theories grounded in research and practice, which may serve as a topic for potential further research in the S-LCE field.

Another apparent limitation is the lack of effective assessment practices in faculty development programs. The results of this literature review and survey reveal assessment is primarily limited to participant self-report participant satisfaction surveys (63%). More rigorous forms of direct assessment, including pre/post measures of faculty knowledge, analysis of faculty work products like syllabi or written reflections, and formal focus groups or interviews were used by less than 40% of respondents. Assessment of impact on other stakeholders and in other domains, such as student course evaluations and community partner feedback solicitation also fell short of 40% of the respondents. Thus, though assessment is one of the top six themes covered in S-LCE faculty development programs, it is not actually implemented in a robust, intentional, and effective way by the majority of S-LCE professionals in the very same programs.

Competency-Based Models of Professional Development

As the study previously discussed reported, competency-based models appear to be an emerging trend in professional development. Competency-based faculty development incorporates specific knowledge, skill sets, and attitudes deemed as salient attributes for competent professional performance. Rychen and Salganik (2001) noted that the word *competence* is derived from the Latin roots of *cognizance* and *responsibility* (cited in Dostilio, 2017). This is noteworthy as it reminds S-LCE professionals of both a scholarly and ethical awareness coupled with a commitment to adhere to and implement best practice in our work. Many programs that use this approach include assessment methods to verify and assess implementation.

Over 20 years ago, Zlotkowski (1998) proposed a service-learning conceptual matrix to describe polarity between two stakeholder groups along a vertical axis: students and sponsors. The latter included community partners as well as constituents across campus colleagues and administrators. It also comprised two domains at opposite ends of a horizontal axis: expertise and common good. The axes shape four quadrants, including values development, pedagogical strategies, academic culture, and community partners. Within each of these quadrants, Zlotkowski named competencies like reflection facilitation, implementation of active learning models, integration of multifaceted assessment, and the study of the philosophical traditions and epistemological implications of service-learning. Though the matrix appears to (over)simplify and conflate stakeholders and domains, as well as the tensions between them, the article details several dilemmas that shape faculty community engagement and development today. These include balancing the (often) competing priorities of community-identified expectations and student learning outcomes, the challenge of integrating curriculum about social issues into courses that are designed to cover large amounts of disciplinary-specific content, and managing the tension between the pervasive neoliberal culture of higher education and the expectation that institutions act as sites for students' civic education and development.

In fact, the competencies in Zlotkowski's 1998 model are present in Blanchard and colleagues' 2009 article arguing for community-engaged faculty development programs to focus on honing faculty members' skills and perpetuating an academic culture that supports community engagement. Competencies are leveled from novice to advanced and include things like knowing and applying CES principles, theories, and evaluation practices; being able to transfer skills to the community; and describing CES activities in tenure and promotion portfolios. The article suggested faculty development formats, content, incentives, and documentation for each level of expertise to be attained and noted interventions across school, university, and organizational domains.

Though Wade and Demb (2009) did not propose a model for faculty development per se, their conceptual model argues that faculty perceptions of factors such as the benefits, challenges, barriers, and supports to integrating CES are crucial indicators of whether faculty initiate, maintain, and/or advance CES practices. The authors organize these factors into a conceptual framework that encompasses three dimensions (or domains): institutional, professional, and personal. Within each dimension, multiple factors are at play, ranging from institutional mission to faculty racial identity to disciplinary socialization.

Axtell (2012) developed an in-house competency-based framework for faculty development at the University of Minnesota consisting of two broad domains, each incorporating five categories or competencies consisting of a comprehensive list of knowledge, skills, and attitudes. This faculty development domain consists of (a) an engagement framework, (b) career development, (c) critical reflection, (d) building and sustaining relationships, and (e) navigating and changing the institutional system. The domain of the community-engaged scholar includes (a) teaching, (b) research, (c) practice, (d) outreach, and (e) administration.

The model developed by Jordan and colleagues (2012) grew out of a grant-funded initiative developed collaboratively by the Community Campus Partnership for Health (CCPH), the University of Minnesota, and the University of North Carolina at Chapel Hill. The Faculty for the Engaged Campus (FEC) initiative built on previous work of CCPH, integrating and assessing faculty CES competencies established by Blanchard and colleagues (2009). The University of Minnesota instituted a one-year faculty development program focused on building or enhancing faculty members' CES competencies and fostering participants to be ambassadors for CES in accordance with Rogers's (1962) diffusion of innovations theory. Program participants completed retrospective pre/post assessment surveys meant to measure faculty perceptions of their level of mastery of a variety of CES competencies. Results from the qualitative component of their mixed methods study showed that faculty could situate their work within a broader CES framework, were enthusiastic about their CES work, and felt better equipped to integrate CES theories and concepts into teaching and research. However, results of the study do not account for changes in faculty practice and related student, institutional, and community outcomes. Finally, Dostilio (2017) identified and enumerated a set of competencies for S-LCEs organized into six broad categories, one of which details the knowledge, skills, and dispositions necessary for facilitating faculty development and support (see Table 1.3).

A Meta-Model for a Holistic Framework for Professional Development

The emerging body of knowledge regarding best practice and competency-based professional development as previously presented can be synthesized into a meta-model for a holistic framework to develop, implement, and assess continuing professional education for the various S-LCE stakeholders in an array of contexts or settings. Our approach is derived from the literature on the evolving roles and responsibilities of community engagement professionals (Dostilio, 2017) and relevant constructs from other competency-based models cited previously. The framework presented here entails providing professional education through direct and indirect means across a complex web of interrelated domains for an array of stakeholders in a variety of settings and contexts. An essential element of this model of professional education is multifaceted, direct, and authentic assessment of impact. Building from the narrative presented previously, we have conceptualized a model that consists of (a) two domains of stakeholders and contexts, (b) four stakeholders, (c) four contexts, (d) conceptual framing factors, (e) faculty competencies, (f) locus of change, and (g) impact assessment (see Table 1.4).

TABLE 1.3
Knowledge, Skills, and Dispositions for Facilitating Faculty Development

Knowledge	Skills and Abilities	Dispositions
• How to approach differently motivated faculty using different strategies • How various departments or disciplines place value on categories of faculty work—teaching, research, and service • Institutional constraints and possibilities that prevent or support faculty engagement • The logistic support needed to implement engaged teaching and research • The needs, research interests, and areas of expertise of faculty engaging in CES • Various faculty career stages and ranks	• Articulating the pressures or existential unease of engagement without alienating or discouraging faculty • Customizing developmental training and support to fit each faculty member's needs and interests • Empathizing with faculty and understanding possibly conflicting demands on faculty time • Facilitating critical reflection wherein faculty encounter the limits of their own experience and value of leveraging community expertise • Facilitating faculty learning from one another • Helping faculty brainstorm how to incorporate community engagement into teaching and research • Helping faculty synergize their teaching, research, and community engagement	• Humility • Innovation/ designing and implementing new programs • Patience • Persuasion • Multidisciplinary and inter-disciplinary collaborations

Source: Adapted from Dostilio, 2017.

Stakeholders and Contexts

Given that effective design and implementation of engaged teaching and scholarship extends outside the confines of a classroom, we have come to realize there are multiple stakeholders and contexts to the process of continuing professional education. The model described here reflects the stakeholders within the SOFAR (students, organizations, faculty, administrators, and residents) model developed by the Center for Service and Learning in the Indiana University Purdue University–Indianapolis Office of Community

TABLE 1.4
Holistic Framework for Professional Development to Advance Community Engagement

Domains	Factors to Consider	Necessary Faculty Competencies	Locus of Change	Measures of Impact
STAKEHOLDERS				
Faculty	Discipline Social identity and background Prior life experiences Nature of faculty role (e.g., tenured, adjunct, etc.) Level of professional experience with CES Other professional commitments	Describe CES concepts, terms and principles (novice) Demonstrate familiarity with CES history and seminal literature (novice) Identify personal motivations and commitments that drive interest in CES (novice) Apply CES principles, theoretical frameworks, and pedagogical strategies when implementing CES (intermediate) Identify potential CES outcomes and a plan for assessing them (intermediate) Develop and deepen cultural competence and critical consciousness (intermediate) Effectively describe CES activities for promotion and tenure review (advanced) Engage in reflection about professional practice and identity through the lens of CES (advanced)	Course design and pedagogical practice Scholarly identity Sense of belonging to other community engagement (CE) scholars Behaviors and beliefs rooted in cultural competence and critical consciousness Promotion & tenure (P&T) preparation Reflective practice	Pre/post measure of knowledge Course syllabus and related documents developed that meet designation and incorporate benchmarks of best practice Focus groups and interviews Awards (e.g., Lynton, Ehrlich) Written and oral reflection Faculty participation in professional development (PD)

Students	Social identity and demographics Prior life experiences Developmental stage/level (Constraints on) time (Constraints on) funds Perception of purpose of higher education and/or degree attainment Perception of community Values and beliefs	Understand need for community-engaged experiences, reflection, and assessment that align with course content and outcomes (novice) Attend to student diversity of student developmental stages, social identities, and life experiences when designing course (intermediate) Integrate community engagement into a class as an integral component of learning process (intermediate) Supplement community experience with content that allows students to reflect on systems of power, privilege, and oppression (intermediate) Effectively facilitate oral and written critical reflection (intermediate) Implement authentic assessment of student learning from CE (advanced)	Student achievement of disciplinary outcomes Student achievement of civic outcomes (knowledge, skills, and dispositions) Student sense of connection to community Student self-efficacy as a civic actor and social change agent Student civic behaviors Student vocational calling and professional trajectory	Scholarly work products Project deliverables for community partner (CP) Reflections Surveys Interviews and focus groups Community partner evaluation of student performance

(Continues)

TABLE 1.4 (Continued)

Domains	Factors to Consider	Necessary Faculty Competencies	Locus of Change	Measures of Impact
Administrators	Organization structure (org chart) Individual roles and responsibilities Power dynamics Disciplinary field Professional pathway and aspirations	Describe community-engaged practices happening across campus (novice) Describe history, principles, and practices of CES in higher education (intermediate) Use data to advocate for funds, policies, and practices that support CES (advanced)	Articulate public purpose of higher education, and specifically CES Know and value existing CES activities happening at institution Know and value CES principles, practices, and trends Promote and support CES	Oral and written public statements Allocation of funds and awards Discussions and interviews Participation in committees, working groups, meetings about CES
Community Partners	Mission of organization Staffing and leadership Services provided Nature of "service" (e.g., advocacy, direct service, education)	Knowledge of potential community partners, their missions and services (novice) Understand community partner role as coeducator (novice) Understand concept of reciprocity (novice)	Build capacity to provide services and/or assess impact Partnership reciprocity Shift power dynamics toward equity	CP-generated data on outcomes/impact for organization Surveys Focus groups and interviews

A HOLISTIC FRAMEWORK FOR PROFESSIONAL DEVELOPMENT

			Grow awareness of and advocacy for CP work	Written narratives and reflections Student reflections on CP Grants and awards for CE work
	Capacity to partner with courses/host students Community/clients served Funding and budget considerations Partnerships and collaborations with other institutions	Communicate effectively with community partners about expectations, needs, and challenges of partnership (intermediate) Integrate community partners into course planning, content delivery, and assessment (intermediate) Maintain equitable balance (reciprocity) between student and community outcomes in achievement of CES partnership activities (advanced) Collaborate with community partners to cocreate knowledge, learning experiences, and capacity-building opportunities (advanced)		
CONTEXTS				
Higher Education and Academic Discipline	Existence of journals, texts, conferences, and so on National awards and recognitions Accreditation and assessment Research, teaching, service paradigm	Familiar with CES history and seminal literature (novice) Write and speak about CES work in a compelling way for grants, scholarly articles, and conference presentations (intermediate) Collaborate with colleagues across institutions, disciplines, and communities to produce innovative scholarship on CES (advanced)	Dissemination of CE practices and research across CE field New paradigms of engaged research, teaching, service Transinstitutional and transdisciplinary collaborations	Publications Conference presentations Grants National awards and classifications (e.g., President's Honor Roll, Carnegie)

(Continues)

TABLE 1.4 (Continued)

Domains	Factors to Consider	Necessary Faculty Competencies	Locus of Change	Measures of Impact
	History and nature of discipline Relative "value" of discipline as perceived by various groups		More equitable, inclusive, democratic higher education spaces (campuses, conferences, etc.)	Host meetings and conferences
Institutional	Mission and vision Logistics and administration of CE Policies and procedures Culture and values Accreditation status Departmental politics Budget and funding	Connect with campus CE center and other colleagues doing CES (novice) Evaluate scholarly content of CES narratives and scholarship in P&T portfolios (intermediate) Act as a mentor and resource to novice CE faculty (intermediate) Understand institutional support structures and barriers that affect the practice of CES (intermediate) Work with other CE stakeholders to bring about institutional changes that sustain and enhance CE practices and outcomes (advanced)	Policies and procedures Organization culture and values P&T review guidelines, policies, and practices Funding priorities Whose voice matters? Infusion of CE across departments and schools Incentives and reward for CE Recruitment and retention of CE faculty and administrators	Funding for CES Awards and compensation for faculty Existence of a center or office supporting CES Engaged departments Survey of faculty, staff, administrators National awards and recognitions (e.g., Carnegie Classification for Community Engagement)

A HOLISTIC FRAMEWORK FOR PROFESSIONAL DEVELOPMENT

				Community partner representation in decision-making bodies and processes
Reports and white papers
Institutional self-assessment
Classroom	Layout of classroom
Number of students
Structure, format, and timing of course sessions
Quarter or semester system
Disciplinary content and outcomes	Organize the classroom space to reflect multidirectional teaching and learning (novice)
Invite diverse voices by including underrepresented narratives and community partners/members as guest speakers (intermediate)
Recognize and navigate inherent classroom power dynamics based on role, race, class, and other aspects of identity (intermediate)
Use a range of techniques to facilitate group discussion and reflection (intermediate)	Student engagement
Integration of content that reflects diverse voices and perspectives
Shift classroom power dynamics toward more democratic, inclusive, equitable paradigm
Create space for multiple epistemologies and learning styles	Tracking student participation and completion of service commitments
Student reflections
Observation of teaching
Review of course content
Review of course activities and assignments

(*Continues*)

TABLE 1.4 *(Continued)*

Domains	Factors to Consider	Necessary Faculty Competencies	Locus of Change	Measures of Impact
			Identify and utilize appropriate community spaces as classrooms for student learning and integrate community members as course participants and colearners (advanced)	
Community	Assets and resources Challenges and barriers Social justice issues History and current status Demographics and juxtaposition of diverse groups Nature of relationships between service providers and residents/recipients	Recognize community as a collection of diverse groups and individuals with both converging and diverging interests, needs, and assets (novice) Understand complex systemic nature of social justice issues (novice) Develop and act in accordance with a commitment to fostering social change (novice) Work effectively with diverse community constituencies (intermediate)	Address community-identified priorities and needs Build trust and sustained partnerships between "town" and "gown" Build individual and collective capacity of community to drive positive social change	Community presence on campus Faculty and student presence in community Feedback from community members and leaders: survey, focus groups, interviews

	Transfer and/or apply skills to the community to build capacity (intermediate) Leverage CES to support community empowerment and social change (advanced)	Sustained collaborative projects and programs Asset maps Public policy, economic development metrics, and/or interventions resulting from CES collaborations

Note: Necessary Faculty Competencies (column 3) adapted from Blanchard et al., 2009, and Axtell, 2012.

Engagement. However, we extend our analysis beyond stakeholders to include related contexts of classroom, community, the college or university (institution), disciplinary fields, and the broader landscape of higher education. Serving S-LCE stakeholders in a variety of contexts requires the S-LCE professional to consider a litany of elements, including the factors that support or inhibit implementation of community engagement; competencies faculty need to develop to engage across constituencies and contexts; desired change in behaviors, processes, practices, and culture; and methods for assessing impact of professional development programming that go beyond participant satisfaction surveys.

Faculty
Although this chapter advocates a broader view of professional educational development to include a variety of stakeholders, we also recognize that S-LCE professionals will spend the majority of their time and energy working directly with faculty. In turn, much of that work will indirectly serve other stakeholders. Support for continued professional education of faculty can take many forms in addition to traditional approaches of workshops and cohorts. The research conducted by Dostilio (2017) on professional competencies noted this by including the ability to customize developmental training and support to fit each faculty member's needs and interests as a salient and necessary skill of S-LCE professionals. In addition to forming workshops and learning community cohorts, Welch (2016) enumerated other methods such as consulting one-on-one, forming book clubs, hosting informal brown bag lunch discussion workshops, creating a resource library, providing e-mails and newsletter updates of funding opportunities, and providing minigrants. Perhaps more importantly, robust professional development can help individual faculty members establish their identities as engaged scholars and professionals.

Students
Professional development indirectly serves students by empowering faculty and community partners to create, implement, and assess robust engaged teaching and learning experiences. This includes teaching and practicing professionalism and cultural competency. In essence, the student dimension in this context is a key driving force to professional development. It is incumbent on S-LCE professionals and faculty to use best practice not only in implementing engaged pedagogy but also in assessing its impact on students' cognitive, attitudinal, vocational, and civic development. Similarly, the collective leadership of S-LCE professionals can influence policy and procedure overseen by administrators of the institution in ways that support students' civically engaged

experiences. This may and could include directly serving students by preparing student leaders to take the role of engaged teaching and learning assistants to serve as liaisons between instructors and community partners for logistical coordination of activities, which is now common at many institutions.

Administrators
The S-LCE professional essentially provides continued professional education when working with administrators to advance engagement that is aligned with the institutional mission (Hubler & Quan, 2016). Further, the S-LCE professional can shape institutional policies and practices in areas like risk management, tenure and promotion, course development funding, and community-campus partnerships. Depending on position and status, the S-LCE professional may directly wield influence with campus administrators or leverage the influence of a critical mass of faculty who can advocate for changes that foster and support engaged teaching and scholarship. In this way, the work of the S-LCE professional reflects the elements of transformative and collective leadership described previously.

Community Partners
S-LCE professionals should consider why and how community partners can get involved with service-learning and community engagement, not only on a course level but also as allies and advocates for institutional and community change. If this is the role we want community partners to play, what sort of professional development and support do they need? How can S-LCE professionals deliver that support directly through workshops and consultations and indirectly by coaching faculty on how to structure courses in a way that infuses community partner expertise?

Classroom
Though the classroom is the most immediate and obvious context in which service-learning and community engagement is implemented, S-LCE professionals and faculty must still devote broad and deep consideration to influential factors, faculty competencies, areas of change, and assessment. The infinite variability of these conceptual elements means that each S-LCE course is unique in how it unfolds, and therefore requires stakeholders to analyze and adapt their practices accordingly. In other words, teaching a community-engaged course isn't just a plug-and-play activity.

Discipline
Effective and comprehensive professional development efforts must acknowledge the reality that faculty work is directly tied to their discipline in what

Benson, Harkavy, and Hartley (2005) refer to as *disciplinary guildism*. This often manifests as faculty having greater loyalty to their discipline than to the institution and its mission (Welch, 2016). Adding to this dynamic of isolated disciplinary silos is the fact that the academic culture of the institution itself values disciplinary work as part of the promotion and tenure system, necessitating the dissemination of new knowledge within disciplinary venues. Comprehensive professional educational development programs must be aware of and take into account this pragmatic factor by including it as part of the programming. In this way, intentional guidance, planning, and effort are given to disciplinary dissemination as part of professional development.

Institution

As mentioned previously, the S-LCE's collective and transformative leadership role can have a profound impact on the institution itself. Educating administrators and faculty about S-LCE can influence the institutional mission, or at least the way the mission is understood and operationalized by stakeholders. Specifically, it can impact hiring practices, resource allocation, public statements, and financial aid priorities. At a larger, macro level, the S-LCE professional typically plays a major role in achieving external recognition of the institution's efforts to embrace community engagement through the application to and awarding of the Carnegie Classification for Community Engagement or the President's Honor Roll for Community Service, both of which help the institution garner recognition and prestige.

Higher Education

Related to this, S-LCE professionals have the power to both directly and indirectly assist their institutions in attaining national recognition for service-learning and community engagement endeavors and disseminating information about those programs and practices to inform changes to S-LCE in higher education. Whether the S-LCE professional functions as a practitioner-scholar who conducts research and publishes or presents on it or simply supports faculty in doing engaged research and disseminating it in journals focused on the S-LCE field, this form of professional development is essential as it facilitates a return to what Saltmarsh and Hartley (2011) refer to as the democratic public purpose of higher education. They characterize this purpose as serving with rather than for the community in ways that "locate the university within an ecosystem of knowledge production, requiring interaction with other knowledge producers outside the university for the creation of new problem-solving knowledge through a multidirectional flow of knowledge and expertise" (p. 21).

Community

Professional development in the community context requires taking into account factors like culture, demographics, and the nature of relationships among residents, service providers, and the university. Further, S-LCE professionals must be aware of the gaps between traditional research and teaching practices, and the forces that lead to community change. Borrowing from the medical field, it is paramount to practice a *do no harm* ethos when working in and with the community. Faculty scholarship and student learning should not come at the expense of community agencies and those they serve.

Conceptual Framing Elements

The elements enumerated in the column headings in Table 1.4 hold influence over the extent to which stakeholders and contexts undergo change through professional development interventions to achieve desired impact. For S-LCE professionals to provide effective support and professional development, they must not only consider but also address situational factors, professional competencies, locus of change, and measures of impact.

Factors to Consider

Building on the work of Wade and Demb (2009), Table 1.4 describes numerous factors that might either support or inhibit the implementation of service-learning and community engagement. For S-LCE stakeholders, internal factors can be static (e.g., race) or change over time (e.g., perception of social issues). External factors affecting individuals might include institutional norms (e.g., publish or perish) or competing time commitments (e.g., students balancing work, full course load, and family responsibilities). Contextual factors range from use of physical space (e.g., classroom setup) to historical narrative (e.g., evolution of town-gown relations over time). Whatever the source of these factors, they can heavily influence the extent to which stakeholders are willing and able to engage in, and enhance, S-LCE practices.

Necessary Faculty Competencies

The faculty competencies column in Table 1.4 reflects the work of Blanchard and colleagues (2009) and Axtell (2012). It is built on the assumption that faculty are responsible for not only learning knowledge, skills, and dispositions required for effective community-engaged teaching and scholarship but also for fostering their capacity to support the professional development of other stakeholders and catalyze positive change in a range of contexts with the end goal of fulfilling the aspirations of S-LCE as a transformative practice. This work should be done in tandem with S-LCE professionals and other stakeholders as their community-engaged capacities and commitments flourish.

Locus of Change
Historically, faculty development has been focused on course development in which the locus of change and impact has been on student performance in a classroom setting. Community engagement extends beyond the four walls of the classroom to various settings and constituencies. As such, a holistic framework for professional educational development must explicitly name the elements that should sustain the intended changes, so that interventions can be built to effectively stimulate these desired changes. This also has implications for how assessment is conceived and implemented. To be able to assess an impact, one must first be clear about the impact one is trying to make.

Measures of Impact
The review of current trends we have presented clearly documents that assessment of professional educational development programs is limited, if not altogether nonexistent. We argue this presents both a pedagogical and ethical issue as our field cannot empirically document or claim to have made an impact on the continued education of professionals. The holistic framework presented in Table 1.4 offers various ways to directly and indirectly assess the impact of professional educational development. As the adjective implies, direct impact assessment is somewhat straightforward as specific targeted goals, such as faculty knowledge of reflection strategies, can be readily measured by a pre/post survey or observed on a course syllabus and/or applied in a class discussion. Indirect assessment involves determining if new knowledge and skills assimilated through professional educational development have been evident and/or applied in other settings and contexts with participating stakeholders such as students or community partners.

Discussion

The broader scope of professional development put forth through this holistic framework accounts for the ethical implications of CES for individuals, institutions, and community. In other words, it assumes that service-learning and other forms of engaged scholarship are high-stakes endeavors that can transform individual worldviews and macro-level systems of oppression when done well but can reinforce oppressive ways of thinking and functioning when done poorly. Thus, faculty members, as the fulcrums around which service-learning courses move, must be informed in their practice. The framework centers the S-LCE professional not only as a provider of faculty development but also as a transformative leader with a moral imperative to engage and develop the skills, knowledge, and values of all community engagement stakeholders while also influencing institutional culture, policies, and practices vis-à-vis community.

As transformative leaders, S-LCE professionals must consider how multiple domains shape, and are shaped by, faculty professional development for community engagement. S-LCE professionals need to account for a variety of push and pull factors, not only those directly related to faculty but also to other stakeholders like students, administrators, and community partners when designing and implementing professional development offerings. This shifts the traditional locus of impact of professional development from classroom and the community to the institution and discipline. In other words, effective professional development transcends developing and delivering effective "workshops" limited to a few hours on the "nuts and bolts" of course construction to using collective action to transform the institution and advance the public purpose of higher education.

Plater (2011) described collective leadership, which manifests itself through the following developmental stages: (a) interpreting the institutional mission to reflect engagement with a variety of audiences and constituencies, (b) defining and proposing specific objectives and goals to realize that mission, (c) cocreating and articulating the steps to achieve those goals, and (d) demonstrating commitment through personal interactions (Sandmann & Plater, 2009). Successful completion of these stages demonstrate knowing how to work with, rather than against, administrators as S-LCE professionals use their collective leadership to influence change (Meyerson, 2003) that will advance and support this work.

These combined components embody and reflect key tenets of transformational leadership theory (Kezar, Gallant, & Lester, 2011; Sandmann & Plater, 2013) because the evolving role of the S-LCE professional goes beyond merely providing direct and discrete skill sets to individual instructors through traditional notions and practice of faculty development to assuming informal and formal leadership within and outside the academy to advance community engagement. Transformational leadership is a process in which leaders, colleagues, and partners collaboratively identify a need for change coupled with collectively developing a plan for implementing that change to empower others in ways that promote social change (Kezar et al., 2011). In this way, Kezar and colleagues (2011) assert that the leadership process "allows scholars to embrace dynamic, process-oriented, collective, context bound, nonhierarchical perspectives of leadership focused on mutual power and influence that emphasize collaboration, cultural understanding, and social responsibility" (as cited in Sandmann & Plater, 2013, p. 514).

Conclusion

This chapter has reframed and expanded traditional approaches to faculty development to create a broader holistic framework of advancing engaged teaching and scholarship with multiple stakeholders in various settings. This process requires the S-LCE professional to take on an array of roles and responsibilities that include yet transcend incorporating customary methods of one-on-one consultation and informal workshops. The remaining chapters and case studies build from this foundation, providing S-LCE professionals strategies and models to use, as well as elucidating how these considerations are framed within larger contexts of broader nationwide initiatives and considerations surrounding the intersections of this work with scholarship.

References

Axtell, S. (2012). *Creating a community-engaged (CES) faculty development program: Phase one—Program and skill mapping.* Retrieved from http://www.engagement.umn.edu/faculty/tools (University of Minnesota Office for Public Engagement)

Beere, C. A., Votruba, J. C., & Wells, G. W. (2011). *Becoming an engaged campus: A practical guide for institutionalizing public engagement.* San Francisco, CA: Jossey-Bass.

Benson, M., Harkavy, I., & Hartley, M. (2005). Integrating a commitment to the public good into the institutional fabric. In A. J. Kezar, A. C. Chambers, and J. C. Burkhardt (Eds.), *Higher education for the public good: Emerging voices from a national movement* (pp. 185–216). San Francisco, CA: Jossey-Bass.

Blanchard, L. W., Hanssmann, C., Strauss, R. P., Belliard, J. C., Krichbaum, K., Waters, E., & Seifer, S. D. (2009). Models for faculty development: What does it take to be a community-engaged scholar? *Metropolitan Universities, 20*(2), 47–65.

Blanchard, L. W., Strauss, R. P., & Webb, L. (2012). Engaged scholarship at the University of North Carolina at Chapel Hill: Campus integration and faculty development. *Journal of Higher Education Outreach and Engagement, 16*(1), 97–128.

Boyte, H., & Fretz, E. (2011). Civic professionalism. In J. Saltmarsh & M. Hartley (Eds.), *"To serve a larger purpose": Engagement for democracy and the transformation of higher education* (pp. 82–101). Philadelphia, PA: Temple University Press.

Campus Compact. (2014). *2014 Campus Compact member survey.* Retrieved from http://compact.org/wp-content/uploads/2015/05/2014ALLPublicInstitutionsReport.pdf

Development [Def. 2]. (n.d.). In Merriam-Webster online. Retrieved from http://www.merriam-webster.com/dictionary/development

Dostilio, L. D. (2017). *The community engagement professional in higher education: A competency model for an emerging field.* Boston, MA: Campus Compact.

Dostilio, L. D., Benenson, J., Chamberlin, S., Crossland, S., Farmer-Hanson, A., Hernandez, K., and colleagues (2006). Preliminary competency model for community engagement professions. In L. D. Dostilio (Ed.), *The community engagement professional in higher education: A competency model for an emerging field*. Boston, MA: Campus Compact.

Furco, A., & Moely, B. (2012). Using learning communities to build faculty support for pedagogical innovation: A multi campus study. *Journal of Higher Education, 83*(1), 128–153.

Gelmon, S. B., & Agre-Kippenhan, S. (2002). A developmental framework for supporting evolving faculty roles in community engagement. *The Journal of Public Affairs 6*(Suppl. 1), 161–182. Retrieved from Academic Search Complete database (accession no. 8657855)

Gelmon, S., Blanchard, L., Ryan, K., & Seifer, S. D. (2012). Building capacity for community-engaged scholarship: Evaluation of the faculty development component of the faculty for the engaged campus initiative. *Journal of Higher Education Outreach and Engagement, 16*(1), 21–45.

Green, P. M., Harrison, B., Jones, J., Shaffer, T. J. (2016). Paving new professional pathways for community-engaged scholarship. In M. A. Post, E. Ward, N. V. Longo, & J. Saltmarsh (Eds.), *Publicly engaged scholars: Next-generation engagement and the future of higher education* (pp. 141–155). Sterling, VA: Stylus Publishing.

Holland, B., & Langseth, M. N. (2010). Leverage financial support for service-learing: Relevance, relationships, results, resources. In B. Jacoby, & P. Mutascio (Eds.), *Looking in/reaching out: A reflective guide for community service-learning professionals* (pp. 185–210). Providence, RI: Campus Compact.

Hubler, R., & Quan, M. (2016). Envisioning, leading, and enacting institutional change for the public good: The role of community engagement professionals In L. D. Dostilio (Ed.), *Community engagement professionals project: Establishing a preliminary competency model for second generation CEPs* (pp. 76–91). Boston, MA: Campus Compact.

Jaeger, A. J., Jameson, J. K., & Clayton, P. (2012). Institutionalization of community-engaged scholarship at institutions that are both land-grant and research universities. *Journal of Higher Education Outreach and Engagement, 16*(1), 149–167.

Jameson, J. K., Clayton, P. H., Jaeger, A. J., & Bringle, R. G. (2012). Investigating faculty learning in the context of community-engaged scholarship. *Michigan Journal of Community Service Learning, 18*(2), 40–55.

Jones, S. R., & Palmerton, A. (2010). How to develop campus-community partnerships. In B. Jacoby and P. Mutascio (Eds.), *Looking in/reaching out: A reflective guide for community service-learning professionals* (pp. 163–184). Providence, RI: Campus Compact.

Jordan, C., Jones-Webb, R., Cook, N., Dubrow, G., Mendenhall, T. J., & Doherty, W. J. (2012). Competency-based faculty development in community-based scholarship: A diffusion of innovations approach. *Journal of Higher Education Outreach and Engagement, 16*(1), 65–95.

Kezar, A., Gallant, T., & Lester, J. (2011). Everyday people making a difference on college campuses: The tempered grassroots leadership tactics of faculty and staff. *Studies in Higher Education, 36*(2), 129–151.

Lawler, P. A. (2003). Teachers as adult learners: A new perspective. *New Directions for Adult and Continuing Education, 98*, 15–22.

Little, D. (2014). Reflections on the state of the scholarship of educational development. *To Improve the Academy, 33*(1), 1–13.

McKee, C. W., & Tew, W. M. (2013, Spring). Setting the stage for teaching and learning in American higher education: Making the case for faculty development. *New Directions for Teaching and Learning, 133*, 3–14.

Meyerson, D. E. (2003). *Tempered radicals: How everyday leaders inspire change at work.* Boston, MA: Harvard Business School Press.

Orphan, C. M., & O'Meara, K. (2016). Next generation engagement scholars in the neoliberal university. *Publicly Engaged Scholars: Next Generation Engagement and the Future of Higher Education*, 214–231.

Plater, W. M. (2011). Collective leadership for engagement: Reclaiming the public purpose of higher education. In J. A. Saltmarsh and M. Hartley (Eds.), *"To serve a larger purpose": Engagement for democracy and the transformation of higher education* (pp. 102–129). Philadelphia, PA: Temple University Press.

Rogers, E. M. (1962). *Diffusion of innovations.* New York, NY: Free Press.

Rychen, D. S., & Salganik, L. H. (2001). *Defining and selecting key competencies.* Cambridge, MA: Hogrefe & Huber.

Saltmarsh, J., & Hartley, M. (2011). Democratic engagement. In J. Saltmarsh and M. Hartley (Eds.), *"To serve a larger purpose": Engagement for democracy and the transformation of higher education* (pp. 14–29). Philadelphia, PA: Temple University Press.

Sandmann, L. R., & Plater, W. M. (2009). Leading the engaged institution. In L. R. Sandmann, C. H. Thornton, & A. J. Jaeger (Eds.), *Institutionalizing community engagement in higher education: The first wave of Carnegie Classified institutions.* (pp. 13–24). San Francisco, CA: Jossey-Bass.

Sandmann, L. R., & Plater, W. M. (2013). Research on institutional leadership for service learning. In P. Clayton, R. Bringle, & J. Hatcher (Eds.), *Research on service learning: Conceptual frameworks and assessment* (pp. 505–535). Sterling, VA: Stylus.

Savaki, V. (2008). *Developing intercultural competence and transformation: Theory, research and application in international education.* Sterling, VA: Stylus Publishing.

Seifer, S. D., Blanchard, L. W., Jordan, C., Gelmon, S., & McGinley, P. (2012). Faculty for the engaged campus: Advancing community-engaged careers in the academy. *Journal of Higher Education Outreach and Engagement, 16*(1), 5–20.

Wade, A., & Demb, A. (2009). A conceptual model to explore faculty community engagement. *Michigan Journal of Community Service Learning, 15*(2). Retrieved from http://quod.lib.umich.edu/m/mjcsl/3239521.0015.201?rgn=main;view=fulltext

Welch. M. (2010). A travel guide on the culture, mission, and politics of academia to promote service-learning. In B. Jacoby & P. Mutascio (Eds.), *Looking in/reaching out: A reflective guide for community service-learning professionals* (pp. 55–72). Providence, RI: Campus Compact.

Welch, M. (2015). Unpublished faculty development workbook. Moraga: CA: Saint Mary's College of California.

Welch, M. (2016). *Engaging higher education: Purpose, platforms, and programs for community engagement.* Sterling, VA: Stylus.

Welch, M., & Plaxton-Moore, S. (2017). Faculty development for advancing community engagement in higher education: Current trends and future directions. *Journal of Higher Education Outreach and Engagement, 21*(2), 131–166.

Welch, M., & Saltmarsh, J. (2013). Current practice and infrastructures for campus centers of community engagement. *Journal of Higher Education Outreach and Engagement, 17*(4), 25–55.

Zlotkowski, E. (1998). *Successful service-learning programs: New models of excellence in higher education.* Bolton, MA: Anker.

2

FACULTY AS COLEARNERS

Collaborative Engagement and the Power of Story in Faculty Development

Timothy K. Eatman

Although many patterns of traditional ivory tower life persist, faculty in twenty-first-century institutions of higher education navigate very different terrain than their counterparts a generation ago. As an example, an important data point reflecting what I call the "75% faculty shuffle" is revealing. Kezar and Maxey (2013) reported trend data on faculty in academe demonstrating that 75% of full-time faculty in 1969 were counted among the ranks of those with tenure. Almost 50 years later, roughly 75% of the corresponding group are neither tenured nor on the tenure track. The reality of this shift alone is significant, holding far-reaching implications because the faculty largely shape institutional culture and climate. Students spend intensive but limited time on campus, and this is increasingly true for many administrators, but faculty are central to the traditions, character, and ethos of an institution over time (Post, Ward, Longo, & Saltmarsh, 2016; Schuster & Finkelstein, 2006; Thelin, 2011).

Extant literature documents the current dynamic landscape of higher education with its myriad changes, including demographic shifts, fluctuating fiscal models, pedagogical innovations, and technological approaches, to name a few (Dolgon, Mitchell, & Eatman, 2016; Eatman, 2012; Kezar, 2012; Lewis & Cantor, 2016; Schuster & Finkelstein, 2006). Within the landscape of higher education, scholars are becoming increasingly more strategic and imaginative about ways to connect with, and pursue democratic purposes in, the larger society (Boyte, 2015; Coles, 2014; Sousanis, 2015). In this regard, many institutions of higher education throughout the country are exploring and embracing community engagement in its sundry forms and definitions. In fact, thought leaders in the academy point to the prevalence or "Centrality of Engagement in Higher Education," actually the title of an important article (Fitzgerald, Bruns, Sonka, Furco, & Swanson, 2016). Publicly engaged scholarship (PES) in particular, with its determined focus on a collaborative knowledge-making enterprise, is an increasingly important aspect of this landscape (Association of American Colleges & Universities, 2012; Eatman, 2012).

Faculty development is very important in this context; regardless of how it is defined and operationalized, it is a useful mechanism for equipping faculty with the necessary tools to navigate their work and to operate as knowledgeable and effective agents within the institutions they serve. One may argue that faculty development writ large is a critical aspect of strategic institution-building in that it provides channels for faculty to be involved in and contribute to the development of institutional vision, mission, values, goals, and to go beyond strengthening teaching, to policy, governance, strategic planning, and other aspects of institutional life. This is to say that the principle of agency lies at the core of faculty development. Institutional aspirations and vision can be fueled by strong administrative leadership, but faculty represent the engine of amelioration. A model of such agency will be presented here and discussed further in chapter 12 as a potential theory of change regarding faculty development. Faculty curate student learning experiences, prepare and socialize students for professional careers, and foster subsequent generations of faculty who take up the mantle. Perhaps most importantly, they cultivate and pass along institutional memory. And for all the leadership that faculty provide and the information they share, I submit that we are at our best when we operate as colearners and understand the power of such a posture in our work. An exploration of this notion of faculty as colearners is becoming more widely pursued within the academy.

Goals and Objectives

This chapter was developed with three objectives intended to advance the purpose of the book. First, I reflect on the current landscape of higher education, lightly tracing the history of the engagement movement and using the collaborative engagement paradigm introduced in recent scholarship by Post and colleagues (2016) as a pivot point. Second, I expound on key elements of publicly engaged scholars as I have referred to them elsewhere (Eatman, 2012) to emphasize the expansiveness and generativity of knowledge-making that colearning can yield. The notion of faculty as colearners breathes within these complementary frameworks. Here I also discuss the politics of PES and the implications of engagement for institutional change. My third objective is to share gleanings from exemplary models that I have witnessed in my own consultations and opportunities to help design and facilitate faculty development initiatives. Drawing on my experience as faculty codirector of Imagining America: Artists and Scholars in Public Life, I hope in this chapter to urge an opening up of faculty development models to the power of story and public narrative as tools to deepen effectiveness and impact.

The Ever-Evolving Landscape: Ebbs and Flows of Engagement

In *The Wisconsin Idea*, written a little more than a century ago, Charles McCarthy (1912) formally described a philosophy that had been gestating under the leadership of Charles Van Hise, who served as president of the University of Wisconsin from 1903 to 1918. His vision was for a vibrant university with tentacles that would reach and positively impact every family of the state. Elsewhere, the 1960 California Master Plan for Higher Education, also known as the Donahoe Higher Education Act, championed by Clark Kerr, who in 1958 was chosen by the regents to lead the entire university system, was signed into law by Governor Brown on April 27, 1960. The plan revolutionized the university system within the state of California despite the fact that gains across social groups have been uneven since its inception. These examples represent two of the most striking twentieth-century vision and policy efforts that demonstrate the potential power of higher education when it advances an anchor institution mission, working together with community-based organizations addressing public purposes and community engagement; however, the academy has struggled to consistently live up to these ideals (Association of American Colleges & Universities, 2012; Coles, 2014; Finkelstein, 2001).

The shift in recent years toward a hyperfocus on economic, individual interest in higher education institutions has many tuned into the civic-minded aims of the academy. Maurrasse (2001) reflects on the role of higher education in communities, observing that, "while corporations meet some particular societal demands, they primarily are driven by the bottom line—profits. Institutions of higher education ideally are driven by the fulfillment of a social mission" (p. 11). A similar expression of this idea is presented by Bowen and the Carnegie Council on Policy Studies (1977), who argue "the goals of higher education are concerned with the development of the full potentialities of human beings and of society" (p. 54). Scholars committed to the democratic purposes of higher education support this conception, agreeing that "the function of American Scholars is to act as engaged 'Public Intellectuals,' not as solipsistic scholastics engaged in intramural battles for power, prestige, and cash within an Ivory Tower" (Benson, Harkavy, & Puckett, 2007, p. 51).

To be sure, the university has a complex history that runs the gamut in its demonstrated commitment to democratic ideals both in rhetorical and actual priorities. Michael Roth (2015), in his compelling book *Beyond the University: Why Liberal Education Matters*, traces the evolution of American higher education in a powerful and accessible way, reflecting its larger purposes while demonstrating the complex ebbs and flows of lofty aspirations and stifling limits.

Engaged Scholarship Across Faculty Roles

In his influential work, Boyer (1990) integrates the mission of the university beyond the three-tier objects of research, teaching, and service to a four-part inclusive definition of *success within institutions*, including the scholarships of discovery, integration, application, and teaching. This broadens all scholarship within the university beyond that which would typically fall under research, allowing for more expansive possibilities in the cocreation of knowledge (Colbeck & Michael, 2006; Schön, 1995). Boyer (1996b) reframes these notions of scholarship in "The Scholarship of Engagement," intending especially to clarify his position that engagement can enrich the knowledge-making enterprise, increasing the value of scholarship.

Boyer viewed the scholarship of discovery and inquiry as governed by the normative model of scholarship and wrestled with ways to open it up. In particular the *assumptive world* of the research university was the system that he was trying to make more flexible and democratic, without sacrificing intellectual rigor (Rice, 2006). Boyer's exasperation with the refusal of the system to grant scholarly legitimacy to crucial domains of knowledge-making is both powerful and warranted. Nonetheless in his effort to elevate the scholarship of teaching, for example, to the status of research, Boyer may have reinforced the dominant prestige hierarchy within higher education against which he focused his concept of the "New American College," inadvertently strengthening the difficulty of finding a home for emerging forms of engaged scholarship within the academy. This may have been useful as a strategic and politically persuasive approach at the time but clearly emphasizes a segmented notion of knowledge-making where each category is compelled to demonstrate that it rises to a privileged level—research. It is important to note that Boyer uses the term *scholarship* in very different ways between *Scholarship Reconsidered* (1990) and "The Scholarship of Engagement" (1996b). His latter framing has much more to do with a particular process of conducting research across all forms of research.

These critiques notwithstanding, notions and practices of engaged scholarship insist on a deeper exploration of the epistemology of knowledge-making.

The conceptual and scholarly efforts of Boyer and John Dewey, whom he frequently references, advance the movement in significant ways. It is equally important, however, to note other intellectual harbingers who are seldom identified as progenitors of the movement for engaged scholarship but deeply embody the essence of this work.

One notable example is found in the distinguished publicly engaged scholar W.E.B. Du Bois, whose transformational work established the first school of scientific sociology (Morris, 2015). His Atlanta school model exemplifies faculty and researchers as colearners and can serve as a strong case example of PES in action. His work is especially prescient in the way that it pushed back against blind adherence to established conventions about race. Morris (2015) observed about Du Bois:

> Because he believed that an authentic social science was possible and that inferior and superior races did not exist, Du Bois was the first social scientist to establish a sociological laboratory where systematic empirical research was conducted to determine the scientific causes of racial inequality. (pp. 437–439)

It lies beyond the scope of this chapter to name the diverse collection of scholars who could be included on the roster of those whose work shaped and advanced the mission and goals of engaged scholarship (Evans, 2009; Iton, 2008; Ransby, 2003). However, it is worth noting the example of Du Bois, and equally important not to miss in his work the critical intersection between PES and issues of social equity. These issues are germane both within the larger society and the community of scholars based in the academy as Morris so masterfully notes. The collaborative engagement paradigm to which we turn now is a useful framework to illuminate such important intersections and implications.

Collaborative Engagement Paradigm

In *Publicly Engaged Scholars: Next Generation Engagement and the Future of Higher Education* (Post et al., 2016), Longo and Gibson (2016) present the *collaborative engagement paradigm*, which they describe as "a new approach for understanding the theory and practice of engagement on college campuses" (p. 62). Collaborative engagement, they posit,

> recognizes that in a networked society, where information is no longer proprietary or the exclusive purview of experts and gatekeepers, the most robust forms of knowledge are cocreated by a wide range of actors.

It involves more than just a professor and students; it includes practitioners and those in the larger community affected by an issue. It recognizes that students and community partners have valuable contributions to make to the learning process and creates space to make that happen. (p. 62)

Collaborative engagement represents a conceptual and practical shift among institutions of higher education from organizing pedagogy around a focus on teaching or instruction to learning (Barr & Tagg, 1995). In this view, it is prudent to emphasize creating learning spaces and widening the circle of such spaces. Located at the intersection of deliberative dialogue, democratic engagement, and community engagement, collaborative engagement underscores the generative work that colearning offers. It arouses a knowledge ecology where the boundaries among and between formal learning spaces, typical learning hierarchies, and informal and even extracurricular learning spaces are blurred and challenged.

Examples of such spaces increase in the academy and often take the form of learning communities like the Honors Living-Learning Community (HLLC) at Rutgers University-Newark (in which I have the honor to serve as inaugural dean) and the CIVICUS Living and Learning Program at the University of Maryland. Emerging postbaccalaureate programs like Imagining America's Engagement Scholars, or even entire college models like College Unbound in Providence, Rhode Island, provide strong examples of knowledge ecologies in this regard. In each of these contexts the role that faculty play is critical to setting the tone and creating a thriving culture. The HLLC, for example, organizes a network of faculty to engage each other around innovative pedagogies for honors program students who are from communities traditionally underrepresented in higher education. Every aspect of the honors program experience, from the admissions process which includes staff and community members to the design of the new building under construction, pivots on the principles of collaborative engagement.

Both encompassing and extending research on high-impact practices for student success (Bonet & Walters, 2016; Kuh, 2008; Priest & Clegorne, 2015; Strom & Strom, 2013; Talbani, 2013; Tukibayeva & Gonyea, 2014), the collaborative engagement paradigm suggests opportunities to leverage the essential components of high-impact practices (curricular interventions, student life experiences, off-campus engagement, and classroom practices) toward faculty development. In a similar way, I believe this relates to best practices of faculty development. Malcolm Brown (2016), for example, has observed that the growing focus on learning-centered approaches apparent in pedagogical development in undergraduate and graduate education "is also informing—and perhaps transforming—the practice of faculty development.

Perhaps the shift can be best characterized as one from viewing faculty members as users of applications to seeing them as adult learners developing a craft" (p. 118). Brown's *craft development* mind-set is compelling and timely in a landscape where innovative and collaborative pedagogical practices are valued.

Collaborative engagement reaches beyond teaching and learning, foregrounding the ameliorative role that higher education can play in democracy. In particular, the deliberative dialogue dimension of collaborative engagement operationalizes how diverse perspectives among a range of stakeholders can be valued. Precisely because higher education has such a deeply embedded culture of exclusion and gatekeeping, it is essential to establish, initiate, and advance models that account for inevitable blind spots and missing voices. This affirms democratic principles and decision-making. In effect, PES supports collaborative engagement in many ways.

Key Elements of PES

As we consider faculty as colearners and the collaborative engagement paradigm, it is important to be clear about how *PES* is defined and operationalized. Although there are several useful definitions available, one that resonates most powerfully for me comes from the Imagining America report *Scholarship in Public: Knowledge Creation and Tenure Policy in the Engaged University* (Ellison & Eatman, 2008):

> Publicly engaged academic work is scholarly or creative activity integral to a faculty member's academic area. It encompasses different forms of making knowledge about, for, and with diverse publics and communities. Through a coherent, purposeful sequence of activities, it contributes to the public good and yields artifacts of public and intellectual value. (p. 6)

This definition offers room for creative transdisciplinary thinking and work. It calls for the expansion of knowledge-making beyond the ivory tower, emphasizing the critical importance of reciprocity and diverse collaborations. And it also celebrates the rigorous disciplinary and methodologically sound nature of knowledge creation while at the same time recognizing that this can manifest in a range of forms and artifacts with important implications for supporting social development and strengthening democracy.

Figure 2.1 employs conceptual mapping to illustrate 10 key elements of PES as I have described them elsewhere (Eatman, 2012). For the purposes of this chapter, I draw attention to the complementarity of the collaborative engagement paradigm and these key elements. Engaging the map like a story

Figure 2.1. Conceptual map of 10 key elements of PES.

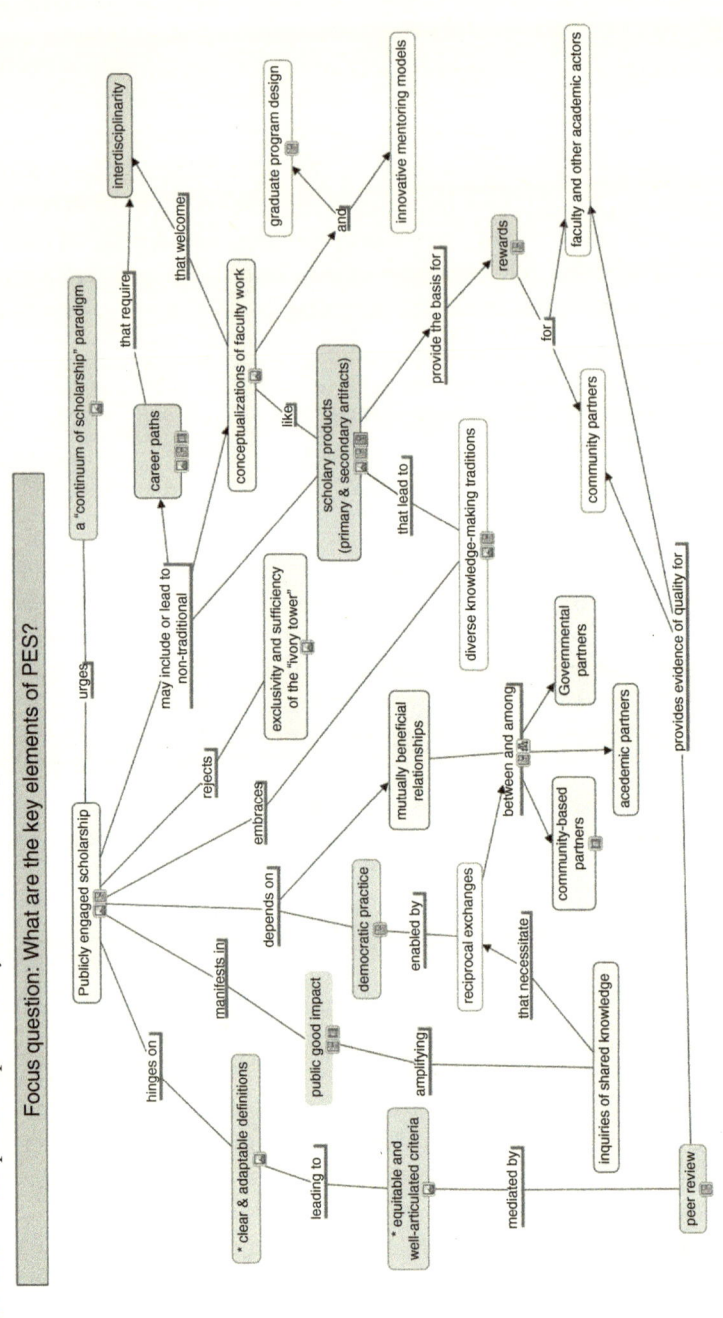

may help illuminate part-whole relationships among the key elements and connections to the collaborative engagement paradigm. I offer it as a tool for reflection and action toward the development of a consciousness, particularly among faculty, about the opportunities of PES for knowledge creation fit for twenty-first-century academy needs.

The PES story begins with emphasis on clear and adaptable definitions (top, left node). The map suggests this should lead to equitable and well-articulated criteria. Such criteria codify the principles of PES so that the work has full standing within academic systems. In a mature expression of collaboratively engaged PES, peer review processes mediated by refined definitions and criteria about knowledge-making are opened up. Thus, we can invite other perspectives, including those of community-based partners and students, into peer review processes. Reimagining peer review can provide evidence of quality for community partners as well as academic actors concerned about impact and/or who require robust assessments about the form and gravity of knowledge-making that expands the evidentiary base.

It is important to note that like collaborative engagement, PES depends on democratic practice enabled by reciprocal exchanges between and among a range of partners, certainly not limited to those in the academy. Locus of impact, especially in the public, amplifies inquiries of shared knowledge. This can help mitigate the pervasive and dominant myth of pure objective research, which serves most powerfully as a gatekeeping mechanism. The myth has a sustained deleterious impact on the manifestation of a full range of scholarly products, including but not limited to articles and books. It also has implications for the career paths that scholars choose and how they navigate opportunities to develop interdisciplinary and transdisciplinary intersections of their work (Eatman, Cantor, & Englot, 2016). The extant literature has established the critical nature of PES formulations and faculty rewards (Boyer, 1996a; Burack, 2010; Diamond, 1999, 2002; Ellison & Eatman, 2008; O'Meara, 2011; Sturm, Eatman, Saltmarsh, & Bush, 2011; Vogelgesang, Denson, & Jayakumar, 2010; Zahorski & Cognard, 1999).

It is important to emphasize here that PES urges a *continuum of scholarship paradigm* (Figure 2.2), which reminds us that knowledge-making is both expansive and replete with nuance. Scholarship at its best requires a deep and abiding sense of agency. Knowledge-makers decide where along the continuum of scholarship to locate themselves; this will likely evolve with the cycle of one's career. This is not only healthy but also essential in the academy of the twenty-first century. It is a kind of academic self-care, in a context that increasingly pitches toward narrow specialization. Faculty development models that keep this in view are sensitive to the dynamic needs of faculty

Figure 2.2. Continuum of scholarship paradigm.

and will be well positioned to be understood as a space of true professional support, nourishment, and even reinvention.

Faculty as Colearners: Cocreation of Knowledge and Public Scholarship

Many scholars have outlined the importance of researching faculty relationships with outside constituencies (Ehrlich & Jacoby, 2009; Harkavy & Wiewel, 1995; Kezar, Chambers, & Burkhardt, 2005). There is an extensive body of literature on the process of practical approaches to creating and sustaining successful university-community partnerships (Baum, 2000; Bowdon & Carpenter, 2011; Dugery & Knowles, 2003; Gass, 2007; Maurrasse, 2001, 2004; Rowley, 2000; Vollmer et al., 2009). Institutional leaders and faculty members from a number of disciplines are cocreating knowledge with communities that extend and test original theory in new contexts. This way of thinking, coupled with a shift of emphasis on problem-centered student learning outcomes, creates room to balance these ideas and promote knowledge creation locally with communities and universities working together (Berberet, 2002).

Calhoun (2006) points out the important but healthy tension of the creation of knowledge as simultaneously authoritative and democratic. Training supplies the former, and the sharing and dissemination supplies the latter. He writes:

> Collapsing the boundaries in favor of the broader public would undermine the capacity to produce authoritative knowledge. Enforcing overly strong boundaries would limit the extent to which research can be informed and challenged by practical problems, the extent to which knowledge is effectively communicated, and the likely support of the broader public for academic work. (p. 23)

The structure of rewards in higher education institutions favors the authoritative dimension of knowledge; some would argue to a fault. True to the structure and function of any traditional gatekeeping mechanism, exclusion and deference buttress this approach. The balance that Calhoun suggests is embodied at the nexus of the collaborative engagement paradigm and PES. It is naïve not to acknowledge that PES, like traditional modes of scholarship, is fraught with myriad challenging political considerations.

Politics of PES in Academe

In recent years, the research on university-community partnerships has flourished. However, the value of PES work and the public service mission of higher education are hotly debated across and within disciplines; this may be further complicated by political agendas at the local, state, and national level. Complying with Cantor and Levine's (2006) call for national attention to the tenure system related to PES, several university-affiliated organizations focus on the importance of these issues. An increasing number of educational institutions and associations, such as Community Campus Partnerships for Health (Seifer & Connors, 2007), Imagining America: Artists and Scholars In Public Life, and the National Forum on Higher Education for the Public Good, focus their work on understanding and analyzing the social role of the university and how it is institutionalized. Similarly, higher education institutions across the country have developed centers to form partnerships with local community partners to cultivate mutual benefits.

As Diamond and Adam (2004) point out, there are few careers beyond becoming a faculty member that offer such rich and diverse opportunities to contribute to the public good. However, these opportunities are often overshadowed by the political tensions within higher education institutions. Checkoway (2001) argues that few faculty members see community improvement as central to their role. Prins (2006) concurs based on her findings of a school-community partnership looking for more rewards for faculty who need to increase coordination without additional burden. However, public engagement work by faculty members is rarely valued in tenure and promotion, allowing little reward for work deemed important (Cantor & Levine, 2006; Diamond & Adam, 2004). Glassick, Huber, and Maeroff (1997) argue that scholarly work should not be exclusively measured by the research aims proposed by Boyer. That is, they emphasize shared standards of excellence defined by clear goals, adequate preparation, appropriate methods, significant results, effective communication, and reflective critique.

Change and Engagement Politics of Public Scholarship

Organizational change is difficult, and academic organizations are particularly difficult to change (Ramaley & Holland, 2005). Directed organizational change is complicated, and Fairweather (1996) notes that most of the major changes in higher education institutions are credited to external factors, despite what faculty members think about the internal debate necessary for such change. So, although many on the inside are resistant to change, academic institutions are capable of it. Change is possible.

An often-cited challenge in directed change efforts is the misalignment of rhetoric from leaders in the institutions with the actions of policy toward engagement in the community. But according to Cantor and Levine (2006), change is in the air. Lately there is a shift in constituencies supporting public scholarship. As mentioned earlier, national organizations are focusing on examining the process, and the Modern Language Association is moving toward greater flexibility in the tenure review process, including outlining the type of work that will influence tenure decisions.

One of the most frequently cited changes necessary to support this type of work is a realignment of the evaluation process for faculty to better meet community needs (Cantor & Levine, 2006; Checkoway, 2001; Dubb & Howard, 2007; Maurrasse, 2003). Dubb and Howard (2007) urge a broader understanding of scholarship that will include and enable change to the tenure process. Ramaley and Holland (2005) apply Glassick and colleagues' (1997) previously mentioned criteria of quality in scholarship to institutional change toward public scholarship. They argue that in order to achieve change, there must be clear goals, adequate preparation, appropriate methods, significant results, effective communication, and reflective critique. And whereas a plan is an essential step in any directed organizational change effort, in addition many in the field note the importance of leadership to implement that change both in policy and culture, especially in terms of tenure practices (Fairweather, 1996; Ramaley & Holland, 2005). Fairweather (1996) writes that "creating substantial changes in faculty and institutional roles to meet changing social and economic needs implies that academic leaders must confront the nature of faculty work and the incentives for maintaining existing faculty norms" (p. 2). Maurrasse (2003) highlights the asymmetrical impact of research universities on the higher education system to set standards and, thus, to impact change. Therefore, leaders in these institutions have a tremendous amount of power. However, as Maurrasse (2003) notes, these premier universities are often not at the forefront of creating new knowledge with their local partners. Ivory tower mentality, as I have called it elsewhere (Eatman, 2016), tends to reify the dominant position of the university and disparage contributions from community-based partners.

All of this is further complicated by the fact that higher education is often polarized between at least two politics as related to engaged scholarship. Public intellectual Harry Boyte (2015) aptly identifies the first of these as the objectivist politics of positivist social science. Its deformations, which are rampant in higher education, include the *experts know best* and *customer service type* approaches and paradigms. The second, subjectivist politics, describes Boyte, is alive in the service-learning/community research cultures. It counterposes *community* and *culture* and *storytelling* to the mainstream academic enterprise, which are basically seen as evildoers, with colleges and universities their bastions. There are exceptions, of course; many people in service-learning and community-based research have good intentions, and are major allies in the movement. But it is naïve not to recognize that in many cases the service-learning and community-based research culture has promoted a politics about blame-gaming, with the enemy being mainstream academia. These tensions can (intentionally or unintentionally) serve to undermine the PES movement, so an awareness of them and the development of strategies for navigating them is imperative.

Exemplars: Collaborative Engagement and Faculty Development

Academic politics notwithstanding, the extant literature demonstrates compelling examples of faculty development tuned to issues of engaged scholarship (Blanchard et al., 2009; Boyte, 2004; Brown, 2016; Furco & Moely, 2012; Hurtado & Pryor, 2005; McKee, Johnson, Ritchie, & Tew, 2013; McKee & Tew, 2013; Salsberg, Seller, Shea, & Macaulay, 2012; Steinert et al., 2009; Warren et al., 2014; Zahorski & Cognard, 1999; Zlotkowski, 1998). Such examples span a range of models from those that use a Dreyfus skill acquisition approach (Blanchard et al., 2009) where learners navigate through five distinct stages of skill acquisition (Dreyfus & Dreyfus, 1980) to themed working groups (Warren et al., 2014) to multiyear faculty learning communities and institution-wide models that bring issues of community, engagement, and student success together with diversity, access, and inclusion (Sturm et al., 2011), to name a few.

Given the emphasis of this chapter I find it useful in this section to point out two examples of faculty development that honor and draw on the principles of collaborative engagement and PES. The first example, Imagining America, is consortial in nature, and the second is institution-based (i.e., Rutgers University-Newark). It is important to note that for each type there are a number of stellar examples, a full accounting of which is beyond the scope of this chapter. Chapters 4, 5, and 6 of this edited volume, however, feature case studies from a variety of institutions that may provide alternative examples. In the spirit of storytelling I draw on my own experiences to illuminate what I've described.

Imagining America: Cultural Organizing Institutes

Although it may be difficult for many academics to concede, our work around institutional transformation is very much community organizing. I have seen this manifest in powerful ways in my work with Imagining America: Artists and Scholars in Public Life (IA) as director for research (2005–2007) and faculty codirector (2012–2017). IA is a national consortium of about 100 higher education institutions and community-based partners working at the nexus of the cultural disciplines' (humanities, art, and design) methodologies and thinking and PES. During my codirectorship with Scott Peters, the IA central office staff and national advisory board began to explicitly explore broad-based community organizing strategies for our consortial work. We learned much about the philosophies and tools of community organizers and it quickly became clear that although hard-core community organizing strategies would not be appropriate for our context, we could flavor such approaches with methodologies from the cultural disciplines, namely public narrative, story circles, community-engaged theater, and other approaches based in arts and design.

The IA brand of cultural organizing was born at our first named cultural organizing institute in 2014 held at the University of Southern California. Drawing on action research convening models that were already in progress, like the Tenure Team Initiative on Public Scholarship (Ellison & Eatman, 2008) and the Full Participation initiative (Sturm et al., 2011), we began to craft an institute model designed to cultivate skills among teams comprising faculty, staff, students, and community partners from our member institutions. The institute design was deliberately embedded in the principles of PES but we did not have the language of collaborative engagement (Post et al., 2016) at that time.

To be sure, IA's cultural organizing institutes are not exclusive spaces for faculty, and yet there is much in the way of faculty development that takes place in them. We use it not only as an opportunity for cultivating learning communities throughout the consortium but also as a device for building capacity among our members to advance their organizing work across campus and community. In this model, we hosted teams from as many as 10 institutions for two- to three-day institutes usually connected to planning for our national conference or a signature initiative (e.g., Full Participation, Performing our Futures). We impressed the importance of diversity among teams (staff, students, partners, faculty) and facilitated democratically enabled sessions pivoting on the power of public narrative (Ganz, 2011) and the arts. Skill sharing and action planning are part of these institutes, but not in a heavy-handed way. Participants are invited to share their stories and the stories of their contexts; they find themselves both on the giving and receiving ends of constructive critique for building their work back at home.

There are other dynamic consortium-based examples of this kind of faculty development, like the Association of American Colleges & Universities (AAC&U) suite of summer institutes. As a member of the faculty for AAC&U's Summer Institute on High Impact Practices since 2010, it has been a privilege to work with colleagues in transdisciplinary contexts focused around student success. Campus Compact also has a strong record of faculty development that reflects the principles of collaborative engagement and PES (Burack, 2010; O'Meara, Eatman, & Petersen, 2015). I have also been quite encouraged by the faculty development approaches employed by the Center for Collaborative Research for an Equitable California (CCREC), an exemplary system-wide research and training enterprise that was established within the University of California System (Baloy, Sabati, & Glass, 2016).

Rutgers University-Newark: P3—A Collaboratory for Pedagogy, Professional Development, and PES

Through leadership in IA, I have had the good fortune to help design and participate in very dynamic faculty development work at institutions of higher education both nationally and internationally. Some of the most well-developed U.S. models were used at institutions like University of North Carolina-Greensboro, Vanderbilt University, University of Florida, University of Northern Iowa, Loyola University Chicago, Auburn University, Rochester Institute of Technology, Georgia College, Fairfield University, Portland State, Kansas State University, Oregon State University, University of New Mexico, University of North Florida, University of Northern Colorado, Bellarmine University, Widener University, and the University of Indiana–Purdue University Indianapolis. In South Africa, the University of the Free State and the University of South Africa also warrant naming here.

In each case, the aforementioned institutions are moving toward more integrated approaches to faculty development where members are seen as adult learners developing a craft (Brown, 2016). In many cases, they are also reaching beyond the traditional faculty-exclusive approach to models that are more intentional about attending to the structural challenges at institutions. I believe that Rutgers University-Newark (RU-N) is a harbinger in this regard with its emergent P3 Collaboratory.

Coming out of the RU-N strategic plan developed under Chancellor Nancy Cantor, P3 is a comprehensive development center designed to cultivate a diverse faculty of dedicated instructors who often connect the institutional learning experience to the lived work experience outside academia. I highlight P3 here because of its utter resonance with both collaborative engagement and PES. Employing principles of democratic practice, subcommittees worked on the three content areas of pedagogy, professional development, and PES (P3), leading to a report and three-phase plan for implementation, including a conference sponsored by the chancellor.

Leaders of the New Professoriate Study Group at RU-N conducted listening sessions, visited institutions, and learned of exemplar models to construct one that would fit the RU-N context. It is important to note that the extent of the structural changes have even impacted the physical space of the institution, as a major renovation of the library's third floor is underway as a concrete investment designed to help manifest the vision. The authors of the report summarize:

> The P3 Collaboratory is a place for scholars to come together across disciplinary, rank and professional boundaries to engage in critical challenges facing our community and society; to be a part of teaching, scholarship and leadership learning communities; and to join in discussions that are of utmost importance to us as a university community-all in a dynamic, flexible and creative space. (Veysey & Askew, 2016, p. 2)

Such spaces are critical for the necessary work of institutional transformation.

Collaborative engagement provides a useful framework for twenty-first-century faculty development. It can stimulate and set the stage for a robust knowledge ecology where faculty are focused on establishing nourishing spaces for intellectual growth and professional development that align with their desire for democratic engagement. The aforementioned examples provide a taste of how one consortium and one institution are exploring and organizing to maximize this opportunity.

Conclusion: The Power of Story

"Creating spaces where hearts and spirits meet minds for deep, impactful, sustained knowledge-making and healing" (Eatman, 2016, p. 70), this chapter uses a sketch of the current landscape of higher education as a springboard to consider compelling models of faculty development. Pivoting on the principles and key elements of PES as they intersect with the collaborative engagement paradigm, I argue that this is a new era—not your adviser's faculty development. In this context, faculty development can be seen as an important channel for advancing the mission and vision of an institution, a way to maximize agency especially among academics who identify as publicly engaged scholars. And yet, the importance of the elements and paradigms notwithstanding, we must be cognizant of the real power that undergirds transformational change.

There is an underestimated power—the power of story. Stories abound. They are, at times, inspiring or energizing and, other times, sad or depressing. It is not surprising when they hold in tension elements both of lift and decline. But there are always stories that reveal the deeper context of an individual, of a matter. Create the right space and even the most repressed, stubborn, and undisclosed stories emerge. Provide a compelling channel with companion methodology and rich gleanings and insights come pouring out. The enigmatic match between invitation and storyteller yields precious fruit, so much of which otherwise has withered on the vine.

My best sense is that the work of higher education transformation in general, and of necessity, harnesses the power of story. The case studies featured in later chapters highlight this point. Building on emerging models of faculty development, the power of story can reveal faculty as colearners and may serve to strengthen faculty development approaches. Learning community models as well as single-standing workshops can be enhanced by employing narrative approaches giving place to the complex interplay of identity, inclusion, and transdisciplinary issues. In the ever-evolving landscape of higher education, can we continue to fetishize traditional gatekeeping approaches?

Receive the quote that opens this conclusion as a challenge and a charge to think and act in more expansive ways about the opportunity of faculty development. How can we create holistic spaces where the community of academe can commit to the endless pursuit of a culture where rigorous and humanistic engagement abounds?

References

Association of American Colleges & Universities. (2012). *A crucible moment: College learning and democracy's future—A national call to action*. Retrieved from https://www.aacu.org/crucible

Baloy, N. J., Sabati, S., & Glass, R. D. (Eds.). (2016). *Unsettling research ethics: A collaborative conference report*. Santa Cruz, CA: UC Center for Collaborative Research for an Equitable California.

Barr, R. B., & Tagg, J. (1995). From teaching to learning: A new paradigm for undergraduate education. *Change, 27*(6), 12–25.

Baum, H. S. (2000). Fantasies and realities in community university partnerships. *Journal of Planning Education and Research, 20*(2), 234–246.

Benson, L., Harkavy, I. R., & Puckett, J. L. (2007). *Dewey's dream: Universities and democracies in an age of education reform—Civil society, public schools, and democratic citizenship.* Philadelphia, PA: Temple University Press.

Berberet, J. (2002). Nurturing an ethos of community engagement. *New Directions for Teaching and Learning, 90,* 91–100.

Blanchard, L. W., Hanssmann, C., Strauss, R. P., Belliard, J. C., Krichbau, K., Waters, E., & Seifer, S. (2009). Models for faculty development: What does it take to be a community-engaged scholar? *Metropolitan Universities Journal, 20*(2), 47–65.

Bonet, G., & Walters, B. R. (2016). High impact practices: Student engagement and retention. *College Student Journal, 50*(2), 224–235.

Bowdon, M. A., & Carpenter, R. G. (Eds.). (2011). *Higher education, emerging technologies, and community partnerships: Concepts, models, and practices.* Hershey, PA: IGI Global.

Bowen, H. R., & Carnegie Council on Policy Studies in Higher Education. (1977). *Investment in learning: The individual and social value of American higher education.* San Francisco, CA: Jossey-Bass.

Boyer, E. L. (1990). *Scholarship reconsidered: Priorities of the professoriate.* Princeton, NJ: The Carnegie Foundation for the Advancement of Teaching.

Boyer, E. L. (1996a). From scholarship reconsidered to scholarship assessed. *Quest, 48,* 129–139.

Boyer, E. L. (1996b). The scholarship of engagement. *Journal of Public Service & Outreach, 1*(1), 11–20.

Boyte, H. C. (2004). *Going public: Academics and public life.* Dayton, OH: Charles F. Kettering Foundation. Retrieved from http://www.kettering.org/media_room/publications/going_public

Boyte, H. C. (2015). *Democracy's education: Public work, citizenship, and the future of colleges and universities.* Nashville, TN: Vanderbilt University Press.

Brown, M. (2016). Faculty as learners: The new faculty role through the lens of faculty development. In A. J. Kezar & D. Maxey (Eds.), *Envisioning the faculty for the twenty-first century: Moving to a mission-oriented and learner-centered model* (pp. 117–226). New Brunswick, NJ: Rutgers University Press.

Burack, C. (2010). *New paradigms for faculty rewards: Resources and an action planning workshop to support engaged scholarship.* Retrieved from https://kdp0l43vw6z2dl-w631ififc5-wpengine.netdna-ssl.com/wp-content/uploads/2011/04/CC-Faculty-Rewards-Institute-Guide_FINAL1.pdf

Calhoun, C. J. (2006). The university and the public good. *Thesis Eleven, 84*(1), 7–43.

Cantor, N., & Levine, S. D. (2006). Taking public scholarship seriously. *The Chronicle of Higher Education, 52*(40). Retrieved from https://www.chronicle.com/article/Taking-Public-Scholarship/22684

Checkoway, B. (2001). Renewing the civic mission of the American research university. *The Journal of Higher Education, 72*(2), 125–147.

Colbeck, C. L., & Michael, P. W. (2006). The public scholarship: Reintegrating Boyer's four domains. *New Directions for Institutional Research, 2006*(129), 7–19.

Coles, R. (2014). Transforming the game: Democratizing the publicness of higher education and commonwealth in neoliberal times. *New Political Science, 36*(4), 622–639.

Diamond, R. M. (1999). *Aligning faculty rewards with institutional mission: Statements, policies, and guidelines.* Bolton, MA: Anker Publishing.

Diamond, R. M. (2002). Defining scholarship for the twenty-first century. *New Directions for Teaching and Learning, 2002*(90), 73–80.

Diamond, R. M., & Adam, B. E. (2004). Balancing institutional, disciplinary, and faculty priorities with public and social needs: Defining scholarship for the 21st century. *Arts and Humanities in Higher Education, 3*(1), 29–40.

Dolgon, C., Mitchell, T. D., & Eatman, T. K. (2016). *The Cambridge handbook of service learning and community engagement.* Cambridge, UK: Cambridge University Press.

Dreyfus, S. E., & Dreyfus, H. L. (1980). *A five-stage model of the mental activities involved in directed skill acquisition.* Berkeley, CA: University of California Operations Research Center [Reproduced by N.T.I.S.].

Dubb, S., & Howard, T. (2007). *Linking colleges to communities: Engaging the university for community development.* College Park, MD: The Democracy Collaborative at the University of Maryland.

Dugery, J., & Knowles, J. (2003). *University and community research partnerships: A new approach.* Charlottesville, VA: Pew Partnership for Civic Change.

Eatman, T. K. (2012). The arc of the academic career bends toward publicly engaged scholarship. In A. Gilvin, G. M. Roberts, & C. Martin (Eds.), *Collaborative futures: Critical reflections on publicly active graduate education* (pp. 25–48). Syracuse, NY: The Graduate School Press, Syracuse University.

Eatman, T. K. (2016). Reflections on the center of the civic. In A. Finley (Ed.), *Civic learning and teaching* (Bridging Theory to Practice Monographs: The Civic Series) (pp. 69–78). Washington DC: Association of American Colleges & Universities.

Eatman, T. K., Cantor, N., & Englot, P. (2016). Real rewards: Publicly engaged scholarship, faculty agency, and institutional aspirations. In C. Dolgon, T. D. Mitchell, & T. K. Eatman (Eds.), *The Cambridge handbook of service learning and community engagement* (pp. 359–369). Cambridge, UK: Cambridge University Press.

Ehrlich, T., & Jacoby, B. (2009). *Civic engagement in higher education: Concepts and practices.* San Francisco, CA: Jossey-Bass.

Ellison, J., & Eatman, T. K. (2008). *Scholarship in public: Knowledge creation and tenure policy in the engaged university.* Syracuse, NY: Imagining America.

Evans, S. Y. (2009). *African Americans and community engagement in higher education: Community service, service-learning, and community-based research.* Albany, NY: State University of New York Press.

Fairweather, J. S. (1996). *Faculty work and public trust: restoring the value of teaching and public service in American academic life.* Boston, MA: Allyn and Bacon.

Finkelstein, M. (2001). Toward a unified view of scholarship: Eliminating tensions between traditional and engaged work. *Journal of Higher Education Outreach and Engagement 6*(2), 35–44.

Fitzgerald, H. E., Bruns, K., Sonka, S. T., Furco, A., & Swanson, L. (2016). The centrality of engagement in higher education. *Journal of Higher Education Outreach and Engagement, 20*(1), 243–253.

Furco, A., & Moely, B. E. (2012). Using learning communities to build faculty support for pedagogical innovation: A multi-campus study. *Journal of Higher Education, 83*(1), 128–153.

Ganz, M. (2011). Public narrative, collective action, and power. In S. Odugbemi & T. Lee (Eds.), *Accountability Through Public Opinion* (pp. 273–289). Washington DC: World Bank.

Gass, E. (2007). *The path to partnership: Assessing a new model of university community partnerships.* Retrieved from http://www.profdevjournal.org/articles/83012.pdf

Glassick, C. E., Huber, M. T., & Maeroff, G. I. (1997). *Scholarship assessed: Evaluation of the professoriate.* San Francisco, CA: Jossey-Bass.

Harkavy, I., & Wiewel, W. (1995). University-community partnerships: Current state and future issues. *Metropolitan Universities: An International Forum, 6*(3), 7–14.

Hurtado, S., & Pryor, J. H. (2005). *The American college teacher national norms for the 2004–2005 HERI Faculty Survey.* Los Angeles, CA: Higher Education Research Institute, UCLA.

Iton, R. (2008). *In search of the Black fantastic: Politics and popular culture in the post-Civil Rights era.* Oxford, UK: Oxford University Press.

Kezar, A. J. (2012). *Embracing non-tenure track faculty: Changing campuses for the new faculty majority.* New York, NY: Routledge.

Kezar, A. J., Chambers, T. C., & Burkhardt, J. (Eds.). (2005). *Higher education for the public good: Emerging voices from a national movement.* San Francisco, CA: Jossey-Bass.

Kezar, A., & Maxey, D. (2013). The changing academic workforce. *Trusteeship, 21*(3), 15–21.

Kuh, G. D. (2008). *High-impact educational practices: What they are, who has access to them, and why they matter.* Washington DC: Association of American Colleges & Universities.

Lewis, E., & Cantor, N. (2016). *Our compelling interests: The value of diversity for democracy and a prosperous society.* Princeton, NJ: Princeton University Press.

Longo, N. V., & Gibson, C. M. (2016). The collabortive engagement paradigm. In M. A. Post, E. Ward, N. V. Longo, & J. Saltmarsh (Eds.), *Publicly engaged* scholars: Next generation engagement and the future of higher education (p. xxiv). Sterling, VA: Stylus.

Maurrasse, D. J. (2001). *Beyond the campus: How colleges and universities form partnerships with their communities*. New York, NY: Routledge.

Maurrasse, D. (2003). Higher education-community partnerships: assessing progress in the field. *Human Resource Abstracts, 38*(2). Retrieved from https://www.worldcat.org/title/higher-education-community-partnerships-assessing-progress-in-the-field/oclc/366382608&referer=brief_results

Maurrasse, D. (2004). *A future for everyone: Innovative social responsibility and community partnerships*. New York, NY: Routledge.

McCarthy, C. (1912). *The Wisconsin idea*. New York, NY: Macmillan.

McKee, C. W., Johnson, M., Ritchie, W. F., & Tew, W. M. (Eds.). (2013). *The breadth of current faculty development: Practitioners' perspectives* (New Directions for Teaching and Learning No. 133). San Francisco, CA: Jossey-Bass.

McKee, C. W., & Tew, W. M. (2013). Setting the stage for teaching and learning in American higher education: Making the case for faculty development. *New Directions for Teaching and Learning, 2013*(133), 3–14.

Morris, A. D. (2015). *The scholar denied: W.E.B. Du Bois and the birth of modern sociology*. Oakland, CA: University of California Press.

O'Meara, K. (2011). Inside the panopticon: Studying academic reward systems. In J. C. Smart & M. B. Paulsen (Eds.), *Higher Education: Handbook of Theory and Research* (pp. 161–220). New York, NY: Springer Education.

O'Meara, K., Eatman, T. K., & Petersen, S. (2015). Advancing engaged scholarship in promotion and tenure: A roadmap and call for reform. *Liberal Education, 101*(3). Retrieved from https://www.aacu.org/liberaleducation/2015/summer/o%27meara

Post, M. A., Ward, E., Longo, N. V., & Saltmarsh, J. (Eds.). (2016). *Publicly engaged scholars: Next generation engagement and the future of higher education*. Sterling, VA: Stylus.

Priest, K. L., & Clegorne, N. A. (2015). Connecting to experience: High-impact practices for leadership development. *New Directions for Student Leadership, 2015*(145), 71–83.

Prins, E. (2006). Individual roles and approaches to public engagement in a community-university partnership in a rural California town. *Journal of Research in Rural Education, 21*(7), 1–15.

Ramaley, J. A., & Holland, B. A. (2005). Modeling learning: The role of leaders. *New Directions for Higher Education, 133*, 75–86.

Ransby, B. (2003). *Ella Baker and the Black freedom movement: A radical democratic vision*. Chapel Hill, NC: University of North Carolina Press.

Rice, E. (2006). Rethinking scholarship of engagement: The struggle for new meanings. *College Compact Reader, 4*(1), 1–9. Retrieved from http://www.solent.ac.uk/ExternalUP/318/eugine_rice_s_paper.doc

Roth, M. S. (2015). *Beyond the university: Why liberal education matters*. New Haven, CT: Yale University Press.

Rowley, L. L. (2000). The relationship between universities and Black urban communities: The clash of two cultures. *Urban Review, 32*(1), 45–65.

Salsberg, J., Seller, R., Shea, L., & Macaulay, A. C. (2012). A needs assessment informs development of a participatory research faculty development workshop. *Journal of Higher Education Outreach and Engagement, 16*(1), 183–194.

Schön, D. A. (1995). Knowing-in-action: The new scholarship requires a new epistemology. *Change, 27*(6), 26–34.

Schuster, J. H., & Finkelstein, M. J. (2006). *The American faculty: The restructuring of academic work and careers.* Baltimore, MD: Johns Hopkins University Press.

Seifer, S., & Connors, K. (Eds.). (2007). *Community Campus Partnerships for Health. Faculty toolkit for service-learning in higher education.* Scotts Valley, CA: National Service-Learning Clearinghouse.

Sousanis, N. (2015). *Unflattening.* Cambridge, MA: Harvard University Press.

Steinert, Y., Mann, K., Centeno, A., Dolmans, D., Spencer, J., Gelula, M., & Prideaux, D. (2009). A systematic review of faculty development initiatives designed to improve teaching effectiveness in medical education (BEME Guide No. 8). *Medical Teacher, 28*(6), 497–526.

Strom, P. S., & Strom, R. D. (2013). Collaboration and support for student success. *Community College Journal of Research and Practice, 37*(8), 585–595.

Sturm, S., Eatman, T., Saltmarsh, J., & Bush, A. (2011). *Full participation: Building the architecture for diversity and public engagement in higher education* (Catalyst Paper). New York, NY: Columbia University Law School. Retrieved from http://cmapspublic3.ihmc.us/rid=1KH181R4C-VHDNKF-Y5D/Flyer_FullParticipationPaper.pdf

Talbani, A. (2013). High-impact practices for cultural competency. *New England Journal of Higher Education.* Retrieved from http://www.nebhe.org/thejournal/high-impact-practices-for-cultural-competency/

Thelin, J. R. (2011). *A history of American higher education* (2nd ed.). Baltimore, MD: Johns Hopkins University Press.

Tukibayeva, M., & Gonyea, R. M. (2014). High-impact practices and the first-year student. *New Directions for Institutional Research, 2014*(160), 19–35.

Veysey, B., & Askew, C. (2016). *Preliminary recommendations report for The P3: A collaboratory for pedagogy, professional development and publicly-engaged scholarship.* Newark, NJ: Rutgers University. Retrieved from http://www.newark.rutgers.edu/sites/default/files/preliminary_p3_recommendations_report.pdf

Vogelgesang, L. J., Denson, N., & Jayakumar, U. M. (2010). What determines faculty-engaged scholarship? *Review of Higher Education, 33*(4), 437–472.

Vollmer, D. (rapporteur), National Research Council. (2009). *Enhancing the effectiveness of sustainability partnerships: Summary of a workshop.* Washington DC: The National Academies Press.

Warren, M., Saltmarsh, J., Krueger-Henney, P., Rivera, L., Uriarte, M., Friedman, D. H., . . . Ramos, L. (2014). *Advancing community engaged scholarship and community engagement at the University of Massachusetts Boston: A report of the working group for an urban research-based action initiative*. Retrieved from https://www.umb.edu/editor_uploads/images/research/Report_on_Community_Engaged_Scholarship.pdf

Zahorski, K. J., & Cognard, R. (1999). *Reconsidering faculty roles and rewards: Promising practices for institutional transformation and enhanced learning*. Washington DC: Council of Independent Colleges.

Zlotkowski, E. (1998). A service learning approach to faculty development. *New Directions for Teaching and Learning, 1998*(73), 81–89.

PART TWO

MODELS OF FACULTY DEVELOPMENT IN SERVICE-LEARNING/COMMUNITY ENGAGEMENT

3

MODELS AND GENRES OF FACULTY DEVELOPMENT

Emily O. Gravett and Andreas Broscheid

Over the last several decades, the faculty developer's toolbox has grown beyond individual instructional consultations and workshops to include a wide variety of programming types, formats, approaches, models, and genres (see Beach, Sorcinelli, Austin, & Rivard, 2016; Ellis & Ortquist-Ahrens, 2010; Lee, 2010). Sorcinelli, Austin, Eddy, and Beach's (2006) research shows that the choice among these programs, whether they are provided by centralized units with dedicated staff, individual faculty developers, or faculty development committees, is typically the result of the faculty's own interests and concerns, the priorities of the director or person leading faculty development efforts, and the priorities of senior-level administrators. As more institutions of higher education begin to focus on service-learning and community engagement (S-LCE) efforts, community interests are added as an influential factor.

In this chapter, we build on these observations by arguing that, in order to select faculty development programming to best support S-LCE, our choices should be informed by the outcomes we want to achieve. What are the objectives—for students, faculty, and/or community partners—of specific S-LCE programs? What objectives do our institutions and/or units pursue, and how can we link strategically to them? What products are the programs expected to create? What processes are they intended to promote? What undesirable outcomes do they wish to avoid?

Backward Design: Beginning With Objectives

Our argument is guided by the backward design approach to education (see Fink, 2013; Hansen, 2011; Wiggins & McTighe, 2005). In contrast to approaches that begin with a focus on the content, schedule, or instructional activities and tools, backward design utilizes learning outcomes and objectives as starting points. Once the desired outcomes and objectives—that is, the knowledge, skills, and/or attitudes that students are expected to learn or know by the end of a learning experience—have been defined, faculty can develop assessments that document to what extent such outcomes or assessments have been attained. And once the needed assessments have been determined, faculty can then develop the learning activities that will help students succeed in the assessments. In other words, backward design approaches focus on aligning learning outcomes, learning assessment, and learning activities (Biggs & Tang, 2011).

We can transfer this backward design framework to the faculty development context by basing our programming choices on considerations of learning outcomes for faculty. The choice of faculty development programming formats should be the result of "what faculty will know, do, and find valuable as a result of their participation in center programming" (Hurney, Brantmeier, Good, Harrison, & Meixner, 2016, p. 70). This approach also allows, as Hurney and colleagues (2016) demonstrate, faculty developers to create a multitiered assessment framework that captures more than demographics or satisfaction. For example, although common program assessments ask participants whether they were satisfied, multitiered assessments may add questions about the programming format (e.g., whether participants had an opportunity to apply the content in a workshop setting), change in faculty behaviors, or the impact on student learning. This way of assessing can be particularly helpful when trying to demonstrate the value or measure the impact of faculty development programs, S-LCE or otherwise.

Before determining the faculty learning outcomes for S-LCE programming, it is advisable to consider the student learning outcomes of S-LCE. After all, faculty developers have to enable faculty to help students achieve such outcomes. Student learning outcomes of S-LCE programs may overlap with those in more traditional learning experiences (e.g., students may be expected to understand a certain amount of foundational knowledge and to be able to apply it). Yet they can also include outcomes that are not always part of more traditional classroom learning: growth of social problem-solving and citizenship skills, a better understanding of others, heightened empathy, ability to work with others, development of affective orientations that support interest in a field of study, creation of professional and disciplinary identities, increased curiosity, and intellectual risk-taking. Eyler and Giles (1999) note that good service-learning has to place students into situations in which they face real-world, "ill-structured" (p. 16) problems, which not only require them to apply a range of information and skills but also challenge their "prejudices, previous experiences, and assumptions about the world" (p. 17). Such experiences, if well supported, can lead to developmental changes that go beyond a list of specific learning outcomes. A good summary of the learning outcomes associated with S-LCE programs can be found in the Association of American Colleges & Universities *Civic Engagement VALUE Rubric* (2010).

Creating high-level, applied, authentic learning experiences may be a daunting task for faculty, and this is reflected in the objectives faculty pursue as they participate in professional development programs. Although there are objectives or outcomes that are fairly small scale (e.g., learning how to create memoranda of understanding or other documentation for community partners, developing grading rubrics for reflective student essays, exchanging experiences with other faculty involved in S-LCE work), the central aims of faculty development for S-LCE are mostly large scale and interconnected. Faculty have to cultivate relationships with support units on campus as well as partners in the community, learn how to support students who face ill-structured problems and potentially disorienting transformative experiences, develop ways for students to effectively close the loop to learn from those experiences, assess the effectiveness of S-LCE experiences, and keep track of their viability in the community, all while maintaining their own motivation in pursuit of such major and complex projects. Each of these interconnected aims houses further interconnected objectives. For example, supporting students immersed in difficult and ill-defined situations requires not only pedagogical and disciplinary competence but also interpersonal skills that can foster student development.

In addition to helping faculty develop educational tools and skills, faculty development programs that support S-LCE have to pursue goals that go beyond teaching support. Truly engaged projects encourage the integration of teaching, scholarship, and service. For example, a faculty member could embark upon an S-LCE project that serves a local community by engaging students as mentors in a Big Brothers Big Sisters program and then use this experience to study the effects of mentoring on at-risk youth (see Peaslee & Teye, 2015; Teye & Peaslee, 2015). Or a collaborative project between engineering and kinesiology faculty members might work with students to create and construct vehicles designed for the needs of children with cerebral palsy (see Nagel, Gipson, Nagel, & Moran, 2014). Faculty involved in such programs may ask not only for pedagogical support but also for programs on creating, evaluating, and publishing interdisciplinary scholarship, as well as programs for making and maintaining connections with community partners, assessing student learning outcomes, publishing on the scholarship of teaching and learning, integrating engaged and interdisciplinary scholarship into their career trajectories, or determining when in one's career to pursue this sort of project, just to name a few examples.

Of course, faculty development programs that support S-LCE not only at student and faculty learning but also must include community partners. Community partners are affected by the actions of faculty and students, but they are also one of the main influences on student learning in S-LCE. At the very least, universities and colleges have to cultivate strong relationships with community partners who will have to comply with institutional rules and regulations, even if it is only at the level of, for instance, completing internship provider reports. Furthermore, from an ethical perspective, S-LCE programs must be guided by respect and reciprocity among community partners, students, and educators (Butin, 2003). This means that the engaged aspects of teaching and learning have to benefit community partners, not just the students, faculty, and/or institutions. At the same time, faculty and students have to avoid assuming or imagining themselves in the role of "white knights" whose actions treat community partners as the passive recipients of benevolent service they may or may not want. In order to ensure that community partners are viewed and treated as coequal participants, the selection of faculty development programming should always consider whether and how community partners are included.

Selecting Programming to Support S-LCE

As noted, there is a rich array of models and genres of faculty development that can support an integrated approach to S-LCE. Across chapters 4, 5, and 6 of this edited volume, exemplars of these models and genres are explored through multiple case studies. Throughout this section, we describe this rich array. A summary of our discussion is provided in Table 3.1. We wish to emphasize that programming selection should always be guided by objectives, as previously discussed. For example, if the S-LCE outcome is providing an opportunity for faculty to build meaningful, long-term relationships with potential community partners, then a one-off workshop, wherein faculty will likely be the only participants and will be gathering together only for a limited period of time, would not be the best choice.

In addition, the decision of which S-LCE faculty development programs to pursue should be informed by campus-wide needs assessment surveys (e.g., Witkin & Altschuld, 1995); strengths, weaknesses, opportunities, and threats (SWOT) analyses (Gelmon, Blanchard, Ryan, & Seifer, 2012); or even informal listening tours. Before investing resources, it is crucial to first gather data from a wide range of institutional stakeholders, including faculty, staff, students, administration, community members, and even alumni.

TABLE 3.1
Summary of Programming Types

Categories	Types	Audience	Resource Needs	Strengths	Shortcomings	Example Outcomes
Information Resources	Libraries Websites E-mail lists Blogs Social media	Anyone with Internet access	Web servers Web design Writing skills Personnel to update resources	Open to anybody Flexible time/space Public presence	Low impact Maintenance needed Impersonal Duplication	Determined by users Communication of support for S-LCE
Support, Incentive, and Recognition Programs	Grants and stipends Travel funding Awards and recognitions	Faculty, staff	Money Award criteria Personnel to select recipients	Flexible time/space Motivates and rewards Low personnel needs	Costly Focus on external motivation Difficult to sustain	Generate excitement Increase buy-in Pilot programs Highlight local expertise, accomplishments
Short-Term Programs	Consultations	Faculty, staff Organizational units Community partners	Expert consultants	Need-targeted Individualized Follow-up possible Confidential Low cost with in-house experts	Time-intensive with many clients	Determined by users Program development Overcoming specific challenges

(*Continues*)

TABLE 3.1 (*Continued*)

Categories	Types	Audience	Resource Needs	Strengths	Shortcomings	Example Outcomes
	Workshops Roundtables Scholarly Talks Internal conferences and symposia		Few (1–6) facilitators and presenters Space Food, drink (optional)	Easy to schedule Participatory	One-off Little follow-up May not have long-term impact	Exchange of ideas Skill development
Extended and Immersive Programs	Institutes Faculty learning communities Mentoring programs Faculty-student partnerships Fellowship programs	Faculty, staff Students Community partners	Facilitators, presenters Space Food, drink (optional)	High impact Participatory	Time intensive Needs advance planning Logistically complex Can be costly	Increased sense of belonging Lasting relationships Program development

Identifying gaps, weaknesses, problems, or ignorance about current support; discovering aspirations, wish lists, or requests; and gauging the interest in and commitment to S-LCE will provide additional rationale and facilitate buy-in for whatever faculty development is implemented. It will also ensure the programs match what faculty and community partners want and/or need.

More generally, it is prudent to form intentional collaborations with those other stakeholders who are interested in, or already supporting, S-LCE. Offices or centers of academic success, student support, disability services, talent and development, faculty development, teaching and learning, civic engagement, experiential learning, volunteerism, internships, entrepreneurship, career services, and study abroad, as well as any center(s) devoted specifically to service-learning and/or community engagement, can join together to offer more diverse, robust faculty development opportunities than any one entity can on its own. In particular, some of these units may be able to manage the administrative work of creating and maintaining S-LCE opportunities (e.g., securing sites to visit, coordinating transportation, etc.), such that faculty even have time to participate in developmental opportunities, rather than spending it all trying to learn and manage these parts of S-LCE work. It may also be beneficial to develop connections beyond campus, by joining, for instance, a national alliance or consortium, such as Campus Compact.

Informational Resources

At a very basic level, faculty developers, together with associated units such as libraries or the other campus resources previously listed, can provide informational, financial, and organizational resources to jumpstart or support S-LCE. These resources can help faculty understand basic concepts and teach themselves how to engage further in S-LCE. Additionally, in our experience, the provision of these resources implies an institution's generally positive attitude toward and commitment to S-LCE endeavors. Because such programs require more limited involvement of faculty development personnel and can make use of existing institutional information technology resources, they are easy to implement at a relatively low cost. Additionally, because use of library and online resources is not bound to a specific point in time, such programs can easily accommodate varying schedules of faculty and community stakeholders.

The faculty learning outcomes that these activities can achieve are not clearly defined and primarily depend on the individual objectives pursued by the faculty who use the resources. Moreover, the impersonal nature of informational programs can limit their impact. Faculty developers should also be careful not to waste time and funds on duplicating resources that exist elsewhere, for example at other institutions' websites. Yet, by piquing faculty interest or by providing foundational knowledge that can later be built on, these informational resources can still serve an important function—as a gateway into other programming with more clearly defined objectives.

Library
One basic informational resource is a physical or virtual library of S-LCE books or journals. Books might include *Service-Learning in Higher Education: Concepts and Practices* (Jacoby, 1996), *Experiential Learning: Experience as the Source of Learning and Development* (Kolb, 2014), *Evaluating Service-Learning Activities and Programs* (Payne, 2000), *Faculty Toolkit for Service-Learning in Higher Education* (Seifer & Connors, 2007), and *Where's the Learning in Service-Learning?* (Eyler & Giles, 1999). The library can also point faculty toward journals, such as the *Purdue Journal of Service-Learning and International Engagement* or the *Michigan Journal of Community Service Learning*. As a partner, the institution's library may be willing to be responsible for purchasing, cataloguing, and managing the checkout process. Otherwise, these responsibilities and modest costs will fall to the unit, center, or individual supporting S-LCE. Faculty can take advantage of these resources if they are interested in learning more but are not yet ready for, or have the time to commit to, a more intensive program with more clearly defined objectives.

Website
If there is a website affiliated with S-LCE faculty development, it can also serve as a resource for faculty who wish to develop their own skills at their own pace. For instance, the Eberly Center at Carnegie Mellon offers webpages where one can "explore the learning objectives that service-learning can address," "examine issues unique to designing and teaching a service-learning course," and "locate resources, examples, and references" (Eberly Center, 2015). S-LCE websites may also include video testimonials from faculty and students as well as community members, a list of potential community partners interested in participating in faculty S-LCE projects, links to other units or centers that support S-LCE on campus, blog entries that share personal experiences with S-LCE, or sample S-LCE syllabi or assignments. If S-LCE events are recorded, the website can house those video recordings for later viewing, which would expand the reach and impact of programming. These websites can also link to other centers' websites, such as Miami University's Office of Community Engagement and Service, which provides a *Faculty Resource Guide for Service-Learning* (Miami University, n.d.), or Vanderbilt University, which offers a teaching guide titled "What Is Service Learning or Community Engagement?" (Bandy, n.d.).

Electronic Mailing Lists
The provision of online resources can be enhanced by the use of social media tools, such as electronic mailing lists, which make it easy to keep information up-to-date and permit users to respond, ask questions, and otherwise engage with faculty developers. It may also be an additional avenue for linking faculty, students, and community members, who might not otherwise have the opportunity to interact. Typically, however, these lists are internal to the institution, with faculty (and sometimes staff or students) being the primary subscribers. Despite their old-time character, e-mail lists are frequently quite active: see, for example, the list of the Professional and Organizational Development (POD) Network in Higher Education or the Higher Education Service-Learning (HE-SL) lists of the National Youth Leadership Council, which are found in Google Groups and are open to nonmembers. Other e-mail lists are subscription only and are more selective of who receives information and who can respond, such as the server at Indiana University–Purdue University Indianapolis or at the Center for Community Engagement and Service Learning at the University of Denver.

Blogs
Blogs enable institutions to reach a wider audience that may include students, faculty, staff, community partners, alumni, and even other professionals (Stephens, 2016). As the Sonoma State University Center for Community Engagement (n.d.) and the University of North Carolina School of Government (n.d.) demonstrate, blog posts can provide faculty development by highlighting ongoing S-LCE projects, announcing and summarizing S-LCE faculty development events, or discussing broader theoretical questions related to S-LCE. Individual faculty developers may even decide to integrate articles on S-LCE into their own blogs and tag them for easy retrieval, such as the *servicelearning* tag employed by the Northern Illinois University Faculty Development and Instructional Design Center (n.d.).

Social Media
For flexible and speedy information provision and interaction with stakeholders, other social media services such as Facebook, LinkedIn, or Twitter can also be useful faculty development tools. Good examples are the Twitter accounts of the Northeastern University Service-Learning Program (@NU_SLearning), the Iowa Campus Compact (@IACampusCompact), Engage IUPUI (@engageiupui), Miami University Engagement and Service (@miamioh_oces), and University of Virginia Learning in Action (@uvaservice). The hashtags #servicelearning, #civicengagement, #participation, #publicengagement, and #citizenengagement are commonly associated with tweets related

to S-LCE work, providing an easy way for faculty to link into a broader network of support and resources.

Support, Incentive, and Recognition Programs

Besides providing informational resources on S-LCE, faculty development centers or individual faculty developers, typically in collaboration with other interested units, can support S-LCE by providing monetary resources and/or by rewarding and publicizing exemplary work. Providing monetary resources will primarily be feasible for institutions or centers with a robust budget committed to supporting S-LCE. Rewarding and publicizing exemplary work may be well suited for smaller or newer programs with more minimal budgets. Although these types of programs do not necessarily help faculty learn how to conduct S-LCE projects, they can support S-LCE in becoming a normalized part of the institutional culture and to grow in recognition. In addition, grants and stipends can be helpful in recruiting participants for pilot programs that are aimed at introducing S-LCE programs to an institution that has not yet integrated them into its faculty reward structure. On the downside, by providing extrinsic rewards, the faculty attracted to S-LCE may be motivated by more than an interest in engaged learning, making it potentially difficult to build a sustainable S-LCE structure.

Grants and Stipends

Many institutions or faculty development centers offer grants or stipends to fund smaller-scale innovations in individual courses or large-scale integration across the curriculum and into the community. For instance, as with the community engagement funding available at Virginia Commonwealth University (2017), faculty can receive a sizable stipend for working on projects that initiate or deepen relationships with community members/organizations or that increase engagement with the broader community. Other large grants can support whole-course or curriculum design or redesign toward S-LCE outcomes. Likewise, smaller minigrants can incentivize more targeted innovation or experimentation, such as the inclusion of a service-learning or community-engagement project in a single course. In addition to whatever budget constraints exist for S-LCE faculty development, the amount of these grants should be determined by other similar grants and stipends so that S-LCE support is comparable and thus its value is clear. These grants are usually application-based and, like service-learning itself, require some kind of follow-up, such as a presentation or a written report. The requirement of this kind of follow-up may help recruit faculty who are in fact interested in

S-LCE and not primarily motivated by the monetary reward. This is a side effect of grants and stipends that we have observed on occasion.

In and of themselves, grants and stipends are not connected to specific faculty learning outcomes, though they can be paired, as recommended previously, with other forms of faculty development that are (e.g., as part of the stipulation for receiving a financial incentive). Instead, they help achieve institutional outcomes, such as the development of S-LCE programs in various disciplines, an increase in faculty members involved in S-LCE, or the public institutional recognition of S-LCE projects. This recognition may make it easier for faculty to divert their time from more readily rewarded activities, such as traditional scholarship, to S-LCE. In this respect, support for external grant applications is particularly valuable, as it may lead faculty to develop externally confirmed profiles of excellence that can further their careers.

Another way faculty development for S-LCE can be financially supported is through funding for faculty conference travel, if a budget is available. There are numerous conferences across the country and the world, such as the National Service-Learning Conference and International Association for Research on Service-Learning and Community Engagement, which gather together professionals who are committed to S-LCE. In addition, attending disciplinary and subdisciplinary conferences may provide faculty with the opportunity to use S-LCE work to contribute to their own disciplines and to raise their own professional profiles. As with any conference, outcomes may include gaining new knowledge, discovering or honing skills, networking and expanding one's professional circle, or encountering new research. These outcomes can extend to nonattending faculty if those who received funding are required to offer some kind of follow-up. For example, faculty might be asked to share a new idea or framework from the conference with their department or college. As with other grants and stipends, funding conference participation gives faculty involved in S-LCE the opportunity to gain external recognition through the presentation of their work and through scholarly exchange with other S-LCE practitioners. This, in turn, may provide incentives for faculty to shift the professional focus at their institutions toward more applied and engaged work, even if it means spending less time on the traditional scholarship of discovery (Boyer, 1990).

Awards and Recognitions
Institutional awards and recognitions can be an important tool for recognizing faculty achievements and for helping faculty create the documentation of success that enables them to use S-LCE work to advance their careers.

Providing internal rewards or recognitions with no financial component or coaching and supporting faculty who apply for external awards and recognition can be low-cost options, ideal for those faculty developers, centers, or institutions that do not have an extensive budget for S-LCE. Internal service-learning or community engagement awards not only reward faculty, staff, students, and/or community partners for excellent work but also highlight outstanding S-LCE work to the campus community. Although there are specific awards for S-LCE, such as the Thomas Ehrlich Civically Engaged Faculty Award (Campus Compact, n.d.), more general awards can acknowledge high-quality S-LCE work. For example, the Outstanding Faculty Awards of the State Council of Higher Education for Virginia recognize, among other things, faculty integration of teaching, research, and service, providing opportunities for those engaged in S-LCE. Faculty developers can play an important role in external award processes by identifying promising candidates, recruiting and training coaches who help candidates prepare strong applications, and guiding faculty through the application process.

Short-Term Programs

The bulk of faculty development is offered in the form of comparatively short, one-off programs that focus on narrowly defined topics. These programs can be effective in introducing participants to specific learning they may need, allowing for the exchange of ideas among participants, and helping participants begin to network. The main advantage of these short-term programs is the fact that they are versatile and require comparatively few resources—a room with one or a few expert facilitators, often recruited from inside the institution, who have prepared in advance. It is comparatively easy for faculty to devote time to these programs because they do not require multiday or even longer-term commitments. The one-off nature of short-term programs also supports the participation of community partners who may not be able or willing to enter into long-term commitments for programs that are marginal to their jobs and careers. Another advantage is the fact that these short-term options can be combined into larger programs, such as conferences or symposia, discussed later in this section. The main disadvantage of short-term programs is that they tend to have limited success in creating lasting change that goes beyond specific teaching tools or processes and in building long-term professional relationships among participants.

Workshops

Workshops have become a staple program in faculty development, and the formats can vary widely. Some last for 60 or 90 minutes, whereas others can fill up a whole day. Some may be open to the entire campus, or even community members, whereas others are tailored for particular units, departments, colleges, or schools. Participation can also vary. In our experience, faculty have the most difficulty making time for workshops and other face-to-face programming around the midsemester point, especially if the experience is not novel or their participation is not incentivized in some way. If the participants are to include community partners, we recommend scheduling the event toward the end of the workday or even the end of the workweek. Workshops typically introduce participants to evidence-based practices and theoretical frameworks, as well as implementable ideas—all focused on a specific theme, such as "Teaching Students How to Write Reflectively" or "Service-Learning 101." It is also possible, as Purdue University has done, to host entire workshop series for service-learning, on topics such as grading, using case studies, or creating community partnerships.

At their best, workshops are active and interactive, giving participants ample time to think about their own contexts and to generate actionable ideas in conversation with colleagues. The facilitators—usually drawn from the staff of a particular unit or on a volunteer basis—should model pedagogical strategies relevant to the workshop topic. There is some question as to the longer-term impact and efficacy of this programming type (see Ebert-May et al., 2011), so it may be wise to invest resources in more extended, immersive alternatives. Nevertheless, the workshop remains a popular offering in faculty development programs.

Workshops are particularly appropriate if the faculty learning outcomes revolve around the acquisition of discrete knowledge, skills, or abilities that require only limited practice or follow-up feedback. In addition, workshops may be useful for faculty to exchange experiences with, and ideas for, S-LCE programs. For a number of other outcomes that are central to S-LCE, more extended, immersive programs may be preferable. Examples include the development of S-LCE programs, the integration of S-LCE projects into individual course designs, or the development of skills to form relationships and address potential conflicts between students and community members. Still, workshops can be a practical, though suboptimal, choice in such circumstances, due to the increased choice and flexible scheduling they offer participants.

Roundtables
Roundtables offer another short-term programming option for bringing together a group of faculty to discuss topics related to S-LCE. Typically, a skilled facilitator provides a short overview, reading, or activity related to a specific topic and then leads the group in an informed conversation about

the material. During the roundtable, faculty have the opportunity to reflect on how the topic relates to their context, to share ideas, to ask questions, to listen to others' perspectives, and to build relationships with their colleagues, often from different disciplines. Roundtables, like workshops, may also benefit from inviting community members into the discussion, not only as participants but also as experts who can partner with the facilitators in shaping the discussion. After all, community leaders and civic professionals frequently have backgrounds in education and expertise with facilitating community interaction, providing valuable contributions to roundtable facilitation.

Scholarly Talks
Scholarly talks invite experts from the faculty or the community to offer an organized presentation in order to engage colleagues in academically informed inquiry. These talks provide an opportunity to highlight expertise and to share important information related to a topic. If the scholarly talk involves short presentations by a panel of experts, it may take on some of the characteristics of a roundtable—interactive and informed dialogue between panelists and audience.

Roundtables and scholarly talks are particularly useful for providing persons involved—or interested—in S-LCE work with the opportunity to learn about existing programs and to exchange information and experiences with each other. Because they are typically one-off events of short duration that require little participant preparation, they can be appealing to participants and are well suited for community partners who otherwise might not be willing or able to invest their time into activities that may be seen as primarily benefiting the academic side of the partnership. If the experts and facilitators in both roundtables and scholarly talks are internal to the institution, such programs can be fairly low-cost affairs; if the experts are external, honoraria of various amounts will have to be budgeted in.

Consultations
Consultations are the bread and butter of faculty development programs, whether at the individual or organizational level. It is during these private conversations that faculty seek guidance and receive support from an empathetic listener, mentor, and possibly coach (see Little & Palmer, 2011). Rather than adopt an expert stance, in which the consultant tells the faculty member what to do, consultants listen, ask questions, and empower faculty members to commit to taking actions that make sense given their particular contexts. Consultations can be based on a variety of data, including video recordings, course materials, peer observations, or student surveys.

To establish a consulting program, an institution needs to identify a pool of experts with experience in S-LCE and prepare them using consulting best practices (see Brinko, 2012; Lewis & Povlacs Lunde, 2001). Among the advantages of consultation programs are the use of existing resources and the ability to tailor the program to participant needs. On the flipside, such programs can be fairly inefficient if they require a large number of individualized meetings with different actors who could just as well meet in a workshop, faculty learning community, or other group experience. Consultations are easy for newer S-LCE faculty development programs or even individuals to start out offering support, but if demand gets too high they may become untenable.

Internal Conferences and Symposia
Internal conferences and symposia can offer a mix of S-LCE faculty development options, often provided by numerous facilitators, usually volunteers, in a schedule of concurrent sessions and plenaries or keynotes. Sessions can be by invitation or by proposal, usually vetted by some kind of campus-wide committee. If funds are available, this can also be a prime opportunity to invite well-known experts in the field to speak, usually for the cost of an honorarium, lodging, and travel expenses. If the conference or symposium becomes an annual offering, choosing a rotating central theme, such as "Building Bridges With the Community," may renew interest every year.

Although internal conferences and symposia inherit the faculty learning outcomes of their constituent programs—workshops, roundtables, keynote addresses (i.e., scholarly talks), and the like—they can also add to them. For one, the sequence of time slots in a full-day or multiday event permits the sequencing of constituent events. It may thus be possible to create mini-institutes out of a series of workshops so that participants can acquire S-LCE skills or knowledge that may not be possible in a single workshop or roundtable. In addition, conferences and symposia may serve as focal points that allow for more intensive networking and relationship-building than shorter, stand-alone programs. Participants can exchange ideas with other faculty engaged in S-LCE work, get inspired by what others are doing, and initiate or deepen relationships with other S-LCE practitioners. Conferences and symposia are also excellent opportunities to invite community partners to present their perspectives on completed or ongoing work, to get to know more of the university's work in the community, and to become a more integral part of S-LCE initiatives.

Although it is usually possible to recruit in-house presenters and facilitators for conferences and symposia and thus keep costs comparably low, the logistical effort is extensive, such as reserving a large number of rooms at coordinated times or managing a substantial number of attendee registrations. Larger faculty development centers may thus be better able to support this type of programming, as they usually employ more administrative support staff. Furthermore, conferences and symposia typically involve the provision of food services and thus come with additional catering costs, which can be quite steep with larger participant numbers. Short-term programs tend to aim for fairly limited outcomes. They help participants exchange or discover ideas, get acquainted with specific concepts or approaches related to S-LCE, and learn discrete skills that may improve their work in this area.

Extended and Immersive Programs

If the desired outcomes of faculty development for S-LCE revolve around lasting changes, then more extended, immersive programs may be needed. For instance, curricular changes, consistent integration of S-LCE into pedagogies, use of assessment and other scholarly approaches to teaching, or creation of communities of S-LCE practitioners may prove to be more time and resource intensive. This is borne out in the research literature, which documents the effectiveness of immersive programs, such as course design institutes (Palmer, Streifer, & Williams-Duncan, 2016) and faculty learning communities (Furco & Moeli, 2012).

Institutes

Institutes are multiday programs that consist of presentations, workshops, roundtables, consultation blocks, as well as opportunities to work individually or in groups to complete a set task, such as the design or redesign of a course, the start of a scholarship of teaching and learning project, or the completion of an academic portfolio. Course design institutes are popular faculty development offerings across the country and they can be effectively adapted to focus on specific types of courses, such as those incorporating S-LCE. Institutes are typically offered for faculty participants on consecutive days, for example over the course of a week during breaks between semesters or spread out over several weeks throughout the semester to accommodate busy schedules. Thus, like the labor-intensive conferences and symposia, they require a great deal of planning and coordination, as well as more extensive time commitments by participants.

Faculty and community partners may or may not be compensated or incentivized for their attendance and participation. Some newly established institutes do offer some financial incentive for attendance. After the value of the institute becomes known, faculty may be asked to attend without compensation or even to pay for participation. Some institutes allow for participation from members outside of the institution, such as neighboring academic institutions or civic organizations. This inclusion is an opportunity to hear alternative perspectives, build bridges, and seek new ways of collaborating to engage the community, which is especially important in the context of S-LCE. If outside participants pay to attend, it can be a way of bringing in funding direct toward other faculty development efforts.

Faculty Learning Communities
Formally defined faculty learning communities (FLCs)—further explored with practical examples in chapter 5—bring together a small group of multidisciplinary faculty members around a common interest, theme, concern, or question over the course of a semester or year (Cox, 2004). FLCs usually consist of fewer than 10 participants to promote depth and relationship-building among the group. The FLC's activities can consist of a common book or readings and discussions involving the study of a topic such as S-LCE or the creation of a common project, such as service-learning components for the participants' courses. Although the objectives of institutes tend to focus on a tangible product (e.g., redesign of a course and syllabus, setup of a new S-LCE program, etc.), FLCs are more about long-term learning, community-building, and the creation of lasting change.

Many FLCs are encouraged to take some kind of action, whether during or after their experience. In contrast to institutes, which tend to have a set curriculum, it is possible for FLCs to be created and organized mainly by participants. Faculty are responsible for facilitating, deciding on topics for the meetings, and setting the group's goals and norms. FLCs tend to require less logistical heavy lifting than many of the previously discussed programming types, given their grassroots nature. Such grassroots initiatives can be especially potent in the context of newer S-LCE faculty development programs; in our experience, it is crucial that such efforts not appear to be top-down or coming from the administration only. They are also usually low cost, though some institutions or centers may choose to pay for the text, food, or even participation.

Because participants have to commit to meet on a regular basis over an extended period of time, it can be difficult to attract the needed number of participants to institutes and learning communities. Additionally, attendance is likely to be subject to attrition over time, particularly if community partners, whose workplaces are not located at the host institution, are part of the cohort. If FLCs are too large, they may not only encounter logistical problems such as finding common meeting times but also fail to achieve some of their more valuable outcomes, such as building a strong sense of community among participants.

Mentoring Programs
Mentoring programs can provide powerful and personalized faculty development opportunities by joining two or more people interested in S-LCE in a supportive, long-term partnership. Although mentoring programs aim at helping mentees perform effectively in a new field of activity, their psychosocial objectives such as support for mentees' (and mentors') understanding and valuation of themselves as professionals are just as important (Ragins & Kram, 2007). Faculty are usually matched with colleagues outside of their area of expertise or department/unit to facilitate networking beyond disciplinary bounds. We have found that partnerships outside the department or unit are more conducive to honesty, as faculty do not have to worry, or at least can worry less, about disclosing information that may affect their standing with department chairs or promotion and tenure committees. Whereas many mentor partnerships are between people with differing levels of experience (e.g., a faculty member who has routinely incorporated S-LCE into her or his courses and someone who is just beginning), peer or mutual mentoring is also possible, with people having similar levels of experience coming together to provide feedback, share ideas, and suggest possible areas of growth, as well as offer support and encouragement.

Mentoring programs do not impose high direct costs, as mentors are typically volunteers from the institution and receive recognition as part of the service component of their positions. Yet their time commitment can be sizable, making it difficult to recruit sufficient or high-quality mentors, potentially impacting resulting S-LCE endeavors. As a result, an S-LCE mentoring program may require the provision of modest stipends to mentors, especially if it is new. As a program gains success and mentors realize that they, too, gain from mentoring relationships, they may be willing to participate without stipends.

Faculty-Student Partnerships
Another type of programming that facilitates the formation of relationships, faculty-student partnerships can provide faculty with alternative perspectives and additional support not always utilized when planning and executing S-LCE opportunities. In one-off interactions or over the course of longer-term relationships, students can give valuable feedback to faculty about S-LCE course materials, potential S-LCE research questions and projects (particularly helpful when the faculty might involve student researchers), or

what S-LCE opportunities and experiences they find valuable. This feedback can be based on their own or observed S-LCE experiences, providing faculty with information or a perspective to which they might not otherwise have access.

Students embedded in S-LCE courses can also provide support for their classmates through peer mentoring or even more formal teaching assistantships, such as the Service-Learning Teaching Assistant Program at Northeastern University (Northeastern University Center of Community Service, 2017). Of course, faculty have to be open to engaging in this kind of relationship with students, which may depend on their career stage, the culture of their discipline or department, as well as the degree to which students are prepared for such partnerships. S-LCE student partners, of course, need to be interviewed, hired, and trained, usually a time-intensive process, as well as compensated or recognized fairly for their time, often in the form of hourly wages or a stipend.

Fellowship Programs
Perhaps the most immersive of all, fellowship programs provide faculty members the opportunity to become active contributors to faculty development. In contrast to the other programs described in this chapter, which aim at helping faculty develop new knowledge and skills for their teaching and scholarship, fellowships pursue the further objective of enabling faculty to help other faculty develop their knowledge and skills. Typically, this involves some kind of affiliation with a well-established faculty development center. Fellowship programs can supplement the S-LCE support already provided by the center while offering the fellows advanced professional development opportunities. Tenures can vary (in some fellowship programs, faculty work for a year; in others, faculty stay on for several, in multiyear rotations). Faculty usually work part time during the academic year, compensated with a course release or a comparable stipend. As such, this is a budget-intensive program.

Fellows might work to support various already existing initiatives or programs related to S-LCE—or the fellowship might provide fellows the opportunity to develop their own S-LCE assignments, courses, or curricula, or to integrate S-LCE into their service and scholarship. Although fellows may come to serve as S-LCE champions, leaders, liaisons, or mentors across campus, they may also need a good deal of support themselves. In our experience, it is essential to take the time to provide adequate orientation and ongoing development opportunities for these faculty.

Conclusion

From the broad overview provided in this chapter, it is clear that there is a wide variety of faculty development programming types that can be marshaled to support S-LCE. It should go without saying that our list is not complete and that there are additional kinds of programs that faculty developers may find helpful as they support faculty. We should also note that faculty development terminology is not always fixed; expert roundtables are sometimes called workshops, institutes are sometimes called learning communities, and so on. Furthermore, the type of programming created by faculty developers is always in flux, due to the creative potential of the profession. We encourage readers to adopt, adapt, improve, mix, and match to their heart's delight. Our central message is that when deciding which type of program in which to invest time, money, and people, faculty developers should carefully consider the goals they are trying to achieve; the needs that faculty, institutions, and communities articulate; and the likely effectiveness of different programming types to meet those goals and demands.

References

Association of American Colleges & Universities. (2010). *Civic Engagement VALUE Rubric*. Retrieved from https://www.aacu.org/civic-engagement-value-rubric

Bandy, J. (n.d.). "What Is Service Learning or Community Engagement?" [blog]. Retrieved from https://cft.vanderbilt.edu/guides-sub-pages/teaching-through-community-engagement/

Beach, A. L., Sorcinelli, M. D., Austin, A. E., & Rivard, J. K. (2016). *Faculty development in the age of evidence: Current practices, future imperatives*. Sterling, VA: Stylus.

Biggs, J., & Tang, C. (2011). *Teaching for quality learning at university*. New York, NY: McGraw-Hill International.

Boyer, E. L. (1990). *Scholarship reconsidered: Priorities of the professoriate*. Princeton, NJ: Carnegie Foundation for the Advancement of Teaching.

Brinko, K. T. (2012). *Practically speaking: A sourcebook for instructional consultations in higher education*. Stillwater, OK: New Forums Press.

Butin, D. (2003). Of what use is it? Multiple conceptualizations of service learning within education. *Teachers College Record, 105*(9), 1674–1692.

Campus Compact. (n.d.). *The Thomas Ehrlich Civically Engaged Faculty Award*. Retrieved from https://compact.org/initiatives/awards-programs/the-thomas-ehrlich-civically-engaged-faculty-award/

Cox, M. (2004). An introduction to faculty learning communities: Utilizing FLCs to solve problems and seize opportunities. *New Directions for Teaching and Learning, Special Issue: Building Faculty Learning Communities, 97*, 5–23.

Eberly Center. (2015). *Service learning*. Retrieved from https://www.cmu.edu/teaching/designteach/teach/instructionalstrategies/servicelearning/index.html

Ebert-May, D., Derting, T. L., Hodder, J., Momsen, J. L., Long, T. M., & Jardeleza, S. E. (2011). What we say is not what we do: Effective evaluation of faculty development programs. *Bioscience, 61*(7), 550–558.

Ellis, D. E., & Ortquist-Ahrens, L. (2010). Practical suggestions for programs and activities. In K. J. Gillespie, D. L. Robertson, & Associates (Eds.), *A guide to faculty development* (2nd ed., pp. 177–134). San Francisco, CA: Jossey-Bass.

Eyler, J., and Giles, D. E. (1999). *Where's the learning in service learning?* San Francisco, CA: Jossey-Bass.

Fink, L. D. (2013). *Creating significant learning experiences: An integrated approach to designing college courses.* San Francisco, CA: Jossey-Bass.

Furco, A., & Moely, B. E. (2012). Using learning communities to build faculty support for pedagogical innovation: A multi-campus study. *The Journal of Higher Education, 83*(1), 128–153.

Gelmon, S., Blanchard, L., Ryan, K., & Seifer, S. D. (2012). Building capacity for community-engaged scholarship: Evaluation of the faculty development component of the faculty for the engaged campus initiative. *Journal of Higher Education Outreach and Engagement, 16*(1), 21–45.

Hansen, E. J. (2011). *Idea-based learning: A course design process to promote conceptual understanding.* Sterling, VA: Stylus.

Hurney, C. A., Brantmeier, E. J., Good, M. R., Harrison, D., & Meixner, C. (2016). The faculty learning outcome assessment framework. *The Journal of Faculty Development, 30*(2), 69–77.

Jacoby, B. (1996). *Service-learning in higher education: Concepts and practices.* San Francisco, CA: Jossey-Bass.

Kolb, D. A. (2014). *Experiential learning: Experience as the source of learning and development* (2nd ed.). Upper Saddle River, NJ: Pearson Education.

Lee, V. S. (2010). Program types and prototypes. In K. J. Gillespie, D. L. Robertson, & Associates (Eds.), *A guide to faculty development* (2nd ed., pp. 21–34). San Francisco, CA: Jossey-Bass.

Lewis, K. G., & Povlacs Lunde, J. T. (2001). *Face-to-face: A sourcebook of individual consultation techniques for faculty/instructional developers.* Stillwater, OK: New Forums Press.

Little, D., & Palmer, M. (2011). A coaching-based framework for individual consultations. *To Improve the Academy, 29*, 102–115.

Nagel, R. L., Gipson, K. G., Nagel, J. K., & Moran, T. (2014). Impacting the community through a sophomore design experience. *International Journal for Service Learning in Engineering, 9*, 439–459.

Northeastern University Center of Community Service. (2017). *Service-Learning Teaching Assistant Program.* Retrieved from https://www.northeastern.edu/communityservice/for-students/programs/service-learning/service-learning-teaching-assistant-program/

Northern Illinois University Faculty Development and Instructional Design Center. (n.d.). *Service learning.* Retrieved from http://facdevblog.niu.edu/tag/service-learning

Office of Community Engagement and Service, Miami University. (n.d.). *Faculty resource guide for service-learning.* Retrieved from http://miamioh.edu/student-life/_files/documents/community-engagement/service-learning/faculty-resource-guide-sl.pdf

Palmer, M., Streifer, A. C., & Williams-Duncan, S. (2016). Systematic assessment of a high-impact course design institute. *To Improve the Academy, 35*(2), 339–361.

Payne, D. A. (2000). *Evaluating service-learning activities and programs.* Lanham, MD: Scarecrow Education.

Peaslee, L., & Teye, A. C. (2015). *Testing the impact of mentor training and peer support on the quality of mentor-mentee relationships and outcomes for at-risk youth* (Final Report, OJJDP Award 2011-JU-FX-0002). Retrieved from www.ncjrs.gov/pdffiles1/ojjdp/grants/248719.pdf

Ragins, B. R., & Kram, K. E. (2007). The roots and meaning of mentoring. In K. E. Kram and B. R. Ragins (Eds.), *The handbook of mentoring at work: Theory, research, and practice* (pp. 3–15). Los Angeles, CA: Sage.

Seifer, S. D., & Connors, K. (2007). *Faculty toolkit for service-learning in higher education.* Learn and Serve America's National Service-Learning Clearinghouse. Retrieved from www.eastfieldcollege.edu/Assets/ServiceLearning/faculty-toolkit-for-service-learning.pdf

Sonoma State University Center for Community Engagement. (n.d.). *CCE blog.* Retrieved from http://www.sonoma.edu/cce/blog/

Sorcinelli, M. D., Austin, A. E., Eddy, P. E., & Beach, A. L. (2006). *Creating the future of faculty development: Learning from the pasts, understanding the present.* San Francisco, CA: Jossey-Bass.

Stephens, J. B. (2016, Summer). Blogging for community engagement learning—An experiment. *National Civic Review, 105*(2), 52–59.

Teye, A. C., & Peaslee, L. (2015). Measuring educational outcomes for at-risk children and youth: Issues with the validity of self-reported data. *Child & Youth Care Forum, 44*(6), 853–873.

University of North Carolina School of Government. (n.d.). *Community Engagement Learning Exchange.* Retrieved from http://cele.sog.unc.edu

Virginia Commonwealth University. (2017). *Community engagement.* Retrieved from https://community.vcu.edu/faculty-support-/

Wiggins, G., & McTighe, J. (2005). *Understanding by design.* Alexandria, VA: Association for Supervision and Curriculum Development.

Witkin, B. R., and Altschuld, J. W. (1995). *Planning and conducting needs assessments: A practical guide.* Thousand Oaks, CA: Sage.

4

SUPPORTING PROFESSIONAL DEVELOPMENT FOR COMMUNITY ENGAGEMENT

Three Institutional Case Studies

Amy Spring

Case studies contributed by *Caile Spear, Kara Brascia, Mike Stefancic, Anna Bailey, Kristin English, Julia Metzker, Chavonda Mills, Sandra Godwin, Sherril B. Gelmon, Kevin Kecskes, Devorah Lieberman, and Leslie McBride*

Welch and Saltmarsh (2013) published a comprehensive study that identified the components and characteristics of established community engagement centers. This chapter builds on that work by featuring case studies from Boise State University, Georgia State College & University (GSCU), and Portland State University (PSU), each of which have integrated service-learning and community engagement into their curricula. The case studies also feature institutions that have mobilized resources to support professional development for faculty, staff, students, and community partners engaged in community-based teaching, learning, and research. The organizational contexts, the scale of their respective community engagement programs, and the methods used to support the expansion and quality of practice are unique to each institution.

Teams from each of the featured institutions developed the case studies included in this chapter. Boise State University's case study illustrates how the systematic recruitment and retraining of faculty through customized support, online infrastructure, and strategic campus collaborations results in a campus culture that embraces service-learning (SL) at all levels. GSCU details the programs and institutional structures that have helped them develop a large-scale program that serves student learning. And last, the Portland State University case offers an illustration of a teaching and learning center that was simultaneously providing professional development for faculty teaching and doing scholarly work in communities while also engaged in institutional development meant to help create an engaged campus. Each case study provides an overview of the institution and its community engagement commitments, a profile of some of the methods used to support professional growth for their constituents, a set of lessons learned, and recommendations intended to be informative and transferable to those seeking to deepen their institution's community engagement capacity.

Boise State University

Caile Spear, Kara Brascia, Mike Stefancic, and Anna Bailey

Boise State University Context

Boise State University, a recipient of the Carnegie Classification for Community Engagement, is a public, four-year doctoral research university with an enrollment of 22,000 students. Utilizing Boyer's (1990, 1996) approach to the scholarship of engagement, the provost set a strategic goal of expanding experiential learning opportunities. Within this supportive climate, faculty are provided with incentives to explore SL. Each year, more than 2,800 students participate in over 150 SL classes, with an average growth of 10 to 15 new SL classes per year. In 2016, 41% of all graduating seniors had taken an SL class. Faculty enjoy the support of a strong, well-respected, centralized Service-Learning Program (SLP), housed in the Center for Teaching and Learning, under Academic Affairs. Three staff members and a graduate assistant focus exclusively on SL, administering an appropriated budget of $230,000. The SL director (20 years of experience) oversees faculty development and is assisted by an SL faculty liaison (20 years of SL experience). The evolution of the Boise State University SL program, including objectives, challenges, and successes, is outlined in Table 4.1.

The rate of new faculty trying SL has varied over the last 15 years. The diffusion of innovation model (Rogers, 1971) aptly describes how faculty have adopted SL pedagogy. During the early years of the SL program, innovator and early adopter faculty readily saw the benefits of using SL pedagogy and how adult learners benefit from applied learning. After this first wave of adopters slowed, SL staff reached out to new segments of faculty. These groups of early and late majority adopters had competing priorities, different motivations, and less willingness to invest time in extensive planning. As

TABLE 4.1
Timeline of Boise State University Organizational and Program Implementation

Early (2000–2003)	Midway (2004–2009)	Advanced (2010–2017)
Objectives/Successes		
Generated interest and understanding of SL Established credibility and visibility of SL and SLP Developed web-based materials, workshops, networks Recruited strong senior faculty for SL advisory board Streamlined SL project registration using online database Instituted SL on transcripts Learned about community needs/strengths	Launched SL faculty learning communities (FLCs) at different levels Increased faculty incentives and rewards for teaching with SL Gained new funding to hire student support coordinator and team of teaching assistants; later hired a community partnership coordinator Hired five student leaders to support community partners (CPs) and students on site Passed 10,000 students enrolled in SL classes since 2000	Implemented phased approach to faculty development Hard-wired community engagement into university's revamped general education Integrated SL into annual faculty review system Supported faculty with their SL scholarship Connected campus with established community-wide initiatives
Challenges		
Danger of heavy recruiting leading to stretched class/community fit and compromised learning Adherence to evidence-based practices during periods of intense growth Lack of reciprocity in SL process and projects	Meeting varying needs of late adopter faculty Facilitating close, reciprocal relationships between CPs and faculty Core CPs overcommitting or overstretched Bottleneck for program growth in developing and managing CPs	Empowering faculty to be self-sufficient, independent of SL staff support Build SLP staff expertise to facilitate large-scale partnerships for the whole campus Some students taking too many SL classes at the same time; some departments seeing diminishing returns

time progressed, we developed different entry pathways to accommodate the various motivation levels of new faculty and address the perceived costs of incorporating SL methods (McKay & Rozee, 2004). Although participation increased, we soon observed some of these faculty were not returning after they taught SL for the first time. One common factor was their minimal contact with SL staff, which often left faculty isolated. To increase faculty retention, we began providing more customized faculty development for all first-time faculty.

Boise State's customized phase model of SL faculty development has three entry pathways, determined by the following factors: (a) faculty motivation, (b) willingness to invest time up front, (c) amount of staff support needed, and (d) potential complexity of the SL experience. For each pathway, SL staff use different planning strategies, tools, training, timing, and levels of contact to help faculty succeed with their first SL teaching experience (see Table 4.2). The three entry pathways fit with certain faculty profiles—fast trackers, planners, and deep planners—used internally to guide staff efforts (not necessarily shared with faculty).

The first path, the fast trackers, appeals to two different groups of faculty: (a) autonomous faculty with project-based teaching experience, who are just looking for SL tools and/or community connections and (b) faculty with less patience for extensive SL planning, wanting to get started and figure it out as they go. The second track, planners, involve faculty who are enthusiastic; eager to take advantage of planning tools, tips, and feedback; and generally follow suggested protocol carefully. The third track, deep planners, are self-driven, careful, thorough, willing to invest substantial time, and see connections to research interests and scholarship.

After faculty teach with SL for the first time, most move from the entry phase to the practice phase, then to the advanced phase, and ultimately the mentor phase (see Table 4.3). During each phase, SL staff provide ongoing support and faculty development appropriate to the faculty member's motivation, level of SL proficiency, confidence, and career development. Faculty development activities range from staff modeling in-class reflection to intensive one-on-one mentoring and FLCs. This customized, phase-based approach helps faculty achieve SL competencies at their own pace, based on their own style. Many reach the mentor stage where they are invited to advise new faculty and serve as SL ambassadors in their college.

Boise State SL staff base the SL entry process and faculty development programs on several assumptions:

1. Faculty development begins during the first consultation and includes most components of staff support, as well as more formal group offerings.

TABLE 4.2
Entry Pathways for New SL Faculty (First Phase of Faculty Development)

Aspects of Faculty Development	Faculty Entry Phase		
	Fast-Track Path	Planner Path	Deep Planner Path
Typical Faculty Profile	Autonomous (experienced with project-based learning) OR Less patient with planning, wanting to dive in and figure it out as they go For less complex SL project	Enthusiastic Eager to take advantage of planning tools, tips, and feedback Follows suggested protocol carefully	Self-driven, careful, thorough Willing to invest substantial time Sees connection to research interests and scholarship
Staff Support Strategy	High support during semester	Front-loaded support	Front-loaded support
Planning/ Consultation Strategy	Focused consultation on SL mechanics and essential elements; offer of plug-ins and templates	Thorough discussion of SL essentials and options, followed by customization to specific course	Same as with planners, plus additional meetings to review feedback, discuss reflection strategies, and create detailed timeline
Community Partnership Strategy	Staff development of CP contact list or pre-established projects; staff-provided faculty/CP discussion checklist and syllabus plug-in language to guide students	Staff development of curated list of CPs, facilitation of site visits, and posting of projects	Same as with planners, OR faculty develop and manage their own CPs, involving CP in designing the project

(*Continues*)

TABLE 4.2 (Continued)

Aspects of Faculty Development	Faculty Entry Phase		
	Fast-Track Path	Planner Path	Deep Planner Path
Classroom Support Strategy	Faculty autonomy OR Staff orientation of students via classroom presentation, then facilitation of project selection/ tracking, reflection, significant student troubleshooting, and evaluation	Staff helping faculty plan intentional framing of SL; staff discussing potential student questions/challenges, and planning proactive solutions; staff offering classroom presentation and reflection facilitation	Same as with planners, but recognizing that deep planners often want to walk through possible scenarios and carefully map out strategies for promoting student success, OR faculty managing their own logistics
Toolkit	Quick checklist, plug-in syllabus language, time-tested reflection questions, suggested timeline, and sample grading system	Planning worksheet, detailed checklist, SL assignment template	Same as with planners, plus foundational SL literature and online SL workshops/webinars
Evaluation and Debriefing	Abbreviated planning worksheet review, syllabus review/approval, midsemester check-in, end-of-semester debrief, review of students' SL evaluations	Planning worksheet and syllabus review/approval, end-of-semester debrief, review of students' SL evaluations	Same as with planners
Faculty Development Recommendation	Drop-in "community of practice" brown bags	FLC	SL literature and theory FLC

TABLE 4.3
Faculty Development by Phase

	Entry Phase: Build Foundation	Practice Phase: Gain Experience	Advanced Phase: Expand Boundaries	Mentor Phase: Lead and Mentor
Goal of Phase	Learn and practice basics of SL pedagogy through pilot semester Increase confidence and commitment to teaching again with SL	Increase sense of self-efficacy with SL and gain autonomy	Build a sense of community with other SL faculty	Sustain high levels of involvement and leadership
Faculty Role	Integrate essential SL principles into course plan Reach out to CPs Reflect on pilot, plan revisions Consider being a mentee	Explore alternate SL models and reflection Take the lead on facilitating SL while SL staff step back Communicate steadily with CPs Attend FLC	Teach SL in other types of classes Build long-term CPs Explore opportunities for SL scholarship Begin planning SL in promotion and tenure review	Cofacilitate SL workshops Mentor other faculty Integrate SL into research and scholarship Build or lead interdisciplinary project
Faculty Development Strategies	Repeated individual consultation with SL staff Facilitated site visits to CPs SL staff modeling of reflection facilitation SL community of practice Mentoring Minigrants	FLC on SL best practices Minigrants Highlight faculty in campus news outlets Appreciation letter from provost to faculty and their chair	FLC on SL scholarship Presentation and proposal assistance Workshops on how to incorporate SL activities in tenure portfolio	Mentorship and campus leadership opportunities Nominate faculty for awards

2. Customization of faculty development is necessary; faculty motivations determine support needs, and class situational factors highly influence the entry pathway, faculty development, and staff support needs.
3. Faculty become learners themselves when integrating a new pedagogy, and they require various types of support and development to meet them at their current level. This process evolves over many semesters.
4. Teaching with a learner-centered pedagogy requires additional support up front.
5. Developing community partnership is a collaborative, reciprocal dynamic process, and faculty will need different levels of guidance.

The SL director and faculty liaison developed our phased approach to faculty development in 2007 after observing that faculty have different knowledge and experience levels, which require different phases of faculty development and corresponding support resources. In 2015–2016 we refined our strategy in response to the unique needs of late-adopter faculty. Specifically, we designed and piloted an expedited (fast-track) process and built in multilevel assessments, including review of SL plans, midsemester check-in, end-of-semester debriefing, and review of student SL evaluations. Initial results indicate this fast-track process has filled a gap in our faculty development program.

Methods

Faculty development starts with the entry phase, where SL staff spend significant time working with instructors new to SL. The goal is to support faculty in integrating essential SL principles into their course plan and to achieve basic skill competency. The first step is the initial consultation, when SL staff engage with and assess the faculty member's motivation and willingness to invest time in planning. We also evaluate the potential complexity of the SL experience based on key factors: class level, size, number of community partners (CPs), whether *new* CPs would need to be cultivated, whether to assign group or individual projects, required or optional SL, and staff support needed. The essential triage that assesses those factors includes the following questions:

- What brings you to SL?
- What is your previous experience with SL, project-based teaching, or experiential learning?
- Describe your class and how you currently structure it.
- What are your initial ideas for SL? What do you want students to gain?

- What is your planning time frame?

These details help us gauge the depth and type of preparation, support, and faculty development to offer this faculty member. After weighing all key factors, SL staff explain the purpose of SL, principles, models, staff support, and what to expect. Then we offer a toolkit for the recommended pathway. The second step, which may occur in separate meetings, is to provide customized support and faculty development, based on specific pathways and phases. We divide the staff support into three linked focus areas: course planning, CP development, and classroom support. See Table 4.2 for a detailed explanation of each path, staff support strategies, toolkits, and faculty development. The tools mentioned in the table, as well as detailed explanations about terms, can be found on the SL website for Boise State University (2017).

Generally, fast trackers opt for minimal resources upfront. If we anticipate their project will be complex, we stay in close touch, troubleshoot as needed, and provide support. After they teach for the first time, they see what is involved and they seek out faculty development, either because they ran into challenges and want to learn to avoid them or they worked in isolation and are excited to share ideas with other SL faculty. The other pathways (planners and deep planners) are offered the same full range of classroom support and faculty development. They generally choose the up-front support focused on course planning, community partnership development, and student preparation; they also take advantage of FLCs during the semester. As a result, planners need less staff support during the semester.

After faculty teach for the first time, they move from the entry phase into the practice phase, and hopefully continue to the advanced phase. The goal of the practice phase is to deepen their use of SL best practices, increase their sense of self-efficacy with SL, and gain autonomy. Once faculty achieve this level of self-efficacy with SL, they developmentally move into the advanced phase. In this phase, they request staff support much less. However, in a proactive effort to retain faculty, SL staff stay in touch with advanced faculty each year, help them build a sense of community with other SL faculty, recognize their efforts, and share opportunities for SL scholarship. Some faculty reach the mentor phase, in which they take on leadership roles. Faculty progression through these phases is for internal staff planning and program evaluation. On a logistical front, tracking the pathway and progress of 10 to 15 entry faculty plus more than 60 returning faculty is streamlined by using a project management system like Smartsheet.

Faculty retention cannot be taken for granted, so an essential step is faculty recognition. SL staff highlight faculty SL stories in campus-wide online newsletters and share the story link with the faculty member's chair and dean, pointing out how the SL experience relates to campus strategic goals. SL staff also facilitate a letter of appreciation from the provost to each SL faculty member and his or her chair. SL staff leverage all opportunities to highlight SL faculty, especially in venues viewed by campus leaders and faculty peers. This recognition strategy also builds a supportive campus climate for faculty.

Results

Boise State measures the success of our faculty development program through both qualitative and quantitative measures. Three quantitative indicators tell us if we are moving in the right direction: students' SL evaluations, faculty retention, and CP feedback. Recent results of these indicators are very positive.

- On student SL evaluations, 79% of students reported that their instructor integrated SL in a way that enhanced their understanding of course content (increase of 8% from previous year); 80% of students reported they would recommend that the instructor continue to use SL in the course (increase of 26% from previous year).
- Faculty retention is on the rise. Last year's SL faculty attrition (accounting for faculty who left the university or did not teach their SL course) was only 3.8%, continuing a steady improvement from 11.8% attrition in 2010.
- CP survey data from 2015 showed that 94% of our partners said that SL students expanded their capacity, 91% said it was worth the time commitment, and 78% of partners felt like a coeducator.

Because we direct significant staff resources to entry-level faculty, we closely examined their results. Data from students' SL evaluations from 30 entry-level faculty last year was 4.01 out of 5 on questions related to SL integration and whether students would recommend that SL continue in that class. We also looked for differences between faculty using different entry paths. Preliminary data from our pilot year (2015–2016) suggest that faculty in all three entry paths experienced similar results on student SL evaluations, taking into account all levels of staff support and faculty development. This data may indicate that staff support serves as a leveler. More data are needed to be conclusive.

Lessons Learned and Advice

The customized, phased approach to faculty development is a framework that categorizes faculty strengths and support needs, as well as the tools, staff support, and faculty development to address those needs. After piloting this approach, we found that many faculty demonstrate a mixture of characteristics, so categorizing is just a guide. High levels of faculty support and development require substantial staff resources, which must be intentionally allocated to fit campus-specific SL growth and retention goals. SL staff must continually balance between quantity and quality; some years we feel pressure from above to increase numbers, so we need to adjust our level of staff support to faculty. For program sustainability, the goal of increasing faculty autonomy must be prioritized. We find that customized faculty development is important because faculty learn differently and motivations vary. Our customized approach evolved from a model of one size fits all, which worked for most early adopter faculty. Over 15 years, as we reached out to later faculty adopting SL pedagogy, we needed to offer multiple entry pathways and a variety of faculty development activities. Forecasters of higher education trends predict the demand for hands-on learning will expand throughout the curriculum, so new situational factors may require SL programs to be even more creative and strategic with faculty support and development.

Georgia College & State University

Kristin English, Julia Metzker, Chavonda Mills, and Sandra Godwin

GSCU Context

GSCU is a small university of 6,600 students situated in a rural county with a public liberal arts mission placing high value on teaching and public service. Consequently, faculty are encouraged to participate in community-based teaching, research, and service. A five-year university-wide quality enhancement plan (QEP), adopted in 2014 as part of our institutional accreditation, aims to make community-based engaged learning (C-bEL) a central component of the undergraduate experience. As such, C-bEL is one of six university-identified transformative experiences required by students during their time at GSCU. *C-bEL* is defined as learning in academic and cocurricular settings in which students directly participate in community experiences which require the integration of theory and practice as well as systematic critical reflection. This initiative, designed by a broad coalition of faculty, staff, students, and community members, brought existing projects sequestered in departments into a holistic institutionalized office, ENGAGE, which provides all levels of support for community-based work. An overview of the work of the office is outlined in Table 4.4. Throughout the last two decades, the programs and structures have grown slowly, but the core work showed progress at every step. The project presented here outlines the program structure and its challenges, anchored by a large-scale study assessing the impact of C-bEL on student learning and development. Methods include standardized pre/post surveys for students and community partners along with common assessment rubrics.

ENGAGE was motivated, in part, by two primary elements—the impact of the Great Recession on the surrounding community, creating a significant disparity between our students and community members, and the desire to address the issue of exposing students to diverse populations. Since 2008, the community has lost over 30% of the county's jobs, making GSCU the largest employer. The median family income for Milledgeville, where the college is located, is approximately $32,460 per year, whereas the median family income for GSCU students is over $80,000 per year. The racial composition of the student body and faculty provides an additional element of distance between the institution and the surrounding community. GSCU is a predominantly White institution (82.4% of its students identify as White), surrounded by a more racially diverse city and county. Whereas the student population is only 7.5% African American, the city is 42.2% African American. These socioeconomic disparities and stark racial differences have contributed to a perception among many local residents that GSCU, although a public institution, does not do enough to serve the local community.

Program Model

A core value of ENGAGE is to engender learning and meet community needs. The rural nature of the surrounding community means there are a limited number of organizations available to partner with the university, and many lack formal organizational structures. These constraints require authentic partnerships to sustain over time, which makes partnership-building a core component of our model. Thus, *faculty development* has become *practitioner development* and intentionally includes faculty, staff, and community members. Building reciprocal relationships is complex and requires practitioners to navigate thorny issues such as institutional bureaucracy, conflicting calendars, student needs, and community issues. Our model addresses these barriers by bringing practitioners together to collaborate on project design, student assessment, and project evaluation.

TABLE 4.4

Timeline of GSCU Organizational Program and Implementation

Early (1996–2001)	Midway (2002–2008)	Advanced (2009–2017)
Objectives/Successes		
Established standards for SL and experiential learning	Integration into the curriculum; ensuring that standards are followed; solicitation of administrative support	Establishing institutional structure and support for activities
Establishment of SL and experiential learning offices; integration into faculty development	Establishment of American Democracy Project presence; grassroots, interdisciplinary faculty development group formed	Implementation of program at the institutional level through our QEP; establishment of a formal structure of definition, development
Providing development opportunities; educating faculty on opportunities	Creation of more opportunities for faculty development	Providing support from development to implementation to inclusion in promotion and tenure process
A few strong collaborations developed between faculty and community partners	Faculty work to build individual SL experiences; creation of grassroots group out of need for consistency	Establishing incentives, development opportunities, and a place to go for resources and assistance
No clear objectives; partnerships evolving as result of faculty connections	Building community partner capacity for providing SL opportunities	Establishment of office as consistent presence for partners
A few fleeting partnerships developed based on individual relationships	Very strong relationships formed with a few nonprofits and community organizations	Systemization of partnership criteria through agreements
Challenges		
Lack of coordination between academic and student affairs divisions	Variable support across academic departments despite strong demand from students and upper administration	Preserving the core values that spawned the project in the face of growing S-LCE structures and assessment demands
Insufficient reward/support system for S-LCE	Insufficient reward system for S-LCE	Developing policies through governance procedures that reward S-LCE
Lack of a structure to sustain partnerships beyond personnel changes	Core community partners overcommitted or overstretched	Insufficient support for grassroots community groups with limited leadership capacity
	Limited partnerships with small community organizations or grassroots community groups	

Recognizing practitioners will have varying degrees of experience with C-bEL, our four-tiered model meets individuals where they are and provides the resources required to sustain partnerships and projects over time. These tiers provide a pathway to evolve from an apprentice to a master practitioner:

- *Apprentice.* A cohort model for novices supported by peer mentoring with experienced practitioners and workshops to build essential skills
- *Journeyman.* Small grants to support implementation or expansion of projects
- *Master.* Grants to support institutionalization in the curriculum through multiyear funding of sustainable collaborations
- *Fellow.* Fellowships awarded to expert practitioners who have demonstrated exemplary work and desire to become mentors to apprentices and journeymen

Due to the direct link between ENGAGE and institutional accreditation, the program is anchored in the assessment of student learning. University practitioners provide reports on student learning, reflections on their own

Figure 4.1. Assessment toolbox, GSCU.

learning, and evidence of impact of the project on the community and institution through periodic project reports.

An assessment toolbox (Figure 4.1) of instruments has been developed to evaluate student growth with respect to a tightly defined set of student learning outcomes (Figure 4.2). Direct measures of student learning most commonly emerge from students' critical reflections assessed by a common rubric adapted from the Association of American Colleges & Universities (n.d.) Valid Assessment of Learning in Undergraduate Education (VALUE) rubrics. Indirect measures come from attitudinal surveys administered to students at the beginning and end of their C-bEL experience.

An annual project report provides a critical opportunity for practitioners to reflect. Arguing that reflection for teachers is as important as reflection for students, Brookfield (1995) writes, "In their attempts to make sense of the chaos they confront on a daily basis, college teachers must evolve new meaning schemes and perspectives for the sake of survival" (p. xv). We have found this theme to be true especially for those involved in community work. Educators, along with students, are likely to find themselves branching out into new territory and building relationships across difference.

The formal development opportunities are supported by less formal activities including monthly faculty development workshops, sharing potlucks, and a blog (ENGAGE, n.d.) to provide just-in-time support to

Figure 4.2. ENGAGE Learning Outcomes.

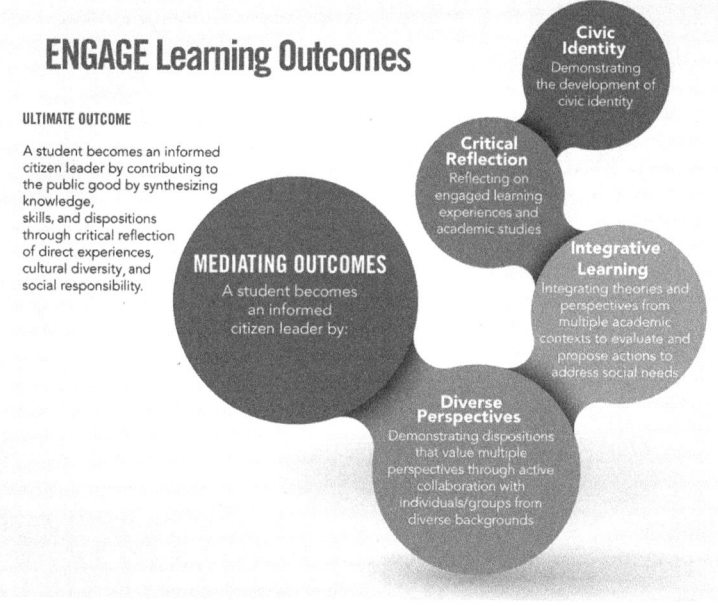

practitioners as they navigate uncharted territories. The sharing meetings have proved essential to growth and engagement as they facilitate ongoing discussions of challenges in course design, assessment strategies, mechanisms for strengthening community ties, and other issues that may arise.

Results

Since implementation began in 2014, several promising practices have emerged related to faculty involvement:

- Introducing first-year faculty to the program and potential partners through a community bus tour of the Milledgeville community has proven to be a successful method of recruiting faculty to the program.
- Strategic nominations of C-bEL practitioners for institutional, regional, and national awards provide valuable recognition for faculty to administrators and encourage continued participation.
- Annual reporting of C-bEL activity in the institutional faculty activity database allows faculty to receive recognition for their contributions in the annual faculty evaluation process—including tenure and promotion portfolios.
- Dissemination of C-bEL work through scholarly venues validates faculty participation—to date, 34 presentations and publications have been made.
- Providing informal opportunities for engaging in "small talk" over a meal is a powerful platform for spawning innovation and strengthening practitioner commitment.

Student Participation

In 3 years, 125 C-bEL experiences have been developed in curricular and cocurricular settings. Approximately 2,600 students have participated in projects as diverse as theater to international global health to art to digital media. These projects have contributed over 51,000 ENGAGE service hours to the community, totaling $1.2 million in value to community partners (Independent Sector, 2016).

Practitioner Participation

The ENGAGE program has benefited from a high level of exposure through university and community marketing efforts. A commendable percentage of instructional staff (23%), from a cross-section of departments, participated in the program tiers in the first few years. It is worth noting that a significant portion, 56% of all C-bEL experiences, have been led by STEM faculty.

With that said, the tier levels have been at or near capacity each semester with the exception of the most recent due to a program transition and personnel shift. The master and fellow tiers require high levels of commitment and participation. In just 2 years, 6 master grants have been awarded to support sustainable, long-term community engagement programs embedded in the curriculum. In just 3 years, 18 fellows (9 faculty, 2 staff, 53 community members, and 2 students) have been recognized for exceptional contributions to C-bEL and enlisted as advisers to the program and mentors to apprentices and journeymen.

Practitioner Retention

The retention and continuation of participants in C-bEL activities are crucial to institutionalization. Roughly one-third of our ENGAGE practitioners transition between one or more tiers. These transitions demonstrate the ability to sustain interest beyond attending development workshops or receiving a grant and, ultimately, build strong community engagement projects and relationships. For example, a Food Justice Road Tour, where students explored sustainable farms in central Georgia, was initiated from a C-bEL course, The Sociology of Food, and received funding from a journeyman minigrant. The tour, open to students, faculty, and community members, has become a highly anticipated annual community event and is sustained by funding provided by ENGAGE.

Although these numbers, examples, and financial incentives (e.g., grants) are important measures of the success of the program, an intentional value was placed on the quality of the experience for student development. That value is a continuing challenge to all community engagement work and not the only one faced in the implementation of the ENGAGE program.

Challenges and Lessons Learned

The ENGAGE program is unique in its comprehensive structure and the prioritization of building quality relationships with community partners, and the program and relationships have prospered overall. Yet we have also experienced some of the same challenges noted by other scholars of community-based work in higher education (Berilla, 2015; Mitchell, 2008; Stoecker & Tryon, 2009). We focus on two: lack of an executive-level evangelist for community engagement and the "White savior" complex.

Because ENGAGE is directly tied to our accreditation review, executive-level leaders prioritized quantitative measures over program quality and relationship-building. Although quantitative measures such as number of community-based courses, number of practitioners, hours spent in service, or the amount of funding provided are important measures of success, administrators must be willing to serve as advocates for quality experiences. We have since learned relationship-building is a key motivator for ENGAGE practitioners and results in high-quality community experiences. A misstep in our planning was not involving administrators directly in this relationship-building, and thus our administrators were not adequately aware of the importance of this work to the success of the program. As shifts in leadership may result in conflicting perspectives, it is crucial to bring institutional leadership into close proximity to the work. This weakness was exposed during a recent program transition and personnel shift. The resulting challenges may have been avoided if administrators had been directly involved in the program implementation process.

As an institution where students involved in community-based work are more often than not White from class-privileged backgrounds and are working with poor or low-income communities of color, we face the challenge of exhibiting a White savior complex. We have observed students (and faculty) who hold beliefs promoting the assumption they are reaching "down" to help a community of color and, as a result, establish themselves as superior to the community partners. Students' experiences of class privilege can reinforce this superiority complex, particularly when they are working with a community or group who are predominantly poor or low income. Students of color from class-privileged backgrounds are not immune to the class dimension of this set of beliefs where they assume they are helping the economically "unfortunate."

The lesson we have learned is that students and practitioners need formal opportunities to reflect on their privilege vis-à-vis the groups with which they are working. Ideally, through the experience, they become familiar with participatory models of engagement that require reflection (Freire, 1986; Smith, 1997). Without continuous reflection on their growth and development as a result of working across differences, they are more likely to come away from the community experience thinking they have "saved" the community and not recognize their own growth—looking outward and not inward. At the same time, it is important to build support in the classroom for students as they branch out beyond the campus and stretch their ability to build relationships with people from backgrounds different from their own.

We have found a sustained culture of community-based engaged learning is achievable only with dedicated participation from all constituents (students, faculty, staff, administrators, and community members). Our program model provides the support and resources necessary to ensure continued faculty participation, continued course and project development, and ultimately an expansive community of C-bEL educators beyond the campus. The ENGAGE program exhibits both examples of success and challenge in the ever-changing world of community engagement. For a program of this nature to become institutionalized, the complex structure, recommendations, and adaptiveness presented here are required of all constituents. Quality community engagement work requires long-term commitment to creating a culture of engaged learning.

Portland State University

Amy Spring, Sherril B. Gelmon, Kevin Kecskes, Devorah Lieberman, and Leslie McBride

PSU Context

The Center for Academic Excellence served as the teaching and learning center for the PSU community. Central to its work, the center was the primary unit to offer professional development resources and programs for community-engaged teaching and scholarship. Although the center no longer operates at PSU, the expertise developed over its 18-year history is being replicated in the distributed model of community-engaged professional development currently being used at PSU.

As an urban-serving university, PSU enrolls more than 22,000 undergraduate and 5,600 graduate students. For over 25 years, PSU has successfully incorporated its motto of "Let Knowledge Serve the City" into teaching, learning, and research experiences through engagement opportunities that bring the campus community into partnership with community organizations. In the early 1990s, PSU transformed its overall undergraduate general education approach into a program known as University Studies. This reform effort was a faculty-led process aimed at bringing more structure and coherence to PSU general education. The University Studies requirements include a 6-credit, senior-level, multidisciplinary, community-based capstone course. In the capstone, students and faculty work collaboratively with community partners to respond to a community-identified concern. This ambitious curricular revision effort helped to build the foundation for PSU's reputation as a national and international leader in community-based learning and community-university partnerships (White, 1994).

In 1995, PSU's Center for Academic Excellence was founded with a mission to "support and promote academic excellence in teaching, assessment, and community-university partnerships in order to enhance faculty scholarship, improve student learning outcomes, and contribute to the Portland metropolitan community" (Kecskes, Spring, & Lieberman, 2003, p. 290).

TABLE 4.5
Time Line of PSU Organizational and Program Implementation

Early (1995–2000)	Midway (2001–2007)	Advanced (2007–2012)
Objectives/Successes		
Capstone program FLCs Faculty in Residence program Identifying and supporting faculty leadership Inclusion of community-based learning workshop in new faculty orientation Rigorous assessment practices beginning to create a culture Opening discussions recognizing community-based approaches in promotion and tenure considerations	Deepening and expanding beyond CBL and focusing more broadly on civic engagement Beginning to develop strategies to support scholarly work connected to community engagement activities Establishment of regularly occurring, highly visible events focused on civic engagement topics Launching of Engaged Department initiative	Expansion of national and international leadership roles Integration of community-based experiences with other campus programs, including the development office, alumni relations, and student affairs Introduction of biannual international symposia and conferences focused on community engagement Selection as 1 of 12 to create and test the Carnegie Classification for Community Engagement Choice for first-ever Jimmy and Rosalynn Carter Award for community engagement
Challenges		
Limited resource allocation Defining excellence standards for the pedagogy Clarifying SL versus volunteerism	Lack of clarity about promotion and tenure standards Meeting varying needs of middle to late adopter faculty	Sustaining momentum and creativity during times of center personnel and institutional leadership changes

(Continues)

TABLE 4.5 (Continued)

Early (1995–2000)	Midway (2001–2007)	Advanced (2007–2012)
Challenges (Continued)		
Tracking partnerships in a decentralized model like PSU's Limitations in staff capacity to support the matching role	Better tracking of capstones and connection to other community-based learning courses to get more complete picture of campus engagement activities	Movement from individual course and partnership focus to collective focus to sequence courses creating continuity of work with community partner Expansion of community-based learning into online courses

Table 4.5 outlines the evolution of the program elements of the center. The founding of the center, as well as the simultaneous launch of undergraduate curricular reforms that required a community-based learning experience, necessitated the inclusion of professional development for community partnerships and community-engaged teaching as a signature aspect of the center's portfolio.

The time line outlines the objectives, successes, and challenges at each of the center's developmental stages. In the table we offer some important milestones of activity that helped to support faculty and the institutional changes needed to advance community engagement at PSU. After 18 years, the center as reviewed in this case formally closed and a new faculty development unit was created to take its place, responding to the need for professional support of online learning. With that organizational change, the center was renamed the Office of Academic Innovation. This case study will provide the organizational framework and program activities that were foundational to the work of the center and continue to inform the professional development approach used at PSU today.

Program Methods and Models

The center was built on the following programming pillars: (a) teaching and learning excellence, (b) community partnerships and support of community-university engagement strategies, and (c) assessment strategies that inform the effectiveness of institutional change. These programmatic approaches focused overall staff initiatives on three levels of mutually reinforcing and often simultaneous activities.

The first level of activities focused on individual faculty development to support teaching and learning excellence, as well as engagement strategies. This level typically centered on a one-on-one consultation format, addressing faculty questions regarding community-based learning (CBL)/civic engagement course design, midterm feedback, evaluation, and professional portfolio development. Given PSU's clearly articulated, lived tradition of community engagement, much of the staff's work focused on individual faculty-community partnership development for the purposes of deepening and extending CBL and/or community-based research (CBR) efforts.

The second level of activities engaged small faculty groups, or theme-based cohort efforts, and used the FLC model as a core design feature. The FLCs met biweekly for up to 20 weeks and involved 6 to 10 faculty members from a variety of disciplines. At times, these cohorts included faculty with their community partner or a student leader. FLCs typically attracted participants with some but limited experience teaching community-based courses. These program participants sought to deepen their practice and integrate their community-based teaching into a scholarly output. Kecskes, Collier, and Balshem (2006) studied the effectiveness of this program model and found that FLCs (a) promote community-based scholarship and productivity, (b) provide a support community for faculty with a shared interest in scholarship connected to community work, and (c) help develop a shared campus meaning of what is meant by *engaged scholarship*. Within this edited volume, further information on FLCs is offered in chapter 5.

Focusing on the connection between a particular domain of knowledge and community-identified interests led PSU to implement one of the nation's first campus-wide engaged department initiatives, building on the foundational work of Campus Compact's Engaged Department initiative (Battistoni and Campus Compact, 2003). Over a 5-year period, engagement staff at the center formally worked with 22 academic departments. This entailed working with teams of faculty within a department in examining learning goals, inventorying courses, and making modifications to the curriculum. Curricular modifications included sequencing courses, articulating community engagement learning outcomes, and committing to offering engaged experiences within the curriculum. Together, these efforts maximized student learning by offering increasingly more challenging applied learning experiences for learners as they progressed through the educational experience. Kecskes and Spring's (2006) review of specific implementation strategies and reflective insights describes the implementation of an interdisciplinary learning community model focused on salient themes, including the scholarship of teaching and learning, sustainability, internationalization, and diversity.

The center's third level of activities was designed to maximize campus-wide and community impact. Activities included large public events where relevant topics in the field of engagement were shared with audiences of faculty, staff, students, and community partners. The center used these events to highlight scholarship relevant to the advancement of community engagement and attract new participants into the programs offered. Activities varied from developing a faculty-wide electronic mailing list and faculty-focused newsletter to facilitating critical conversations and large-group topical exploration such as the Civic Engagement Breakfast series and monthly faculty-community conversations. The center also sponsored the annual Civic Engagement Awards Celebration each spring, which was a high-profile event well attended by faculty colleagues and university leaders. Lastly, leveraging PSU's community engagement leadership position at an increasingly international level led to the development and implementation of four international symposia on the PSU campus.

All three levels of the center's development activities were mutually reinforcing and intentionally designed to develop both faculty expertise and leadership in a variety of scholarly practice areas. One of the advantages of this three-level approach over the 20-plus-year history of this work at the institution is that it provided staff the ability to monitor program offerings across all three levels, thereby helping to ensure that the frequency, depth, and breadth, as well as allocated resources for activities and events at each level, aligned with center goals.

Across these levels of activity, multiple initiatives related to assessment were developed and integrated into this work, reflecting the third pillar of the center's programming, specifically assessment strategies that inform the effectiveness of institutional change. In the very early days of the center (see Table 4.5), a major initiative of one of PSU's first Corporation for National Service grants was to develop a robust set of assessment strategies and tools to help in understanding the impact of the new curricular strategy of CBL (Driscoll, Holland, Gelmon, & Kerrigan, 1996). At the time, there were few resources available to assist institutions in developing strategies to understand the implications of their community engagement strategies. The PSU assessment model, which presented a multiconstituency approach considering student, faculty, institutional, and community perspectives, continued to be developed with center and faculty leadership and ultimately was published as a monograph by Campus Compact (Gelmon, Holland, Driscoll, Spring, & Kerrigan, 2001). This assessment work contributed to PSU's reputation for national and international leadership in engagement. This work also informed the ongoing assessment strategies in community-engaged classes, particularly the capstone classes that are part of the general education program.

Measures of Success Include Robust Faculty Engagement

Successful faculty development centers must continually balance the need to be responsive to emerging trends in higher education with the need to maintain support for existing program and institutional priorities. The ability to access and deploy available resources, creating programs that implement institutional priorities, was an important function of the center. The role of the administration and center staff accompanied by faculty engagement and leadership were essential to the success of the center's activities.

For the individual faculty member, especially one just beginning to explore community engagement, what was most important was easy access to expert staff, faculty mentors, and various resources (i.e., print, online, and experiential) in order to build relevant knowledge. A center-created website, electronic mailing lists, and event notifications were all methods of inviting faculty engagement in the programs. The center website would receive an average of 18,000 visits annually. However, one of the most effective methods of engaging faculty in this work has been through personal outreach to faculty by center staff and colleagues familiar with resources available in the unit. Center staff had face-to-face, individual consultations with up to 150 faculty annually.

Although staff expertise was recognized by faculty, the lived experiences of faculty colleagues on similar professional trajectories of tenure and promotion may be more relevant. Among the successes at PSU has been the appointment of a series of faculty leaders as short-term faculty-in-residence. These leadership roles have been an effective way to maintain the engagement of experienced, senior-level faculty in the activities of the center while making their teaching and scholarly expertise available to junior faculty seeking mentors, identifying models and methods of doing effective engagement work, and meeting essential tenure and promotion benchmarks. Up to 89 new faculty hires were served by this unit annually through faculty-in-residence-led programs. Engaging faculty expertise in sharing wisdom about how to create, conduct, and disseminate community-engaged scholarship across disciplinary boundaries has informed creative research methods and broadened interdisciplinary partnerships.

Center staff, serving as the first response to faculty inquiries, used their knowledge of the campus and broader community to connect people to campus colleagues with relevant or related interests. Center staff were well positioned to cultivate relationships with community partners and make those relationships accessible to faculty and students, offering resources and recommendations as they created community-based learning courses. Program success was best achieved when center staff created venues for faculty to inform each other's work and support one another in their own professional growth. Kecskes and colleagues (2006) outline that learning communities where faculty are able to inform one another's work see an increase in (a) scholarly products produced, (b) social support among a scholarly community, and (c) understanding of the scholarship of engagement. This program evaluation points to the power of programming that puts faculty in situations where professional development happens through a facilitated scholarly network.

Implications and Recommendations for Other Campuses

The recommendations offered here are ones that have been used to shape the development of community-based professional development activities at Wagner College and LaVerne University, institutions where one of the center's founding directors went to work in the years after leaving PSU. Recognizing that not all the recommendations offered apply to or work on every campus, the following structural and organizational factors may have utility for other colleges and universities.

Reporting Structure

For campus-wide and regional credibility, some campuses have found a center is best positioned under the provost's office (Welch & Saltmarsh, 2013). This reporting structure allows the center to respond with programs that support the priorities of the individual academic units and the emerging institutional priorities as identified by the provost, president, and others that serve in executive leadership roles at the institution. This positions the center as an action-oriented unit that helps to convene, discuss, and implement campus initiatives and policy.

Physical Location

The center's location communicates credibility and purpose when it is visible and accessible. The center at PSU was located in an office next to the Office of Academic Affairs in the center of campus, increasing program visibility, success, and perceived importance. Centers that include offices as well as spaces for faculty development programs and community/campus meetings are most effective.

Organizational and Staffing Structure

The mission of the center determines the ideal organizational and staffing structure. The center director and dedicated staff overseeing programming for each of the stated unit goals are essential for the center to be able to initiate and offer programs that are responsive to campus needs. PSU's center had staff dedicated to community partnerships and engagement as well as teaching, learning, and assessment, which helped make the organizational goals consistent with the staffing structure (see Figure 4.3).

Budgeting

Establishing a budget that allows for the hiring of program staff dedicated to the essential goals of the unit is a priority. Early on, the center allocated resources from private foundations and federal grants to provide minigrants to faculty to accelerate their adoption of CBL, with programming support from center staff. The PSU center creatively expanded its personnel capacity by sharing administrative support with the Office of Academic Affairs, securing faculty-in-residence who shared responsibility among academic departments, administrative structures, and the center. Unique to the community partnerships and engagement portfolio in the center at PSU, a student

Figure 4.3. Center for Academic Excellence organizational chart, PSU.

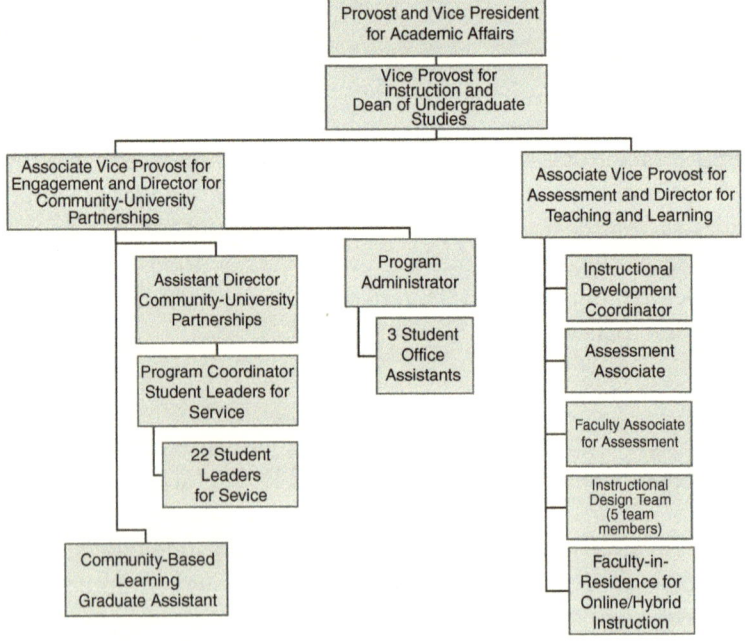

leadership team was created that offered a small stipend to students who worked in community-based settings and assisted students and faculty in connecting with a variety of community-based sites.

Credibility
Center credibility is enhanced when the center director and personnel themselves engage in teaching, learning, scholarship, and service. These are the measures of success within the academy, and center personnel should lead by example.

Sustainability
Tying the goals of the center to the institutional mission provides it with opportunities to serve as a unit that can implement institutional initiatives and priorities. Given this overarching institutional directive, the center is perceived as a necessity to the future success of the institution. The more the faculty and staff voice opinions about the invaluable contributions made by the center, the more it is perceived as a necessity for the future. Creating an advisory board comprising campus and community leaders increases visibility, credibility, awareness, and commitment from those who may influence campus politics during times of campus tension.

Organizational Demands Lead to Organizational Evolution

Currently the Office of Academic Innovation (OAI), the Institute for Sustainable Solutions (ISS), and the University Studies program all provide targeted professional development programs to support community engagement. The practices used in these units build on the foundational vision of the center that continues to inform current faculty development approaches in use today at PSU. The OAI and the University Studies program combine personal outreach with online resources to invite and support faculty engagement in activities. Both units have developed resource materials that are accessible online at PSU's page on community-based learning (Lifting Bridges, n.d.) and PSU's website on the senior capstone for University Studies (Portland State University, 2017).

Conclusion

The three programs presented as case studies in this chapter represent a range of institutional contexts—small and large, urban and rural, long established and nascent programs. This diversity of institutional type and the variety of program models presented offer useful tools for the development or enhancement of faculty support programs in the context of community engagement and SL. Implications from these case studies indicate the importance of (a) establishing strong organizational support structures with appropriate levels of staffing, (b) designing programmatic approaches that scaffold faculty learning and address the unique and complex needs of faculty-community partnerships, and (c) involving all levels of stakeholders from students to administrators as advocates for the success and sustainability of S-LCE programs on campus. The case studies also demonstrate how institutions evolve and centers respond to organizational changes over time.

References

Association of American Colleges & Universities. (n.d.) *VALUE: Valid assessment of learning in undergraduate education*. Retrieved from www.aacu.org/value

Battistoni, R. M., & Campus Compact. (2003). *The Engaged Department toolkit*. Providence, RI: Campus Compact.

Berilla, B. (2015). *Integrating mindfulness into anti-oppression pedagogy: Social justice in higher education*. New York, NY: Routledge.

Boise State University. (2017, January). *Faculty toolkits*. Retrieved from https://servicelearning.boisestate.edu/faculty-toolkits/

Boyer, E. L. (1990). *Scholarship reconsidered: Priorities of the professoriate*. Princeton, NJ: Princeton University Press.

Boyer, E. L. (1996). The scholarship of engagement. *Bulletin of the American Academy of Arts and Sciences, 49*(7), 18–33.

Brookfield, S. D. (1995). *Becoming a critically reflective teacher*. San Francisco, CA: Jossey-Bass.

Driscoll, A., Holland, B., Gelmon, S., & Kerrigan, S. (1996). An assessment model for service-learning: Comprehensive case studies of impact on faculty, students, community, and institution. *Michigan Journal of Community Service Learning, 3*, 66–71.

ENGAGE. (n.d.). Community-based engaged learning [blog]. Retrieved from https://engageatgc.wordpress.com

Freire, P. (1986). *Pedagogy of the oppressed* (M. B. Ramos, trans.). New York, NY: Continuum.

Gelmon, S. B., Holland, B., Driscoll, A., Spring, A., & Kerrigan, S. (2001). *Assessing service-learning and civic engagement: Principles and techniques*. Providence, RI: Campus Compact.

Independent Sector. (2016, May). The value of volunteer time [Blog]. Retrieved from http://www.independentsector.org/resource/the-value-of-volunteer-time/

Kecskes, K., Collier, P. J., & Balshem, M. (2006). Engaging scholars in the scholarship of engagement. In K. McKnight Case, G. Davidson, S. H. Billig, & N. C. Springer (Eds.), *Advancing knowledge in service-learning: Research to transform the field* (pp. 159–181). Greenwich, CT: Information Age.

Kecskes, K., & Spring, A. (2006). Continuums of engagement at Portland State University: An institution-wide initiative to support departmental collaboration for the common good. In K. Kecskes (Ed.), *Engaging departments: Moving faculty culture from private to public, individual to collective focus for the common good* (pp. 219–242). Bolton, MA: Anker.

Kecskes, K., Spring, A., & Lieberman, D. (2003). The Hesburgh Certificate and Portland State University's faculty development approach to supporting service learning and community-university partnerships. *To Improve the Academy, 22*, 287–301.

Lifting Bridges. (n.d.). *Community-based learning.* Retrieved from http://liftingbridges.weebly.com/

McKay, V. C., & Rozee, P. D. (2004). Characteristics of faculty who adopt community service learning pedagogy. *Michigan Journal of Community Service Learning, 10*(2), 21–33.

Mitchell, T. D. (2008). Traditional vs. critical service-learning: Engaging the literature to differentiate two models. *Michigan Journal of Community Service Learning, 14*(2), 50–65.

Portland State University. (2017). *University Studies: Senior Capstone.* Retrieved from http://capstone.unst.pdx.edu/resources

Rogers, E. M. (1971). *Communication of innovations: A cross-cultural approach.* New York, NY: The Free Press.

Smith, S. E. (1997). Deepening participatory action-research. In S. E. Smith, D. G. Willms, & N. A. Johnson (Eds.), *Nurtured by knowledge: Learning to do participatory action-research* (pp. 173–263). Lanham, MD: Apex Press.

Stoecker, R., & Tryon, E. A. (2009). Unheard voices: Community organizations and service learning. In R. Stoecker & E. Tryon (Eds.), *The unheard voices: Community organizations and service learning* (pp. 1–18). Philadelphia, PA: Temple University Press.

Welch, M., & Saltmarsh, J. (2013). Current practice and infrastructure for campus centers of community engagement. *Journal of Higher Education Outreach and Engagement, 17*(4), 25–55.

White, C. R. (1994). A model for comprehensive reform in general education: Portland State University. *The Journal of General Education, 43*(3), 168–229.

5

LEARNING COMMUNITIES AS A CREATIVE CATALYST FOR PROFESSIONAL DEVELOPMENT AND INSTITUTIONAL CHANGE

Star Plaxton-Moore, Julie Hatcher, Mary Price, Carey Borkoski, Vanya Jones, and Mindi Levin

Research suggests that faculty in higher education institutions increasingly understand the value of community-engaged scholarship, including using service-learning (SL) and community-engaged learning (CEL) pedagogies in their classrooms. Nationally, based on research from the Higher Education Research Institute, faculty across all ranks and institutional types increasingly report that they have "collaborated with the local community in teaching/research" (Saltmarsh & Hartley, 2016, p. 26). Yet faculty participation continues to face a variety of challenges and barriers such as time constraints, competing roles and responsibilities, institutional and disciplinary culture/expectations, and campus policies including promotion and tenure that do not explicitly endorse community-engaged practice (Demb & Wade, 2012; Furco & Moely, 2012; Wade & Demb, 2009).

Faculty learning communities (FLCs), considered by some to be a particular type of *community of practice* (CoP), represent opportunities to address many of these barriers. Often, these terms are used interchangeably, but the literature makes a slight distinction between the two approaches. A CoP is group of people who informally come together for further inquiry into a topic of interest, whereas an *FLC* is defined as "a small group learning structure with a process that enables its participants to investigate and provide solutions for about any significant problem or opportunity within higher education" (Cox, 2016, p. 89), with an emphasis on the scholarship of teaching and learning, group membership from across disciplines, and well-articulated roles for facilitation; further resources are available from Miami University (Faculty Learning Communities, n.d.). Both approaches incorporate known faculty motivations toward increasing interest and participation in active learning pedagogies like SL (Furco & Moely, 2012; Harwood et al., 2005). Such communities, connecting members around a topic such as S-LCE course design, offer faculty a chance to ask questions, share resources, give and receive support, and expand their networks with like-minded faculty (Rice & Stacey, 1997). Such faculty development programs represent a mechanism for exploring dimensions of community-engaged practice and offer the potential to influence broader institutional culture and policies related to community engagement. This chapter presents three case studies of faculty development programs, offering lessons learned and recommendations for effectively implementing and understanding outcomes of learning communities for both participants and institutions.

Literature Review

Empirical literature suggests that building faculty competencies in SL course design requires collegial networks focused on instruction and teaching strategies (Hill & Haigh, 2012). Developing faculty competencies in SL requires understanding individual perspectives, attempting to better match faculty members' identified interests and values with teaching capacity, and creating a network of supportive relationships linking instructors and researchers (Hill & Haigh, 2012). Wright (2005) reported that individual faculty members travel on an "instructional pathway" (Wright, 2005, p. 347) and often move in isolation, resulting in a need for more social interactions to improve their chances of developing a sustained interest in teaching. Nicolle (2005) and Senge (2000) agreed that a university climate where faculty function as individual entrepreneurs makes collaboration difficult, and Lave (1991) posited that faculty reportedly value dialogue with their peers, especially when considering the adoption of innovative teaching strategies. Remmik, Karm, Haamer, and Lepp (2011), through interviews with early career university teachers, demonstrated the importance of CoPs in enhancing faculty learning.

FLCs are a specific type of CoP, with a focus on shared learning building on the transdisciplinary expertise of each member. FLCs can focus on modifying teaching strategies, supporting in-depth inquiry, promoting the scholarship of teaching and learning, or facilitating campus policy change (Richlin & Cox, 2004). Similar to a student learning community, a high-impact learning approach that fosters student success through creation of shared learning experiences and support structures, the FLC approach is experiential in nature and generates shared knowledge among participants through reading, reflection, and collective action. Research has shown FLCs to be effective in encouraging reflective practice, strengthening collegial relationships, facilitating pedagogical sophistication, and advancing adoption of SL and other innovative practices (Cox, 2004; Furco & Moely, 2012; Rice & Stacey, 1997).

FLC facilitation is a distinctive technique that attends to group norms, requiring self-awareness and recognition of core commitments in regard to both intellectual work and administrative processes for the FLC (Ortquist-Ahrens & Torosyan, 2009). Facilitation necessitates a balance between relationship-building and productivity, and FLCs strive to be balanced between cultivating a sense of community among participants and achieving agreed-upon goals (Cox, Richlin, & Essington, 2012). Acknowledging that all participants are experts in their own right and have important contributions to make is a key aspect of creating the safe and respectful environment that an FLC requires for success (Layne, Froyd, Morgan, & Kenimer, 2002). Although all participants must commit themselves to these values of mutual respect, responsibility for orienting the group to this mode of learning lies with the facilitator, who needs to foster an ethos of "genuine community, deep learning, and projects of significance" (Ortquist-Ahrens & Torosyan, 2009, p. 32) by listening, observing, and gently steering the process. Within the field of service-learning and community engagement (S-LCE), there is strong evidence of the value of FLCs to support curricular change (Furco & Moely, 2012; Rice & Stacey, 1997), but little is known to date about how this type of faculty development ultimately changes campus culture and policy to further support community-engaged scholars.

Overview of Case Studies

The following three case studies from different institutions illustrate various approaches to the design and implementation of FLCs (see Table 5.1). These faculty development initiatives are shaped by particular campus contexts, are informed by a range of goals, and represent different ways to implement FLCs to improve practice and influence change in campus culture and policy as it relates to community-engaged scholarship.

TABLE 5.1
Overview of Case Studies

Case Study	Institutional Context	Office/Center Leading Initiative	Name of FLC/CoP Initiative	Initial Goals of FLC/CoP
Case Study 1	University of San Francisco (USF) Urban Jesuit Catholic four-year institution that includes a College of Arts & Sciences, School(s) of Education, Law, Nursing and Health Professions, and Management Carnegie Classification for Community Engagement 2007, 2015	Leo T. McCarthy Center for Public Service and the Common Good (funding, content, and faciliation) Center for Teaching Excellence (funding and design)	Faculty Learning Community on Community-Engaged Learning (FLC-CEL)	Engage faculty with current critical scholarship in the community engagement field and inform their individual purpose and practice Develop a cross-disciplinary learning community to support each other and departmental peers to engage in reflective and innovative community-engaged teaching
Case Study 2	Indiana University–Purdue University Indianapolis (IUPUI) Urban comprehensive public research university comprising 18 schools and 350 degree programs Carnegie Classification for Community Engagement 2007, 2015	Center for Service and Learning (funding, design, content, and facilitation) Academic Affairs (cosponsor and collaborator)	Faculty Learning Community on Public Scholarship (FLC-PS)	Define *public scholarship* in the context of campus-level promotion and tenure guidelines; identify criteria to assist faculty in documenting and evaluating public scholarship Provide resources to deans and department chairs for adapting these criteria into school-level promotion and tenure materials and guidelines
Case Study 3	Johns Hopkins University (JHU) Research I institution and the largest anchor institution in Baltimore, Maryland University's health professional schools	Student Outreach Resource Center (content, design, and facilitation) University president (funding)	SOURCE Online Community of Practice Fellows Program (SoCP)	Build an online network of faculty and community leaders Share resources and offer course development support Leverage the knowledge, experience, and skills of the SL Fellows cohorts

University of San Francisco

Star Plaxton-Moore

This case study describes an FLC comprising experienced community-engaged faculty seeking to enhance their own practice on CEL, build connections with like-minded peers, and influence institutional culture and policies to strengthen and expand community-engaged scholarship.

Context and Goals

USF is a mission-driven Catholic institution committed to educating "leaders who will fashion a more humane and just world" ("Vision, mission, and values statements," n.d.). In alignment with this core aspect of USF's institutional identity, the university approved and enacted an SL course requirement for all undergraduates in fall 2002. To achieve the SL designation, a course must meet five criteria and eight learning outcomes ("Community Engagement and Service-Learning at USF," n.d.). Most graduate programs also include community-engaged courses ranging from professional practica to community-based research. The Leo T. McCarthy Center for Public Service and the Common Good (McCarthy Center) supports SL and community-engaged courses by facilitating an array of faculty development programming, including a cohort-based fellowship on CEL, workshops, book clubs, panels, and discussions ("Leo T. McCarthy Center for Public Service and the Common Good," n.d.).

In 2014, in an effort to enhance support for more experienced community-engaged faculty, the McCarthy Center leveraged the FLC program coordinated by USF's Center for Teaching Excellence (CTE). McCarthy Center staff worked with a faculty member to secure funding for an FLC focused on CEL.

Design

Although FLCs have very few guidelines at USF, there is a recommended structure to foster desired outcomes. Faculty members submit a proposal to CTE for a topic of focus and, once selected, the FLC meets twice a month throughout the academic year, with a shared budget of up to $3,000. The learning community comprises 6 to 10 faculty members from diverse disciplines, and the faculty facilitator receives a course release to compensate for the workload. The FLC must produce final deliverables to be shared with CTE and the broader faculty. Beyond these parameters, there is significant flexibility in regard to recruitment of participants, identification of outcomes and deliverables, content selection, and meeting format.

For the CEL FLC (FLC-CEL), the McCarthy Center worked with the faculty facilitator to reach out to faculty members with at least a few years of experience teaching community-engaged courses. The FLC-CEL launched with 10 faculty participants, including 2 from each college and school at USF and 1 McCarthy Center staff member. All faculty participants were tenured or pretenure, and they self-identified along a continuum of novice to advanced in terms of community-engaged scholarship experience. The FLC met twice a month for 90 minutes throughout the year. Participants used the first three meetings to develop a shared understanding of CEL and craft outcomes for the group. To support the former endeavor, the McCarthy Center staff member compiled resources, including articles and media that explained theoretical foundations, essential elements, and inherent dilemmas of CEL. The FLC implemented an online course management system known as Canvas to organize and share these and other resources contributed by all participants.

Implementation

With this common content as a starting point, the FLC identified the following goals: (a) educate FLC participants and the broader USF faculty about current research, practices, and principles of community-engaged teaching and learning; (b) identify and celebrate exemplary community-engaged teaching happening across campus; and (c) provide informed recommendations to administrators about how to expand and enhance community-engaged teaching and learning.

The FLC-CEL implemented two strategies to achieve the first goal. In the fall, FLC participants were responsible for presenting their community-engaged course models to the group and sharing the literature that informed their designs. In this way, the FLC members' teaching practices were enriched by a multiplicity of disciplinary perspectives, theoretical frames, and research. In spring, the FLC invited Jeffrey Howard, editor of the *Michigan Journal of Community Service-Learning*, to campus for two workshops: the first on critical reflection and assessment of student learning and the second on getting community-engaged scholarship published. In total, approximately 30 faculty members attended one or both workshops. Howard also met separately with the FLC to help situate its work within the broader higher education community engagement context.

To achieve the second goal, the FLC-CEL designed a publication entitled *Profiles in Community-Engaged Learning*. FLC participants committed to contributing their own profiles and collecting at least one other profile from colleagues in their schools. The profiles are approximately 1,000 words long and structured around a common set of questions illuminating community-engaged course details, successes, challenges, and faculty motivations. The inaugural edition of *Profiles in Community-Engaged Learning* featured 18 faculty members, and hard copies were disseminated to all administrators and other key stakeholders on and off campus, including the university's board of trustees.

The third goal of the FLC-CEL, to provide informed recommendations to new and incoming institutional leaders, drew heavily on the input collected through the previously described activities. In addition, the FLC met with both the outgoing provost and the newly appointed university president. The purpose of these meetings was to get a sense of how the leadership perceives, thinks about, and talks about CEL, but also to share the data gathered by the FLC on faculty community engagement and broader CEL trends.

The FLC's final deliverable was a four-page *Executive Report on the Current Status of Community-Engaged Learning at USF and Recommended Future Directions*. In the report, the FLC provided an overview of the context of CEL at USF and presented the following recommendations: (a) reframe SL as CEL; (b) develop consistent alignment between how we talk about and conduct CEL as a part of USF's mission; (c) establish higher-quality standards for CEL courses and develop a CEL requirement for graduate programs; and (d) cultivate an academic community that develops, supports, and incentivizes community-engaged faculty (Faculty Learning Community on Community-Engaged Learning, 2015). The FLC also shared the executive report with the president, provost, vice provosts, deans, and associate deans.

Outcomes

In alignment with previous studies on FLC outcomes (Furco & Moely, 2012; Harwood et al., 2005), the FLC-CEL fostered a sense of competence in implementing community-engaged teaching and scholarship strategies among participants. Though the FLC did not conduct a formal assessment of its outcomes, participants were queried with open-ended reflection questions about their learning experiences after the program ended. The participants' responses serve as qualitative data that illuminate outcomes from the FLC. For example, one faculty participant from the Department of Rhetoric and Language described the change he made in framing the community experience for his students:

> I now frame it as community-engaged learning in my syllabus instead of service-learning. My students and I have conversations during the first week of class about different models of community-engaged learning, and discuss what we should do . . . to keep from replicating a charity model. It's a way of addressing that White savior complex before we engage.

Additionally, one faculty participant from the School of Education articulated modifications in her community-engaged research:

> My original intention was to conduct research on the education of Gitano (gypsy) students in the local schools in Granada, Spain, particularly in regard to experiences of discrimination. Inspired by my work in the FLC, I shifted my orientation away from being a detached researcher . . . toward becoming more involved in work being carried out by Gitanos in local organizations. This shift enabled me to build much more respectful and productive relationships with Gitano leaders.

Of further importance, participants also developed a sense of community and an actual network of supportive peers. In fact, peer relationships continue to be nurtured, as described by participants who said, "I think that the experience of being in the group together for a whole academic year forged friendships that are enduring," and "I've maintained relationships [with other FLC members] mostly through informal conversations about how our courses are functioning."

Although individual professional development and community cohesion are important outcomes, the most significant and somewhat unexpected impact of the FLC-CEL has been on institutional culture, practices, and policies related to community-engaged teaching and learning. The *Profiles in Community-Engaged Learning* publications (a first and second volume have been published) (Lo et al., 2015) have contributed to a culture shift by celebrating more diverse and inclusive forms of engaged pedagogies beyond undergraduate SL courses. Among the 26 faculty profiles included in the publications, 12 describe undergraduate SL courses and 14 describe graduate community-engaged courses representing all colleges at USF. Additionally, subsequent to the FLC, participation in faculty development programming offered by the McCarthy Center has increased and reflects greater diversity of representation across undergraduate and graduate programs, schools, and departments. We have run two faculty fellows cohorts since the culmination of the FLC-CEL, with a total of 13 participants representing three schools; moreover, 42 faculty members have participated in the past four faculty development workshops, representing all schools across USF. For the first time, the center also welcomed two librarians and one administrator as workshop participants. Indeed, this appears to indicate that there is growing interest in building relationships across community-engaged faculty and enhancing professional practice.

Culture shifts at the college level are occurring as FLC participants exert their influence in a number of ways, including as department chairs and/or advocates for curriculum changes informed by the work of the FLC. The two participants from the School of Education (one of whom is a department chair) drew on learning from the FLC to shape revisions to USF's Doctor of Education (EdD) program:

> We applied the learning from the FLC in developing the syllabus for a new doctoral course in the School of Education, Introduction to Public Scholarship and Community-Engaged Learning. Adding this course is a major achievement in re-envisioning our doctoral program with a stronger focus in community-engaged learning.

The faculty facilitator of the FLC credited his experience with the FLC as "a springboard for becoming chair of the department" and an "important developmental turning point" in his desire to move beyond faculty work into a leadership position. As chair, he has prioritized support for the School of Management's undergraduate SL course, which is usually offered in 10 to 12 sections each semester, by facilitating faculty check-ins and resource sharing as well as recommending new faculty to participate in the McCarthy Center's faculty development programs (every new hire since 2015 has participated).

To catalyze changes at the institutional policy level, the FLC and McCarthy Center staff have drawn on the executive report to inform strategic priorities. Members of the FLC were invited to the Provost's Council meeting to present proposed revisions to CEL policies and practices, leading the associate vice provost for academic affairs to convene a faculty working group to research and design a process for transitioning from a *service-learning* to *community-engaged learning* course designation and revise the related student learning outcomes and course criteria. Representation on this working group includes two McCarthy Center staff, three faculty members who teach undergraduate SL, and two faculty who teach community-engaged graduate courses. All USF schools are represented on the working group with the exception of the School of Law.

Indiana University–Purdue University Indianapolis

Julie Hatcher and Mary Price

This case study describes a three-year FLC program, now in its second year, designed to result in institutional change by improving campus promotion and tenure (P&T) guidelines for public scholarship.

Context and Goals

Like many institutions of higher education, IUPUI takes seriously its role as a public metropolitan university. The campus of 30,000 students, located in the heart of the state capital, is in close proximity to government agencies, public schools, nonprofit organizations, museums, and urban neighborhoods. Strategic neighborhood partnerships, community-engaged research, and anchor institution initiatives support economic and workforce development and provide additional ways for faculty to work *in and with* communities in educationally meaningful ways (Bringle, Hatcher, & Holland, 2007). The Center for Service and Learning (CSL) is a centralized campus unit charged with deepening the campus culture for community engagement through program initiatives with students, staff, and faculty (Indiana University–Purdue University Indianapolis, 2017). Over the past decade, CSL has sponsored and cosponsored with other campus units a number of FLCs to support faculty (i.e., research on SL, international SL courses, integration of SL into themed learning communities, and first-year seminars).

In 2014, an identified weakness and recommended area of improvement for IUPUI from both the Carnegie Foundation and the North Central Accreditation Higher Learning Commission was to better align campus mission and faculty roles and rewards as related to civic engagement. Based on positive outcomes of prior FLC initiatives, CSL invited Academic Affairs to cosponsor a three-year FLC on public scholarship (FLC-PS) to address this issue. All FLC funds ($5,000 annually) and programmatic support come through CSL and colleagues in Academic Affairs provide critical institutional support and collaboration to enact collective goals.

Design

The goals of the FLC-PS include defining *public scholarship*, identifying criteria at the campus level to assist faculty in documenting their community-engaged work, and providing resources to deans, department chairs, and school-level committees for adapting these criteria into P&T materials and guidelines. At the advice of the senior vice chancellor for academic affairs, the membership of the FLC-PS was selected and invited from tenured faculty across campus with experience in, or commitment to, supporting public scholarship. Now at the beginning of the third year, nine tenured faculty from six schools on campus have participated in the FLC-PS. This multidisciplinary perspective has been an inherent strength, as various disciplinary norms for evaluating excellence in scholarship have informed the process and the products developed. As was featured in chapter 2 and will be showcased in chapter 11 of this volume, it is important to consider designing for scholarship opportunities when engaging with faculty.

Implementation

The CSL executive director and director for faculty development share responsibility for the program and work closely with two faculty cochairs to facilitate the FLC. The FLC-PS is a combination of retreat style format (4–5 hours) and meetings (1.5–2 hours) with the goal to meet 3 to 4 times each semester. Center staff and cochairs collaborate to create the agenda. We have learned that there is a fine balance between functioning as a community and functioning as a committee. To cultivate a sense of community, coffee and food are typically a part of each meeting, whether at a restaurant near campus or enjoying homemade soup or dessert. We value the power of coffee and food to facilitate meaningful dialogue and cultivate relationships that support collective action (Sandy & Holland, 2006).

CSL staff members identify reading material for each FLC session and upload materials to an open-access file-sharing account. Having materials readily available, particularly for new FLC members and other stakeholders across campus, is very helpful. These include resources from national organizations (e.g., Community-Campus Partnerships for Health, Imagining America: Artists and Scholars in Public Life), examples of tenure review guidelines from other universities (e.g., Michigan State University, Portland State University, Syracuse University, University of Minnesota), and articles and book chapters (e.g., Cavallaro, 2016; Ellison & Eatman, 2008; Jordan, 2007; Peters, 2010; Post, Ward, Longo, & Saltmarsh, 2016; Sandmann, 2009). The cochairs and CSL staff colead discussions and guide the FLC to identify and prioritize short- and long-term goals.

Due to the disciplinary expertise of one of the initial cochairs, the FLC has benefited from using design thinking strategies to generate ideas, create timelines for task completion, make sense of data, and envision next steps. Design thinking approaches intentionally gather input from all stakeholders, foster transparency as ideas are put forth and analyzed in a systematic way, build trust among participants, and facilitate discussions to shape meaning (Brown & Katz, 2009; Cross, 2007). In practice, design thinking often asks participants to brainstorm and jot ideas on sticky notes, draw diagrams, or create flowcharts of key action steps, and these strategies are often used in the campus workshops offered by the FLC-PS.

Outcomes

There are a number of positive outcomes from the first two years of the FLC-PS. These include deliverables and products, outcomes for participants, and institutional effects in terms of changes in campus-level P&T guidelines. The FLC wrote a concept paper, *Public Scholarship at Indiana University–Purdue University Indianapolis* (Wood et al., 2016), which included a definition of *public scholarship*, critical insights from the literature, and proposed criteria to evaluate quality in public scholarship. In addition, FLC-PS members collaborated with CSL and Academic Affairs to implement a new series of campus workshops for faculty called the Pathways to Public Scholarship Workshop Series. The FLC hosted visits by Timothy K. Eatman, Scott Peters, and David Scobey from Imagining America, a national consortium of publicly engaged scholars. These scholars consulted with senior administrators, facilitated workshops for faculty and graduate students, and advised FLC members on principles of cultural organizing for institutional change. Formal presentations about the FLC-PS have also been made at national and disciplinary conferences (e.g., Association of American Colleges & Universities, Imagining America).

In terms of outcomes for participants, anecdotal evidence suggests that it is a very beneficial experience. Of the seven FLC-PS members in the first year, five elected to remain involved across all three years of the program, an indicator of a high level of satisfaction with the FLC experience. Two members have used the definition of *public scholarship* and criteria outlined in the concept paper as the framework for their dossiers for a successful promotion from associate to full professor. Three members have used their involvement in the FLC to highlight excellence in service. Three FLC members have been asked to make presentations and lead similar approaches within their school-level P&T committees. Four members serve as department chairs and have integrated public scholarship more intentionally into graduate programs (i.e., American Studies, Design) as well as formal program reviews (i.e., Museum Studies, Religious Studies). Participants have also strengthened their ties to CSL staff, faculty governance, and administrators in Academic Affairs. Each of these relationships is valuable to furthering faculty development and deepening the campus culture for community engagement.

In terms of outcomes for the institution, campus-level P&T guidelines now include the definition of *public scholarship* and give guidance to candidates on documenting their work in public scholarship. Additionally, important work is underway to replicate this approach in three schools (i.e., the School of Liberal Arts, the Herron School of Art and Design, and the Fairbanks School of Public Health) as a result of campus-level FLC-PS work. The concept paper has also been shared at the Indiana University system level with colleagues on the regional campuses who are responsible for leading applications for the Carnegie Elective Classification for Community Engagement. There is enthusiasm among this group to replicate a similar FLC-PS approach on each regional campus.

Johns Hopkins University

Carey Borkoski, Vanya Jones, and Mindi Levin

This case study describes an online CoP for faculty and community members to support professional development related to teaching an SL course by deepening shared understanding of good practice.

Context and Goals

The Student Outreach Resource Center (SOURCE) is the S-LCE center for the JHU health professional schools. Established in 2005, it represents a unique resource that promotes, coordinates, and offers community engagement opportunities for students, staff, and faculty. Since its inception, SOURCE has supported faculty by providing connections with community agencies and consulting on developing practicums and courses with community engagement components. In 2012, the president provided funding for SOURCE's yearlong SL Fellows program to train faculty, alongside community partners, in SL pedagogy. SL Fellows reported positive outcomes including increased knowledge of SL instruction and relationships with a cohort of like-minded individuals interested in community engagement, as well as a need for more ongoing support. An online CoP emerged as a promising way to create space for discussions, resource exchange, and sharing of common issues and successes, resulting in a better model for sustained support.

Design

The SOURCE Community of Practice (SoCP) includes faculty and community partners from current and past SL Fellows cohorts. During the 2015 pilot year, 33 invitations were sent to faculty and community fellows. Sixteen (46%) faculty ($n = 12$) and community fellows ($n = 4$) joined the online community. Faculty participants represent each of the health professional schools, including medicine, public health, and nursing. The SoCP included faculty members with varying experiences with SL. Community members included individuals from SOURCE community partners in Baltimore engaged in SL either through classes or other SOURCE programs. Convening faculty and community partners in the same space provided an opportunity for important stakeholders to share their unique and different experiences with SL.

The virtual community included development of an online platform accessible to participants, facilitation of discussions and catalog of responses, and creation of an online resource library. Google Communities serves as a free host platform for the SoCP and provides a way to invite a diverse group of members to the online community for exchanging resources and ideas.

In the first year of the SoCP, a faculty facilitator encouraged participation. The role of facilitator was to create and post weekly discussion topics and questions, troubleshoot member issues and questions, monitor discussions, and respond to questions. The facilitator also identified a schedule of discussion topics, potential reflection questions, activities, and resources. A list of planned topic titles included What is SL?; Learning Theory Relevant to SL; Reflection; Curriculum Design; Assessment of SL; Power and Privilege; Cultural Humility; and Asset Building. The proposed plan included a first week for posing questions, introducing members, and polling them on topics they wanted to discuss in the online community. The facilitator role also included setting up member access to the virtual community and instruction on how to navigate and use the various tools available.

Implementation

After the initial meeting, the SoCP members started to post their own discussion questions soliciting advice and ideas from peers. In one case, a faculty member was in the middle of an SL course and made a specific request for examples of reflection activities and/or questions that others had used in their own classes. Within a few days, members (including the facilitator) responded with questions they had used and advice for how to engage with students around these questions. Subsequently, the facilitator planned weekly discussions around various topics and encouraged participants to provide discussion topics based on their interests. SoCP members participated in a total of 14 weekly discussions (86% facilitator and 14% participant generated) in this online community but most of the conversations only included a small but consistent group of 5 to 6 members. This translated into a 30% total participation rate. Furthermore, 56% of the replies from individuals were in response to just 3 of the initial facilitator posts.

A review of community activities revealed that general discussion, the advice column, and resources were the most common areas for posting. General discussion focused primarily on time-sensitive questions and tips around implementation and management of SL courses in progress. Faculty posted requests for examples of assessment tools, reflection questions, and other activities to motivate student engagement. Advice topics focused more on time-independent SL questions and suggestions that faculty might consider as they plan for future SL courses. Resources included teaching tips, activities, reflections, relevant articles and books, and other media sources like YouTube videos. As a new endeavor, it seems that multiple topics beyond advice and resources were unnecessary for member discussions and community content.

Outcomes

The program evaluation describes faculty and community involvement in the CoP. The impact of the CoP was measured through two focus groups. CoP participants were invited by e-mail to participate in a focus group about their experiences, opinions, and attitudes regarding the online community. One-hour focus groups were recorded and transcribed to learn more about the opinions and experiences of the CoP community members. A phase of qualitative data analysis known as a priori coding was used to identify codes and subcodes, which were grouped into themes. Some of the main themes included *characteristics of fidelity* (Dusenbury, Brannigan, Falco, & Hansen, 2003); elements from Wenger's (1998) *social learning framework—community, practice, identity, meaning-making, and attributes of value creation*; and *immediate, potential, and applied value* based on Wenger, Trayner, and de Laat's (2011) research. In the focus groups, members shared a variety of reasons for low participation and suggestions for improving future iterations of SoCP.

Nine (56%) of the CoP members participated in the focus groups. The themes that emerged from the focus groups included technological barriers to participation, a need for scaffolding to train faculty on how to use the virtual space, and the need for prompts and reminders to help integrate this faculty support into day-to-day workflow. Individuals reported that although they use mobile technology including phones, tables, and computers, they did not understand or feel comfortable with Google Communities. Community members reported a strong interest in participating but did not have the time to stop and learn how to use this "new" tool. Participants also noted that additional training on how to interact in the Google Community (i.e., posting and responding to discussions, sharing resources) may have increased participation. Chapters 4 and 6 (the other case study chapters) in this volume also discuss some of the pros and cons of online S-LCE faculty groups within their specific institutions, and chapter 3 gives a comprehensive overview of the specific context within which online development may be the best fit.

Vygotsky (1978) would suggest that even members with expertise and rich experiences need scaffolding across their zone of proximal development (ZPD). Scaffolding or ZPD refers to the guidance and assistance individuals receive to eventually master previously difficult skills. It is important that implementers offer teaching, training, and simulations to bridge the known and unknown elements of these faculty development efforts. In fact, a respondent in the focus group noted that "with just a little scaffolding" the value of the community would expand. Finally, the focus group participants also noted a need for prompts and notifications from the facilitator to not only reward members for participation but also remind them to participate.

Implications for Practice and Research

Each of these case studies offers a different approach in supporting the development of faculty as community-engaged scholars, yet collectively they give insight into improving practice and research on the value of FLCs to support community-engaged scholars. In terms of practice, there were many observed challenges and strengths (see Table 5.2). From these, a number of implications for both practice and research are identified.

Identifying explicit goals for learning communities and aligning the goals with current campus priorities helps to gain buy-in from key stakeholders and recruit members who have shared interest in working collectively with others on the topic at hand. There are many benefits to collaborating with other campus units on the design and implementation of learning communities (e.g., Academic Affairs, Center for Teaching Excellence, Division of Equity and Inclusion, Division of Undergraduate Education, International Affairs), and this approach is effective in advancing shared goals for faculty development. Although initial goals and deliverables should be realistic and well communicated during recruitment, it is equally important to see how the goals and deliverables evolve and shift across time. As members gain deeper understanding and share ideas with one another, they are more likely to take ownership for their collective work and generate new goals to accomplish.

The facilitator needs to identify resources and scaffold learning, yet honor the expertise among participants who may choose to alter and lead the group in a slightly different direction. Time is a limitation for all of the case studies presented, and likely a function of the increasing challenges in faculty time (Demb & Wade, 2012). The facilitator's role is critical in terms of scheduling meetings far in advance, sending reminders, and providing an online platform for resources in case members cannot attend.

Across these case studies, facilitators used various approaches to describe outcomes for participants and the institution, yet only one described a formal program evaluation. This points to the need for assessment, both formative and summative, to be an integrated aspect of design and implementation (Cox et al., 2012). None of the cases included formative assessment within the program design, and this is a weakness. Summative assessment at the end of the program provides valuable information for scholarly products and

TABLE 5.2
Case Studies Challenges and Strengths

Challenges	Strengths
Case Study 1: Faculty Learning Community on Community-Engaged Learning (FLC-CEL)	
Irregular attendance by FLC members due to schedule conflicts Two FLC members leaving the group after first semester No formal assessment of the FLC conducted	Self-selected group of faculty committed to CEL and improving their practice Institutional support in the form of funding and resources from CTE and McCarthy Center University leadership meeting with FLC members to discuss new directions for CEL Well organized in the use of meeting times and online platform for sharing resources Deliverables directly aligned with the FLC's intended outcomes and prompting subsequent positive institutional changes related to CEL
Case Study 2: Faculty Learning Community on Public Scholarship (FLC-PS)	
Irregular attendance by FLC members in year two due to unanticipated roles and responsibilities Difficult to acclimate two new FLC members in year two who lacked shared knowledge of public scholarship Sometimes trick to balance the leadership roles of CSL staff and faculty cochairs No formative or summative assessment of the FLC conducted	Collegial cross-disciplinary group able to debate ideas with mutual respect Strong support from Academic Affairs, Faculty Council, and deans Deliverables directly aligned with the FLC's intended outcomes and prompting subsequent positive institutional changes related to PS Success at the campus level leading to replication in three schools the following year Presentations on FLC-PS at four national conferences
Case Study 3: SOURCE Online Community of Practice Fellows Program (SoCP)	
Significant technology barrier due to lack of knowledge about Google Community tools and processes; needed scaffolding lacking to prepare group for online format	Faculty underscoring the benefits of convening a group of faculty and community partners around SL Facilitation of collegial support for teaching at a research university; requests by participants for additional types of programming to support SL teaching

(Continues)

TABLE 5.2 *(Continued)*

Challenges	Strengths
After early sessions, use of the online format as a means for discussion and resources by only a few members Time constraints limiting participation Lack of integration of the CoP processes into workflow/routine of members	Participant report of increased confidence to confirm opinions and ideas about SL Connections for faculty with a common interest in SL Formal assessment of SoCP conducted and outcomes summarized

improved practice, but formative assessment gathers feedback during the program in order to modify the program to better address participant needs. Issues such as comfort with online tools could be easily addressed if identified during formative assessment of the program.

In terms of program evaluation research, there are various components of FLC design that warrant further investigation. The length of time of an FLC may be an important variable to explore, particularly if one of the intended outcomes is institutional change. These case studies represent a semester model, a yearlong program, and a three-year initiative. Are there added benefits that emerge through multiyear programming? Another variable to examine is the range of campus stakeholders interested in the goals associated with outcomes for FLC participants and the institution. Might it increase the likelihood for institutional change if more than one campus unit is sponsoring and funding the initiative? In terms of research, the relationships among the amount of meeting time, the nature of the interactions during the meetings, and the types of deliverables and outcomes for both individuals and the institution could be explored. Another unstudied outcome in the research to date (Furco & Moely, 2012) is the degree to which FLC participants go on to assume other leadership roles within their school or on campus and the extent to which participants develop scholarly products of their own as an extension of their involvement in the learning community.

Conclusion

This chapter highlights three case studies that demonstrate how faculty-led and institutionally supported FLCs can be vehicles for supporting teaching innovation, building community across disciplines, improving campus understanding of public scholarship, and catalyzing institutional change. Consistent with experiential learning theory (Kolb, 1984), this approach to faculty development is well aligned with the theoretical framework for SL that values reflection on experience and translates knowledge into new and improved practice. Experienced community-engaged scholars have agency and confidence to enact their commitment to innovative teaching and institutional improvement, but perhaps they can leverage this agency most effectively when doing so as a cohesive group. These programs have potency; two case studies saw movement beyond development of SL practice to the shaping of institutional policies, illuminating faculty development as a form of leadership cultivation beyond pedagogical training.

References

Bringle, R. G., Hatcher, J. A., & Holland, B. (2007). Conceptualizing civic engagement: Orchestrating change at a metropolitan university. *Metropolitan Universities, 18*(3), 57–74.

Brown, T., & Katz, B. (2009). *Change by design: How design thinking transforms organizations and inspires innovation.* New York, NY: Harper Business.

Cavallaro, C. (2016). Recognizing engaged scholarship in faculty reward structures: Challenges and progress. *Metropolitan Universities, 27*(2), 2–5.

Cox, M. D. (2004). Introduction to faculty learning communities. *New Directions for Teaching and Learning, 97,* 5–23.

Cox, M. D. (2016). Four positions of leadership in planning, implementing, and sustaining faculty learning community programs. In J. L. Bernstein & B. A. Flinders (Eds.), *New Directions for Teaching and Learning, 2016*(148), 85–96. San Francisco, CA: Jossey-Bass.

Cox, M. D., Richlin, L., & Essington, A. (2012). *Faculty learning community planning guide.* Los Angeles, CA: Alliance Publishers.

Cross, N. (2007). *Designerly ways of knowing.* Basel, Switzerland: Birkhäuser.

Demb, A., & Wade, A. (2012). Reality check: Faculty involvement in outreach and engagement. *The Journal of Higher Education, 83*(3), 337–366. Retrieved from https://doi.org/10.1353/jhe.2012.0019

Dusenbury, L., Brannigan, R., Falco, M., & Hansen, W. B. (2003). A review of research on fidelity of implementation: Implications for drug abuse prevention in school settings. *Health Education Research, 18*(2), 237–256.

Ellison, J., & Eatman, T. K. (2008). *Scholarship in public: Knowledge creation and tenure policy in the engaged university* (Imagining America Paper 16). Retrieved from http://surface.syr.edu/cgi/viewcontent.cgi?article=1002&context=ia

Faculty Learning Communities. (n.d.). *What is a faculty learning community?* Retrieved from http://www.units.miamioh.edu/flc/whatis.php

Faculty Learning Community on Community-Engaged Learning. (2015). Executive report on community-engaged learning at University of San Francisco [Unpublished internal document].

Furco, A., & Moely, B. E. (2012). Using learning communities to build faculty support for pedagogical innovation: A multi-campus study. *Journal of Higher Education, 83*(1), 128–153.

Harwood A. M., Ochs L., Currier D., Duke S., Hammond J., Moulds, L., . . . Werder, C. (2005). Communities for growth: Cultivating and sustaining service-learning teaching and scholarship in a faculty fellows program. *Michigan Journal of Community Service Learning, 12*(1), 41–51.

Hill, M. F., & Haigh, M. A. (2012). Creating a culture of research in teacher education: Learning research within communities of practice. *Studies in Higher Education, 37*(8), 971–988.

Indiana University–Purdue University Indianapolis. (2017). *Center for Service and Learning.* Retrieved from http://csl.iupui.edu/

Jordan, K. (Ed.). (2007). *Community-engaged scholarship review, promotion, & tenure package.* Peer Review Workgroup, Community-Engaged Scholarship for Health Collaborative, Community-Campus Partnerships for Health. Retrieved from http://depts.washington.edu/ccph/healthcollab.html

Kolb, D.A. (1984). *Experiential learning: Experience as the source of learning and development.* Englewood Cliffs, NJ: Prentice Hall.

Lave, J. (1991). Situating learning in communities of practice. In L. Resnick, J. Levine, & S. Teasley (Eds.), *Perspectives on socially-shared cognition* (pp. 63–82). Washington, DC: American Psychological Association.

Layne, J., Froyd, J., Morgan, J., & Kenimer, A. (2002, November). Faculty learning communities. In *Frontiers in Education, Proceedings of the 32nd Annual Conference* (Vol. 2, pp. F1A–13). Piscataway, NJ: IEEE.

Lo, K. D., Fuentes, E., Holler, D., Iglesias, T., Katz, S. R., Moore, S., . . . Sears, S. (2015). *Profiles in community-engaged learning* (McCarthy Center Faculty Publications Paper 12). Retrieved from p://repository.usfca.edu/mccarthy_fac/12

Nicolle, P. S. (2005). Technology Adoption into Teaching and Learning by Mainstream University Faculty: A mixed methodology study revealing the "How, when, why, and why not," *Journal of Education Computing Research, 39*(3), 235–265.

Ortquist-Ahrens, L., & Torosyan, R. (2009). The role of the facilitator in faculty learning communities: Paving the way for growth, productivity, and collegiality. *Learning Communities Journal, 1*(1), 29–62.

Peters, M. (2010). Community engagement and social organization: Introducing concepts, policy and practical applications. In M. Peters, S. Fudge, and T. Jackson (Eds.), *Low carbon communities: Imaginative approaches to combatting climate change locally* (pp. 13–33). Cheltendam, UK: Edward Elgar.

Post, M. A., Ward, E., Longo, N. V., & Saltmarsh, J. (2016). Introducing next generation engagement. In M. A. Post, E. Ward, N. V. Longo, and J. Saltmarsh (Eds.), *Publicly engaged scholars: Next generation engagement and the future of higher education* (pp. 1–11). Sterling, VA: Stylus.

Remmik, M., Karm, M., Haamer, A., & Lepp, L. (2011). Early-career academics' learning in academic communities. *International Journal for Academic Development, 16*(3), 187–199.

Rice, D. L., & Stacey, K. (1997). Small group dynamic as a catalyst for change: A faculty development model for academic service-learning. *Michigan Journal of Community Service Learning, 4*, 64–71.

Richlin, L., & Cox, M. D. (2004) Developing scholarly teaching and the scholarship of teaching and learning through faculty learning communities. *New Directions for Teaching and Learning, 97*, 127–135.

Saltmarsh, J., & Hartley, M. (2016). The inheritance of next generation engagement scholars. In M. Post, E. Ward, N. Longo, & J. Saltmarsh (Eds.), *Voices of next generation engagement: Toward a more collaborative, publicly engaged future in higher education* (pp. 15–33). Sterling, VA: Stylus Publishing.

Sandmann, L. R. (2009). Second generation: Community engagement promotion and tenure issues and challenges. In J. Strait & M. Lima (Eds.), *The future of service-learning: New solutions for sustaining and improving practice* (pp. 67–89). Sterling, VA: Stylus.

Sandy, M. & Holland, B.A. (2006). Different worlds and common ground: Community partner perspectives on campus-community partnerships. *Michigan Journal of Community Service Learning, 13*(1), 30–43.

Senge, P. M. (2000). *The academy as learning community: Contradiction in terms or realizable future. Leading academic change: Essential roles for department chairs* (pp. 275–300). San Francisco, CA: Jossey-Bass.

University of San Francisco. (n.d.). Community engagement and service-learning at USF. Retrieved from https://myusf.usfca.edu/mccarthy/programs/community-engagement

University of San Francisco. (n.d.). Leo T. McCarthy Center for Public Service and the Common Good. Retrieved from https://myusf.usfca.edu/mccarthy

University of San Francisco. (n.d.). Vision, mission, and values statements. Retrieved from https://www.usfca.edu/about-usf/who-we-are/vision-mission/

Vygotsky, L. S. (1978). *Mind in society: The development of higher mental processes.* Cambridge, MA: Harvard University Press.

Wade, A., & Demb, A. (2009). A conceptual model to explore faculty community engagement. *Michigan Journal of Community Service Learning, 15*(2), 5–16.

Wenger, E. (1998). *Communities of practice: Learning, meaning, and identity.* Cambridge, UK: Cambridge University Press.

Wenger, E., Trayner, B., & de Laat, M. (2011). *Promoting and assessing value creation in communities and networks: A conceptual framework.* Ruud de Moor Centrum: Open University of the Netherlands.

Wood, E., Hong, Y., Price, M. F., Stanton-Nichols, K., Hatcher, J. A., Craig, D. M., ... Palmer, K. L. (2016). *Public scholarship at Indiana University-Purdue University Indianapolis.* Retrieved from https://scholarworks.iupui.edu/handle/1805/9713

Wright, M. (2005). Always at odds?: Congruence in faculty beliefs about teaching at a research university. *The Journal of Higher Education, 76*(3), 331–353.

6

MISSION-DRIVEN, LOW-COST CREATIVE PRACTICES

Ann E. Green, Ann Marie Jursca Keffer, Kim Jensen Bohat, Melody Bowdon, and Amy Zeh

The three case studies in this chapter—Saint Joseph's University (SJU), Marquette University, and University of Central Florida (UCF)—present innovative approaches to faculty development for service-learning and community engagement (S-LCE). Creative practices use original ideas in mission-driven contexts and adapt limited resources in innovative ways. Although the schools represented range from medium-sized, comprehensive SJU to large, research-oriented UCF, the approaches to faculty development at all three institutions have arisen organically from their particular contexts. Each uses evidence-based practices to encourage the pedagogical development of their faculty and enhance overall teaching quality. Although each program has developed to reflect local circumstances (e.g., institutional mission), the practices described can be adapted with limited resources. For example, the largest resource for SJU's mentoring model is time from the faculty mentor and mentee; the university's S-LCE director supports the pair, celebrating successes and resolving tensions along the way.

In each case, the programs described draw from institutional expertise to facilitate conversations and foster collaboration between faculty members and service-learning administrators in intentional best practices. SJU draws from a community of experienced staff and faculty to create mentoring relationships. Marquette reaches outside of institutional resources drawing from professional networks and merging community-based learning with e-learning. UCF runs a robust service-learning track in its faculty summer development conference. Regardless of how the programs are designed, each emphasizes a dialogue between the local and the larger community of service-learning scholars and practitioners.

Building Relationships, Creating Community: Mentoring as Professional Development for New Service-Learning Faculty at Saint Joseph's University

SJU, Philadelphia's Jesuit university, is located on the border between Philadelphia and its more affluent suburbs. According to SJU's mission statement, "We prepare students for personal excellence, professional success, and engaged citizenship. . . . We encourage and model lifelong commitment to thinking critically, making ethical decisions, pursuing social justice, and finding God in all things" (www.sju.edu/about-sju). The Saint Joseph's University Service-Learning Program, implemented through the Faith-Justice Institute, is an interdisciplinary curriculum based on a pedagogy emphasizing the integration of traditional coursework, reflection, and mutually beneficial campus-community partnerships. SJU's program provides faculty with resources and opportunities to design and implement rigorous community-based learning courses that develop students as whole persons ethically, intellectually, and spiritually. Through a lived experience of the Jesuit mission, especially considering solidarity with those most in need, we hope students will engage compassionately with what Peter Hans-Kolvenbach (2000) calls "the actual world as it unjustly exists."

Design and Implementation

A focus on interpersonal relationships is a hallmark of SJU's Ignatian mission, and one faculty development opportunity offered is faculty-to-faculty mentoring. Pairing faculty new to service-learning with experienced faculty members expands the new faculty member's access to resources and collegial support while providing an open space for dialogue regarding pedagogical implementation. Thus, one of the most important characteristics in matching mentor and mentee is an ability to be professionally vulnerable, a trait that is explored later in this chapter.

Identified by the service-learning director, mentors may come from the same or a different department/college as the new faculty, and face several expectations:

- Coordinating and debriefing class visits for new service-learning faculty to witness service-learning pedagogy in action
- Performing routine in-person visits, e-mail communication, and a review of the syllabus as mutually agreed upon with the new faculty member during course development and first semester of teaching a service-learning course

- Visiting the new faculty member's classroom during the first semester of teaching, offering constructive and developmental feedback
- Serving as an additional resource to service-learning staff on topics such as syllabus construction, integration and reflection techniques, course materials, and interrelating student service experiences
- Working with service-learning staff to provide pedagogical resources that meet individual faculty needs

In addition to these task-specific requirements, the faculty mentor and director must discern how to balance tasks with relational expectations. Because relationship-based service-learning is the core of the institute's work, faculty development privileges the relationship over task-based requirements. An underlying goal is a long-term relationship between the new service-learning faculty member and the community of faculty and staff affiliated with the institute. After the official mentoring relationship ends, we hope new service-learning faculty are integrated into a supportive network where they can participate in additional opportunities offered by the institute like lectures, learning communities, and pedagogy discussions.

Mentor Pairing
The institutional context is of utmost importance in forming the mentoring pair. The relationship between the mentor and mentee is intended to parallel the relationship-based approach that students undertake as a cornerstone of SJU's service-learning program. Rather than focus on task-oriented service, the program nurtures intentional relationships between students and clients at the placement. This philosophy is mirrored in the relationships fostered through faculty mentoring partnerships. This parallel practice fosters growth in both the mentor and the mentee in part because of its deliberate design.

A faculty member new to teaching service-learning works with the director on pedagogy, logistical resourcing, and facilitation of the mentoring opportunity. Through working with the new faculty member in developing an understanding of service-learning pedagogy and syllabus construction, the director offers mentoring as an additional resource. The positionality of the director as a professional staff allows for an initial, authentic dialogue with the new faculty member describing different facets (not individuals) to consider when identifying a mentor. A new faculty member should consider contextual questions such as the following:

- Is the new faculty member early career or tenured in rank/status?
- Does the new faculty member's home department have strong positive working relationships?

- Does the new faculty member have an existing collegial relationship with an experienced service-learning faculty member?
- Are there disciplines that share a similar philosophy or language?

Naturally, answers to these questions inform the matching process, helping the new faculty member and director navigate an established community of scholars to create a short list of potential mentors. Then, the director serves as intermediary, approaching the prospective mentor and facilitating an introduction between the pair.

Intertwined within the contextual questions is the trait of professional vulnerability. Professional vulnerability creates an authentic relational space for professionals to safely expose areas of growth, earnestly seek new pedagogical tools, and develop a collegiality founded in trust and mutuality. The director has a selected list of faculty, several of whom have won teaching awards as selected by their peers and who have demonstrated pedagogical flexibility, active listening, and critical reflection, and who have demonstrated (through their engagement with service-learning) their professional vulnerability. The faculty mentors have an ability to reflect on their own practices, articulate areas for growth, and be open to change. The director individually checks in with both mentor and mentee to ensure that both people find the relationship productive. The new service-learning faculty member receives support for vocational formation and resources that meet course development needs. By mentoring a less experienced faculty member, the mentor can critically reflect on her or his past practice and consider ways of modifying and enhancing her or his pedagogy according to the changing needs of students, service partners, and the service-learning program. The dialogue rooted in an authentic and transparent relationship ultimately serves as a foundation fostering a community of scholars with service-learning experience.

For faculty mentors, the relationship with the mentee differs from other relationships with pretenure faculty because this relationship is intentionally reciprocal. At SJU, it is uncommon for a junior faculty member to visit a more senior colleague's classroom, but in the mentoring relationship fostered by the service-learning program, reciprocity is built into the program. As a senior faculty member, I (coauthor Ann Green) welcome the opportunity for class visits from a more junior colleague. Although having anyone visit changes the class dynamic, visits from a junior colleague also help me reflect on why I do what I do. This helps me reflect on practices that may have been long established in my pedagogy and refine them for this evolving generation of students.

To further expand on what is gained through service-learning mentoring, a faculty colleague in philosophy stated the following in a critical self-evaluation:

> In the service-learning mentoring program, my mentor welcomed me into her own practice of gracefully interlacing competing demands like balancing the ideal of "freedom to form your own beliefs and values" with the idea that some values (racism, classism, sexism, sanism) simply aren't acceptable, and other values (solidarity, equality) are required. I am truly grateful for being invited to witness the practice of someone so experienced and skilled. I was able to visit my mentor's classes, talk with her about syllabus design, have detailed conversations about grading, and discuss my own style of teaching after she visited my classroom. She raised ideas that deeply challenged my own preconceptions about pedagogy—including how correcting grammar in a way that may seem "nitpicky" could have complex effects on how students related to both me and the course. This program helped me tremendously with teaching in general—not just service-learning. I am someone who is hungry to see as many different approaches to teaching, and to learn as many teaching strategies, as possible. Books on pedagogy are helpful, but being able to see and interact with an experienced mentor was so much more effective in helping me understand the less "tangible" parts of teaching—body language, the messages I send to my students with my demeanor, and several other elements of teaching as a practice. (V. Hoffman, personal communication, January 2, 2017)

As this faculty member articulates, the mentoring relationship influences other aspects of new faculty's teaching. We believe it assists an untenured professor in more effectively refining her critically reflective practices prior to tenure and in more clearly articulating these practices in annual reports and tenure narratives.

Social Capital
Additional benefits from the mentoring program include the social capital created for faculty and the program alike. The service-learning program benefits are seen at the department and college level through faculty members who have participated as mentee and/or mentor and are now in administrative leadership positions (e.g., chair, dean). Within these positions the leader has the opportunity to advocate for the program and support for additional external professional development opportunities (e.g., service-learning conferences, external training, and professional presentations). In addition to providing opportunities for critical reflection for the mentor and the mentees, the success of these relationships includes the mentor's ability to direct the mentee to additional resources (e.g., discussion guides, reflection rubric, and learning communities).

Finally, by having faculty mentor other faculty, the program ensures that goals and objectives are implemented organically, throughout the relationship. Often faculty are independent about their pedagogy, but an aspect of a service-learning program is maintaining shared pedagogy, particularly critical reflection and community experience as texts. Through the mentoring relationship, new faculty are coached and guided in their pedagogy. Furthermore, the close collaboration between the director and mentor allows for specific resource dissemination to the mentee as per identified needs and ongoing development. For example, during a meeting which provides resources and an introduction to service-learning pedagogy, including SJU service-learning criteria, faculty members are encouraged to speak about related previous experience and/or identify areas of growth. Therefore a faculty member who had little experience in designing intentional, challenging, and connected reflections might be paired with a mentor who specializes in this area, or a faculty member who expresses a desire to learn more about teaching race and racism might be referred to a faculty mentor who specializes in pedagogy that addresses race.

Challenges

There are several challenges to the mentoring relationship. The first and most critical for the faculty involved is time. Faculty who are teaching service-learning courses are already involved in more labor-intensive teaching. In order to ask faculty to participate, reward structures are important. In an institution where high-quality teaching is the first criteria in a tenure application, new faculty are often unfamiliar with critical reflection in pedagogy. SJU's faculty development programs provide new faculty with concrete ways to address teaching and pedagogy. In this case, an additional reward is often the letter that the more senior faculty member may write for the mentee documenting the work for her or his tenure file. Senior faculty often appreciate the opportunity to discuss pedagogy with a colleague and can cite the mentoring program as an aspect of leadership, which is an additional criteria for promotion to professor. In addition, the director will write a support letter for faculty mentors applying for professor.

Other challenges include the power differential between the junior and senior faculty members. Although mentors and mentees are often from different departments, there is still tension around even the most informal appraisal of one's teaching. For example, on occasion, a mentee has questioned a mentor's assessment of student participation, perceiving that more students spoke than the mentor documented in the notes. Although this is a point of tension, having the service-learning director as a mediator is helpful in facilitating these conversations or advising the mentor and mentee on conflict. It is our experience that these conflicts can produce learning opportunities and greater opportunity for reflection for both mentor and mentee.

Faculty in some disciplines are resistant to the pedagogy of service-learning and concerned about losing course content. The mentoring relationship helps to address such issues. As a faculty member in finance stated,

> I was initially hesitant that students would take my service-learning course. The course is an upper-level finance course and requires a significant amount of work. In contrast with my mentor, I thought adding a service-learning component would deter students from taking the course. I was pleasantly surprised that students not just excelled at service-learning but also showed improved performance in their regular course work. My mentor let me know of potential issues and solutions, which helped me navigate some of the more challenging aspects of the course. Her insights toward logistics, grading, and assignments provided for a seamless course. (R. Sharma, personal communication, December 20, 2016)

Strong mentoring relationships are the cornerstone of the program, requiring institutional organization but minimal financial resources. Responsibilities for the formation and implementation of service-learning courses and oversight of mentoring are built into the director's role. In the beginning of the initiative, the institute funded a nominal stipend for faculty mentors. Currently, faculty mentors receive reimbursement to fund one meal with their mentee to build relationship and discuss pedagogy. Finally, the dedicated cohort of faculty who serve as faculty mentors demonstrate exceptional personal and professional vocation and leadership in fostering academically rigorous, pedagogically sound community-based learning courses aligned with the university's mission.

In summary, the Ignatian mission of social justice is embedded throughout the service-learning mentoring relationship. Like the best of Ignatian pedagogy, intentional, reciprocal, relationship-based mentoring mirrors the relationship between the students and the community partner placement. A dedicated community of scholars and intentional institutional organizations facilitates deep, authentic, and vulnerable mentoring relationships that embrace social justice pedagogy.

Innovative and Integrated Faculty Development: Faculty Learning Communities and Reflection Models at Marquette University

Since 1994, the Marquette University Service-Learning Program (SLP) has manifested Marquette's Jesuit character and core values. The SLP serves as a catalyst for promoting a culture of pedagogical excellence at Marquette and is rooted in the Ignatian tradition and the scholarship of teaching and learning. The SLP strives to both provide transformational learning experiences for students and have a positive and bidirectional relationship with the Milwaukee community. Since 2011, the SLP has been situated within the Center for Teaching and Learning. As such, the SLP has focused heavily on faculty development in an effort to improve the quality and impact of service-learning as a high-impact practice across the university. To date, the SLP has offered extensive professional development opportunities to both faculty and future faculty, including, but not limited to, facilitated reading groups around issues of diversity and intercultural competency for faculty, workshops on assessment and community partnership, faculty field trips, one-on-one consultations, and community-faculty roundtables.

Among these faculty development efforts, two particular opportunities—detailed in this chapter—have proven very successful for the SLP, as evidenced by assessment data. The first initiative is a faculty learning community (FLC) which worked with new and veteran faculty members to improve the integration of service-learning within a course. The second initiative is the creation of online reflection modules that have assisted faculty in integrating critical, continual, contextual, and challenging reflection into their courses (Eyler & Giles, 1996). Together, these two efforts have helped faculty to create more impactful service-learning courses, inciting new vigor for the pedagogy across campus. These programs are adaptable to other university programs that seek high-quality impactful service-learning experiences.

Design and Implementation: Faculty Learning Community on Integrated Course Design

Like most service-learning programs, there is a wide variety in the quality of service-learning implementation at Marquette. Some faculty members are intentional about integrating service-learning into their courses. These faculty use service-learning as text, have multiple assignments dealing with community-based learning, and use service-learning examples during lecture and course discussions. Other faculty use service-learning as an optional assignment, doing very little to draw service-learning into formal pedagogy and assessment. When faculty and students view service-learning as peripheral to learning outcomes and proficiencies, they are less engaged in the richness of the experience (Eyler & Giles, 1996). Further, student reflections are often superficial because students do not make the connections between community experience and academic content.

To address these concerns, the SLP turned to pedagogical theory and curriculum design literature from the educational development field.

Specifically, the program utilized L. Dee Fink's (2003) work on integrated course design, from his signature text, *Creating Significant Learning Experiences: An Integrated Approach to Designing College Courses*. Fink's model for course design introduces a clear strategy for helping faculty to integrate and align pedagogy (e.g., service-learning) with their learning goals and assessment activities.

The pilot of this FLC, Designing Effective and Integrated Service-Learning Courses: The Community Engaged Learning Institute, occurred during the spring 2016 semester and was led by the SLP director. The learning goals for the FLC, listed in Table 6.1, are mapped to the taxonomy of learning (e.g., foundational knowledge, application, integration) expressed in Fink's text.

Applying best practices in course design, faculty participants were encouraged to assess their syllabi critically, with willingness to create an entirely new course. Applying Fink's (2003) taxonomy of significant learning, including instruction on how to use backward design, integration, active learning, and assessment, the FLC also spent significant time discussing

TABLE 6.1
FLC Learning Goals and Connection to Fink's Taxonomy

FLC Learning Goal	*Type of Significant Learning From Fink's Taxonomy of Significant Learning*
Faculty will understand service-learning as a pedagogy and will define key service-learning and integrated course design terminology.	Foundational knowledge
Faculty will apply techniques for critical reflection and connected assessment strategy.	Application
Faculty will identify how service-learning will intersect with their particular learning objectives.	Integration
Faculty will feel more confident in helping their students understand social justice considerations central to their service-learning experience.	Human dimension
Faculty will be excited about creating impactful service-learning courses for their students.	Caring
Faculty will design a new integrated course and will use this technique in future course design.	Lifelong learning

important elements of service-learning courses, including community partnerships (Stoecker & Tryon, 2009), critical reflection (Ash & Clayton, 2009), and diversity education (Mitchell, Donahue, & Young-Law, 2012). Already nationally recognized as an exemplar program, the Marquette SLP creatively built on its success by drawing on the literature and best practices outlined by the Association of American Colleges & Universities (AAC&U), the Professional Organizational Development Network (POD), and scholarship of teaching and learning (SOTL) work.

Nine faculty members, accepted through an application process, participated in the community in the inaugural semester. They received a $1,000 stipend for participating in the eight-week session, which met each week for two-hour sessions. Participants were responsible for completing homework assignments and creating and submitting a new course syllabus. One-on-one consulting with the SLP director was available throughout the process, and almost half of the faculty set up private consultations to go over potential reflection assignments, course sequencing, and community partnership opportunities. The FLC sessions drew rich interdisciplinary conversations between veteran and new service-learning faculty. These interdisciplinary connections proved very fruitful, as many of the faculty speak in each other's courses or are planning ways to partner on service-learning projects.

Faculty completed a post-FLC assessment; they requested that they continue meeting because they appreciated both Fink's (2003) course design process and the opportunity to discuss the pedagogical approach to service-learning with interdisciplinary colleagues. After faculty submitted both their old and new syllabi, they received feedback from the SLP director and a Center for Teaching and Learning faculty consultant, based on a rubric SLP created that assessed both integrated design and the effectiveness of the service-learning experience. Table 6.2 is a sample of the integrated design rubric used for faculty feedback.

As a whole, the new syllabi reflected more opportunities for active learning throughout the course. Many faculty moved from lecturing to using more case studies, forward thinking assignments, and group learning opportunities. Further, the new syllabi integrated and developed service-learning experiences that clearly aligned with course learning goals, with newer and more innovative projects. Some faculty adopted project-based models, some moved to working with individual partners, and some created intensive projects that included taking the entire class to visits with community members and bringing community members into classrooms. Faculty also offered more opportunities for critical reflection. Instead of thinking about reflection as one culminating assignment, they utilized reflection opportunities throughout the entire class.

TABLE 6.2
Sample of Rubric Used for Syllabus Assessment

Aspects of Integrated Course Design	Poor (0–1 points)	Fair to Good (2–3 points)	Excellent (4–5 points)	Score	Comments
Learning goals, learning activities, and assessment are integrated throughout the course.	Goals, activities, and assessment are not aligned and do not support significant learning.	There is some alignment of goals, activities, and assessment.	The goals, activities, and assessment are interactive and connected. They are reflective and support each other.		
Aspects of Successful Service-Learning Courses	**Poor (0–1 points)**	**Fair to Good (2–3 points)**	**Excellent (4–5 points)**	**Score**	**Comments**
Pre-, mid-, and postservice critical reflection opportunities are integrated into the course.	Reflection assignments or discussions are not defined within the syllabus.	Some reflection opportunities appear to be integrated into the course.	Reflection exercises are integrated throughout the course.		

Improvements to the syllabi and assignments included enriched opportunities for feedback on academic and civic learning, through the use of student self-evaluation, peer feedback, and faculty evaluations with structured rubrics for grading. Currently, the SLP is working to assess if curricular changes were indeed implemented during the following school year and how those changes impacted the participants' teaching and their teaching scores.

Challenges

Related to the challenge of creating integrated service-learning courses is the difficulty involved with creating meaningful critical reflection assignments. In evaluations and feedback collected by the SLP, faculty often articulated dissatisfaction with their reflection assignments and discussions. Specifically, faculty expressed concern about their students' abilities to draw connections between course content and their community experience, as well as students' abilities to critically analyze social justice topics, understand their social identities, and discern how the community experience shaped personal values. In many instances, feedback came from faculty in disciplines that did not traditionally use critical reflection as a learning technique and were ill-equipped to facilitate sometimes unwieldy, sometimes politically charged, classroom conversations. Other faculty members felt conflicted about how much time they could allow for reflection discussions in content-heavy courses or were unsure how to grade reflections appropriately and fairly. Across the 55 to 60 Marquette faculty members who have integrated service-learning each year, there has been a great deal of variation in the quality of reflection assignments, the amount of actual reflection assignments students completed, and the quality of in-class discussion.

To respond to these concerns, the SLP staff partnered with instructional designers and e-learning experts with the Center for Teaching and Learning to create online reflection modules that assist faculty integration of critical reflection into service-learning courses. The primary goal of these reflection modules was to guide faculty in using a research-based critical reflection process and thus model best practices for faculty. Enriching the opportunities for quality critical reflection in the classroom ideally would result in a more impactful learning experience for students.

David Kolb's (1984) experiential learning model served as a guide for the creation of the modules. The prompts guide students through the *What? So What? Now What?* reflection model derived from Kolb's work. Within these assignments, students are asked to consider course application and integration as well as social justice and/or social identity issues. Rubrics were also created to help faculty assess the quality of the critical reflection and to give students an important feedback loop that is necessary for learning and growth. The rubrics are viewable to the students as they develop their assignment responses, so expectations are clear and guided.

If a faculty member indicates an interest in using them, the modules are loaded into their service-learning course's learning management system. Of note, the prefabricated modules can be used as is, because they are content-agnostic. That is, the questions that prompt reflections stress an individual's ability to connect community experience with course learning objectives. The beauty of these content-agnostic prompts is that they can be used in courses ranging from biomedical engineering to theology, from psychology to nursing courses. Modules include preservice, midservice, and postservice reflection options for faculty to use. Each point-in-time module includes the option of an essay, discussion board, multimedia project, or blog assignment. Faculty can choose to use whatever assignment or combination of assignments they like. For example, they may use a preservice discussion board, opt to facilitate an in-class discussion instead of the midservice web-based assignment, and then use the postservice essay assignment. They can also customize the modules to address particular course material and academic questions. Figure 6.1 presents an example of a prompt for a postservice discussion board post (Bohat, Schweizer, & Hayslett, 2012).

No financial incentive is given to faculty who use the modules, and all of the instructional design for the project has been done within the department. There is essentially no operating cost for the modules. Initially, large-group training was held to introduce faculty to the reflection tool and to show them how to customize the modules to fit with their course objectives. Currently, new faculty are introduced to and educated on the tool individually.

In 2015, higher education graduate students from Patrick M. Green's curriculum class at Loyola University Chicago assisted Marquette's program through a service-learning experience of their own by building out additional reflection modules that examined particular topics such as citizenship, stereotypes, and root causes of social justice, providing faculty with a menu to choose from when selecting reflection assignments for their courses. Moving forward, the Marquette SLP plans to continue to build out the menu of options for faculty interested in using the modules.

To date, the online reflection modules have been adopted by about 70% of faculty who use service-learning at Marquette. Faculty report that they have observed an increase in the depth of their student critical thinking ability because of the quality of the prompts. Faculty are also satisfied with the rubrics because they offer an objective grading system and feedback loop that is connected to learning objectives. The vast majority of faculty continue to use the modules in succeeding semesters. On the Graduating Senior Survey,

Figure 6.1. Prompt for postservice discussion board.

Begin your participation in this discussion by posting your response to the following two-part prompt:

- Part 1
  - What have you learned from this experience that you could not simply learn from reading a textbook or sitting in class? Explicitly describe, using terminology from the course, the ways in which your service-learning experience clarified, illuminated, troubled, and/or expanded the theories, course concepts, principles, issues, and learning objectives you investigated, examined, and/or explored in this course. Describe the insights you have drawn from the connections you have made. How do those connections inform your understanding of the course material? What conclusions have you reached? About what are you still curious? List questions you still have or that have been piqued by your service-learning experience.

- Part 2
  - What has been your role in perpetuating social injustice? How have your personal values changed as a result of your service-learning experience? What is your responsibility and how will you behave going forward based on your service-learning experience?

---

students are asked how impactful service-learning was to their education. Since 2013, the number of students reporting that service-learning was either highly impactful or somewhat impactful to their learning has grown 10%. Although other efforts and programs have likely also played a role in increasing this number, the reflection modules have helped the SLP ensure that high-quality reflection is happening in service-learning courses.

Marquette's SLP has impacted students' learning by working with faculty to create service-learning-centered integrated course design and by helping faculty to implement critical reflection assignments. These creative approaches to faculty development provide an example of the importance of grounding work in educational theory and providing new, innovative models of professional development experiences. Creating an opportunity for an interdisciplinary community of faculty to apply integrated course design to service-learning course development is an innovative way to support faculty in creating stronger service-learning courses. Modeling a structure to support continuous, contextual, and challenging reflection by drawing on the assets of an online environment is an original idea. These two examples demonstrate how inventive approaches to faculty development can be used to improve service-learning courses.

The Summer Faculty Development Conference: An Immersive Service-Learning Training Experience for Faculty at the University of Central Florida

When President John C. Hitt took the helm at UCF in 1992, one of the core goals he set for the growing institution was to become America's leading partnership university. Since that time, the UCF student population has expanded from nearly 20,000 to more than 64,000 and the partnership commitment has flourished. Related efforts have had profound impacts on our students as well as the local, state, regional, national, and international communities of which UCF is a part. Service-learning pedagogy is a key tool UCF employs to honor twin commitments to community engagement and excellence in education, and a robust faculty development ecosystem helps to support and promote those efforts. In this case study, we describe one component of our comprehensive faculty development model, the service-learning track of UCF's annual Summer Faculty Development Conference.

UCF is a public research-intensive university and one of the largest institutions of higher education in the nation. More than 17,000 of the nearly 55,000 undergraduate students enrolled at UCF this year will participate in experiential learning activities as they pursue their degrees. That emphasis is regularly renewed, with service-learning figuring significantly in UCF's 2016 strategic planning efforts, which challenges the university to engage all students in service-learning and to increase designated service-learning courses by 50% within the coming years.

Service-learning has been included in UCF courses since at least the mid-1990s, but formal program development began in 2001 when a team of faculty and administrators began to think intentionally about how to operationalize the values of service-learning pedagogy on a large scale across campus. Since that time, more than 200 faculty members from over 40 departments have taught more than 140 service-learning courses, many of which were initially developed through faculty participation in the program we call *summer conference*.

Design and Implementation: The Summer Faculty Development Conference

UCF's annual Summer Faculty Development Conference engages 200 to 300 faculty and staff members across UCF's multiple campuses in conversations about improving the educational experiences of students. The four-day event is collaboratively designed and planned by a diverse campus team and coordinated by the Karen L. Smith Faculty Center for Teaching and Learning. Typically the first three days include theme-based plenary events, morning workshops (both track-specific and general interest), and afternoon time slots that provide opportunities for work on projects with access to a variety of resources from colleagues to technologies to subject matter experts. The conference culminates in a showcase event on the fourth, which features presentations and interactions among participants and guests.

Each year the core planning team works for several months to identify current needs among colleagues and to consider current university-wide opportunities and concerns as they develop a theme for the annual conference. Service-learning is one track among 8 to 10 offered each year, which might include diversity and inclusion, internationalization, writing across the curriculum, curriculum mapping, active learning, integrative learning, undergraduate research, teaching with technology, and more. The event and its planning and debriefing phases provide a space for meaningful cross-pollination of ideas and approaches, and encourage the development of a program that invites faculty members from all tracks to think about their projects and topics from multiple perspectives. Although a faculty member working to increase international components of a course or to add writing assignments may not be focused significantly on service-learning, well-planned cross-referenced programming may promote interest in future faculty development activities and can lead to valuable collaborations and innovative curricular decisions.

The Office of Experiential Learning and the Faculty Center for Teaching and Learning collaborate to provide programming for a service-learning track at the conference and beyond. Although service-learning efforts require year-round support and engagement, the intense and focused summer conference model is an effective and creative way to help faculty members take a deep dive into service-learning at a time in the academic year when they can realistically make solid planning decisions for the coming year.

Longtime program leaders have identified several key elements that have contributed to its success.

- *Faculty-driven and led programming.* Based on the details of the specific projects proposed by selected applicants, the service-learning program director recruits faculty members who have previously participated in the summer conference service-learning track and who have successfully taught service-learning courses to create and offer

workshops during the conference. Offerings typically include a mix of the following:
- Introductory topics such as definitions and models of service-learning, relevant campus policies, and key effective practices
- Advanced issues such as managing service-learning projects, assessing learning outcomes in service-learning classes, balancing the emphasis on service and learning in course planning, and the procedure for getting a course approved as an official UCF service-learning course
- Topics that target specific course models such as online and blended learning, service-learning in high-enrollment courses, or managing large service-learning programs
- Partnership-focused topics such as learning with community partners or service-learning opportunities in the campus environment
- Topics that address course content concerns such as service-learning in the sciences or service-learning and integrative learning

- *Compensation for faculty members' time.* Faculty members who participate in the Summer Faculty Development Conference receive a grant of $800 in recognition of their time both during the event and in follow-up phases, which include the writing and submission of an implementation report and revised syllabus to the service-learning program. This compensation helps to make it possible for faculty members to clear their schedules and concentrate fully on developing courses during this time period.
- *Competitive application process.* Faculty members interested in being part of the track apply to be selected. The application includes a request for the course number and title; instructor, college, and department; a brief description of the project; list of specific goals; changes in methodology (current and proposed practices); and an assessment plan for the project. This information allows the director to select track members from a variety of disciplines and to create a programming plan that is clearly relevant to participants' needs.
- *Connections to scholarship of teaching and learning initiatives.* The UCF Faculty Center is a hub for educational research on campus, and the collaborative support and development model we employ allows a connection between service-learning faculty and SoTL programming. Faculty members who participate in a summer conference become part of a service-learning community and receive announcements about calls for articles and conference presentations on campus and beyond as well as invitations to local workshops and special events.

This creates a culture where faculty presentations and courses can be informed by and contribute to relevant research beyond our university.
- *Sustainability as promoted through connections with university initiatives and values.* Like many colleges and universities, UCF is engaged in a number of broad, student-focused initiatives and efforts at any given moment. The collaborative model for planning, implementing, and assessing the service-learning summer conference track allows the program and involved faculty members to make connections between their individual courses and projects and the broader vision at the university. For example, the College of Undergraduate Studies leads a Unifying Theme initiative that promotes exploration of revolving themes across the curriculum and into cocurricular projects. Previous themes have included environmental issues, and our collaborative program support model has allowed faculty members to make connections to their service-learning courses and take advantage of campus-sponsored speakers and special events to enhance service-learning classes. Our university's commitment to large-scale student success initiatives is also relevant. We hope to apply tools such as predictive analytics to look at particular courses in the curriculum and determine what kinds of pedagogies might be valuable and relevant and to create plans of study that spread experiential learning activities across the students' careers to promote increasingly complex assignments and activities.

Challenges

Although overall the conference results in thoughtful and thorough service-learning curriculum planning and strategies, there can be challenges. One relates to the conference project deliverable. One of the requirements of receiving the grant to participate in the conference is that faculty members complete their service-learning course syllabi by January 31 of the year following the event. The generous time frame provides participants ample time to create a successful and rigorous learning experience for their students that meaningfully addresses a need in the community. It further allows faculty members time to gain approval from their administrative staff as well as possibly move through the process of designating their course with the "SL" code that appears in the course description once approved by the service-learning curriculum committee.

Although the timing of the conference is convenient in many ways, its separation from the beginning of the academic year can make it difficult to attain these deliverables, as once faculty members finish their conference work in early summer, they move on to other things (e.g., research, committee work, publishing, heavy teaching loads) that limit their ability to not only implement but also complete the course or program syllabi. This is particularly true given the fact that department supervisors may prioritize other efforts or initiatives over service-learning.

These conflicting priorities point to another challenge—tensions surrounding promotion and tenure and advancement more generally. Though improvements are evolving, some departments do not recognize service-learning as a pedagogical innovation or as a field of meaningful inquiry but rather as a service activity, which is not typically valued as highly as other efforts. To address this challenge, we contact the track participants throughout the year to see if they need further assistance (e.g., further course development, finding strong community partner matches, and simply letting them know that they have a support network). By reaching out to each individual, we hope to create an environment that both promotes a feeling of safety in trying new pedagogies and fuels the desire and passion to extend the classroom into the community and utilize newly learned skill sets to improve our partners' programming and give our students the opportunity to connect academics and civics.

Programs like this, which rely on faculty leadership and peer mentoring, also run the risk of becoming cliquish, when the same faculty members repeatedly take leadership and participation roles in an annual event. To combat this phenomenon, we are purposeful in giving faculty members who have not previously participated in the track priority for acceptance and by rotating the track workshops and presenters to keep this long-standing event fresh and relevant.

Despite these challenges, the service-learning track of UCF's summer conference is a model of which we are proud. It promotes faculty-to-faculty mentoring and sharing, provides a context for faculty members from various disciplines to engage and share ideas, establishes a culture of peer mentoring, connects service-learning with other key initiatives across campus, and productively solidifies the connection between the faculty center and the service-learning program.

Conclusion

Although service-learning is an increasingly important pedagogy at universities across the country, service-learning offices often remain relatively poorly funded, particularly in areas like faculty development. Service-learning directors and faculty leaders must often create faculty development programming with limited resources. Each of the three creative practices explored in this chapter offer innovative cases of successful faculty development programming with limited resources. Each institutional practice has aligned service-learning work with the institution's mission and maximized limited resources through inventive designs. Building on S-LCE's established evidence-based practices, these examples highlight how relationships, technology, and faculty/administrator leadership within different institutional contexts can achieve the shared goal of well-informed faculty and effective service-learning programs.

As with the faculty communities featured in the case studies found in chapter 5, cohorts of S-LCE pedagogically informed faculty create spaces for faculty to utilize newly developed techniques to improve teaching quality in all areas of teaching, not just service-learning. The deliberate programming models for the greater institution facilitate communities of dialogue and shared engagement for the successful delivery of academically rigorous community-engaged student coursework. By showing how these three programs emerged from different institutions and contexts, we hope we have provided inspiration for other service-learning programs that may devise even more innovative and creative programs using limited resources.

References

Ash, S. L., & Clayton, P. H. (2009). *Learning through critical reflection: A tutorial for service-learning students.* Raleigh, NC: Authors.

Bohat, K. M., Schweizer, H., & Hayslett, C. (2012). *Service learning online reflection tool.* Milwaukee, WI: Marquette University.

Eyler, J., & Giles, D. E. (1996). *A practitioner's guide to reflection in service learning: Student voices and reflections.* Nashville, TN: Vanderbilt University.

Fink, L. Dee (2003). *Creating significant learning experiences: An integrated approach to designing college courses.* San Francisco, CA: Jossey-Bass.

Hans-Kolvenbach, P. (2000, October). *The service of faith and the promotion of justice in American Jesuit higher education.* Presentation at the Commitment to Justice Conference, Santa Clara University, Santa Clara, CA.

Kolb, D. A. (1984). *Experiential learning.* Englewood Cliffs, NJ: Prentice Hall.

Mitchell, T. D., Donahue, D. M., & Young-Law, C. (2012). Service learning as a pedagogy of whiteness. *Equity & Excellence in Education, 45*(4), 612–629.

Stoecker, R., & Tryon, E. (2009). *The unheard voices: Community organization and service-learning.* Philadelphia, PA: Temple University Press.

7

DYNAMICS ON THE EDGE

Exploring Roles and Intersections of Service-Learning and Community Engagement and Educational Development

Cara Meixner, Becca Berkey, and Patrick M. Green

> *Over the decades, faculty development has proven its capacity to anticipate and respond to changes in higher education. It has opened opportunities for teaching as well as scholarly development. It has recognized changes in students—their increasing diversity, their different learning needs, and their new demands as consumers of education. It has evolved from a focus on individual to collective development and from singular to multidimensional purposes.*
>
> M.D. Sorcinelli, A.E. Austin, P.L. Eddy, and A.L. Beach,
> *Creating the Future of Faculty Development*

Faculty developers—and the centers or offices with which we are affiliated—are regarded for the pivotal role we play in the professional development of instructional faculty. The field is now preferably referred to as *educational development*, which also takes into account the growth and development of a future professoriate (e.g., graduate students) and the contributions of nonfaculty participants (e.g., community partners, students, staff, academic administrators). Given this work, educational developers occupy liminal roles that transgress silos and divisions. Sometimes, our work is fused with service-learning and community engagement efforts; in other cases, educational developers are service-learning/community engagement (S-LCE) novices, relying on powerful campus and community partnerships to create transformative learning experiences for college and university students—and the communities we serve. There are also S-LCE professionals, who may or may not report within a center for teaching and learning, with rich backgrounds in faculty development.

This chapter is coauthored by three educational developers, two of whom formally direct S-LCE initiatives at their respective institutions. Having entered into our work from varied yet intersected perspectives and roles, we have positioned this chapter at the intersection of theory and practice, with the following outcomes in mind: (a) developing an appreciation for the roles that educational developers and centers play in faculty and institutional success; (b) identifying opportunities for powerful partnerships among S-LCE professionals and other educational developers; (c) exploring—through practical, lived vignettes—shared intersections of work among S-LCE professionals and other educational developers; and (d) considering shared pathways to evidence success in our work. In pursuing these outcomes, it is our hope that this chapter will serve as a bridge from the case study chapters in the first half to the second half of the book. Although the case study chapters elucidated promising practices across institutional contexts, they were predominantly written from the perspective of those in primarily S-LCE professional roles. This chapter connects the work of both S-LCE professionals and educational developers in part three, "Challenges and Opportunities in Pedagogy and Partnerships," and part four, "Engendering Change in Educational Development"; it is applicable to both S-LCE professionals and educational developers who find themselves engaged with this work in the borderlands (see the introduction for an overview of this concept).

With these aims in mind, we will first consider the nuanced history, role, and evolution of the educational development field. Therein, we acknowledge the silo-crossing and boundary-spanning work of all educational developers, including S-LCE professionals. Several heuristics frame this work, which maps to an evolving, growing academy and the many cultures that inhabit higher education. From there, we identify the core work of S-LCE professionals, tracing a tendency, for some, to "back into" educational development. The chapter segues from history and theory to practice and application, wherein we explore vignettes that call for professional expertise—and partnerships—in pedagogy, service-learning, and organizational development. We conclude with an opportunity to envision a future of shared pathways and partnerships linked to trends in higher education, the need to evidence learning improvement, and the call to engage and transform our communities.

History, Role, and Evolution of Educational Development

Most known within the academy are educational development efforts manifest in programs and services that advance faculty as teachers, scholars, and to a growing extent institutional and public citizen leaders. Recognizing the intersectionality among the varied contributions that faculty make (e.g., advisers, program chairs, faculty senators), many educational development centers now provide initiatives that focus on career and leadership development, often homing in on the needs of faculty within a caucus (e.g., contingent/adjunct faculty) or career stage (e.g., midcareer). Some centers formally house S-LCE, whereas others work closely with S-LCE professionals reporting through the same division (i.e., academic affairs), or others such as student affairs or outreach divisions. Systematically, the field of educational development has embraced organizational development initiatives, wherein efforts have attended to issues such as institutional effectiveness, curriculum reform, and inclusive excellence. More than half of all educational development centers, for instance, are now involved in accreditation efforts (POD Network, 2016).

History of Educational Development

A brief review of the history and evolution of educational development reveals its arc, situating its impact on faculty, academic programs, and institutions of higher education. This history is also one that is aligned, philosophically and practically, with the evolution of S-LCE as a field. Educational development extends back to 1810 at Harvard University, wherein the sabbatical was first introduced (Eble & McKeachie, 1985). Leaves were the dominant genre of faculty development until the 1970s (Sorcinelli, Austin, Eddy, & Beach, 2006), by which time the field had blossomed and "a raft of new terms hit college and university campuses" (Albright, 1988, p. 3), such as *faculty development, academic development, professional development, instructional development*, and *instructional improvement*.

In a thorough review of educational development's evolution, Sorcinelli and colleagues (2006) conceptualized five periods characterizing the field's proliferation: the Age of the Scholar, the Age of the Teacher, the Age of the Developer, the Age of the Learner, and the Age of the Network. Table 7.1 summarizes each of the periods with reference to characteristics and key influencers.

Across each of these periods, educational development practices have retained some constancy while innovating to meet the needs of a changing professoriate, diversifying cadres of learners, and evolving institutional cultures. For instance, the sabbatical, though not always the province of educational development centers, retains its status as one of the most privileged and coveted forms of faculty professional development. Several dimensions of professional development have been offered by centers since the 1970s, guided by frameworks introduced by Gaff (1975) and Bergquist and Phillips (1975). Both frameworks suggest initiatives supporting instructional

TABLE 7.1
A Brief Historical Progression of the Educational Development Field

	Characteristics and Goals	Key Influencers
Age of the Scholar (mid-1950s–1960s)	Focus on "improving and advancing scholarly competence" (Sorcinelli et al., 2006, p. 2), with the goal of enhancing content expertise	• Expansion of higher education • Public prestige of the professoriate
Age of the Teacher (late 1960s–1970s)	Focus on teaching development, namely skills and evaluation processes, supported by the recognition that faculty should develop as teachers—not just scholars	• Boomers enter the academy • Rise of activism • Retrenchment; lack of mobility • Forming of POD Network (1974)
Age of the Developer (1980s)	Expansion and assessment of teaching development initiatives, namely the evaluation of faculty members. Broadening of educational development programs focused on faculty career span	• Surge in educational development programs • Tightened budgets • Foundation support (e.g., Lilly) • Attention to quality of undergraduate education
Age of the Learner (1990s)	Focus on development "for a greater range and variety in teaching and learning methods, skills, and sensitivities" (Sorcinelli et al., 2006, p. 4), technology adoption, assessment, and attention to all facets of the faculty role	• Focus on learning over teaching • Diversification of higher education • Change in faculty roles • Competition for funding • Introduction of technologies

Age of the Network (2000s)	View of educational development as "a central strategy for assisting faculty in balancing multiple responsibilities and taking on new and different roles" (Sorcinelli et al., 2006, p. 161); focus on improving practice with scholarship, continuing to broaden educational development beyond teaching and learning, and strategically linking individual and institutional needs	• Awareness of educational development as a global enterprise
		• Heightened expectations:
		  ○ collaboration
		  ○ assessment
		  ○ accountability
		  ○ diversity
		  ○ sustainability

development (e.g., teaching methods, course design) and organizational development (e.g., leadership development for administrators). Gaff (1975) offers a third dimension, faculty development (i.e., improvement over the career span) paralleling the Bergquist and Phillips (1975) notion of personal development, which promotes growth and development long-term. Within each of these dimensions—instructional, organizational, faculty/personal—reside the genres of programming explored by Gravett and Broscheid in chapter 3 of this volume.

Structurally, educational development centers vary from institution to institution in ways that bear resemblance to stand-alone centers for S-LCE (notably, no concrete data exist on the percentage or number of educational development centers that house S-LCE). Surveying 494 educational developers at 300 institutions, Sorcinelli and colleagues (2006) reported the following core structures characterizing the delivery of educational development across institutions of higher education: a centralized unit with staff (54%), an individual faculty member or administrator (19%), a committee supporting development (12%), other/combination (11%), or a clearinghouse (4%). Notably, of the respondents who directed centers, 60% also held a faculty appointment; Sorcinelli and colleagues (2006) opine that these individuals "may be perceived as more credible on issues of teaching and learning because of their direct involvement in the classroom" (p. 32). More recent data (POD Network, 2016) indicate a trend toward professionalization of educational development, "reflected in the fact that the percentage of [educational developers] who are Center for Teaching and Learning (CTL) staff (including directors, associates and assistants) has grown steadily from 1996 (23%) to 2016 (60%)" (p. 5).

Educational Developers as Migrants and Navigators

Like their S-LCE counterparts, educational developers inhabit many roles, navigating and negotiating a diverse topography of academic life. All at once, most educational developers are teaching faculty, researchers and scholars within their discipline, members of academic tribes, consultants and coaches, academic administrators, campus leaders, and community-engaged citizens. Some of these arenas overlap whereas others are distinct and sometimes in conflict with one another.

Seminally, Green and Little (2012) suggest that educational developers thrive *in the margins*; this is a liminal place "located between and among other units, as simultaneously inside and outside, and neither completely dominant over, nor subordinate to, other overlapping cultures within a given institution" (p. 214). Acting from the margins is not to be confused with being marginalized (Green & Little, 2012, 2013); rather,

Locating ourselves in the interstices, with the double vision of the marginal person, lets [an educational developer] play the role of collegial provocateur: the person who spots discrepancies and contradictions, who names or questions the unspoken agendas, and who plays devil's advocate to sharpen colleagues' thinking if no alternative viewpoints materialize. This space is intellectually engaging, and one that many of us are apt to assume as academic developers. (p. 535)

Occupying the margins, educational developers may also be thought of as arbiters among the six cultures described by Bergquist and Pawlak (2008) and summarized in Table 7.2.

Intersections With Literature on Service-Learning and Community Engagement Professionals

Like that of the educational developer, the position of the S-LCE professional has evolved in the past several decades. SLC-E, as a field, has been informed by many of the same trends evident in the establishment of educational development (e.g., expansion, activism, learning focus, collaboration). Further, we can map the work of the S-LCE professional onto the heuristic explored in Table 7.2. S-LCE professionals, in their faculty development work, travel within and outside of the six cultures of the academy. Although their role may be most dominant in the advocacy culture (Bergquist & Pawlak, 2008), it is important to underscore the work of the practitioner in navigating multiple cultures, often all at once.

As S-LCE professionals traverse evolving networks and cultures, the naming of their work remains an important consideration. Dostilio and Perry (2017) explore and challenge the nomenclature around practitioner or service-learning/community service director and the evolution of terms around staff-focused titles. Ultimately, the suggestion for articulating the broad title *community engagement professional* both engages the multifaceted dimensionality of this role while pushing on its necessarily hybrid nature. Further exploring the complexities of the S-LCE professional role, and its evolution within the service-learning and community engagement field, demonstrates the necessity for educational development as a significant function.

Backing Into Educational Development

Because *service-learning*, by definition, does not exist without faculty involvement and engagement, the S-LCE professional engages in and with faculty development for a variety of purposes and enters into the work of

TABLE 7.2
Summary of Six Cultures of Educational Developers

Culture	Description	Educational Developer Role
Collegial	Typically affiliated with instructional faculty, this culture values the disciplines (and disciplinary sovereignty), knowledge generation and dissemination, autonomy, and faculty governance. The doctrine of academic freedom is integral to this culture.	Many educational developers began their careers as faculty; thus, they understand and empathize with the norms within this culture. Such credibility engenders opportunities to disrupt the status quo and introduce facets germane to the other five cultures (e.g., curriculum reform, transdisciplinary collaborations).
Managerial	Synonymous with *administrative*, this culture values competency, hierarchy, and efficiency. In response to external pressures, accountability is a necessary hallmark.	Educational developers report through managerial channels and may be responsible for assuring institutional aims are met. Often, educational developers represent the interests of other cultures, helping faculty grow as competent leaders in their service roles.
Developmental	As described by Bergquist and Pawlak (2008), this culture cultivates "programs and activities furthering the personal and professional growth of all members of the higher education community" (p. 73) and values openness, collaboration, and learner-centered education.	Educational developers embrace and cultivate developmental spaces, calling for collaborative, evidence-informed approaches that engender change (at micro, meso, and macro levels) in the academy.

(*Continues*)

TABLE 7.2 (Continued)

Culture	Description	Educational Developer Role
Advocacy	Valuing equitable practices and procedures, this culture is often affiliated with faculty unionization and collective bargaining. Further, Bergquist and Pawlak (2008) view service-learning as a way of engaging "advocacy-oriented faculty members" (p. 136) with the community.	Educational developers are often familiar with and sensitive to the needs of individuals and groups around whom advocacy efforts are centered (e.g., adjunct faculty, community-based organizations). Further, educational developers, when navigating across cultures, can represent the opportunities afforded through community engagement practices.
Virtual	Responding to imminent change, this culture has emerged from the need to cultivate a global learning network. Herein, organizational boundaries are more malleable than other cultures.	From online learning to certificate programs, educational developers can be particularly helpful in shepherding faculty (and other constituents) through intentional design of courses, curricula, and projects.
Tangible	This culture returns to the genesis of higher education, (re)emerging in partial response to the presence of the virtual world. Herein, academicians value tangible traditions, face-to-face education, student-faculty relationships, and centering in a lived (physical) space.	The cultivation of faculty communities, with an emphasis on relationships and a pedagogy of place, is akin to the world of educational developers.

Source: Bergquist & Pawlak, 2008.

educational development from multiple places. Often, S-LCE professionals facilitate workshops for faculty on how to do service-learning in order to increase the number of service-learning courses on campus. Institutional initiatives to further develop civic engagement opportunities for students may be the driving force on other campuses, in which the S-LCE professional collaborates with faculty and academic programs to institutionalize service-learning. The approach of many S-LCE professionals is to collaborate with faculty to create another service-learning course rather than establish pedagogical foundations in practice. In other words, S-LCE professionals may aim to increase service-learning courses rather than enhance teaching and learning strategies, thus backing into faculty development activities. Although the primary aim may not be teaching and learning enhancement, it consistently tends to be a secondary or tertiary cause for employing the service-learning pedagogy in a course or academic program. Even when it is not a cause at all, the outcome of enhanced teaching and learning through the incorporation of service-learning must be considered and centered by S-LCE professionals in their work with faculty, and understanding the role of (and potential for partnership with) the educational developer in doing so is paramount.

In many ways, the S-LCE professional role mirrors the development of the field, as the emergence of service-learning grew from the adaptations of the civic mission of higher education through the 1980s and 1990s. The evolution of the S-LCE field included a shift from cocurricular programs (e.g., volunteerism) to an emphasis on academic service-learning (Jacoby, 2009; Stanton, Giles, & Cruz, 1999). Building practices from a variety of professional organizations, such as the National Society for Internships and Experiential Education (Kendall, 1990), the most common definition of *service-learning* as well as suggestions for infrastructure emerged in the mid-1990s (Bringle & Hatcher, 1996). Welch and Saltmarsh (2013) traced this evolution of specific infrastructure for service-learning centers that emerged in higher education, noting that an "entire generation of students, faculty, staff, and community partners has thus created a new area of study, professional literature, and set of practices while shaping the design and architecture of community engagement structures on campus" (p. 27). The set of practices and the institutionalization of centers dedicated to service-learning approach the work in a multiplicity of ways.

As indicated in the report by the National Task Force on Civic Learning and Democratic Engagement entitled *A Crucible Moment: College Learning and Democracy's Future* (2010), a general goal is to build the capacity of students as engaged citizens in the twenty-first century. *A Crucible Moment* provided higher education institutions with a framework for a civic-minded campus with certain characteristics:

- Civic ethos governing campus life
- Civic literacy as a goal for every student
- Civic inquiry integrated within the majors and general education
- Civic action as lifelong practice (p. 15)

As the S-LCE field has evolved, this framework demonstrates the evidence of increasing emphasis on learning, with significant implications for academic programs.

Although the service-learning literature has consistently emphasized pedagogy (Ash & Clayton, 2009; Howard, 1993), the increased emphasis on student learning, paralleled in the educational development literature as the Age of the Learner (see Table 7.1), has moved the S-LCE professional more directly into an educational development role. Dostilio (2017) explicitly names "facilitating faculty development and support" (p. 50) as a key competency for community engagement professionals, with the following associated knowledge, skills, abilities, and dispositions:

- Knowledge of how to approach differently motivated faculty using different strategies
- Knowledge of how various departments or disciplines place value on categories of faculty work: teaching, research, and service
- Ability to customize developmental training and support to fit each faculty member's needs and interests
- [Being open] to innovation/ability to design and implement new programs
- [Embracing] multidisciplinary and interdisciplinary collaborations (p. 50)

Although S-LCE professionals have emerged with faculty development a significant function in their role, it is just one of many functions they must engage. As Dostilio's (2017) competency model suggests, the community engagement professional also administers community engagement programs, cultivates community partnerships, institutionalizes mission-aligned initiatives, and leads general institutional change toward democratic engagement (see chapter 2 for a more detailed discussion). This global role hearkens back to the Age of the Network in Sorcinelli and colleagues' (2006) framework (see Table 7.1) and blends together developmental, advocacy, virtual, and tangible approaches from Bergquist and Pawlak's (2008) six cultures of educational developers (as summarized in Table 7.2).

Approaching Educational Development From a Different Direction

S-LCE professionals enter educational development with explicit goals related to the orientation of student learning, ranging from pedagogical approaches (e.g., applied learning, experiential learning, or service-learning) to mission-aligned institutional initiatives (e.g., civic learning, civic engagement, prioritized community partnerships, or community service). Although S-LCE professionals may approach faculty development as a function of their work for a distinct purpose, the role requires them to construct intentional educational development programs. The similarities of this role to educational developers working "in the margins" and as "arbiters of culture" are striking. For example, Dostilio (2017) explicitly states within her proposed competency model how S-LCE professionals lead change within and shape institutional culture in order to "encourage a democratic engagement orientation" (p. 46). The transgressive and advocacy-centered work of educational developers is inclusive of or similar to that of the S-LCE professional, although the point of entry may differ.

We see evidence in the case study chapters of the engagement of S-LCE professionals with the work of educational development, whether directly or indirectly, or in named or unnamed ways. In the chapter 4 case study on Boise State University, the authors describe their customized phase-entry process for faculty interested in incorporating service-learning into their teaching in which they, based on internal assessment methods, place faculty in a track and customize their educational development efforts to match. In the same chapter, the case studies from both Georgia State College & University and Portland State University describe long-standing efforts driven by institutional change initiatives to meaningfully engage faculty in their different contexts. In chapter 5, the three case studies serve as examples of the benefits for educational development outcomes from engaging faculty in learning communities, as well as the potential for those very same faculty learning communities to, in turn, impact institutional change around democratic and civic outcomes as evidenced in organizational policies, procedures, and language (e.g., promotion and tenure). Finally, in chapter 6, we see the borderlands at play as each case study represents the customization of educational development initiatives aimed at S-LCE outcomes with faculty in widely different institutional contexts involving limited resources.

Throughout the nine case studies in these three chapters, however, a direct tie to institutional educational development initiatives and/or direct acknowledgment of the educational development role being played by the S-LCE professionals who authored them is lacking. It is our hope that by bringing these two fields together, our readers will see the potential benefits and impacts of bridging not only theory between these fields but also the potential for collaborative, institutionally contextualized practice. We ask S-LCE professionals and educational developers alike to consider how we are mutually strengthened through discovery and development of the intersections of our work—a blatant call to lean into, rather than shy away from, institutionally imposed roles.

The Impact of Service-Learning and Community Engagement Work

Although building partnerships and community between educational development and S-LCE professionals is imperative, so is highlighting the impact of these partnerships and their resulting S-LCE courses and work on student learning, as well as the community both inside and outside the institution. Toward this end, we turn to Hanleybrown, Kania, and Kramer's (2012) work on collective impact. Being able to discuss collective impact relies on the following key conditions: (a) a common agenda, (b) shared measurement, (c) mutually reinforcing activities, (d) continuous communication, and (e) backbone support. Collective impact differs from isolated impact in important ways. Notably, isolated impact focuses on individual solutions, work that happens in silos, isolation of particular program impacts, and a misassumption that change at a large scale is dependent upon scaling just one organization, or one part of a single organization. Collective impact, rather, is characterized by an understanding of complex problems and the need for networked solutions, collaboration, and synergy among various stakeholders, and the coordination and cultivation of both likely and unlikely partnerships (Hanleybrown et al., 2012). Although the collective impact framework is traditionally utilized to discuss approaches to solving social problems, its parallels with the types of partnerships needed for higher education to fully realize its civic purpose (with S-LCE being part of that) are clear.

Potential for Powerful Partnerships

As illustrated, the professional and institutional spaces occupied by educational developers and by S-LCE professionals overlap in significant and meaningful ways. However, the pathways into roles, the professional and educational backgrounds of those involved in them, and the influence of the institutional structure and mission may differ significantly across individuals and contexts. In these ways, considerations of personal and professional preparation and motivation, as well as what is involved in navigating these multiple roles and identities, are significant. That said, an understanding from both educational developers and S-LCE professionals of the myriad ways that each must maneuver these dynamics is essential for partnership, and ultimately for successful S-LCE efforts to emerge and flourish on a campus. Toward this end, we will next introduce our institutional contexts, missions, and structures as merely three examples of these dynamics at play, and as illustrative of our motivators for compiling this volume and writing this chapter.

Three Institutions, Three Different Structures

Table 7.3 gives an overview of each of our institutions, including a brief profile and the structure of educational development and S-LCE efforts, as well as our own positionality within them.

As illustrated in this table, it is clear just across our chapter author group that a variety of factors bring us to our work. The implications of our unique positionality impact the work we do on our campuses, the partnerships we forge and how we do so, and most importantly, the pathways through which faculty on our campuses who are interested in S-LCE need to travel.

Vignettes

To illustrate these complexities even further, we propose three vignettes (Table 7.4) that draw from our different contexts and varied places of positionality. It is important to note that these vignettes focus on the stakeholder group that is the focus of this volume—faculty—and therefore exclude important dimensions of the student and community partner groups inherent in S-LCE work.

The vignettes offer a snapshot of the complexities faculty experience when navigating institutional structures to integrate S-LCE into their courses. Upon consideration of these three vignettes, the word *partnership* immediately comes to mind. Josiah and Andrea, for example, are unlikely to find solutions to their conundrums without reaching out and building relationships with the S-LCE or educational development professionals on campus, respectively. The point of entry, however, may be through the center for teaching and learning or the S-LCE office on campus. In addition, and referring back to Table 7.2, they also need a broader, more explicit understanding of the culture(s) each is mediating on their respective campuses, whether due to historical context, personal style, office/center culture, institutional priorities and mission, or other cause, to effectively build these partnerships.

TABLE 7.3
Overview of Educational Development and S-LCE Efforts at James Madison University, Loyola University Chicago, and Northeastern University

	Author Name/Position at Institution/Educational Background	Brief Institutional Profile	Structure of Educational Development Efforts	Structure of S-LCE Efforts
James Madison University, Virginia	Cara Meixner, executive director of the Center for Faculty Innovation and associate professor of Graduate Psychology • BS, Health Services Administration • MA, Counseling and Personnel Services • PhD, Leadership and Change	• Public • Carnegie Category: Master's Colleges & Universities • Carnegie Community Engaged Campus Classified • Undergraduates: 19,548; Graduates: 1,722; TOTAL: 21,270 • Full-time faculty: 1,028; Part-time faculty: 472; TOTAL: 1,500	Educational development efforts are housed in the Center for Faculty Innovation (CFI), which is staffed by academics with joint departmental appointments on campus, faculty associates, and an operations team. The CFI reports to the vice provost for academic development.	Curricular service is supported alongside cocurricular service by the Department of Community Service-Learning (CS-L), which is staffed by three full-time professionals, a fiscal technician, an administrative assistant, and two graduate assistants. The CS-L reports to the associate vice president for student affairs.

Institution	Profile	Details	Center 1	Center 2
Loyola University, Chicago, Illinois	Patrick M. Green, director of experiential learning and clinical instructor of experiential learning • BA, History and Literature, Honors Liberal Arts • MA, History • EdD, Educational Leadership and Organizational Change	• Private, Jesuit • Carnegie Category: Doctoral Universities—Higher Research Activity • Carnegie Community Engaged Campus Classified • Undergraduates: 11,129; Graduates: 5,293; TOTAL: 16,422 • Full-time faculty: 799; Part-time faculty: 714; TOTAL: 1,513	The Faculty Center for Ignatian Pedagogy (FCIP) houses resources on teaching, learning, and assessment and offers programming geared toward faculty around engaged teaching, Ignatian pedagogy, and teaching with technology. The center's staff consists of a director, administrative assistant, and coordinator. The FCIP reports to the Office of the Provost.	The Center for Experiential Learning (CEL) is the home for both educational development and service-learning efforts on campus. The seven full-time staff and two graduate assistants in the center have a variety of backgrounds. The CEL reports to the Office of the Provost.
Northeastern University, Massachusetts	Becca Berkey, director of service-learning (codirects the Center of Community Service in this role) and affiliated faculty, Human Services • BS, Biology • MS, College Student Personnel • PhD, Environmental Studies	• Private • Carnegie Category: Doctoral Universities—Highest Research Activity • Carnegie Community Engaged Campus Classified • Undergraduates: 17,923; Graduates: 7,543; TOTAL: 25,466 • Full-time faculty: 1,261; Part-time faculty: 408; TOTAL: 1,669	Four units comprise the Teaching and Learning Group (TLG), which report up through the Office of the Provost and are overseen by the assistant vice provost for teaching and learning. These groups are the Academic Assessment Group, the Center for Advancing Teaching and Learning through Research (CATLR), the Research Institute for Experiential Learning Science (RIELS), and Student Assessed Integrated Learning (SAIL). Across these 4 interrelated groups, there are 16 staff.	The Center of Community Service (CCS) houses both curricular and cocurricular efforts at the university, as well as two AmeriCorps programs. There are nine full-time staff in the center, which is codirected by the director of service-learning and the director of cocurricular community programs. CCS reports to the Office of City & Community Affairs at the institution, which is a branch of the general counsel's operations.

TABLE 7.4
Vignettes Demonstrating the Intersections Between Educational Development and S-LCE

Vignette 1	Josiah is an associate professor of history and educational developer in the Center for Faculty Innovation at James Madison University, He has met several times with Norah, a biology faculty member whose desire to incorporate a community-based component aligns not only with her course outcomes but also with her professional goals to bridge the study of ecology with community needs. While Josiah understands and can communicate the basic premises associated with service-learning, he is unskilled in the logistics and nuances of campus-community partnership-building. Both Josiah and Norah want to ensure the course—and its full design—meet the community's goals as well as the learning objectives of the course.
Vignette 2	Andrea is a faculty member in the Institute for Environmental Sustainability, teaching a capstone course that is also a service-learning course. She is seeking potential community partners with whom to work and working on how to build community-oriented projects into her service-learning course by having students work in groups on projects with environmental agencies and present their projects to the agencies at the end. After receiving advice from the Faculty Center of Ignatian Pedagogy regarding general pedagogical strategies, she now needs to seek support from the Center for Experiential Learning around specific service-learning course design, critical reflection assignments, and service-learning outcomes for the capstone project.
Vignette 3	Cameron is a new computer science faculty member at Northeastern University in Boston with a history of utilizing service-learning. She notices that while service-learning is mentioned during the faculty orientation (which is put on by the Center for Advancing Teaching and Learning through Research), she is not clear on the specific next steps she should take. At the institution where she served as a teaching faculty member while pursuing her doctorate, she was on her own in incorporating service into her course and setting up partnerships. She is new to the Boston area and does not yet have any connections in the community and is also unsure if the university has any resources to help make these connections.

For Cameron, with the knowledge that more emerging and new faculty are showing interest in S-LCE, and therefore this should be featured during orientation, a more proactive partnership between the teaching and learning center and the S-LCE office on campus may have prevented her confusion. If such a partnership already exists, but simply was not displayed effectively during new faculty orientation, Cameron may be able to find the appropriate channels for her inquiries by asking the facilitating staff, who will then point her to the right contact and/or to shared work around S-LCE (e.g., upcoming workshops, fellows opportunities, etc.). For Josiah, Andrea, and Cameron, these new collaborative channels may lead to developing nascent or untapped faculty development and S-LCE skills of their own or could even evolve into a new role supporting faculty who want to incorporate S-LCE (e.g., in a mentoring program or faculty learning community). In all three cases, a more consistent and intentional partnership between the two offices would create clear pathways for faculty and enhance educational development efforts in the S-LCE arena.

All of this said, simply building partnership to help ourselves and others navigate the tricky waters of this work is not enough. Because both educational developers and S-LCE professionals are migrants and navigators within the landscape of higher education, it is essential to build a common understanding of one another's distinct and shared work, and to set parameters of interaction with the multiple ways that faculty may come into one or the other's distinct orbit. Just as S-LCE professionals often find themselves "backing into" educational development, so might the educational developer "back into" S-LCE work. The bottom line is that for a campus to have a successful and thriving service-learning and community engagement portfolio, faculty must be involved, and to accomplish that, all of these professionals need to be working together with common language and toward common goals.

Shared Pathways and Partnerships

In chapter 9, Stephanie T. Stokamer discusses faculty development as it sits at the intersection of institutional characteristics, priorities, and culture (see Table 9.1 for the considerations in each). Not surprisingly, it is often the tensions, rather than the synergies, between these considerations that shape faculty pathways to S-LCE work, as well as the partnership focus areas in the institutional context. This provides a helpful lens through which to view much of what is contained in this book, keeping in mind that what you see forged at different colleges and universities has also been shaped by its own set of unique tensions and synergies. Additionally, location and community culture surrounding service and the relationship of the university to its surrounding communities also shape and influence the work of S-LCE, as she aptly points out. Building on these ideas, chapter 12 (written by Richard Kiely and Kathleen Sexsmith) discusses innovative considerations in faculty development and S-LCE. In doing so, the authors articulate an integrative and transformative model in consideration of the dynamics we have discussed in this chapter. They invite both educational developers and S-LCE professionals to engage in "critical reflection on their own assumptions about what constitutes robust S-LCE theory and practice in (a) teaching and learning, (b) institutional support and change, (c) knowledge generation and application, and (d) community partnerships and capacity building" (p. 283. this volume). As both chapters 9 and 12 point out, the changing context of higher education and the national landscape within which it exists are increasing the need to provide evidence of S-LCE's power to both improve learning *and* to engage and transform our communities. As such, the models and suggestions Stokamer as well as Kiely and Sexsmith highlight are essential to building a bridge between educational development and S-LCE professionals as well as achieving the civic aims of higher education.

Additionally, chapters 8, 10, and 11 offer important insights into the various dimensions of the roles that educational development and S-LCE professionals occupy. Chapter 8, by Chirag Variawa, is written from the perspective of a faculty member who has never served in either of the professional roles highlighted in this book. He discusses both how he has made meaning of the variety of educational development opportunities in which he has participated but also specifically how he has applied those ideas to teaching with S-LCE in a multitude of contexts and with an eye toward special considerations involving inclusion, class size, and delivery format. Gabriel Ignacio Barreneche, Micki Meyer, and Scott Gross discuss the importance of community partnership, monitoring, and assessment for sustainability and reciprocity in chapter 10. They acknowledge the sometimes nebulous nature of work with faculty incorporating S-LCE into their teaching, stating:

> Ideally, community members and community-based organizations are involved in the development of educational experiences, processes, and assessment of learning rooted in the unique and pressing priorities of the community. Although curricular goals and processes are developed, actual outcomes are often unknown due to the shifting conditions, assets, and needs of the community. (p. 242, this volume)

In chapter 11, Sherril B. Gelmon and Catherine M. Jordan expand on some of the ideas presented by Timothy K. Eatman in chapter 2 around faculty commitments to scholarship. They do this by providing an in-depth overview of community-engaged scholarship, as well as its relationship to the scholarship of teaching and learning and to the scholarship of engagement. Through chapters 8 through 12 in this book, it is our hope that both educational developers and S-LCE professionals gain a common understanding of their overlapping and distinct work and, using this, how to support S-LCE faculty more holistically.

Conclusion: Where Do We Begin?

In this chapter, we have presented information about educational development and S-LCE professionals and hope that we have made a compelling case for partnership and shared understanding. We have also emphasized the importance of institutional context—if one thing is clear, fostering S-LCE with faculty requires a great deal of creativity, patience, and relationship-building. That said, we also encourage readers to explore ways to bring educational development and S-LCE professionals together not only with one another but also with faculty. In addition to what you may be able to provide on your campuses, there are many resources and institutes to look into nationally and internationally.

One of the most important organizations in educational development is the Professional and Organizational Development (POD) Network in Higher Education, which hosts many professional development opportunities, helps provide access to resources, and holds an annual conference. In S-LCE, the International Association for Research on Service-Learning and Community Engagement (IARSLCE) serves as an organizing space for exchange and dialogue among people engaged in research on service-learning and community engagement broadly. As the authors of this chapter and part of the coediting team of this book, we encourage educational developers and S-LCE professionals alike to step out of their world and reach across to the other by attending a meeting, conference, or even coattending with your colleagues in other areas of your institution and/or the faculty with whom you work. In addition to these and other important organizations in these niche fields of higher education, the Association of American Colleges & Universities (AAC&U) hosts many network meetings and conferences that focus on faculty, educational, and/or organizational development and civic learning. Participation in these and other professional meetings not only creates new pathways for faculty and professionals to sharpen their skills and gain new insights but also allows for powerful cross-institutional partnerships to form.

Are partnership and shared understanding innovative? In the structural context of higher education institutions, it may be. Bass (2012) challenges higher education institutions to apply concepts of disruptive innovation "asserting one key source of disruption in higher education is coming not from the outside but from our own practices" (p. 24). He calls for us to expand our conception of teaching and learning, specifically from the lens of innovation in instructional support, suggesting a team-based design. How can this team-based approach be applied to educational developers and S-LCE professionals?

As S-LCE professionals and educational developers, we as coauthors draw from our own experiences collaborating with partners across our own institutions. One of our greatest resources at our respective institutions are faculty and staff partners, near and far across campus, who hold knowledge, resources, skills, experiences, and values that may contribute to our shared educational goals. Knowing that such partnerships have strengthened the breadth and depth of our work, through increased programming, broader outreach, and developing networks, we pose the following critical questions to readers to reflect on their own roles as creating disruptive innovation:

- Considering S-LCE professionals and educational developers, with whom do you currently work? How might these partnerships be strengthened?
- With which campus partners do you seek to work? Where is there a natural intersection between your shared work in the academy?
- Where can the common goal of enhancing teaching and learning for increased student success be leveraged with other campus partners?
- What challenges or barriers are inhibiting you from fostering relationships with campus partners to develop common educational goals?
- How can you transcend challenges or barriers in order to initiate mutually beneficial partnerships between S-LCE professionals and educational developers?

By developing partnerships between S-LCE professionals and educational developers on campus, we make more explicit the shared goals of enhancing teaching and learning in order to build educational experiences that support student access, retention, and matriculation toward degree completion.

In partnership, the educational developer and S-LCE professional have the potential to leverage their combined role as culture-creators, advocators, and change-makers to move closer to the intended disruptive innovation (Bass, 2012). Their combined effort may be strengthened when employed in tandem, thus facilitating the very changes needed in higher education. As Bass (2012) concludes, our emphasis on teaching and learning must be connected, meaning both integrated and networked. When S-LCE professionals and educational developers create such a nexus, teaching and learning has the potential to be transformed.

References

Albright, M. J. (1988). Cooperation among campus agencies involved in instructional improvement. In E. C. Wadsworth, L. Hilsen, & M. Shea (Eds.), *Professional and organizational development in higher education: A handbook for new practitioners* (pp. 3–8). Stillwater, OK: New Forums Press.

Ash, S., & Clayton, P. (2009, Fall). Generating, deepening, and documenting learning: The power of critical reflection in applied learning. *Journal of Applied Learning in Higher Education, 1*, 25–48.

Bass, R. (2012, March/April). Disrupting ourselves: The problem of learning in higher education. *EducauseReview, 47*(2), 22–33.

Bergquist, W. H., & Pawlak, K. (2008). *Engaging the six cultures of the academy*. San Francisco, CA: Jossey-Bass.

Bergquist, W. H., & Phillips, S. R. (1975). Components of an effective faculty development program. *Journal of Higher Education, 46*(2), 177–215.

Bringle, R. G., & Hatcher, J. A. (1996). Implementing service-learning in higher education. *Journal of Higher Education, 67*(2), 221–239.

Dostilio, L. D. (2017). Planning a path forward: Identifying the knowledge, skills, and dispositions of second-generation community engagement professionals. In L. D. Dostilio (Ed.), *The community engagement professional in higher education: A competency model for an emerging field* (pp. 27-55). Boston, MA: Campus Compact.

Dostilio, L. D., & Perry, L. G. (2017). An explanation of the community engagement professionals as professionals and leaders. In L. D. Dostilio (Ed.), *The community engagement professional in higher education: A competency model for an emerging field* (pp. 1–26). Boston, MA: Campus Compact.

Eble, K. E., & McKeachie, W. J. (1985). *Improving undergraduate education through faculty development: An analysis of effective programs and practices*. San Francisco, CA: Jossey-Bass.

Gaff, J. G. (1975). *Toward faculty renewal: Advances in faculty, instructional, and organizational development*. San Francisco, CA: Jossey-Bass.

Green, D. A., & Little, D. (2012). Betwixt and between: Academic developers in the margins. *International Journal for Higher Education, 17*(3), 203–215. doi:10.1080/1360144X.2012.700895

Green, D. A., & Little, D. (2013). Academic development on the margins. *Studies in Higher Education, 38*(4), 523–537. doi:10.1080/03075079.2011.583640

Hanleybrown, F., Kania, J., & Kramer, M. (2012, January 26). Channeling change: Making collective impact work. *Stanford Social Innovation Review*. Retrieved from https://ssir.org/articles/entry/channeling_change_making_collective_impact_work

Howard, J. (1993). Community service learning in the curriculum. In J. Howard (Ed.), *Praxis I: A faculty casebook on community service learning* (pp. 3–12). Ann Arbor, MI: OCSL Press.

Jacoby, B. (2009). *Civic engagement in higher education: Concepts and practices.* San Francisco, CA: Jossey-Bass.

Kendall, J. C. (1990). *Combining service and learning: A resource book for community and public service* (Vols. 1 & 2). Raleigh, NC: National Society for Internships and Experiential Education.

National Task Force on Civic Learning and Democratic Engagement. (2010). *A crucible moment: College learning and democracy's future.* Washington DC: Association of American Colleges & Universities.

POD Network. (2016). *The 2016 POD Network membership survey: Past, present, and future.* Retrieved from https://sites.google.com/a/podnetwork.org/wikipodia/pod-sponsored-surveys

Sorcinelli, M. D., Austin, A. E., Eddy, P. L., & Beach, A. L. (2006). *Creating the future of faculty development: Learning from the past, understanding the present.* Bolton, MA: Anker.

Stanton, T. K., Giles, D. E., & Cruz, N. L. (1999). *Service-learning: A movement's pioneers reflect on its origins, practice, and future.* San Francisco, CA: Jossey-Bass.

Welch, M., & Saltmarsh, J. (2013). Current practice and infrastructures for campus centers of community engagement. *Journal of Higher Education Outreach and Engagement, 17*(4), 25–55.

PART THREE

CHALLENGES AND OPPORTUNITIES IN PEDAGOGY AND PARTNERSHIPS

8

SPECIAL PEDAGOGICAL CONSIDERATIONS

Designing Learning in Service-Learning and Community Engagement

Chirag Variawa

This chapter is framed from my perspective as an engineering faculty member learning about and applying service-learning and community engagement (S-LCE) in undergraduate and graduate classrooms with a diverse set of stakeholders. A unique aspect of this discussion is that the first iteration of this instructional approach was implemented at a medium-sized private university in the United States, whereas another iteration was at a large public university in Canada. More specifically, the breadth of perspectives that I came across in using S-LCE across these institutions—concentrating on core engineering design courses—affords an invitation into the insights I have gleaned from my unique vantage point and how I have employed them in my teaching and implementation of S-LCE in these special contexts.

In addition to being an undergraduate student who participated in an S-LCE engineering design experience, I have taught iterations of a large-enrollment S-LCE course as a graduate student teaching assistant (TA) and, more recently, as a faculty member across institutions using S-LCE as a teaching and learning model. This chapter focuses on my unique perspective and the instructional models employed in designing a large-enrollment S-LCE course. Thus, this chapter reflects a faculty perspective pieced together from the literature and implemented in these contexts. In essence, this chapter is a self-study of my teaching and learning practices in the context of S-LCE, with attention to the special pedagogical considerations I have learned to navigate along the way.

This chapter begins with an investigation into the design of the teaching and learning experience in an S-LCE context. I start with a framework for identifying and systematically organizing the pieces of an S-LCE experience, with the goal of creating an inclusive, accessible learning environment for all participants. Then, this chapter engages with the literature about course design, providing an overview of some of the variations used in existing learning experiences. Following this, I introduce several instructional design frameworks I have employed, including universal instructional design (UID), as a set of principles that have guided my course design and delivery. Finally, I discuss the case study of a large first-year engineering design course with a substantial S-LCE component, focusing on its design, challenges, and evolution in the context of the changing needs of the S-LCE environment and the ever-changing landscape of higher education.

Design of the Learning Environment

Early in my university education, I recall having mixed emotions when it came to engaging in teamwork and working collaboratively to learn new material, but I quickly discovered that these were core components for succeeding in S-LCE courses. Like many of our students today, graduating from high school with top grades meant that my identity was linked to scholastic achievement, much of which was based on doing well on tests and exams. Though our students today are often well connected technologically, learning might still be considered an independent interaction between students and the course material, facilitated by an instructor.

As a student entering the field of engineering, many of my courses were principle-based, which meant that the instructor would explain a concept in class, provide resources to scaffold a problem-solving exercise, and evaluate the performance of the responses. This is largely a traditional approach to learning that does not engage much with the community outside of the classroom. This approach is considered a safe bet, often low-stakes, and may have a rather predictable result because the system is limited to the community within the classroom, carefully curated by the instructor. In contrast, today's students live, work, and play in a highly connected world, in which mobile devices and the Internet are core components of their daily operations and checking notifications are part and parcel of daily life. Leveraging this technology-oriented "community presence" is a part of every classroom, whether we, as instructors, acknowledge it or not. Through technology, students are engaging with the outside world, or the community, whether we acknowledge that or engage it purposefully in instruction. However, the teamwork and collaborative nature of solving problems in class might not be as intrinsic to all student learning behaviors, even with so many of them being interconnected. Thus, scaffolding these experiences for them involves careful design of the learning environment.

As a graduate student TA in the early 2000s, I taught a large first-year engineering design and communication course with an S-LCE component just as access to the Internet on mobile devices was becoming more common. In this experience, I saw firsthand that some students gravitated toward using collaborative tools (e.g., Google Docs) and that this was an organic process not originally planned by the instructional team. The litany of other tools to help engage the learning population in engineering problem-solving were also foreign to the teaching and learning environment, some of which were not planned a priori by the instructional team. The challenge with this is that some of these tools may be inappropriate for student use in a given context, and not yet having developed mastery of course concepts, students may not know which tools to use, or how to use them effectively. More broadly, some of the tools better scaffolded into instruction were successful in S-LCE contexts—a lot of that success is attributed to instructors being flexible enough to encourage broad-based thinking, but also constructing the S-LCE learning environment so that it encourages intentional and effective use of learning tools.

In my experience, teaching and learning in S-LCE contexts requires an understanding that multiple stakeholders' interests add layers of complexity not otherwise seen in traditional instructor-to-student classroom lecturing. The shared learning experience comes from interactions among instructors, students, the broader community, and their inherent connections to the course learning outcomes, situational factors, pedagogical approaches, and assessment instruments. Specifically, some of these interactions are outside the locus of control of instructors, and as such, there may be special pedagogical considerations to be aware of, and to design for, when mapping out the course of instruction in S-LCE contexts.

In the case of non-S-LCE learning environments, instructors might be able to carefully curate the learning experience, as they may have a great degree of control over situational factors present in their courses. For example, if everyone in the class is working from the same case study, then there may be less variability in the classroom. In a way, the instructor creates a *high-control* dynamic, because the experiences that the students will have in that environment are modeled in a system that is largely predictable by the instructor. S-LCE, however, is a learning environment in which the instructor may have to forfeit some of this control to balance authenticity of the learning experience, resulting in a *low-control* dynamic. For example, some students may focus their attention on a specific aspect of the service-learning to a greater extent than others, leading to an authentic yet different learning experience from student to student. Appreciating the literature in teaching and learning frameworks, and then designing the S-LCE learning environment, can help build flexibility into the classroom, thus building the motivation for our discussion about S-LCE as a special pedagogical approach.

The construct of *learning environment design* is one where the parameters and expectations of the learning can be approximated, with the understanding that students may have an incongruent set of educational experiences by the end of the course and that this is part of the design (Bransford & National Research Council, 2000). This means that there are several variables whose values are unknown and often changing, and these may impact the learning experiences for those involved. Designing the learning environment enables us to identify some of these variables and then build some flexibility into educational experiences by appreciating the connections among concepts, stakeholders, and their interests.

Engineering the Design of a Learning Environment

My perspective as an engineering instructor lends to my experience designing a learning environment, in that I examine inputs and outputs inherent in designing a product, device, or process. This perspective affords a unique vantage point where we can understand how to systematically optimize a teaching and learning experience. Understanding the context, framing the challenges present, and using a combination of divergent and convergent strategies to solve these challenges are the basis of engineering design thinking. Perhaps the immediate riposte is that learning environments have a humanistic component integral to their function and efficacy toward inclusion. Also, the criticism is that engineers may favor mechanistic, logical, and rational views of the world and try to make sense of it via quantification. By extension, it might seem that these schools of thought are orthogonal to one another. However, contemporary engineering approaches place significant emphasis on human factors in design—wherein the system adapts to the user instead of the other way around—in turn, informing our perspectives on designing the learning environment systematically by understanding the relationships of the user and their environment and the characteristics of the connections between inputs and outputs.

As an engineer, I tend to favor a worldview that attempts to understand functions, objectives, constraints, service environments, and resources available in any given context. This thought process may be roughly translated across disciplines as faculty implement S-LCE within their courses. For example, an instructor may use this worldview to determine what the goals of the learning experience are, how they will be met, by what metrics success will be measured, and so on. Anecdotally, understanding that an airplane will carry a specific mass from one location to another in potentially adverse weather conditions (not knowing what they are at a particular place or time) affords the engineer an opportunity to design a better airplane overall, one that can be better aligned with expectations. By extension, if we know what our student learning outcomes are, we can potentially use an engineering worldview to make sense of how those expectations will be met generally.

In designing first-year undergraduate engineering courses with large team-based S-LCE components, my engineering-based steps were to clearly define the objectives of the learning experience, how the processes of learning would be facilitated in the context of S-LCE (and perhaps the uniqueness that S-LCE brings that a traditional learning experience cannot), and the parameters and resources present. In other words, the design was scaffolded to reflect and articulate the context and intended outcomes. Institutionally, this would involve meeting with stakeholders and clarifying the expectations of the learning experience; this meant that I met with the department chair, the support staff, and also both incoming and graduating students to ascertain their insights. Many of these were then translated into metrics used to determine the success of the learning experience.

Once we have an appropriate understanding of the problems we are going to solve and the metrics by which a successful solution can be measured, it is important to appreciate the relationships between inputs and outputs required so that the solutions use resources wisely. Much like an engineering design process, an informed and systematic strategy can begin to arrange features in a way that leads learners toward expected outcomes, while designing out unintended features that may send students off course. Institutionally, this can mean arranging course topics based on related criteria, having regular teaching-team meetings, polling students for their mastery of course concepts, being aware of student workload generally, and so on. The emphasis here is that educators intentionally design the learning experience for the students without being acutely involved in all aspects of that teaching and learning exchange. The analogy here is as follows: Engineers are designing the vehicle, but the driver and passengers are the students operating that vehicle from start to finish, whichever path they take to get there. Accounting for breakdowns along the way (e.g., briefing student support services before test grades are released), the design of the learning environment accounts for variations in path; speed; complexity; and, for some, irrationality that may become apparent due to taking a more scenic route along the way.

Approaches to Modeling Learning Processes

There are several factors to consider when employing a personalized approach to the creation of an S-LCE experience. Although knowing one's students very well enables an instructor to carefully guide the students on their learning journey, it is only feasible in environments that have a commensurate amount of resources to do so. That is, small class sizes are great candidates, as instructors can get to know their students on a deeper level; by this, the instructor may understand the strengths and weaknesses of each student, mentoring or coaching in ways leading to success in the S-LCE experience. In a small class—where *small* is a relative term depending on the course, institution, and other influences—this individualized instruction can be systematic in designing individual learning plans that map out interests, motivations, goals, and ways each student will work toward achieving those goals (Chen, 2009; Grohnert, Beausaert, & Segers, 2014). The lens used here would be to clearly delineate the individual biases and trajectories of learning toward the development of competency, while being aware of the blind spots and learning barriers of each student (Fenwick, 2008). Although this approach can work well for smaller class sizes and instances where resources are easily accessible, it is much more difficult to employ individualized learning approaches in large classes—another special consideration of teaching and learning in the context of S-LCE.

Large classes can be excellent contexts to use S-LCE pedagogy, even though at face value doing so may seem daunting. There is a spectrum of approaches. On one end is the instructor's ability to employ more individually focused approaches (the left side of Figure 8.1) that are generally better suited to small class sizes and provide opportunities for more personalized instruction and individual student attention by the instructor. The other end of this spectrum (the right side of Figure 8.1) has a less individualized

Figure 8.1. Individualized approach versus a systemic approach to student learning.

approach, possibly due to large class sizes. In large classes, initiating and sustaining high-quality S-LCE experiences requires just as much thought and curation as the smaller classes, perhaps even more, with the understanding that each unique student requires some degree of affordance that is spread evenly across all learners and learning styles in the class. Larger classes, however, need not be any less effective in using S-LCE as a pedagogical approach; this is later demonstrated in my case study of successful S-LCE implementations in a large class.

An advantage of using S-LCE in large classes is that there is a possibility of having many more projects, and more diversity in those projects, in turn leading to a richer learning experience for those involved. This is especially true if this breadth of S-LCE learning experience is shared among project-based teams. In doing so, students can begin to see how their own unique approaches to S-LCE map to the approaches of others, who may or may not have similar S-LCE projects, and begin to understand that, though we live in a complex world, approaches to solving S-LCE projects can be abstractly similar and lead to higher-quality learning experiences overall.

To achieve these higher-quality learning experiences, no matter the class size, the emphasis here is to enable and foster communication among S-LCE project teams and to encourage the students in that experience to share their learning strategies, and in turn their competencies, with one another. Though this can be done in small class sizes, the breadth of information gathered through a large-scale S-LCE experience builds on the individual depth gained by each team in the class. As such, though employing S-LCE in a large class may seem intimidating, the payoff is that when students in that large class share their learning experiences with their peers, they can begin to see that different projects do not necessarily mean a completely different learning experience. This can be especially useful when a learning objective of the course is to apply multidisciplinary approaches to problem-solving—like using both narrative and 3D modeling to represent a physical device—as it cuts across traditional assumptions of competency.

The literature within the scholarship of teaching and learning (SoTL) describes several approaches to designing learning experiences for diverse learners. These approaches systematically organize the instructional design experience into manageable, meaningful steps. One model used in information science and engineering is called ADDIE (analyze, design, develop, implement, and evaluate) (Reinbold, 2013). Applying its principles to S-LCE in the classroom, the structured sequential operation of its phases provides the instructor with a way to lay out the pieces of an S-LCE experience and detangle seemingly conflicting aspects in steps. In a STEM (science, technology, engineering, and math) classroom, this is largely symmetrical to a design process where an instructor would identify and understand a problematic aspect of a learning environment, suggest a reasoned approach for characterizing and solving it, develop the protocol for the solution, implement an intervention, and then measure its success. One example might include understanding why students are not accessing the course website. The instructor may *analyze* trends over time, *design* high-value aspects that would encourage participation, *develop* one (or more) of them into a valuable resource aligned with student learning outcomes, *implement* by uploading the content to the website, and then *evaluate* whether that resulted in any change to website usage.

As such, the ADDIE model can help an instructor trace the thinking around problem-solving in order to better understand and support students as they progress toward the solution. In a large-class environment, structured sequential problem-solving with ADDIE can help groups of students stay on task and also enhance awareness of when they are rushing ahead or falling behind. For example, this approach can inform the design and internalization of phases of problem-solving, where student teams articulate milestones in their learning and check with their instructor before the subsequent phases begins. This can be effectively employed in large-enrollment classes because the students know when to continue and when they ought to check in with their instructors, and instructors can modulate the advancement of a project, especially if insufficient progress has been made in any particular phase.

Backward design is a design model that focuses on the outcome and develops strategies based on meeting that outcome (Reynolds & Kearns, 2017). It has three stages: desired results, assessment evidence, and the learning plan. These stages are, essentially, seen as being performed backward—articulating what the end goal looks like and then working backward from that end goal. In an S-LCE classroom, I have used this approach extensively to clearly articulate to my students what the learning outcomes are. This encourages students to keep the end goals in mind, especially because my final exams are based largely on mastery of course concepts (based in turn on those learning outcomes). Thus I can work "backward" with student teams as they come to understand the S-LCE experience as an environment in which learning outcomes are met. For example, one of my learning outcomes states, "By the end of this course, students will be able to apply basic calculus to model their designs." By highlighting this before students actually engage with the S-LCE experience, they know that mathematics will be a lens by which they can articulate the problem. One of the next steps that students might do for a physical design is to identify change in position over time and use calculus to predict overall displacement (and thus make their product robust enough to withstand a specific distance traveled).

By extension, backward design can be used in an S-LCE context to prime student learning toward specific learning outcomes, so that they know what will be assessed at the end of the course.

The Dick and Carey model (Dick, 1996) is a reductionist strategy used to assess a large problem in smaller, and potentially more manageable, pieces. In other words, it breaks down the instruction into small components. This model focuses more on designing lessons and is objective driven. As applied to the design of learning environments for S-LCE, it enables instructors to create small but impactful learning moments for students as they progress through an S-LCE experience. For students, this could mean a more manageable frame of reference from which to work. For community partners, it could mean a more focused environment to guide student learning. For the instructor, it could mean assessments are aligned with specific student learning. For instance, if students are presented with a large, complex, complicated S-LCE context like "reduce tailpipe emissions from a car," the Dick and Carey model would suggest further refinement into separate aspects: "What is a tailpipe?"; "What are emissions?"; "Why are emissions produced?"; and so on. Each of these smaller, more focused tasks can be investigated piecewise and then added together to respond to the initial design problem.

The Dick and Carey model can enable groups of students to move forward when they may be stuck at a particular point, as it scaffolds an orientation rather than a phase of getting things done. For example, if the learning environment comprises students from very diverse backgrounds and/or competencies, the Dick and Carey model can help an instructor encourage the students to align their thoughts to agree on common elements, such as the development of objectives and an assessment of constraints. These significant learning experiences support alignment within diverse student teams on common issues and testing mechanisms, and this, in turn, can potentially lead to teams forming more inclusively and progressing more smoothly.

Keller's (1987) ARCS (attention, relevance, confidence, satisfaction) model focuses on motivating learners. Used in the context of S-LCE, this can suggest that the instructor selects S-LCE contexts where students are motivated by the authenticity and complexity of the problem(s) being solved. In my experience, I have found it difficult to generate equal levels of interest in S-LCE experiences because some students are fundamentally more motivated than others in S-LCE tasks. A misalignment of motivation among team members in an S-LCE project can lead to teams becoming dysfunctional and eventually falling apart. ARCS, therefore, offers insight on how to compartmentalize aspects of motivation and better understand team dynamics in the classroom.

As an example, instructors may find certain teams not working well and mistakenly attribute this to general motivation, whereas a more educated perspective can isolate the issue to a lack of confidence in getting the job done. Moreover, some of these issues can be addressed by additional resources (e.g., increasing technical competency or becoming cognizant of other challenges that the students may have). In my first-year course, for example, some student teams decided that they were no longer going to work together due to differences related to work ethic; it became clear after speaking with them using the ARCS lens that some of these students just did not possess the confidence in their technical ability to get the job done. Shortly thereafter, the TA assigned to supplement technical education in a specific area supported the team, which became functional again. In similar cases, using the ARCS model, an S-LCE instructor can potentially better understand how teams operate to help design a more inclusive learning environment.

Having situational awareness of the designed learning environment can also help an instructor align inputs, expected outcomes, and actual outcomes. Using this lens, one can begin to use an optimization perspective to investigate and influence how these factors might affect the learning environment. This is akin to a flow problem, or logic-mapping problem, or stress-strain relationship in engineering, where inputs are transformed into outputs, which are then analyzed in the context of expected outcomes. This is in contrast to a prescriptive approach, where all steps are meticulously planned out in advance. In my experience, being flexible yet organized highlights two very important features to consider before teaching using S-LCE, as we will see later again in this chapter.

Course Design as a Framework for Small-Scale and Large-Scale S-LCE Classrooms

The literature on frameworks for course design in higher education offers a wealth of perspectives on increasing the quality of education for students (Chun & Evans, 2016; Roessger, 2012). Though some of this literature is domain specific (Bozorgmehr, Saint, & Tinnemann, 2011), some models cut across disciplines and pedagogical approaches quite well—with some very conducive to the context of S-LCE as the authentic environment for teaching and learning (Ahmed & Palermo, 2010; Clark & Wallace, 2015).

Though the discussion of frameworks on instructional design is not the focus of this chapter, it is a very important consideration in the design of learning environments and useful in creating a systemic lens for S-LCE approaches. Let us begin by thinking of a learning environment where all our learners are unique, special, and have as their common denominator the fact that they are students in one particular class. The students in that class are expected to have some degree of similarity in their prior education; perhaps they all converse in the same language or have passed the same qualifying assessment to be there in the first place. Each learner, however, has traversed a unique path to enroll in that class. With those differences, how are we, as instructors, able to create a learning environment that caters to all of them? Furthermore, what biases or assumptions do these students have about their learning experience, whether these are S-LCE-based or not? How do these biases and assumptions influence their learning?

Some approaches to creating teaching and learning experiences require an acute and deep familiarity with all students in that learning environment. This may be because the class sizes are small enough that an instructor can be very familiar with each individual student's learning style, level of academic competency, and so on, as illustrated on the left side of Figure 8.1. In this environment, it may be possible to curate an individualized learning program for each member of the class so that every student can learn the material in the most appropriate individual manner. Furthermore, knowing each student well leads to enhancing individual learning in a unique and customized way. There are learning frameworks, some of which are rooted in personalized mentoring, that capitalize on the deep individualized knowledge of students, and this can, in turn, be used to craft S-LCE experiences that are truly designed for each student (Bornsheuer-Boswell, 2014; Muschallik & Pull, 2016).

Universal instructional design (UID) is a framework that has as its core the notion that instructional experiences should be designed to be accessible for all populations (Higbee, 2009; Rush & Schmitz, 2009; Samuels-Peretz & Powers, 2014). This is a holistic rather than an individualized approach to teaching in any class environment, but it is particularly well suited for large-scale S-LCE implementations. Specifically, it suggests that objectives should be described for all students in ways that are clear and understandable. It also suggests multimodal instruction and design that can apply to all learning styles regardless of preference. In particular, UID is a strategy that aims to increase access to information in a way that takes into account the diversities of all learners generally while eliminating barriers that may prevent learners from accessing the knowledge and/or instructional material (Ouellett, 2004). In the context of S-LCE instruction, UID can be used to state clear objectives that are applicable to all teams of students—clarifying the expectations for a learning experience while being flexible enough to account for variations in approach used to satisfy those expectations.

The multimodal approach to teaching and learning here can be applied to communication between and among teams of students, making the connections and learning process more transparent and accessible, potentially leading to higher-quality reflective learning experiences. Furthermore, UID suggests that although there are diverse learners in any classroom, S-LCE—engaged or not—increases accessibility to course material, with systemically designed course experiences leading to higher-quality learning experiences for all (Campbell, 2004). This may be due to the fact that UID-inspired course design approaches take into account learning barriers that students may not see for themselves but which leave them out of the learning experience.

As an example, students in a large-scale S-LCE course may not appreciate that they need supplementary instruction on technical communication—but because that is available to them anyway, whether they think they need it or not, such instruction is accessible to them to use. As more and more students begin to use, with curiosity, the resources available to them, they may begin to see the value of supplementary instruction, incorporating that into their learning in the classroom (Mino, 2004). In a large-class environment, this not only increases the quality of learning for those who know they need extended resources but also extends this capacity to those students who do not know they need the resources. Specifically, designing instruction using a UID approach enables students in large-scale S-LCE-based courses to have access to resources, potentially leading to higher-quality teaching and learning as they detect and mitigate learning barriers they may not have known about otherwise. Table 8.1 shows some of the foundational elements of UID and how they can be translated into a learning environment; though Table 8.1 is presented generally, it can be applied to creating a systemic approach to increasing accessibility to all learners, including those in S-LCE-based settings.

Case Study of an S-LCE-Based Course Design and Students in First-Year Engineering

A large first-year engineering course at the University of Toronto provides a case study in which S-LCE was implemented successfully to teach the basics of engineering design, teamwork, and communication. This course, Engineering Strategies and Practice (ESP), was designed for an annual student enrollment of 800 to 1,200 students and a thrice-weekly common lecture in a large auditorium. The class is split into separate tutorial sections of approximately 40 students each, meeting once a week.

The precursors to ESP were a number of engineering design and English writing courses, each with different instructors, all using a traditional, or non-S-LCE, approach to teaching and learning. These courses were independently administered and were variable in student learning experiences. In an attempt to scaffold the development of an engineering identity for

TABLE 8.1
The Seven Principles of Universal Instructional Design and an Example of Its Application in a Learning Environment

UID Principle	Example of Application
Accessible and equitable	Course documents available 24/7 from a website
Flexibility in use—multimodal	Course materials viewable online as well as in print
Intuitive to use	Reduction of excessive instructions on software set-up
Perceptible information—transparency	Schedule of instructions in syllabus
Supportive environment—tolerance for minor error	Due dates with reasonable late policy instead of "nonacceptance"
Low physical effort	Ease of access to learning materials
Physical accessibility—appropriate learning space	Safe learning space

first-year students, ESP was created to blend together significant learning experiences intrinsic to learning the fundamental applications of engineering in society. Instructors across applied science and engineering, and from outside this group of faculty, came together to systematically design the S-LCE experiences that now form the foundation of the largest engineering course in Canada.

ESP is a two-part course—ESP-I offered in September and ESP-II offered in January—that builds on the lecture material presented in class in carefully curated S-LCE learning experiences. ESP-I teaches students the basics of engineering design, teamwork, communication, and the social impact of engineering decisions. The lecture material focuses on theoretical fundamentals, and the tutorials reinforce these concepts by placing students in teams of five to seven individuals and giving all teams the same problem to work on throughout the term. Because all student teams in the large class work on the same problem, the lecture can focus on mapping the theory to practice in a controlled way. The UID approach employed involves a very clear scaffolding of learning across the project-based experience common to all students. This forms the foundation that the students build upon as they transition to ESP-II, the large-scale exemplar in systematically using S-LCE.

ESP-II assigns each of the 800 to 1,200 first-year engineering design students into teams of 5 to 7 students and apportions them a real, authentic, community-based client design problem. Teams are made pseudo-randomly, preferentially assigning students who have similar schedules. There are over 150 projects per term, each carefully curated by course staff. Though this may seem quite challenging, it is particularly noteworthy that the course has developed a reputation at the University of Toronto and the surrounding community over time whereby students can offer engineering expertise for free, with students learning through this process. Each of the student design teams then meet with their S-LCE client and apply the theory learned in the weekly lectures to each unique S-LCE project. The design teams work with the clients to understand the issues present and then determine ways to mitigate those issues, afterward formally drafting and presenting a plan of action whereby that S-LCE project is resolved.

Each of the student engineering design teams has at least three scaffolded interactions with their community client. Prior to the first meeting, the instructor calls and asks the client to submit a one-page description of the engineering problem. These can range from large projects like crafting a strategy to inform public school students about community issues to smaller-scale problems, like designing a front porch, addressing a physical learning disability, or redesigning a senior's home. Once clients submit their proposals, they are reviewed by a member of the teaching team for overall difficulty and verified for consistency as compared to the other projects that term.

Starting with this initial information, the students then work with their tutorial TA to perform a preliminary audience analysis of their client and their values and biases prior to crafting their first internal task of creating a telephone plan. This task brings student teams together to organize their thoughts about client interaction and project description. The objective here is to introduce the design team to the client and set up a date, time, and location for the first meeting. Once the initial phone call is made, the student teams write an interview plan, which includes an opening strategy, several open-ended and closed-ended questions, and some commentary on next steps. This plan is shared with their tutorial TA, who verifies that there is no objectionable content planned, and the students are free to meet with the community client at their discretion. The objective of this first meeting is to better understand the problem(s) the clients are facing from as many perspectives as possible in an authentic, genuine context. In my experience, it is at this point that many of students learn about professionalism and, for the first time, are able to see the potential impact of their design decisions in a societal context. This learning moment is incredible for those involved, as the students begin to grasp the importance of what they are doing. On the other side, many clients enjoy the enthusiasm of the first-year students. The course teaching team is the conduit between abstract and real learning experiences.

There is also some excitement from community partners as they are often eager to meet these students in person and to get the project underway.

Anecdotes suggest that students come prepared to the initial meetings with engineering notebooks and a variety of open- and closed-ended questions. Some students decide to wear business attire, and the student groups often meet separately before the meetings to go over a final meeting plan. Some students are nervous, but the authenticity of the S-LCE experience encourages them to see the interaction as a real-world preparatory experience and this often serves to strengthen students' resolve to do well. Furthermore, as an instructor, I often hear the preparatory conversations our students have, and I am struck by how aligned those conversations are to the course learning outcomes—one of which is to apply professional communication principles in engineer-client meetings.

After the first in-person meeting between the students and their community client, each design team carefully develops a report about their comprehensive understanding of the problem(s), functions, objectives, constraints involved, and the stakeholders affected, proposing at least five approaches to potentially solve or address the problem(s). This report is then the subject of the second in-person meeting between the client and the student team, at which students inform the client of the different approaches and get a sense of what the client may want to see implemented. It is very important, however, that each engineering design team knows that making the client happy is not necessarily going to earn them a good grade. It is by following a systematic design process, informed by the suggestions of the client, that a critically established design decision will be reached. In some cases, the client may suggest alternative solutions, but it is the student team's responsibility to comprehensively reason all possible approaches instead of blindly following what the client wants. The underlying thinking here is that the client may be off base in logic or assumptions, and it is the engineers' responsibility to take into account all possible outcomes while diplomatically working with clients to incorporate their viewpoints and input.

Once the student teams have a sense of direction, they then carefully produce a final design specification, and some teams even design hands-on prototypes using 3D modeling. This then informs the final client report and presentation, both of which are delivered to the client at the end of the term. The final presentation is when all first-year students deliver a formal, professional study on the issues faced, the approaches used, and the suggested implementation of a design solution. All of this occurs in the presence of both the client and the course teaching team, and often many of the designs are ultimately implemented.

The reflection component of this course includes an engineering notebook, which gives an accurate log of the meeting minutes, noting conversations, decisions, sketches, and other communications that occur throughout the course. This is supplemented with a student-written narrative on lessons learned from the S-LCE experience. In all, this very large-scale implementation of an S-LCE experience scaffolds each first-year engineering student's understanding of the real social implications of engineering design decisions and the importance of teamwork in generating relevant, useful outcomes.

The instructional team of ESP-I and ESP-II uses a carefully designed UID-focused approach to ensure that all students have access to the instructional material. They upload videos of all lectures to a course website, clearly state all deliverables and expectations, benchmark assessments regularly, and check in with the rest of the instructional team throughout. The systemic lens used here is to have all students leave the course with an increased awareness of, and competency for, applying engineering fundamentals in the real world and using the systematic design of the course as a scaffold for their own problem-solving approach with the client/team exchange. Every year, each student design team not only learns the fundamentals of engineering but also practices that understanding in authentic contexts using a holistic and accessible approach to teaching and learning.

Conclusion: Designing Learning With Multiple Frameworks

The ESP courses described use S-LCE in a collaborative, rigorous learning environment in a highly team-directed context. The instructional team works very carefully to articulate the design process used in developing the course, identifying the inputs and intended outputs while concentrating on objectives, functions, constraints, and the service environment, trying to optimize each facet along the way. With such a large class and limited resources, it is important to best understand the variables involved in such an undertaking. We have learned from experience that excellent organization and still remaining somewhat flexible to incongruencies in student learning are key parts to a successful S-LCE experience. As a result of our own reflections, we have seen that the learning frameworks and theories identified are not used in isolation, but rather simultaneously. Specifically, we experienced using the ADDIE and ARCS models to categorize learning material and view them from perspectives of supporting student motivation and community engagement, all while optimizing the learning material holistically using the framework of universal instructional design.

Overall, S-LCE experiences benefit from the use of frameworks as organizational tools to scaffold and guide the teaching and learning experience.

For example, they help categorize the many variables that will undoubtedly affect student learning while also informing ways ahead when difficulties emerge. They also assist in mapping the learning process for those involved, so that novice learners can engage even the most complex problems successfully. Though our current work uses only a sample of these organizational aids, they were useful agents in increasing transparency in the learning outcomes that were sought; it is clear that they were valuable and constructive in creating well-received S-LCE experiences.

As we look forward to future iterations of S-LCE in the core curriculum, we anticipate a better understanding of the relationships between our students and their communities, especially with respect to incoming biases and assumptions. By using a variety of frameworks and investigating if and how they intersect, we can survey the impact of S-LCE experiences more comprehensively. Via structured investigation, for example, we may be able to explore relationships between student workload and mental health and how we can identify and optimize learning materials across disciplinary barriers. The effect of these investigations can strengthen the existing frameworks for our S-LCE experiences and better inform teaching and learning for more diverse audiences.

In general, S-LCE has shown to be an excellent pedagogical tool for authentic, rigorous instruction. Though distinct from traditional methods of in-class lecturing, with careful planning and openness to flexibility, we have seen that S-LCE can certainly be used to create a pragmatic learning experience for all involved. With the goal of increasing access to education, S-LCE also has the effect of bringing our learning communities together in ways not commonly seen. With the broader society now an integral part of the learning process, S-LCE can increase value, inclusivity, and access to education for many people—including members of the community.

References

Ahmed, S. M., & Palermo, A. G. S. (2010). Community engagement in research: Frameworks for education and peer review. *American Journal of Public Health, 100*(8), 1380–1387.

Bornsheuer-Boswell, J. N. (2014). Editor's overview—Mentoring in higher education: The keys to success. *Mentoring and Tutoring, 22*(1), 1–3.

Bozorgmehr, K., Saint, V. A., & Tinnemann, P. (2011). The global health education framework: A conceptual guide for monitoring, evaluation and practice. *Globalization and Health, 7*(1), 8.

Bransford, J., & National Research Council. (2000). *How people learn: Brain, mind, experience, and school.* Washington DC: National Academy Press.

Campbell, D. M. (2004). Assistive technology and universal instructional design: A postsecondary perspective. *Equity & Excellence in Education, 37*(2), 167–173.

Chen, C. M. (2009). Ontology-based concept map for planning a personalised learning path. *British Journal of Educational Technology, 40*(6), 1028–1058.

Chun, E., & Evans, A. (2016). Rethinking cultural competence in higher education: An ecological framework for student development. *ASHE Higher Education Report, 42*(4), 7–162.

Clark, S. G., & Wallace, R. L. (2015). Integration and interdisciplinarity: Concepts, frameworks, and education. *Policy Sciences, 48*(2), 233–255.

Dick, W. (1996). The Dick and Carey model: Will it survive the decade? *Educational Technology Research and Development, 44*(3), 55–63.

Fenwick, T. (2008). Understanding relations of individual–collective learning in work: A review of research. *Management Learning, 39*(3), 227–243.

Grohnert, T., Beausaert, S., & Segers, M. (2014). Pitfalls of personal development plans—The user perspective. *Journal of Vocational Education & Training, 66*(1), 74–88.

Higbee, J. L. (2009). Implementing universal instructional design in postsecondary courses and curricula. *Journal of College Teaching and Learning, 6*(8), 65.

Keller, J. M. (1987). Development and use of the ARCS model of instructional design. *Journal of Instructional Development, 10*(3), 2–10.

Mino, J. J. (2004). Planning for inclusion: Using universal instructional design to create a learner-centered community college classroom. *Equity & Excellence in Education, 37*(2), 154–160.

Muschallik, J., & Pull, K. (2016). Mentoring in higher education: Does it enhance mentees' research productivity? *Education Economics, 24*(2), 210–223.

Ouellett, M. L. (2004). Faculty development and universal instructional design. *Equity & Excellence in Education, 37*(2), 135–144.

Reinbold, S. (2013). Using the ADDIE model in designing library instruction. *Medical Reference Services Quarterly, 32*(3), 244–256.

Reynolds, H. L., & Kearns, K. D. (2017). A planning tool for incorporating backward design, active learning, and authentic assessment in the college classroom. *College Teaching, 65*(1), 17–27.

Roessger, K. M. (2012). Toward an interdisciplinary perspective: A review of adult learning frameworks and theoretical models of motor learning. *Adult Education Quarterly, 62*(4), 371–392.

Rush, D. K., & Schmitz, S. J. (2009). Universal instructional design: Engaging the whole class. *Widener Law Journal, 19*, 183.

Samuels-Peretz, D., & Powers, J. (2014). Documentation and Universal Instructional Design: A partnership supporting diverse learners in higher education. *The New Educator, 10*(1), 35–43.

9

THE INTERSECTION OF INSTITUTIONAL CONTEXTS AND FACULTY DEVELOPMENT IN SERVICE-LEARNING AND COMMUNITY ENGAGEMENT

Stephanie T. Stokamer

Faculty development unfolds at the intersection of institutional characteristics, priorities, and culture, each of which shapes and constrains faculty development and compels service-learning and community engagement (S-LCE) professionals to align their efforts with their particular situation in order to maximize their effectiveness (see Table 9.1). Institutional characteristics can be understood as basic, relatively fixed descriptors, such as size, type, and location. Institutional priorities include new initiatives, strategic programs, and curricular emphases, whereas institutional culture encompasses elements such as campus climate and leadership.

As an S-LCE professional, I have had the challenge and opportunity to create a faculty development program for community engagement that reflects the nuances of my institution, Pacific University. This chapter will explore the institutional contexts of faculty development, using Pacific University as an example for analysis. A closer examination of the Pacific University case reveals the ways in which our approach reflects our institutional context, and how we in turn can shape the *characteristics, priorities,* and *culture* that define our campus and approaches to faculty development.

TABLE 9.1
Overview of Institutional Context for S-LCE Faculty Development

Element of Institutional Context	Considerations for Faculty Development
Institutional Characteristics	• Carnegie Classification • Mission • Location
Institutional Priorities	• Strategic plan • High-impact practices • Initiatives and commitments • Curricular emphases
Institutional Cultures	• Campus climate and faculty morale • Tenure and promotion practices • Student body • Leadership

The Pacific University Case

The Pacific University approach to faculty development illustrates many aspects of institutional characteristics, priorities, and culture. Describing our community engagement program in greater detail thus sets the stage for unpacking our work in light of our institutional context. Located in the suburban town of Forest Grove, Oregon, Pacific University enrolls about 3,500 students and has a near 50/50 split between undergraduate and graduate programs. The undergraduate program consists primarily of a residential liberal arts experience in the College of Arts and Sciences (CAS).

Pacific University Institutional Priorities

In 2009, the CAS faculty approved a major curriculum revision that included a new academic civic engagement requirement, deemed the Civic Engagement (CE) Cornerstone, for the bachelor degree. With that requirement, the Center for Civic Engagement (CCE) was formed. In 2011, I was hired as the new director of the CCE and tasked with implementing and supporting curricular and cocurricular civic engagement. The CCE is housed in and primarily supports CAS, though we also support some university-wide functions, such as data collection and reporting. Pacific University now offers over 50 courses in 25 disciplines with a CE designation in CAS, a more than 250% increase in the number of CE classes since 2011. Furthermore, the CCE has earned significant internal credibility among faculty, students, and the administration for its work with faculty and the community, and the CE Cornerstone is now well established, though still a work in progress.

The initial language describing the CE Cornerstone stipulated that CE courses adhere to criteria articulated by a subcommittee of faculty who were already including civic engagement in their courses and were the champions of the new requirement. Differences of opinion among them led to a rather broad catalog statement:

> Civic Engagement (CE) Requirement: Complete a Pacific CE-designated course (2 or more credits) or project. . . . Students who complete the CE Cornerstone requirement will engage in civic engagement projects that:
> - serve the common good
> - involve students in experiential learning outside the classroom and the teaching lab
> - engage students with the campus community or the broader world
> - include appropriate orientation, preparation for the project, and opportunity for thoughtful reflection
> - are shared with the campus community through appropriate means devised in consultation with the Center for Civic Engagement. (Pacific University, 2017, p. 39)

Faculty seeking the CE designation submit a proposal to the CCE explaining how a course would meet each of these criteria, which is then reviewed by a faculty committee.

Though the original designation proposal form asked faculty to describe their intended work with community partners, the CE Cornerstone requirement was driven by internal curricular reform without extensive consideration for community partners or the effects our requirement might have on them. From the lens of best practices in community engagement, this approach was less than ideal. As so often happens in academia, the gaze was inward; immediate pressures and supports for the S-LCE staff reinforced prioritizing an increase in the number of CE courses so that students had available courses to fulfill their requirement. The S-LCE staff encouraged faculty to consider a range of options for civic engagement, including both campus-based and community-engaged experiences such as service, advocacy, awareness-raising, political and electoral activity, research, and activism. As a result, the broad understanding of civic engagement that was useful for encouraging growth was at the same time somewhat vague and not deliberately collaborative with our community.

Pacific University Institutional Characteristics

Over time, there was such variation in CE courses that it became difficult to explain clearly to students, faculty, and community partners what we really meant by civic engagement and, significantly, why some proposed projects seemed outside the spirit of civic engagement whereas so many others were not. For example, one student proposed doing a fundraiser for the owners of a local pub that had been destroyed by fire. Another student wanted to volunteer at her church's after-school program, and a community partner needed students to staff a reception desk. These all seemed like pleasant, prosocial activities, but were they civic engagement? Better articulating what civic engagement means to us at Pacific University was essential to clarifying what counts for the requirement.

Therefore, to clarify and focus our work, the S-LCE staff, working in conjunction with an advisory council of students, faculty, staff, alumni, and community partners, led the creation of the Principles of Quality Academic Civic Engagement at Pacific University (PQACE). These principles are specific to our context, though they may have broader applicability in the field: (a) relevant problem-solving, (b) public interest, (c) meaningful learning opportunities, (d) depth of experience, (e) reciprocity, (f) respectful collaboration, (g) academic integration, (h) reflection on experience, (i) appropriate assessment, and (j) public citizenship. The complete PQACE document includes a detailed explanation and examples for each principle to provide the most useful guidance for all of our stakeholders in what to aim for in their engagement (see Table 9.2).

The PQACE is firmly rooted in the S-LCE literature, best practices, and personal experience. I constructed the first draft of the PQACE, drawing extensively from the S-LCE literature, my experience at other institutions (e.g., Portland State University), and the perpetual conversation within the S-LCE scholarly community around what we mean by *service-learning*, *community-based learning*, *civic engagement*, and similar related terms within the S-LCE field. Through relationships, I cultivated the trust of both faculty and community partners to inform the PQACE and develop a shared understanding that we needed a clear articulation of our work, such that gaining buy-in was not a significant challenge.

Indeed, the role of multiple stakeholders in denoting our principles is noteworthy, as it has led to a stronger foundation for collaborative civic engagement. For example, given the importance of reflection for experiential learning (Dewey, 1938), its appearance among our principles is not surprising. A community partner, however, made a revision encouraging the inclusion of community partners in reflection activities in our explanation of that principle. Once established, the principles immediately became the foundation for multiple civic engagement efforts, such as our student leadership program, our assessment plan, and faculty development. They have also been the basis for sometimes difficult conversations with faculty about whether

TABLE 9.2
Principles of Quality Academic Civic Engagement at Pacific University

Principle 1: Relevant Problem-Solving

- CE projects address a significant social or environmental issue in the community (e.g., education, pollution, immigrant rights, etc.) through actions that can make a difference on those issues.
  - Direct and indirect service
  - Advocacy
  - Activism and nonviolent protest
  - Awareness-raising
  - Action-oriented research
  - Electoral or political involvement
- CE goes beyond being nice to others or pursuing interests that are enjoyable to oneself or others to focus on addressing and ameliorating particular problems.
- When CE projects focus on public problem-solving, students can better see the contribution they are making and are better able to articulate that contribution in terms of specific academic issues or concepts.

Principle 2: Public Interest

- CE projects work for the public interest, not private gain, leading to more just and equitable societies and a more sustainable world.
- Students work with individuals, groups, and organizations, connecting specific tasks being undertaken to social or environmental issues that affect a larger population.
- The CCE does not support civic engagement activities that inhibit social, economic, or environmental sustainability.

Principle 3: Meaningful Learning Opportunities

- The CE experience should offer deep learning potential; the nature of the work performed should be intellectually stimulating (and often involves emotional stimulation as well).
- While mundane tasks are sometimes necessary to support a particular cause, they should be combined with other kinds of tasks in order to have a high-quality CE experience.
- Student learning is facilitated by an intensity in which students experience something new to them, something about which they are particularly passionate, and/or something that presents a real challenge.

Principle 4: Depth of Experience

- CE projects should be in-depth enough for students to learn from the experience and make an authentic contribution.
- Though measuring hours is not necessarily the best way to indicate substance, it is an indication of depth of experience.

(Continues)

TABLE 9.2 *(Continued)*

• CE projects that culminate in some sort of event for which practice or preparation is necessary (e.g., a performance), also need to include enough actual engagement with the community that students can learn more about the problems or issues they are addressing to count for CE credit.
Principle 5: Reciprocity
• CE projects should be mutually beneficial for students and community partners or campus organizations. • CE projects should address community needs and problems, whether that community is on campus or off. • Whereas many CE projects involve observation, students should also be taking action in some way that is useful to others or works toward some kind of change.
Principle 6: Respectful Collaboration
• CE projects should entail respectful collaboration with campus or community organizations. • Partners should benefit from CE efforts, and faculty should work with partners in advance (when possible) to cocreate CE activities and learning objectives, plan supervision, agree upon necessary training or orientation, and determine guidelines for incidents such as absence, tardiness, or rule violations that can disrupt partner operations. • Supervising CE students can take a considerable amount of time and effort invested on the part of campus and community organizations for CE students; therefore, CE faculty and students should be mindful of their actions and effects on partners.
Principle 7: Academic Integration
• CE should have clear and direct integration with academic concepts such that it is woven into the curriculum through readings, assignments, class activities, and assessment techniques that connect that CE experience to the academic content of the course. • CE should not be an "add-on" to a course that lacks connection to other course activities. • With effective academic integration, students are adequately prepared for the CE experience, understand its context in their learning, and are equipped with the knowledge needed to embark on their civic engagement work.
Principle 8: Reflection on Experience
• The process through which students learn from experience is reflection. Reflection takes many forms, but it is an academic exercise guided by faculty and not merely a log of time spent.

(Continues)

TABLE 9.2 *(Continued)*

- High-quality reflection is structured, occurs regularly (e.g., before, during, and after the CE experience), challenges students to apply the CE experience to other course concepts, and includes feedback and assessment.
- Reflection should be rigorous, analytical, creative, and/or emotional, and may also be the basis for additional class activities such as discussion.
- When possible, community partners should also be included in the reflection to strengthen and deepen the experience for everyone.

Principle 9: Appropriate Assessment

- CE projects should be assessed in a way suitable to their design.
- As part of academic integration, the CE experience can be assessed in numerous ways, including written analyses, essays, oral presentations, and contributions to class dialogue.
- Community partners should have an opportunity to provide regular feedback on projects or services provided by individual students and whole classes.

Principle 10: Public Citizenship

- CE is a public process of working to create change, though sometimes the details of that work are private (e.g., how one votes in an election).
- CE projects should be shared with the campus and/or community to provide inspiration, information, and documentation.
- Isolated and invisible efforts are not likely to garner the collective energy that is needed for large scale, systemic change, whereas public displays of civic engagement can inspire others to take action and/or demonstrate how to get involved.

their courses adhere to the principles, though my experience to date is that faculty want to provide a high-quality civic engagement component and the PQACE have prompted useful reflection and iterative teaching rather than pushback.

The PQACE have now been used to ground a variety of faculty development techniques. The flagship program is a minigrant tied to a full-day workshop. With the PQACE woven throughout, the workshop has five main segments: Civic Engagement Theories and Models, Best Practices in Experiential Learning, Selecting and Working With Campus and Community Partners, Facilitating Student Learning From Civic Engagement, and Assessing and Sharing Civic Engagement. In the absence of a center for teaching and learning at Pacific University, the workshop is designed to model and explain effective pedagogical practices in general (e.g., utilizing multiple learning modalities) and specific to civic engagement (e.g., reflection on experience). Recognizing the impossible feat of a thorough faculty development activity in a single day, the workshop is intended to give participants sufficient confidence to continue in community-engaged teaching, especially with our additional supports of one-on-one meetings and a community of practice. Other examples are featured throughout this edited volume in various case studies, as well as specific faculty development activities. Other faculty development activities offered by the CCE include a scholarly reading group and an iterative teaching roundtable (in which faculty reflect on recent courses and prepare for the next semester), both of which are now organized with the PQACE in mind. Indeed, both the PQACE and the faculty development program that has cohered around them emerged from, reflect, and contribute to a particular institutional context marked by characteristics, priorities, and culture.

Institutional Characteristics

Any approach to faculty development for community engagement is likely to be formulated in light of the basic characteristics of an institution. Characteristics such as structure, mission, and location are relatively fixed, though sometimes do change over time, and they provide the basic structure for operations. Other institutional characteristics that could affect faculty development for community engagement include its status as public or private and whether it has a specialized focus, such as being faith-based or minority-serving. Combined, all of these characteristics provide the skeleton that shapes faculty development for community engagement.

Perhaps the most fundamental description of an institution is its structure as indicated by the Carnegie Classification of Institutions of Higher Education. As a way of delineating the kinds of degrees offered and emphasis on research or other areas of specialization, the Carnegie Classification provides a broad view of how community engagement might be construed at a particular institution and therefore some possible considerations for faculty development. For example, Moore and Ward (2010) described the challenges that faculty at research-intensive institutions continue to face in adopting community engagement pedagogies when their contexts so strongly emphasize disciplinary research. They suggested that one area for faculty development could be to help faculty at such campuses envision community engagement aligned with, rather than separate from and in addition to, their scholarly agenda. In contrast, Prins (2002) suggested that because many community colleges emphasize workforce training, faculty development in that environment might be most successful if it highlights the connections between community-engaged learning and career preparation. However, Jeandron and Robinson (2010) also noted that in a time of shrinking budgets, community colleges may need to be creative in seeking opportunities other than conferences for faculty development, such as web-based training and in-house workshops. The case study chapters in this volume feature examples of such opportunities. Moreover, institutions across the spectrum of degree types have achieved the Carnegie Classification for Community Engagement and can serve as exemplars for others with similar structures (New England Resource Center for Higher Education, 2016).

Classified under "Master's Colleges & Universities: Larger Programs" in the Carnegie system, Pacific University has two dominant strands—a residential undergraduate liberal arts college and several nonresidential graduate professional colleges. The latter embed community engagement into their programs through practicum, field experience, and clinical components of the curriculum, but operate relatively autonomously. The CCE primarily serves faculty in the undergraduate liberal arts strand, in which the teaching role is preeminent in the CE Cornerstone part of the core curriculum. As a result of this bifurcation among colleges, faculty development for community engagement offered through the CCE tends to focus on undergraduate teaching. Though research is not as highly prized as at some institutions, a subset of faculty have integrated community engagement into their scholarly work, and the CCE has provided consultation and support when they do. Although action-oriented community-engaged research falls under the civic engagement umbrella, a research-intensive institution might have given it more emphasis than we did in the PQACE.

An institution's mission complements its structure and provides direction that can bolster faculty development efforts. Although the usefulness of a mission statement is debatable, as skeptics may believe that it is meaningless or has largely symbolic value, it can be a powerful tool that drives a deliberate and comprehensive approach to implementation of initiatives and a sense of shared purpose among constituents (Morphew & Hartley, 2006). S-LCE professionals can help faculty connect their work to the institution's mission, thereby highlighting the relevance of community engagement. At Pacific University, our program has benefited from a new mission, adopted in 2012, which includes language of inspiring students "to think, care, create, and pursue justice in our world" (Pacific University, 2017). Civic engagement clearly aligns with that intention, so we are able to encourage faculty to see their efforts as operationalizing our mission.

Another basic institutional characteristic is location. Whether a campus is situated in an urban, suburban, rural, or small town location, and the related variant of a predominantly residential or commuting student body, might influence the content or logistics of a faculty development program. For example, at an urban postsecondary school such as Portland State University, 64% of students are from the Portland metropolitan area (Portland State

University, 2017). S-LCE programs could help faculty localize content or understand the pedagogical implications of students already connected to their communities through earlier educational or civic activities, or bring to light reasons why some may be already disillusioned by negative experiences that have perhaps led to distrust of local government or fellow citizens.

Indeed, a place-conscious approach recognizes the localized nature of community engagement (e.g., the history and civic culture of particular communities) and the pedagogical challenge of appropriate design for engagement in specific civic contexts. Portland, for instance, is widely known as a city with thriving civic engagement, active neighborhood networks, and a large nonprofit sector, in a state with progressive electoral processes that have garnered consistently high voter turnout. With spillover of that civic culture into suburban Forest Grove, Pacific University S-LCE programs do not need to focus as much on the fundamental necessity of civic engagement as perhaps would be warranted at an institution located in a less participatory region. As both part of a larger community and a community unto itself, any college or university is likely influenced by the civic culture surrounding and within it, suggesting that S-LCE professionals attend to the environment in which they are working—which affects faculty, students, and community partners alike—and help faculty do the same.

Faculty development might also take into consideration whether faculty largely live near the institution or commute, which could influence their connection to and understanding of that locale.

Pacific University is in a suburban location, close to the edge of the urban growth boundary of the Portland metropolitan area. As such, it is surrounded by farmland and rural communities though itself situated in Forest Grove, a small town with its own identity, local government, and a few nonprofit organizations. The location is relevant to our work in a few ways, one being that because many partners are outside of our immediate town or even 30 miles away in Portland, faculty development must include how to handle logistical hurdles such as transportation and travel expenses. In addition, because many faculty commute to campus from some distance, they may not know the history, economic forces, and social experiences that have contributed to the challenges facing Forest Grove or have connection to the community assets or potential partners in place for addressing them. For this reason, our faculty development program has included networking opportunities with community partners so that faculty have a chance to learn more about what is already happening in the community and meet representatives from organizations with whom they may find some common interest. This approach also facilitates the principle of respectful collaboration by strengthening the relationships that make a web of community engagement. Furthermore, fleshing out the priorities that give life to the skeleton of structure, mission, and location allows community engagement professionals to more deeply align their faculty development efforts with the direction in which an institution is going.

Institutional Priorities

Successful faculty development is tuned in not only to the basic characteristics of an institution but also to the priorities that enliven it. In 2004, Furco and Holland pointed out that "service-learning is . . . an *integrative strategy* that addresses multiple objectives and brings together a number of disparate units, structures, and programs on campus" (p. 25). S-LCE professionals can garner support for their work by positioning faculty development as part of such an integrative strategy in line with the institution's priorities. Such priorities are often articulated through a strategic plan, propelled by ideals such as equitable educational achievement, diversity, and sustainability, all reflected in the curriculum.

Strategic plans can offer the impetus for institutional support of faculty development efforts, particularly if community engagement is explicitly addressed or implicitly included in focus areas such as experiential or applied learning, career development, pedagogical innovation, and so on. In their examination of factors that can help service-learning endure, Vogel, Seifer, and Gelmon (2010) identified "strategic activities" (p. 60), or those efforts that align service-learning with strategic planning and other institutional initiatives, as key to longevity. Indeed, whether necessary in order to obtain support or not, clearly connecting faculty development efforts to a strategic plan may help legitimize community engagement at institutions where it is still marginalized or curry favor with administrators who are pleased to see their vision implemented.

Pacific University undertook a strategic planning process in 2012–2013, and as the director of the CCE, I was invited to join the college's steering committee. A seat at that table helped elevate our work, and aspects of community engagement appear throughout our college's plan, such as in sections related to integrated and applied learning, well-being, and sustainable practices. At institutions without a strong tie to S-LCE in the strategic plan, professionals may need to translate how their efforts relate in order to gain support, such as framing service-learning in terms of academic excellence.

Indeed, given that institutions generally strive for both financial stability and strong programming (with or without a strategic plan), they may prioritize those practices that are known to facilitate student engagement and college completion. With support from the Association of American Colleges

& Universities (AAC&U), Kuh (2008) reported on the "high-impact" (p. 9) educational strategies that foster student success in higher education. With substantial research indicating their benefit to students in terms of student engagement and educational persistence, these high-impact practices include first-year seminars; common intellectual experiences; learning communities; writing-intensive courses; collaborative assignments; undergraduate research; diversity and global learning; internships; capstone projects; and, of course, community-based learning. Kuh provided a number of reasons for the positive outcomes associated with these practices, such as the deep and active learning they require; the involvement with faculty and diverse peers they engender; and the opportunities for regular feedback, applied learning, and personal transformation that they afford. Perhaps most promising about these practices is that they seem to have compensatory effects for students who have been underserved by the education system, and thus their utilization could be invaluable to educational equity and student achievement.

However, Kuh (2008) emphasized that high-quality implementation is essential to the effectiveness of these practices, thereby suggesting a strong link to faculty development. This point influenced our adoption at Pacific University of principles for *quality* civic engagement and programs designed to help faculty work toward excellence in community-engaged teaching. In addition, the Kuh report encourages colleges to utilize at least two high-impact practices, either in combination or progression, and recognizes their overlapping and intersecting elements. His work thus suggests another strategy for faculty development: focusing on best practices and why they work, alone and in combination, to boost student success. At Pacific University, for example, we have conducted presentations at a retreat for faculty teaching first-year seminar courses. Likewise, S-LCE professionals could create a faculty fellows program such as the one at the University of Massachusetts Amherst, which is designed to help faculty develop service-learning courses (University of Massachusetts Amherst, 2017). Those courses in turn meet the requirements for their Certificate in Civic Engagement and Public Service, which includes substantial service-learning coursework and a capstone project that could involve a practicum or research, thereby incorporating several of Kuh's high-impact practices.

Other common priorities could be embedded in a strategic plan or intertwined with high-impact practices. If, for example, a focus on sustainability has been energizing campus stakeholders, then applying that enthusiasm to community engagement may attract new audiences. At Pacific University, a newly established Center for a Sustainable Society has facilitated collaborative support of student involvement in action-oriented projects (e.g., advocating for a plastic bag ban in Forest Grove), public participation (e.g., serving on the city's Sustainability Commission), cocurricular programs (e.g., Give & Go, our annual move-out program that both reduces waste and donates goods from students to local organizations), and CE courses (e.g., Food for Thought and Action). Other S-LCE professionals may be able to partner with an office of sustainability on campus to host a joint workshop in which faculty receive support related to what can be a challenging concern. In a similar vein, the Netter Center for Community Partnerships at the University of Pennsylvania and its signature program of university-assisted community schools has both grown out of and influenced an institutional commitment to the revitalization of its surrounding neighborhood (University of Pennsylvania Netter Center for Community Partnerships, 2012).

Furthermore, institutional priorities are reflected in the curriculum, and the extent to which community engagement pervades academic programming points to both the strategy and content of faculty development. Young, Shinnar, Ackerman, Carruthers, and Young (2007) suggested that "academic legitimacy" (p. 360) is necessary for service-learning to be institutionalized, and faculty development can help create and confirm such legitimacy. If community engagement has become embedded in the core curriculum or in a critical mass of majors, minors, or other academic programs, then faculty development can focus on quality enhancement and refining existing courses, partnerships, and other processes and structures. If, however, community engagement exists only on the periphery of the curriculum, faculty development may need to focus more on foundations and attempt to tap into faculty motivations to promote participation. We have found that our PQACE (especially meaningful learning opportunities, academic integration, and appropriate assessment) have served to reinforce the academic legitimacy of our community engagement work. For example, as cofacilitators of a faculty workshop about learning objectives, S-LCE staff were able to not only highlight the importance of learning objectives crafted to incorporate community engagement for existing CE Cornerstone faculty but also talk about community engagement in a way that emphasized academic rigor in front of a larger audience, which perhaps added to its legitimacy on our campus. Still, neither understanding an institution's priorities nor its basic features is complete without examining its heart and soul—institutional culture.

Institutional Culture

Regardless of what is written in college catalogs or websites, intangible aspects of campus life also affect what works in faculty development. Vogel and colleagues (2010) identified a supportive institutional culture as one factor influencing long-term sustainability of service-learning, such as a sense of purpose to serve community, faith-driven service, or a strong connection to place. Moreover, administrators, students, and faculty together may influence and be influenced by incidents or trends that affect the campus environment.

One example is the campus climate around diversity, equity, and inclusion. Simmering issues related to different groups on campus, or a history of tension between the student population and community population, for example, could affect community-campus collaboration. The CCE at Pacific University has been an active partner with campus colleagues working on social justice issues, cohosting multiple programs aimed at students and faculty, as well as, to a lesser extent, community partners. One strategy that has worked for us is to collaborate with faculty who are experts in topics such as critical race theory on efforts, such as a jointly held session about addressing microaggressions in the classroom during a campus-based faculty conference. Although the session was not specific to faculty teaching CE courses, our work together allowed me to draw on my colleague's expertise to help faculty in attendance understand what the challenging pedagogical situation of a racially charged comment could look like in CE courses and how to handle it.

Furthermore, S-LCE professionals who are able to be nimble in their operations could make use of critical incidents to offer faculty development opportunities relevant to the current moment in time, such as considering community engagement in light of a natural disaster near campus, an election, or a controversial speaker. Recently, for instance, our S-LCE staff conducted a faculty conversation about facilitating class discussions inclusive of and engaging with diverse political perspectives. Likewise, factors such as faculty culture, student culture, and campus leadership can dramatically affect the tenor of campus pursuits and therefore faculty development.

Faculty culture shapes faculty work beyond the actual job description. Though potentially including such norms as acceptable attire or meeting decorum, more significant issues related to faculty development are enthusiasm for engagement, morale, and promotion and tenure policies. Vogel and colleagues (2010) noted that the existence of faculty champions and a "critical mass" of support among faculty, students, and administrators are correlated with durability in service-learning programs. In contrast, faculty turnover and disinterest in community engagement could pose significant challenges to institutionalization (Prins, 2002; Vogel et al., 2010). Faculty development may require strong incentives to overcome low morale due to issues such as resentment about workload or resistance to curricular innovation. If faculty are disinterested, S-LCE professionals may need to start with a campaign to pique interest, perhaps including guest scholars from varying disciplines, partners who can share opportunities to work together, or students who present how their academic path has been affected by community engagement.

Furthermore, faculty development programs that entail creating a community of practice may be a fruitful antidote to a negative campus climate—as faculty begin to hear more about each other's community work, they can become collectively energized as champions who might otherwise have been isolated. Morale at Pacific University seems to rise and fall with the waves of various activities, announcements, and decisions, but the community of practice we have sought to create is a largely positive and productive environment in which faculty encourage each other and discuss issues specific to civic engagement courses and programs. Our experience suggests that community engagement work, so often energizing for those who undertake it, can bring together disparate faculty in ways that overcome poor morale.

In addition, because our CE requirement was the outcome of faculty-driven curricular reform, it has not met the same kind of resistance that top-down decisions sometimes do. In fact, our S-LCE staff have sought to cultivate some sense of pride in our work through awards, newsletter features, and other forms of recognition so that faculty can see the CE Cornerstone as a successful component of our core curriculum. Although not everyone is an enthusiastic supporter, the combination of faculty empowerment, flexibility, and support provided by the CCE have facilitated the general acceptance of this new academic endeavor, in turn leading to further advances as new hires see opportunities for integrating civic engagement into their work and are now often asked about their interest in civic engagement during the search process.

Of course, faculty morale could also be influenced by promotion and tenure policies and practices. Tenure-track faculty must balance the roles of teaching, research, and service. O'Meara (2005) noted the importance of tenure and promotion policies in how faculty prioritize and report their work. Though many institutions have adopted Boyer's (1990) guidance to acknowledge, value, and reward the scholarship of engagement, institutions vary in how or whether they recognize the engaged scholarship of community-based learning and the relative significance of promotion and tenure with respect to adoption of community engagement practices (Abes, Jackson, & Jones, 2002; Kezar & Rhoads, 2001; O'Meara, 2002, 2005). The possibility remains that tenure and promotion policies could influence the time or motivation faculty have for community engagement. S-LCE professionals may therefore target personnel processes for faculty development, working with faculty to use community engagement to their advantage and advocating for better understanding among those who evaluate faculty portfolios.

Our S-LCE staff are willing contributors to faculty review processes. We write letters in support of faculty promotion, explain our principles to encourage quality, speak to the community-engaged scholarship of faculty, or discuss their participation in our faculty development programs, such as the course development minigrant. We could be more proactive, however, in assessing how community engagement has been a help or hindrance in promotion and tenure processes, and adjusting our faculty development programming accordingly.

Likewise, student culture may also suggest appropriate strategies for faculty development. Some institutions have long traditions of student activism or community service, or a highly engaged subset of students (perhaps affiliated with S-LCE offices or programs). Such exemplars can become part of faculty development efforts as well. For instance, a panel of students could share their community engagement experiences at a faculty workshop. In contrast, at schools in which the student body tends to be more apathetic or focused on other activities, faculty development efforts may need to include strategies for sparking student interest in community engagement. The CCE at Pacific University oversees both curricular and cocurricular civic engagement, and as such can develop programs that complement each other in this way. Though the student body is not best characterized as activist, students do engage with community groups in numerous ways—through athletics, Greek organizations, clubs, community service work-study, and more. The CCE student leadership program also serves a faculty development function as participants go to classes as ambassadors of the CCE, talking with students and their professors about our center, community engagement, logistics, and so on.

Overarching both student and faculty culture is leadership-level support for community engagement. Administrators can be tremendous champions for community engagement. Langseth, Plater, and Dillon (2004) argued that the chief academic officer has a powerful leadership role to play, being the person who often "carries the burden of defining the parameters and importance of service-learning for the institution through advocacy, resource allocation, and intentionality in making service-learning an institutional priority" (p. 3). High-level administrators lending their power and influence to advocate and support service-learning is one factor in program success (O'Meara, Lounder, & Hodges, 2013; Vogel et al., 2010). For S-LCE professionals, such administrators may be a great help in securing resources to support faculty development programs, but they could also be partners in the work, serving, for example, as keynote speakers at faculty development workshops or joining national efforts such as Campus Compact or the Democracy Commitment— both established by college presidents—which offer professional development opportunities relevant to community engagement (Campus Compact,

2017; The Democracy Commitment, 2017). Community engagement at Pacific University has the support, though not deep involvement, of administrators, at least in part as a result of the variety of faculty development programs we offer.

Implications of Institutional Intersections for S-LCE Professionals

Paying attention to the institutional context of community engagement matters because S-LCE professionals are institutional agents who both act on behalf of their colleges and can proactively construct them. The institution's characteristics, priorities, and culture therefore have implications for the ways in which S-LCE professionals exert their own power and lead an institution toward high-impact community engagement through faculty development. This institutional impact will be further explored through a theory of change and framework presented in chapter 12. In attending to institutional context, S-LCE professionals may be able to calculate where their influence can be most efficiently and effectively applied to shift their organizations toward more effective community engagement, and wherein they must adapt their own actions to that context as it is.

All campuses are at least somewhat fluid due to inevitable personnel turnover and inherent movement of the student body through college. In that regard, S-LCE professionals may be able to further their faculty development aims by attending to how institutions change and help bring to bear those mechanisms over which they have some degree of influence. By participating proactively in assessment and accreditation processes, for example, S-LCE professionals can prompt administrators to properly structure or resource their priorities. They may not be able to change the Carnegie Classification for an institution, but they could lead an institutional self-study to determine whether to pursue the Community Engagement elective category. Likewise, although the culture of engagement around campus can be powerful, it is also something that S-LCE professionals are both a part of and can influence. A positive and supportive leader may be able to boost faculty morale with respect to a community engagement initiative, for example, if not larger institutional issues. Moreover, S-LCE professionals can lead by example in using equity as a guiding principle or by ensuring that community engagement faculty have support dealing with diversity issues in their courses or research. Faculty development for community engagement can thus become part of an overall approach to institutional improvement and integrity.

Conclusion

Like most institutions, Pacific University is a work in progress. Our work is not done with respect to building a strong community engagement program, but faculty development has been instrumental to our progress so far. The PQACE have grounded our efforts, providing a clear path for ongoing faculty development. Adopted elsewhere and tailored to that institution's conceptualization of community engagement, they could continue to serve as a focal point for S-LCE offices, as they will for us. Conversely, as our institution changes, we may adapt the principles accordingly.

Indeed, community engagement in higher education necessitates mindful integration of the needs and interests of multiple stakeholders. By attending to an institution's characteristics, priorities, and culture, S-LCE professionals are better positioned to orient their work toward what makes sense for their institutional context, which fosters the credibility essential to effective S-LCE programming. Ultimately, doing so has the potential to increase their achievement of desired outcomes, thus improving both their own educational environment and all of our communities.

References

Abes, E., Jackson, G., & Jones, S. (2002). Factors that motivate and deter faculty use of service-learning. *Michigan Journal of Community Service Learning, 9*(1), 5–17. Retrieved from http://quod.lib.umich.edu/m/mjcsl/

Boyer, E. (1990). *Scholarship reconsidered.* Princeton, NJ: Carnegie Foundation for the Advancement of Teaching.

Campus Compact. (2017). *Overview.* Retrieved from http://compact.org/who-we-are/

The Democracy Commitment. (2017). *Programs.* Retrieved from http://thedemocracycommitment.org/programs-3/

Dewey, J. (1938). *Experience and education.* New York, NY: Simon & Schuster.

Furco, A., & Holland, B. (2004). Institutionalizing service-learning in higher education: Issues and strategies for chief academic officers. In M. Langseth & W. M. Plater (Eds.), *Public work and the academy* (pp. 23–39). Bolton, MA: Anker.

Jeandron, C., & Robinson, G. (2010). *Creating a climate for service-learning success.* Retrieved from http://www.aacc.nche.edu/

Kezar, A., & Rhoads, R. (2001). The dynamic tensions of service learning in higher education: A philosophical perspective. *The Journal of Higher Education, 72*(2), 148–171. Retrieved from http://www.ohiostatepress.org/Journals/JHE/jhemain.htm

Kuh, G. D. (2008). *High impact educational practices: What they are, who has access to them, and why they matter.* Retrieved from http://www.aacu.org/

Langseth, M., Plater, W., & Dillon, S. (2004). *Public work and the academy: An academic administrator's guide to civic engagement and service-learning.* San Francisco, CA: Jossey-Bass.

Moore, T. L., & Ward, K. (2010). Institutionalizing faculty engagement through research, teaching, and service at research universities. *Michigan Journal of Community Service Learning, 17*(1), 44–58. Retrieved from http://quod.lib.umich.edu/m/mjcsl/

Morphew, C., & Hartley, M. (2006, May/June). Mission statements: A thematic analysis of rhetoric across institution type. *The Journal of Higher Education, 77*(3), 456–471.

New England Resource Center for Higher Education. (2016). *Classified campuses.* Retrieved from http://nerche.org/index.php?option=com_content&view=article&id=341&Itemid=92#CECdesc

O'Meara, K. (2002). Uncovering the values in faculty evaluation of service as scholarship. *Review of Higher Education, 26*(1), 57–80.

O'Meara, K. (2005). Encouraging multiple forms of scholarship in faculty reward systems: Does it make a difference? *Research in Higher Education, 46*(5), 479–510. doi:10.1007/s11162-005-3362-6

O'Meara, K., Lounder, A., & Hodges, A. (2013). University leaders' use of episodic power to support faculty community engagement. *Michigan Journal of Community Service Learning, 19*(2), 5–20. Retrieved from http://quod.lib.umich.edu/m/mjcsl/

Pacific University. (2017). *Academic catalog.* Retrieved from https://www.pacificu.edu/sites/default/files/Images/editors/881/Final-Catalog-12-11-17.pdf

Portland State University. (2017). *Profile.* Retrieved from https://www.pdx.edu/profile/snapshot-portland-state

Prins, E. S. (2002). The relationship between institutional mission, service, and service-learning at community colleges in New York State. *Michigan Journal of Community Service Learning, 8*(2), 35–49. Retrieved from http://quod.lib.umich.edu/m/mjcsl/

University of Massachusetts Amherst. (2017). *Civic Engagement & Service-Learning.* Retrieved from http://cesl.umass.edu/

University of Pennsylvania Netter Center for Community Partnerships. (2012). *History.* Retrieved from https://www.nettercenter.upenn.edu/about-us/history

Vogel, A. L., Seifer, S. D., & Gelmon, S. B. (2010). What influences the long-term sustainability of service-learning? Lessons from early adopters. *Michigan Journal of Community Service Learning, 17*(1), 59–76. Retrieved from http://quod.lib.umich.edu/m/mjcsl/

Young, C. A., Shinnar, R. S., Ackerman, R. L., Carruthers, C. P., & Young, D. A. (2007). Implementing and sustaining service-learning at the institutional level. *Journal of Experiential Education, 29*(3), 344–365.

10

RECIPROCITY AND PARTNERSHIP

How Do We Know It Is Working?

Gabriel Ignacio Barreneche, Micki Meyer, and Scott Gross

One might imagine reciprocity and partnership as a tango between the community and the academy, with the goal of good eye contact, strong communication, and coordinated movements, all without too many abrupt pauses. For those whose teaching and scholarship have been heavily influenced by community-engaged work, there is often a shared understanding that reciprocity and partnership are highly participatory; grounded in mutual benefit for community-based organizations, students, and faculty; and transformational for teaching while simultaneously addressing community needs.

Dance partnerships are not always magical. There are often failures and missteps that present opportunities for learning, stronger footing, and growth. For faculty considering active participation in service-learning and community engagement (S-LCE) for the first time, quite often there are moments of pause, reflection, and analysis. Many times S-LCE practitioner-scholars assist these faculty members in mitigating the critical concerns and risks associated with deviating from conventional modes of teaching and research. Such analysis includes exploring new ways of understanding educational partnerships, content, process, and rigor. Common faculty concerns include statements like the following:

- "My colleagues don't understand why I'm interested in a community-based partnership."
- "What if I don't have the same goals as the community-based organization?"

- "I would really like for my students to work with the community, but I want to make sure that I have full control of the learning environment at all times."
- "There is one organization that I'd like to work with, and I have many ideas of how this should work."
- "I'm worried that if this experience fails I will be evaluated negatively in my teaching evaluations and by my institution. Could this prevent me from getting tenure?"
- "You mean I have to give up actual course content for students to engage in community-engaged learning? I don't have time!"
- "I want my students to become invested, but not too invested. They still need to be more focused on the classroom material and what I'm teaching them. Rigor is most important to me."

S-LCE is a fundamental transformation of traditional ways of teaching that can create disequilibrium between the need to control the conditions for learning and the goals of community-centered design and knowledge application. Faculty members relinquish the oversight and control more typical of educational experiences that are limited by the four walls of a classroom. Ideally, community members and community-based organizations are involved in the development of educational experiences, processes, and assessment of learning rooted in the unique and pressing priorities of the community. Although curricular goals and processes are developed, actual outcomes are often unknown due to the shifting conditions, assets, and needs of the community.

Just as with the concerns of faculty members, from our experience as practitioner-scholars, we find that community-based organizations and partners considering active participation in shared projects have reason for pause. Often, S-LCE professionals assist community-based organizations in mitigating many critical questions, concerns, and risks associated with partnership. Such analysis includes a new way of understanding how to engage college students in mission-driven opportunities, navigate college and university structures, and work effectively alongside faculty members. Community partner concerns include statements like the following:

- "I want to build relationships with a college/university, but I'm unsure of the point of entry to get to the right person/people to make a partnership happen."
- "I'm unsure of the language that's used to describe these partnerships and the barriers that exist in the academy that separate faculty, staff, and students who are involved with my organization."

- "What if my organization doesn't have the same goals as the college/university? How can I say no without damaging relationships and future opportunities?"
- "There is one project that I'd like for students to work on, and I have many ideas of what I will need from them and how this should work."
- "I'm worried that I don't have the bandwidth to take on students or additional projects outside the day-to-day needs of the organization."
- "I'm worried that if this experience fails, the college/university will not want to partner with my organization again."
- "What I need from a partnership goes well beyond the scope of one semester. What happens when the students are done with their class?"

Reciprocity and partnership with the community are key ingredients to successful S-LCE learning experiences. We use the word *community* to encompass the individuals, organizations, groups, and conditions that impact social, environmental, and cultural realities. An asset-based approach to understanding community input honors the expertise and contributions of individuals, partners, and organizations (Scheibel, Bowley, & Jones, 2005). As faculty and S-LCE professionals explore reciprocity and partnership, there are a series of considerations central to the process. This chapter reviews this process of building partnerships rooted in reciprocity, including the following:

- Previewing promising practices in reciprocity and partnership in S-LCE
- Navigating the intersecting and divergent needs of community partners and institutions of higher education
- Understanding community partner assets, needs, contexts, and perspectives
- Identifying opportunities for powerful partnerships
- Understanding the conditions for partnership
- Analyzing how the ecosystem of academia and the realities of the faculty tenure and promotion structure can affect the development of campus-community partnerships
- Recognizing the responsibility of S-LCE professionals and faculty when campus-community partnerships are unsuccessful

With this in mind, faculty new to S-LCE are advised to spend considerable time cultivating relationships; assessing community assets and needs directly related to course content; and practicing reflexivity in developing shared goals, projects, and assessments for the course or educational experience.

Promising Practices and Guiding Principles for Campus-Community Partnerships

A great dance partner comes to know the other person to the point of anticipating the partner's movements and needs. With practice, dancers understand the necessity of using multiple methods of communication to achieve their shared goals. They are mutually aware of the conditions that can present challenges, both individually and collectively, to the routine. Dance partners spend considerable time planning, practicing, and executing a routine, while always honoring space to make changes and adjustments. Finally, they rely on visual cues and intuition to meet the needs of the other dancer from start to finish.

Promising practices in campus-community partnerships are grounded in a methodology that equally values the contributions of the academy and the community in S-LCE work. Like dance partners, both faculty and community partners need to be prepared to enter into a relationship that is open-minded, focused, and coordinated with a deep desire to build upon the other partner's strengths for mutual benefit and gain.

Community relationships provide evidence of institutionalization when agency resources are coupled with those of the academy to build reciprocal, enduring, and diverse partnerships that mutually support community interests and academic goals (Bringle & Hatcher, 2000). Principles of promising practice for campus-community partnerships are considered in Table 10.1.

A number of colleges and universities are leading the way in fostering environments for campus-community partnerships to flourish. Many institutions house centers, offices, and S-LCE practitioner-scholars working alongside faculty to develop promising campus-community partnerships. As noted in chapter 7 of this edited volume, S-LCE practitioner-scholars often serve as faculty developers who pair and facilitate faculty interests with community assets in creative ways.

One example is Rollins College, where the Center for Leadership and Community Engagement serves as the point of entry for community-based organizations. Rollins College is a small, private, liberal arts college located five miles north of downtown Orlando, Florida. The institution's mission is grounded in developing responsible leaders and global citizens, and, as such, the college has a tradition of curricular and cocurricular service to the community. The undergraduate population in the College of Liberal Arts is about 1,900 students. S-LCE practitioner-scholars serve as conveners for faculty and community partners to make meaningful connections based on shared goals and mutual benefit. Each year Rollins College hosts a community partner

TABLE 10.1
Principles of Promising Practice for Campus-Community Partnerships

Shared Goals and Outcomes	S-LCE faculty and community partners come to the table with the desire to create shared goals for both students and the community that are grounded in the missions of the institution, organization, and course curriculum.
Equal Distribution of Both Teaching and Learning	S-LCE faculty fully recognize community partners as coeducators in the relationship. They empower community partners to be an integral part of the educational experience, inviting them to share lived experiences and expertise in the field. Faculty understand that they, like their service-learning students, are colearners in the S-LCE process.
Mutual Benefit	S-LCE faculty seek to identify opportunities for synergy between community interests, academic goals, and student learning outcomes.
Open and Fluid Communication	S-LCE faculty make exceptional efforts to create environments for open, honest, and continuous feedback among all participants during the course or project. Faculty work alongside community partners to develop communication strategies at the inception of the relationship while reevaluating strategies frequently.
Assessment and Feedback	S-LCE faculty collaborate with community partners to develop metrics to evaluate shared goals and outcomes, methods of communication, and impacts on student learning and the community. In addition, S-LCE faculty and community partners assess the relationship's strengths, challenges, and future opportunities for growth and/or improvement.

breakfast and fair to connect S-LCE faculty and students with organizations looking to develop relationships to advance their mission and goals.

Another example is California State University San Marcos (CSUSM), where the institutional structure facilitates deep and pervasive campus-community partnerships. CSUSM is a medium-sized public university about 35 miles north of San Diego. Founded in 1989, the university now has over 15,000 students and prides itself on being both community engaged and entrepreneurial. Over half the graduates each year are the first in their families to earn a four-year degree and more than half are students of color. With 4 colleges, more than 80 degree programs, and a focus on high-impact practices, the university boasts that 82% of alumni remain in the region and join the local workforce.

To facilitate its extensive S-LCE endeavors, CSUSM created a Division of Community Engagement in 2011, headed by a vice president. With a full-time staff collaborating with a faculty director, the division hosts mixers every semester, during which faculty and community partners can meet each other, discuss potential relationships, and plan for upcoming collaborations. At a typical mixer, approximately 25 community partners interact with 15 faculty who are exploring new service-learning projects.

Other efforts in campus-community partnerships include the following promising practices:

- *Duke University:* At Duke, the Office of Civic Engagement prepares the campus to be in mutual partnership with the community. Leading through influence, the office works with individual offices and units across the institution in order to create more whole, equitable, and sustainable partnerships. Other programs that work with faculty to guide community partnerships include Duke Service-Learning and DukeEngage.
- *Miami-Dade College.* At Miami Dade College, the Institute for Civic Engagement and Democracy has developed a Community Partner Workshop for nonprofit staff. The workshop introduces partners to the concept of S-LCE, including their role in the educational process; the concept of reflection and how they can help students not only serve but also learn from the experience; best practices of service-learning and how it differs from volunteerism and internships; how to recognize/thank student volunteers; the benefits for their agency and clients, as well as for students, faculty, and the college; how to partner with faculty and the college; and much more.

As showcased in chapters 5 and 6, the University of San Francisco's McCarthy Center for Public Service and the Common Good and the University of Central Florida's Office of Service-Learning are also exemplars of promising practices. Overall, extensive scholarship in the field of S-LCE (e.g., Bringle & Hatcher, 2002) demonstrates a pervasive and ever-growing presence of campus-community partnerships through academic S-LCE efforts. While employing practices that have been recognized in the S-LCE research community, each institution must also develop a plan tailored to its particular context.

Developing an Ethos of Community Engagement Vis-à-Vis Community Partnerships

The interplay between campus and community, grounded in reciprocity and action, is transformational in highly effective S-LCE practices (Clayton, Bringle, Senor, Huq, & Morrison, 2010). S-LCE faculty, professionals, and community partners are part of a larger ecosystem of relationships, partnerships, neighbors, and students that connect academy and community. As such, for any learning or social impact to happen, these complex interrelationships must be understood and nurtured.

There are times when faculty and S-LCE practitioners may not understand how their individual efforts can have a larger impact on the relationship between the institution and the community. As S-LCE faculty and professionals plan for intentional and purposeful engagement with community partners, there are areas to consider that relate to overall institutional impact, such as the following:

- Does a strategy exist at the college/university in regard to cultivating community partnerships?
- Are there social issues within the community that have been identified by both community partners and the institution as priorities?
- What impact does the partnership have overall on the institution's relationships within the community?
- Who should be made aware of the partnership?
- How can I ensure that this partnership will last beyond one semester or course?

In designing partnerships, it is critical to understand the institutional and strategic impact of engagement on the community. As such, these considerations should guide the ways in which faculty and professionals interact with the community.

An Ethos of Community Engagement—"For the Common Good"

Many colleges and universities are returning to the fundamental idea of developing an engaged and active citizenry, which has helped birth a modern-day understanding of the community engagement ethos and its unique conditions. Boyer (1996) called for higher education to serve a greater purpose for the direction of American life, creating a climate where the academy and the community communicate more frequently and cocreate knowledge for the common good. In the late twentieth century, advocates for the S-LCE movement emphasized an ideal of institutionalizing community-based learning and scholarship (Holland, 2011). The main focus was to move the work of community-engaged praxis and research from the periphery to the center of academic, faculty, and student life. Today, hundreds of institutions have committed to fostering campus climates grounded in an ethos of engagement where community partnerships and organizations are part of the very fabric of the educational experience. Relevant research, practices, and tools have emerged to guide S-LCE faculty and practitioner-scholars through the institutionalization of community engagement (Furco, 2002). The Campus Compact website, as well as that of the National Service-Learning Clearinghouse, provide many resources and examples toward this end as well.

Campus-Community Reflections on Engagement and Empowerment

Campus-community partnerships provide an extraordinary opportunity for participants to impact the learning environment inside and outside the classroom. True partnerships have a shared understanding that all participants provide expertise that is meaningful and mutually beneficial to both students and community. Even in the most thoughtful and well-designed partnerships, S-LCE faculty and practitioner-scholars should reflect on their agency regarding the inherent privilege and power that may be associated with their academic roles. Colleges and universities often have access to human and fiscal resources, technology, innovations, and research, and are often influencers within communities where they reside. Similarly, community-based organizations that have access to financial resources or are governed by powerful stakeholders can influence campus-community partnerships in ways that are not mutually beneficial for faculty or students.

The unequal position between the academy and the community can be a source of conflict when entering into a partnership (Scheibel et al., 2005). Faculty, staff, and students are an extension of their institution and have the unique responsibility to engage mindfully and purposefully within the community, making sure the goals of the partnership are always at the center. Partnerships that center on engagement and empowerment spend time in shared compassion and empathy-building, recognizing the opportunity and struggle that each face in their work.

With this in mind, in our experience we have found that S-LCE faculty and practitioner-scholars often encourage community partners to guide the relationship based on their unique contributions, expertise, and experiences (Mitchell, 2008). Additionally, faculty and practitioner-scholars often use language that reflects this ethos when discussing student learning, projects, and experiences. Furthermore, S-LCE faculty and practitioner-scholars ground their work in promising practice and seek out opportunities to leverage institutional resources (e.g., educational experiences, funding, additional campus partnerships) to enhance the mission and work of the organizations with whom they are in partnership.

Identifying and Cultivating Community Partnerships

When identifying community partners and community-based organizations, S-LCE faculty and practitioner-scholars are advised to seek individuals and organizations that see their role as that of a *coeducator* of students. Together, coeducators explore the opportunities that exist to connect the course curriculum with areas of impact and need in the community. In chapter 2, Timothy K. Eatman discusses this as a relationship in which all parties are colearners. Once these opportunities have been identified, S-LCE faculty, practitioner-scholars, and community-based organizations should discuss shared goals, outcomes, available human resources, plans for the oversight of students, and mechanisms for feedback. In addition to identifying overlapping areas of impact on the course or project, campus-community partners should also discuss where professional duties and roles diverge. Separate responsibilities may include faculty oversight for student grading and assessment and community-based organization oversight of operations, fiscal matters, and staff management.

When S-LCE faculty and practitioner-scholars seek community partnerships that are rooted in the mission of the college or university, they have an opportunity to build off existing synergies. Such partnerships can leverage an ethos of engagement that is connected to a greater momentum and focused on sustainable community impact. S-LCE faculty and practitioner-scholars are advised to communicate information about their partnerships with various areas of the institution that work closely with the community to make sure that efforts are being directed toward a larger strategy and the greater good. Such individuals and departments could include offices and centers for civic and community engagement, philanthropy and nonprofit leadership, community affairs, marketing and public relations, and centers for faculty development and/or learning and teaching. Chapter 7 offers a more thorough discussion of the necessity and centrality of these partnerships in achieving student learning and community impact.

A Framework for Partnership

Much of the work of S-LCE is about matchmaking, or finding the ideal partner, which involves technical skill as well as style. This partnership—between an academic partner and a community partner—is dependent on many variables including mission, culture, expectations, communication, planning, liability, and more. To this end, CSUSM has created a framework (Figure 10.1) to make sense of the mechanics behind the university's side of the partnership.

On the left side of the framework is outreach, which signifies a unidirectional relationship where one organization is doing something *to* or *for* the other. On the right side is engagement, which points to a bidirectional relationship of reciprocity and mutual benefit, where partners are working *with* each other. The framework is a continuum in the sense that partnerships can be plotted at numerous points along the spectrum. Where the partnership exists on the continuum does change as circumstances evolve, so the placement may slide one way or another. Further, the framework is an impartial heuristic. Outreach is not better than engagement, nor is the opposite necessarily true. As depicted at the bottom of the figure, all of the work shown—both outreach and engagement, and everything in-between—is referred to as *community engagement.* In other words, both outreach and engagement constitute community engagement at CSUSM.

Although it is important to understand the technical skills of matchmaking, the style of matchmaking is more multidimensional, involving contextual considerations, relationship alignment, shared intentionality, commitment, and willingness to serve as both leader and follower. Is the timing right for both the community partner and the academic partner? Are the styles of the individuals involved compatible? Are motivations complementary? Who takes the lead, and when? Are all parties dedicated to seeing the work through and finishing the project? The answers to these and other questions will help determine when faculty and community organizations are ready to enter into the partnership.

Figure 10.1. Continuum framework for outreach and engagement.

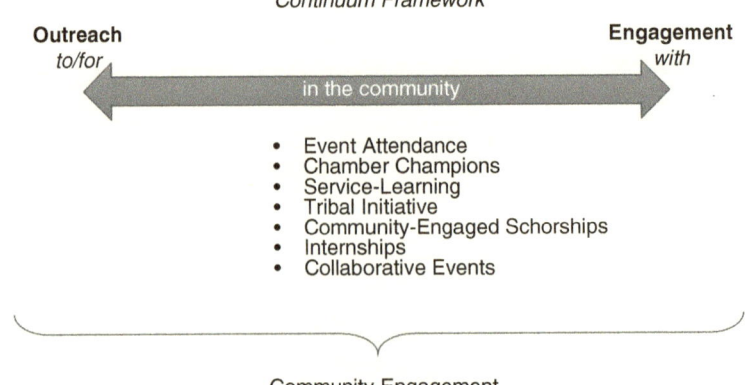

Role of S-LCE Practitioner-Scholars

For faculty unfamiliar with the skill and the style of matchmaking, S-LCE can feel like foreign territory. At CSUSM and at Rollins College, S-LCE practitioner-scholars are the key bridge-builders to community partners. Regardless of how S-LCE is rewarded and recognized in faculty review processes, it is unrealistic to expect faculty to know how to navigate the landscape of community organizations, manage liability and risk, and facilitate all the logistics involved. S-LCE practitioner-scholars have the skillsets necessary for building sustained partnerships and supporting faculty as they learn community-engaged pedagogies. Another consideration when supporting faculty is respect for faculty members' autonomy to decide which pedagogy is best for their courses, even if it may not match the promising practices of partnership development.

With these considerations in mind, scholar-practitioners and faculty at CSUSM consider and engage in a series of steps that help cultivate effective partnerships:

1. *Listen.* In partnership, it is critical that the work is meeting the need of the community. This is learned by asking questions and listening to the community expressing that need. However, it is possible that the community may name a need with which the academic partner cannot help.
2. *Acknowledge cross-cultural interaction.* Institutions of higher education and community organizations have distinct cultures; thus, partnerships become cross-cultural interactions. Explicitly naming norms can be a helpful way of learning to navigate through inherent complexities. A consideration involves properly preparing students to negotiate cultural difference within the ethos of "Do no harm" and "Contribute to the common good."
3. *Adapt and name the purpose.* In establishing purpose, partnerships may require some give-and-take wherein the needs of both dancers shift and recalibrate with the evolving needs of the other. After hearing the needs of the community partner, for instance, the faculty member may modify the readings from the course. As the community partner is made aware of the course's learning outcomes, the community organization may also shift aspects of the project accordingly.
4. *Listen again.* Partners are advised to deliberately create additional times for listening. This can be to simply check in with each other to confirm the project is going as planned. Further, asking for input as part of the assessment strategy will help with any continuous improvement processes (Holland, 2001).

These steps are not a set formula, nor are they an exhaustive list. Yet following these steps will create the beginning of a solid foundation to maximize reciprocity and leverage profound impacts on the campus and community. This sentiment is aptly summarized by Kesler Gilbert, Johnson, and Plaut (2009): "As campuses stretch to co-create knowledge and actions that contribute to positive community change, community partners stretch to co-educate the students in such efforts" (p. 36).

Is Less More? Strategic Partnerships in S-LCE

A challenge to community partnerships is that they are often derived from existing relationships, which can be unsustainable if partners do not plan for the possibility of attrition or transition from the institution or organization (Scheibel et al., 2005). More institutions like Rollins College are looking to strategic partnership models to guide cultivation of community partnerships. Rollins College has consulted the Corella & Bertram F. Bonner Foundation (n.d.) for inspiration on strategic partnership development in the community. Also of note is Eddy and Amey's (2014) *Creating Strategic Partnerships: A Guide for Educational Institutions and Their Partners*. Strategic partnership models are situated to create deeper partnerships with longer-term commitments between a small grouping of partners in order to focus on continued projects with more sustainable and transformative impact on the community. Thus, strategic community partners recognize the institution's potential impact on furthering the community-based organization's mission long term. Strategic community partners value multiple high-impact pathways for student engagement within the organization, such as research, volunteerism, internships, philanthropy, and board membership. Strong candidates for strategic partnership recognize the unique role of coeducation, envision the institution's impact on the organization as central to its mission and day-to-day operations, and have the human resources to accommodate student engagement and partnerships.

Faculty Considerations for Partnership Development

A central element of the development of successful and mutually beneficial campus-community partnerships is the role of the individual faculty member. Given their complex roles on campus, faculty engaging in S-LCE practices must consider numerous factors before entering into these partnerships, including how to institutionalize and standardize S-LCE practices on their campus, how S-LCE work changes their teaching and scholarship, and how to leverage S-LCE to develop professionally.

Standardized Criteria for S-LCE Practices

Institutionally standardized criteria for S-LCE practices engender high-quality partnerships. By establishing standards, stakeholders can avoid common mistakes and pitfalls of campus-community partnerships. For example, faculty members who are new to S-LCE pedagogies can consult with established criteria, examining how best to tailor their courses to community needs. Clear guidelines on how to structure a partnership in the community help ensure that the relationship will be reciprocal, respectful, and mutually beneficial for all individuals involved.

At Rollins College, faculty can request a community engagement (CE) designation for their courses. The impetus for this designation is twofold. First, as students register for classes, they are made aware of the service-learning component of the courses in question. Second, courses with the CE designation are eligible for financial, logistical, and mentoring support from the college's Center for Leadership and Community Engagement. Using the institution's approved standards for S-LCE courses, a team of faculty and practitioners with significant experience in service-learning praxis and theory vets the courses under consideration for the CE designation. More importantly, the CE criteria standardize the practices and expectations for community-based learning. One of the key elements considered by the vetting team is the presence of an intentional plan for including the community partner in the course design and implementation. The following list shows the standards for CE courses at Rollins College, with the community partner's role indicated in italics.

- Identifies and addresses a need in the community (campus, local, regional, or global)
- Meets course objectives and demonstrates a clear connection between the community activity and the course content
- Involves structured student pre/post reflection
- *Involves collaboration with a community organization/agency that is committed to a reciprocal partnership between service and learning*
- *Allows the community partner to share in classroom dialogue, discussion, and scholarship (when appropriate), including reporting feedback, service project results, or research*
- Requires a minimum of 15 hours of direct service/research with the community organization/agency
- Features assignment(s) in which students share their experience with the class community as well as the community organization/agency and address a plan for active citizenship beyond the course

CSUSM has also developed an SL designation for service-learning courses. Different from Rollins College, the designation is at the discretion of the faculty member teaching the course. In the name of academic freedom, faculty determined this designation process through faculty governance. CSUSM has implemented an online database listing institutionally approved partners, allowing students to match with the partner of their choice while also completing all liability paperwork. Additionally, faculty can utilize the database to see which students have matched and which have not. Such technological advances serve as incentives for faculty to designate their courses accurately. Nonetheless, some faculty choose not to work through the system. Consequently, the integrity of the data at CSUSM remains a constant challenge.

Well-crafted, intentional campus-wide criteria for S-LCE practices have the potential to add value to the institution's broader mission while ensuring equity, reciprocity, and mutual benefit. By prioritizing S-LCE projects that have mutually advantageous community partnerships, the institution makes a public statement about relationships with the larger community—namely, through reciprocally beneficial and respectful interaction. Finally, standardized criteria go a long way in mitigating tensions and mistrust within communities that might see or have experienced the institution as exploitative or imperialistic in its work.

The establishment of standard criteria has its shortcomings and might not work on all campuses. For example, the process of establishing what constitutes acceptable S-LCE praxis may alienate faculty who have a different vision or long-standing history of S-LCE engagement. Faculty and practitioner-scholars may need to carefully assess the context of S-LCE practices at their particular institutions, collaborating with faculty leadership and requisite governance structures. In some contexts, a decentralized approach, although more cumbersome and less rigid, may be more effective in delivering the goal of sound campus-community partnerships.

New Paradigms for Teaching, Student Learning, and Scholarship for Faculty

In many institutions of higher education, faculty have been traditionally viewed as "sages on the stage"—experts in their fields of academic research and unquestionable authorities in their classrooms. With a shift in higher education to more learner-centered and collaborative environments, faculty have been challenged to shift dynamics of power, inviting more collaboration with and direction from students in order to enhance student learning (see Weimer, 2002).

Similarly, there has been additional movement to shift the locus of knowledge production from the faculty to community partners. Traditionally, community engagement tended to be initiated by the college or university to benefit institutional needs, such as student experiences, faculty research agendas, and development of the institution; this could be conceived as an imperialistic relationship. Fortunately, promising practices in S-LCE have evolved to recognize potentially exploitative dynamics, advocating for reciprocity in partnerships. In this way, the needs and assets of the community and institution can be of equal footing (see Gelmon, Holland, Seifer, Shinnamon, & Connors, 1998).

Whereas academe once served as a primary source of knowledge creation, best practices in S-LCE situate community partners as coeducators in the student learning experience and cocreators of knowledge. By giving the community partner an active role in student learning, faculty democratize the learning process, modeling behaviors of lifelong learning for their students. In other words, when students see their faculty learning with, from, and beside a community partner, barriers between faculty and students dissolve. The quality of learning is enhanced by the diversity of experiences and knowledge that the community partner brings to the conversation.

One of the more difficult challenges with the coeducator model, however, may be the tenure and promotion system for faculty. If teaching is a primary responsibility for a faculty member, relinquishing autonomy can be a risky proposition. Should the community partner not fulfill obligations, resulting in an ineffective learning experience, the faculty risks negative course evaluations that could adversely affect a case for tenure and promotion. Similarly, success from a service-learning course might not entirely be attributed to the faculty; students may praise the community partner versus highlighting the efforts of the core instructor. Further, not all community partnerships successfully balance fulfilling the community organization's need while enhancing the course's learning outcomes. Although an unsuccessful partnership may not seem out of the ordinary for practitioners of S-LCE pedagogy, an uninformed tenure and promotion committee may not be empathetic to the faculty member's case. As a result of these potential risks, a cautious untenured faculty member may think twice before entering into a partnership. It would simply not be worth the risk if conventional teaching practices, residing within the control of the faculty member, are rewarded the same as S-LCE practices. Faculty should always consult their institution's faculty handbook and governance documents to ascertain if there are already norms and conventions about how S-LCE work (research and teaching) is viewed in a promotion and tenure case. In the absence of these, it is critical to seek clarification from departments and academic administration.

National organizations such as Campus Compact as well as the International Association for Research on Service-Learning and Community Engagement (IARSLCE) can provide guidance and resources.

Related to this matter is the issue of community-based research, explored more thoroughly in chapter 12. With the model of the community organization as coeducator or coauthor, faculty must navigate how their own work on a project is recognized in the context of professional review. Collaborative research efforts often require more time and energy than solo projects; an inexperienced review committee might not recognize the additional efforts involved in a coauthored project with a nonacademic partner. Additionally, a community-based research project must contend with issues related to intellectual property rights and technology transfer, as well as ethics board considerations. Again, when putting all of the potential risks on the scales with potential rewards, some faculty may simply choose to avoid this line of research in favor of more traditional and universally recognized sole-authored opportunities.

Another potential deterrent from the faculty point of view involves finding the right dance partner within an institution's group of established community partners. If an institution has decided to focus energies on a particular set of projects or partners, faculty may find themselves alienated from the process—or hoping to develop a project outside of the more limited scope of the institution. A faculty member from environmental studies, for instance, may be interested in environmental engagement. If institutional efforts privilege and focus on hunger and homelessness, the educator may face limited opportunities. As a result, the faculty member may be more likely to independently develop a less sustainable, more loosely structured partnership.

In order to mitigate such obstacles, a few steps are recommended at the institutional level. Most importantly, tenure and promotion criteria can evolve, under the leadership of faculty governance, to value, recognize, and reward community-based research and service-learning pedagogy. At CSUSM, not all department-level promotion and tenure guidelines specifically recognize S-LCE, though there is movement to revise all evaluation guidelines to include S-LCE. However, such a goal requires the long view. In the short term, a committee of experienced faculty have prepared a rubric for reviewers to support an informed evaluation of S-LCE. The same committee has also written a guiding document to help junior faculty prepare a file that successfully positions community-engaged work. Enos and Morton (2003) rightly note, "Changing or expanding the faculty reward system requires a fundamental shift in campus culture and so is, by definition, a difficult and incremental journey" (p. 36).

Faculty Development to Foster Sustainable Partnerships: Two Approaches

In partnership with campus centers for teaching and learning, S-LCE offices can play a vital role in new faculty orientation programs, professional development opportunities, and faculty mentoring initiatives. One way to introduce new faculty to S-LCE and promote the development of community partnerships is through opportunities afforded to newly hired faculty. At Rollins College, for instance, the Center for Leadership and Community Engagement takes new faculty into the community to meet with civic leaders and community partners. Led by practitioner-scholars, this tour introduces faculty to pedagogical and research opportunities; participants meet and engage with long-established community partners in an informal setting while learning how their faculty peers have forged mutually beneficial community partnerships.

CSUSM exemplifies another approach to faculty development. Through structured workshop sessions, faculty learn the promising practices of S-LCE pedagogy and research while also hearing lessons learned from colleagues. CSUSM also offers working groups during winter and summer break that meet for three sessions: one to discuss the anatomy of a meaningful service-learning experience, one to select potential community partners and review the process for building relationships, and one to review the redesigned course syllabus and answer lingering questions. Feedback indicates that participating faculty feel more prepared to teach the course, are more likely to continue with S-LCE in the future, and are more apt to maintain an ongoing relationship with the community partner.

It is important to note the role of faculty leadership in the development and execution of these professional development opportunities. The model of *faculty serving faculty* can enhance credibility and increase buy-in among the faculty at large. For this reason, CSUSM implemented a Faculty Director initiative, wherein each S-LCE program has a director whose primary responsibility is to serve as a resource for other faculty. Faculty directors receive two course buyouts each semester for taking on this role, which leverages their social capital among the faculty as well as their expertise in S-LCE.

Another strategy that can lead to successful partnerships, especially for established faculty, are mentoring programs—some examples of which are showcased in the case study chapters of this book. The peer-to-peer relationships offered by faculty champions and advocates provide legitimization of S-LCE efforts as well as valuable insight into relationship-building, pedagogical transformation, community-based research, and even tenure and promotion. Rollins College began its mentoring efforts through a Faculty Fellows program. In the early stages of its S-LCE efforts, Rollins College brought together faculty from four diverse academic areas; these fellows received stipends for their work in providing workshops and colloquia for other faculty to learn about S-LCE. Over the years, this growing cadre of early adopters, in concert with practitioner-scholars, forged a critical mass of faculty that have legitimized S-LCE across campus and ensured high-quality partnerships through the mentorship of faculty who have sought the CE designation discussed earlier. Through a robust faculty serving faculty model, campuses can work toward sustainable and mutually beneficial relationships with the community.

Challenges and Pitfalls of Partnerships

Service-learning and community engagement can be messy and unpredictable. Challenges exist in S-LCE, even in the most well-executed and articulated partnerships. Quite often, partnerships and projects will look different from conception to conclusion. Academy and community are themselves in flux, creating conditions that shift both the learning environment and the partnership itself, affecting student participation in turn. As such, S-LCE is often a journey into unchartered territory, with roadblocks, pitfalls, and pathways not yet taken (Cress, Collier, & Reitenauer, 2005).

Campus-community challenges may include any of the following:

- Infrastructure changes at the institution or community-based organization
- Staff turnover in the community-based organization
- Faculty attrition or retirement
- Evolving expectations for the partnership by the S-LCE faculty member and/or community partner
- Lack of reciprocity by the S-LCE faculty member and/or community partner
- Lack of communication between S-LCE faculty and community partner
- Shift in priorities within the community-based organization
- Closure of the community-based organization
- Lack of engagement and follow-through by students

The good news is that faculty and community partners can prepare for many of the challenges during the relationship-development process. Partners should discuss possible risks and pitfalls before embarking on a new partnership. Developing both a communication plan and learning agreement will help faculty and community partners focus on shared goals throughout the partnership. Further, faculty and community partners should schedule opportunities for face-to-face communication throughout the semester, including a midsemester meeting. Finally, faculty and community partners should spend time reevaluating the partnership among the faculty member, institution, and community-based organization, considering helpful questions such as the following:

- What are the successes of the partnership? Challenges?
- Did the partnership meet expectations regarding communication?
- Did the partnership achieve desired goals and outcomes?
- In what ways can successes be shared publicly with the institution and community?
- What could be done differently in the future to achieve greater success?

As facilitators and conveners, S-LCE practitioner-scholars can also be a great resource for faculty and community partners when challenges and pitfalls arise. S-LCE practitioner-scholars can be involved in the creation of a communication plan and learning agreement, supporting faculty and community partners with strategies to move through conflict. S-LCE practitioner-scholars also have the opportunity to nurture relationships with academic deans, department chairs, and leadership within the community-based organization to ensure there is a plan in place for times of unexpected transition. Further, S-LCE practitioner-scholars can leverage strategic community partnerships in the event of unplanned shifts in organizational priorities or closure. Finally, innovative and creative interventions organized by or through S-LCE practitioner-scholars can assist faculty in helping reenergize student engagement in the course.

Conclusion

The search for an ideal dance partner, the choreography of the routine, and the performance itself is a complex and sometimes problematic process for all parties involved: community-based organizations, institutions of higher education, faculty members, students, and S-LCE practitioner-scholars. The intricacy of these relationships and the possibility of failure could seem daunting in many cases. Nonetheless, in spite of these challenges and difficulties, campuses and community-based organizations continue to seek out one another because both the students and the members of the community stand to gain much more through their interactions than by isolation from one another. Furthermore, healthy and productive relationships can fulfill the missions of community organizations while redefining town-gown relationships, many of which have been problematic historically.

In spite of still having to challenge or renegotiate the path to tenure and promotion, many faculty have embraced this dynamic pedagogy while seeking out new lines of community-based research, steeped in the ethos of mutual benefit, shared respect, and sustainable long-term relationships with their community partners. But the steps of the dance must be choreographed with care and intentionality. By following best practices in the field and strategically engaging with community partners to maximize the impact on both the institution and the community partner, success for all parties can be achieved. It really does take two to tango, and what a wonderfully inspiring dance it can be when the community and academia collaborate as equals.

References

Boyer, E. (1996). The scholarship of engagement. *Journal of Public Service & Outreach, 1*(1), 11–21.

Bringle, R., & Hatcher, J. (2000). Institutionalization of service learning in higher education. *The Journal of Higher Education, 71*(3), 273–290.

Bringle, R., & Hatcher, J. (2002). Campus-community partnerships: The terms of engagement. *Journal of Social Issues, 58*(3), 503–516.

Clayton, P. G., Bringle, R. G., Senor, B., Huq, J., & Morrison, M. (2010, Spring). Differentiating and assessing relationships in service-learning and civic engagement: Exploitative, transactional, or transformational. *Michigan Journal of Community Service Learning, 16*, 5–22.

Corella & Bertram F. Bonner Foundation. (n.d.). *Community partners*. Retrieved from http://www.bonner.org/community-partners

Cress, C. M., Collier, P. J., & Reitenauer, V. L. (2005). *Learning through serving: A student guidebook for service-learning across the disciplines.* Sterling, VA: Stylus.

Eddy, P. L., & Amey, M. J. (2014). *Creating strategic partnerships: A guide for educational institutions and their partners.* Sterling, VA: Stylus.

Enos, S., & Morton, K. (2003). Developing a theory and practice of campus-community partnerships. In B. Jacoby (Ed.), *Building partnerships for service-learning* (pp. 20–41). San Francisco, CA: Jossey-Bass.

Furco, A. (2002). Institutionalizing service-learning in higher education. *Journal of Public Affairs, 6*(Suppl. 1), 39–67.

Gelmon, S. B., Holland, B. A., Seifer, S. D., Shinnamon, A., & Connors, K. (1998). Community-university partnerships for mutual learning. *Michigan Journal of Community Service Learning, 5*(1), 97–107.

Gross, S., Prado-Olmos, P. L., & Villarreal, S. (2016, October). *Across the continuum: A framework for community engagement.* Paper presented at the meeting of the Coalition of Urban and Metropolitan Universities, Washington DC.

Holland, B. (2001). A comprehensive model for assessing service-learning and community-university partnerships. *New Directions for Higher Education, 114*, 51–60.

Holland, B. (2011). The engaged campus. In J. Saltmarsh & E. Zlotkowski (Eds.), *Higher education and democracy: Essays on service-learning and civic engagement* (pp. 281–284). Philadelphia, PA: Temple University Press.

Kesler Gilbert, M., Johnson, M., & Plaut, J. (2009). Cultivating interdependent partnerships for community change and civic education. In J. R. Strait & M. Lima (Eds.), *The future of service-learning: New solutions for sustaining and improving practice* (pp. 33–51). Sterling, VA: Stylus.

Mitchell, T. D. (2008). Traditional vs. critical service-learning: Engaging the literature to differentiate two models. *Michigan Journal of Community Service Learning, 14*(2), 50–65.

Scheibel, J., Bowley, E. M., & Jones, S. (2005). *The promise of partnerships: Tapping into the college as a community asset.* Providence, RI: Campus Compact.

Weimer, M. (2002). *Learner-centered teaching: Five key changes to practice.* San Francisco, CA: Jossey-Bass.

PART FOUR

ENGENDERING CHANGE IN EDUCATIONAL DEVELOPMENT

11

CONNECTING SERVICE-LEARNING AND COMMUNITY ENGAGEMENT FACULTY DEVELOPMENT TO COMMUNITY-ENGAGED SCHOLARSHIP

Sherril B. Gelmon and Catherine M. Jordan

The goal of this chapter is to encourage readers to connect faculty development work facilitated by service-learning and community engagement (S-LCE) professionals and faculty to community-engaged scholarship (CES). Based on our collective experience conducting professional development workshops on CES for faculty, this chapter builds on those approaches and offers practical advice addressed to S-LCE professionals. S-LCE professionals are academic administrators who collaborate with faculty to develop their capacity to create and offer service-learning courses and other community engagement activities, both curricular and cocurricular, to students, and then derive CES from those experiences. S-LCE professionals often hold a terminal degree with training in education or an alternative discipline. Service-learning and community engagement professionals may also hold faculty rank and fulfill responsibilities usually associated with faculty positions; we emphasize the academic administrative roles of these professionals in this chapter to distinguish the integration of scholarship into complex and multidimensional roles and responsibilities that are different from the traditional teaching, research, and service roles of faculty. This chapter can help these academic professionals to develop and disseminate engaged scholarship that emerges from the work they do independently, as well as in collaboration with faculty and other colleagues.

Scholarship can be an important part of work for S-LCE professionals, helping them to share and disseminate their learning and insights, establishing their credibility as scholars with faculty colleagues, and creating opportunities to collaborate with faculty. In this chapter, we explore the experiences and perceived impact of a group of S-LCE professionals who already do CES and give some recommendations for the broader community of practitioners. This work is based upon a literature review, our own experiences as CES scholars, and a survey of S-LCE professionals.

Definitions

As is evident from reading the preceding chapters in this volume, multiple terms are used to describe the kinds of scholarship in which S-LCE professionals might engage. Therefore, it is appropriate to begin with some definitions of key terms, including *CES*, the *scholarship of teaching and learning* (SoTL), and the *scholarship of engagement* (SoE).

CES involves the scholar in a mutually beneficial partnership with the community (Commission on Community-Engaged Scholarship in the Health Professions, 2005). *Mutually beneficial* means that the outputs of CES are varied and useful to both the community and to the advancement of knowledge and education (Gelmon, Holland, Seifer, Shinnamon, & Connors, 1998). CES combines the principles of community engagement with accepted standards of scholarship. Thus, high-quality CES will result in both traditional and nontraditional representations of the work when a CES scholar undergoes performance review.

SoTL "encompasses a broad set of practices that engage teachers in looking closely and critically at student learning in order to improve their own courses and programs, and to share insights with other educators who can evaluate and build on their efforts" (Hutchings, Huber, & Ciccone, 2011, p. xix). Boyer (1990) first described the scholarship of teaching as one element of his four-part categorization of scholarship that also included discovery, integration, and application. Hutchings and Shulman (1999) described the scholarship of teaching as a strategy by which scholars investigate questions related to the process of student learning—settings, contexts, breadth, and so on—in order to improve their own teaching and to advance practice more broadly.

SoE was described by Boyer (1996) as the scholarly ways in which university resources are employed to apply any of Boyer's four notions of scholarship—discovery, integration, application, teaching—to address the most "pressing social, civic, and ethical problems" (p. 27). SoE includes explicitly democratic dimensions that encourage the participation of nonacademics in scholarly collaborations in ways that enhance and broaden engagement and deliberation about major social issues inside and outside the university (NERCHE, n.d.). Some authors use CES and SoE interchangeably; others distinguish SoE as the process of studying engagement, as compared to CES, which defines scholarly work that is done through a process of engagement. Barker (2004) suggests that SoE encompasses five practices: public scholarship, participatory research, community partnerships, public information networks, and civic skills or civic literacy. Resolution of these conflicting perspectives is beyond the scope of this chapter. We use *CES* as the broad term, but emphasize the importance of understanding SoE, given its foundational usage in this field.

Each of these forms of scholarship can lead to vastly different kinds of scholarly products, both because of the nature and focus of the scholarly inquiry and also because of the discipline in which the work is grounded and the associated models, methods, and frameworks that may be used (e.g., arts-based research versus social sciences research versus health services research). The context of a project about developing and displaying public art will be very different from a project focused on youth literacy, which again will differ from a project on prenatal nutrition. These varying contexts will lead to alternative forms of scholarly products.

For the purpose of this chapter, rather than parsing definitions to create a narrow perspective, we are taking a broad approach to engaged scholarship that includes all of these—CES, SoTL, and SoE. Scholarship could be generated from community-based learning activities (service-learning or other forms) and relate to teaching and learning; it could be about the process of engagement and focus on, for example, partnership development and maintenance, or it could be about the impact of community engagement on communities and reflect community collaborations. The important point is that S-LCE practitioners have the capacity to do scholarship as part of their work in both academic professional and faculty roles (see chapter 2, which focuses on faculty as colearners), whatever the topical focus. How they disseminate their insights from their faculty development and community-engaged work, and how they ensure they are recognized for it as an important part of their professional work, is central to a continuing commitment to scholarship, let alone the intrinsic motivation of being recognized for valuable contributions in the field, for the community, or at their institution.

To enhance the relevance of this chapter, in addition to reviewing pertinent literature and reflecting on our own experiences conducting CES and leading faculty development workshops on the applicable skills and competencies, we adopted a qualitative data collection strategy to better understand the experiences of S-LCE practitioners with CES. We conducted a survey of current S-LCE practitioners to gain their insights about conducting CES. We invited an initial group of 15 individuals who were either known to us as scholars or were part of a group who led the Practitioner Scholar Forum at the 2016 International Association for Research on Service-Learning and Community Engagement (IARSLCE) annual research conference. An e-mail invitation was sent individually to each person on our initial list. They were asked to complete a brief survey and were invited to identify 2 or 3 additional practitioner-scholars for us to contact. Using this snowball sampling approach, 40 practitioner-scholars were invited to participate, and 21 responded in a 2-week period in December 2016. The survey questions addressed motivations, experiences, and impact regarding conducting CES. All surveys were deidentified upon receipt. Selected responses are used throughout this chapter to reflect the experiences of this sample of practitioner-scholars. All protocols were reviewed and approved by the Portland State University Institutional Review Board.

Why Is Community-Engaged Scholarship Important for the Service-Learning and Community Engagement Professional?

Faculty members' usual roles require that they undertake scholarship, seek peer review, and invest considerable time in disseminating their work for fairly obvious reasons—scholarly activities and publication are the coin of the realm in academia. Faculty members' reputations, job stability, and career advancement typically depend on scholarly productivity. Faculty are motivated by less self-protective factors as well. Disseminating one's scholarship in academic journals is an important way to influence the field and contribute to our collective knowledge. Soliciting and incorporating critical feedback from peers effectively hones focus and improves conceptualization, rigor, writing, and the overall quality of one's work.

Faculty and S-LCE professionals who participate in community-engaged research and other forms of community-engaged scholarly work are also committed to disseminating the products of their collaborative endeavors in order to benefit both the academic and practice communities. They aim to reach diverse audiences, such as community members, practitioners, and policymakers, and may use nontraditional formats (not the academic journal article) to reach these audiences for whom the academic literature is often not digestible or physically accessible.

In addition, some S-LCE professionals often work within a different context on campus. Their job security or reward structure may not be dependent on scholarly productivity. They may be evaluated on metrics such as the number of service-learning courses created, student course evaluations, numbers of trainings offered to build faculty capacity to integrate S-LCE into their courses, and the training evaluations of participating faculty. S-LCE professionals typically are focused on making impact through routes other than writing and dissemination. They may be motivated to excel in their jobs by enhancing community benefit and enriching students' educational experiences and developmental outcomes.

For what purpose and benefit, then, would S-LCE professionals seek to engage in scholarship, peer review, and dissemination? Our qualitative survey of current S-LCE professionals revealed important themes that describe both the purpose and benefits of engaging in CES. Many of these are similar to the motivations of faculty. Several respondents cited the personal benefits, in terms of deepening their own understanding and grounding their practice in evidence. In the words of two respondents:

> I also engage in scholarly work to further my own knowledge in support of my work.

> Writing forces me to organize my thoughts and think about my work differently. Doing this better prepares me to talk with others on campus about what I do, why I do it, and how.

At an academic institution that values scholarship and where publications are the currency of highest value, S-LCE professionals can earn the respect of faculty colleagues and administrators for their contributions to scholarship. Their enhanced credibility, as well as their shared language of scholarship, certainly aids their ability to work effectively with faculty members—and they may coauthor with faculty to be supportive of a colleague's work. This contributes to the professionalization of their roles and may lead to additional professional opportunities such as consultation requests or advancement to more senior positions in administration, as illustrated in several responses:

> Due to the fact that I am not in a faculty role, I feel like (whether true or not) I need to write about this work and have it accepted or at least peer-reviewed so that it has an added layer of value/worth/rigor as perceived by others within my organization. In higher education, something is "believable" and "good" when accepted by others in the academy as such. Otherwise, it is easier to dismiss. While not my proudest reason for doing scholarly work, I do it so that others within my organization will listen and trust/believe me.

Being an active scholar gives me more credibility with the faculty, staff, and graduate students I work with. I can share my experiences writing grants, getting "revise & resubmits" on manuscripts, and publishing. I can lead professional development in a more credible, grounded, authentic way. In other words, because I produce scholarship, I am able to fulfill one of my job responsibilities more effectively.

If I were to leave my institution for another institution (maybe not a research/very high), I will have a track record that demonstrates my scholarly abilities and achievements. In other words, producing scholarship lays the foundation for future/potential job mobility.

S-LCE professionals also feel they have something to say. They have a unique perspective on the work of an engaged institution and make a different contribution to our knowledge base about S-LCE than do the faculty who teach service-learning courses or conduct community-engaged research and publish on these topics. In addition, engaging in scholarship offers the S-LCE professional the opportunity to influence the field by starting a dialogue on teaching and learning strategies, educating others, offering guidance and best practices, and demonstrating the value of S-LCE in higher education and the community. Scholarship also creates a mechanism to influence institutional change on their own campuses and across higher education to better support the work of their peers, campus offices of S-LCE, and the faculty they support in developing SL courses. As several respondents noted:

> I think more diverse ideas and perspectives at the table, talking about and writing about the work, benefits the entire field. In this sense, I see my work as contributing to a larger body of knowledge.

> I enjoy reading and considering the work of others and find, at times, I have unique perspectives to offer. This compels me to want to explore ideas and trends I see through my own work and contribute to the field.

> My motivation for taking a scholarly approach to my professional development work is that I want the next generation of scholars and practitioners to have evidence-based recommendations for respectful and effective community-engaged scholarship and practice. In other words, I want to make sure the next generation has confidence, mind-sets, knowledge, skills, tools, and generative questions to keep making a difference in the world—especially with populations who are typically not included in the process and with the complex natural and social problems we now face.

S-LCE professionals have an ideal opportunity to make scholarly contributions, and the benefits are many. Their work in faculty development, intended to enhance faculty members' capacity to teach using service-learning or similar pedagogies or to conduct community-engaged research, provides important material for their own scholarship. By approaching their faculty development programming in a scholarly manner—in other words by grounding their program design in adult learning theory, implementing their programs with rigor, and engaging in quality evaluation of their programs' impacts—S-LCE professionals can generate and analyze critical data and develop insights to improve S-LCE in higher education.

Examples of Community-Engaged Experiences of Service-Learning and Community Engagement Professionals

Our survey results demonstrate that engaging in CES has a variety of impacts as reported by the current S-LCE professionals who responded. CES has an impact on the S-LCE professional's own work in terms of professional opportunities, identity, and advancement; the reputation of the S-LCE professional's institution or organization unit; advancement of the field of community engagement and practice in general; and enhancement of institutional capacity. These are illustrated through the quotations provided in Table 11.1.

It is clear from the responses that these S-LCE professionals conduct CES in order to both make an impact and share their own learning about the impact of the various activities in which they are involved at their campuses. The motivations are similar to those of faculty, yet the S-LCE professional may have to make more of a case to be recognized and rewarded for scholarship because it often is not required for job responsibilities, performance evaluations, or institutional reward structures. The insights of the survey respondents show that these S-LCE professionals are highly motivated to conduct scholarship, recognizing the value of dissemination that is a central part of the work of faculty colleagues and demonstrating their own contributions to the scholarly community—both independently and in collaboration with other colleagues (e.g., faculty and S-LCE professionals).

Discussion

S-LCE professionals are in a unique position to contribute to scholarship about the need, process, and impact of professional development to enhance faculty capacity for S-LCE. The nature of their roles provides several advantages. S-LCE professionals work across the disciplinary and departmental partitions in the academy, as well as across roles (faculty, administrators, campus partners, students). This provides them with a comprehensive view of faculty development needs and the impact of faculty development programs

TABLE 11.1
Quotations Illustrating S-LCE Professionals' Experiences With CES

Theme	Illustrative Quotations
The S-LCE Professional's Work	It has provided me the opportunity to speak at conferences and on other campuses.
	It has a personal impact—helping me live out my identity as a scholar.
	My scholarship has also been part of what I used for successful documentation of impact for my promotion dossier.
Reputation of the University or Organizational Unit	It has garnered support from my administration, and thus fostered general support for my department from the administration.
	The scholarship has motivated practitioners to contact my institution for countless site visits and correspondence to see how to replicate or modify our model.
	My work and that of my colleagues has certainly had an impact on national organizations such as the Association of American Colleges & Universities who formally promote our program as an explicit exemplar.
Advancement of the Field	I have contributed to the thinking about how to create a democratic classroom.
	I have helped test and refine some assessment tools that are widely used by practitioners.
	I have contributed to the development of models to use student leadership in community engagement work.
	My work has contributed models of thinking (democratically engaged partnerships, community engagement professional) as well as methodological examples (explanatory case study, reciprocal validity).
	My research has helped practitioners more than academics. My research has been read by community partner staff and centers for community engagement/service-learning staff.
Enhancement of Institutional Capacity	My research on types of faculty work has informed other institutions as they put together institutional policies.
	My research about interdisciplinary community engagement journals has been included in trainings at regional Campus Compact events in the past few years.

(Continues)

TABLE 11.1 (*Continued*)

Theme	Illustrative Quotations
	My research that is at the intersection of SoTL and community engagement has informed professional development programs at at least two different institutions.
	Reports I have cowritten have been used on other campuses as frameworks.
	Practitioners at other institutions have read my work and the work of my colleagues at [name of institution] and contacted us to make meaning of how they would apply what we have done at their institutions.

across campus, as well as a broad network of potential faculty partners in scholarly endeavors. They have a broad and specific knowledge of the S-LCE work on their campuses and the role that faculty development plays. As such, S-LCE professionals are uniquely qualified to make the case for the impact of S-LCE on student outcomes, teaching and learning strategies, community benefits, and faculty practices. This positions them uniquely to deliver quality faculty development to realize these outcomes.

Finally, S-LCE professionals may not be hampered by the requirements and constraints of promotion and tenure. Though certainly concerned about the quality of the outlets they may publish in or disseminate through, they are not constrained by metrics such as journal impact scores or order of authorship. This frees S-LCE professionals to focus on the strongest messages, made to the most relevant audiences, and using the most effective mechanisms for dissemination. Such freedom allows S-LCE professionals to explore multiple methodological approaches, to approach research from a variety of paradigms, to engage in creative approaches to scholarship, and to seek varied outlets for dissemination of scholarship.

Recommendations

We offer the following recommendations to assist S-LCE professionals in realizing the potential for scholarship provided by their unique vantage points.

Material for Scholarship

By creating, delivering, and studying the impact of faculty development programs, S-LCE professionals have the opportunity to approach their work in a scholarly manner as well as to develop scholarship from their programmatic activities. The literature on faculty development and other forms of educational development provides information about possible theoretical or conceptual scaffolds, such as adult learning theory, that can undergird the development of sound faculty development programming (Jordan, 2016; Jordan et al., 2012). Intentional developmental and summative evaluation of faculty development programs can then provide the foundation for numerous scholarly products.

Topics that might be addressed through evaluation research include the following:

- The impact of faculty development programming on faculty practices concerning S-LCE, as perceived by faculty participants and/or their students
- The impact of faculty development on the student experience or student outcomes
- Issues at the level of the community, such as benefits to community partners of enhanced faculty capacity for S-LCE through faculty development programming
- Issues at the level of the academic institution, including enhanced campus capacity for S-LCE, changes in policies or support structures for S-LCE, or barriers to faculty involvement in S-LCE or to providing appropriate faculty development
- The benefits and challenges of integrating scholarship into the S-LCE professional's role
- Special faculty development needs, such as tailoring offerings for junior faculty or senior faculty, the ease of aligning the focus and approaches of certain disciplines with S-LCE, or developing the skills for cross-cultural partnerships.

Finally, some authors have pointed to the need to move beyond qualitative, observational program description or case study approaches toward the design and development of more empirical studies to advance the field (see Welch & Plaxton-Moore, 2017).

Partnership Potential
In our survey, respondents reported a wide range of scholarship partners (e.g., faculty colleagues, community partners, students, other local academic professionals such as those in teaching and learning centers, and other S-LCE professionals across other institutions). As mentioned previously, the S-LCE professional tends to work across campus and, through the provision of faculty development, has the opportunity to form relationships with a broad network of faculty. These faculty members provide an important

resource for the S-LCE professional. Faculty are usually interested in opportunities to collaborate on scholarly writing projects as they are motivated by the need to demonstrate scholarly productivity. Faculty bring skill sets and resources that can be useful to such projects. Depending on the individual, a faculty member might bring evaluation capacity, writing talent, the ability to perform rigorous literature reviews, and possibly one or more graduate assistants with interest in contributing to the work. Faculty may have interest in collaborating around any of the topics discussed in the previous section but are likely to be most interested in documenting and communicating about the impact of S-LCE activities on their students or on the community. This documentation would serve the faculty member in making a case within the promotion and tenure process for the impact of teaching and research activities.

There may also be opportunities to collaborate with students through their participation in various activities, especially when students are motivated to develop scholarship that illustrates their community engagement. The presence of other academic professionals on a campus who are also interested in CES, such as those in centers of teaching and learning, may provide yet another collaborative opportunity for S-LCE professionals.

S-LCE professionals often have long-standing relationships with community partners or are familiar with the partners of the faculty they have worked with through faculty development. Sometimes community partners take part in faculty development efforts as guest or coinstructors and therefore have a unique and helpful perspective on the impact of faculty development programs organized by S-LCE professionals. Community partners are potentially valuable collaborators in producing scholarship resulting from faculty development programmatic efforts. Community partners and S-LCE professionals might productively partner on scholarship related to motivations for community partner involvement in faculty development, the impact of community partner participation in faculty development on faculty practices or student outcomes, or the ways in which community partner participation in faculty development facilitates institutional change.

S-LCE professionals on other campuses are a third important potential partner. Combining evaluation research information or conducting collaborative scholarship across campuses might result in the design of faculty development best practices or documentation of strategies for effective institutional change.

Innovative Approaches to Dissemination
Peer-reviewed journal articles are the gold standard in many disciplines within academia. However, journal manuscripts are only one strategy for S-LCE professionals to disseminate their scholarly work related to faculty development. As noted by one survey respondent:

Because I am not in a faculty line and while my identity as a scholar is perhaps valued, my motivations for publishing are very different. Much of what I do write about and still need to write about is about my practice—strategies, methods, implications. And what I create I want to make easily accessible. As such, I am less concerned with the level of peer review and more interested in usability and utility, much of which cannot be captured in traditional peer-reviewed publications or the time it takes to get published.

As noted, the type of work they perform, the unique vantage points they hold, and their relative freedom from typical constraints on definitions of *scholarship* and *impact* offer S-LCE professionals the chance to consider innovative approaches to dissemination, such as the following:

- A training manual for implementing an existing faculty development program
- A model or rubric describing faculty competencies for S-LCE and faculty development approaches to enhance those competencies
- Evaluation tools for measuring impact on faculty, students, community partners, and institutions
- An online toolkit or resource page offering best practices in faculty development for S-LCE
- Undergraduate or graduate course syllabi developed by faculty development participants representing best practices

Publication Outlets With Potential
Every year new journals are launched, filling a gap in the available publication outlets for S-LCE journal manuscripts. An obvious genre is the group of journals about S-LCE, particularly those that focus on higher education. The anchors in the field, such as the *Michigan Journal of Community Service-Learning*, have been joined by newer journals such as the *International Journal of Research on Service-Learning and Community Engagement* and the *Journal of Service-Learning in Higher Education*. Another important genre is the literature on faculty development and other forms of professional development, such as the *Journal on Centers for Teaching and Learning* and the *Journal of Faculty Development*. Unique journal subsections such as "Education & Training," "Works in Progress," "Practical Tools," or "Lessons Learned" might provide the S-LCE professional an entree into these journals, compared to journals that focus more narrowly on original research articles.

A limited number of outlets for dissemination of innovative products of scholarship, such as the training manuals, evaluation instruments, or toolkits already mentioned, also exist. Some are peer reviewed, offering S-LCE professionals important sources of feedback on their work and enhancing the credibility of their scholarship with faculty colleagues. CES4Health .info, operated under the auspices of Community-Campus Partnerships for Health, is a mechanism for rigorous peer review by academic and community peer reviewers, with online, open access publication of innovative products of community-academic-partnered scholarly work addressing human, environmental, and community health (Community-Engaged Scholarship for Health, 2017; Jordan, Gelmon, Ryan, & Seifer, 2012; Jordan, Seifer, Gelmon, Ryan, & McGinley, 2011). Innovative products resulting from collaborative work between S-LCE professionals and community partners would be well aligned with CES4Health's purpose.

The Multimedia Educational Resource for Learning and Online Teaching (MERLOT II, 2017), developed by California State University, is a curated collection of free and open-access peer-reviewed resources for online teaching, learning, and faculty development. Though not specific to S-LCE, resources for online faculty development for S-LCE or syllabi or course content for online courses with service-learning or community engagement components, developed as part of a faculty development program, would be appropriate submissions to MERLOT.

Conference presentations, such as at the conference of the International Association for Research on Service-Learning and Community Engagement (IARSLCE) or the Engagement Scholarship Consortium (ESC), provide other outlets for dissemination of strategies for, and outcomes of, S-LCE professionals' faculty development programming. The POD Network is another online venue for both presentation and dissemination that may be relevant for the S-LCE professional.

Pitfalls to Avoid
Survey responses provided rich evidence of issues to avoid as well as strategies, advice, and tips. The overwhelming sentiment among survey respondents was that scholarship is either a small fraction of their job duties or not expected at all. Consequently, scholarship tends to get pushed to the back burner. Respondents also noted some gaps in skill sets. Others noted, perhaps related to these issues, that they lack the strategies and structures to assist them in producing scholarship. The comments in Table 11.2 illustrate these points.

Helpful Tips
Survey respondents offered numerous strategies that S-LCE professionals can use to enhance their writing skills and practice as well as manage their time and priorities. They also discussed the types of external supports, at the institutional level as well as opportunities at the national level, which would support the scholarly productivity of S-LCE professionals.

TABLE 11.2
Pitfalls Noted by Survey Respondents

Scholarship a Small Fraction of Job Description, or Not Expected at All	I've been able to get it documented to say it's 5% of my time. But the reality is that it is impossible to get the other 95% of the job done at the same time. As soon as one task is finished, they want the next task started and there isn't the ability to say, "Wait, I need to write about that project/activity/idea before I move on to the next thing."
	What gets in the way is always limited time and the pressing need to focus on the "practice" side of my work.
Gaps in Skill Sets	I see many new hires come into outreach and engagement positions with little background in SoTL; they might have amazing community experience but they really struggle with what significant questions are in the field, how to frame a research or evaluation study, what theories they could chose to draw upon, and so on. Many of them are not even aware that SoTL exists.
Lack of Strategies and Structures to Assist in Producing Scholarship	I wish I had better daily practices of research and writing—it's not that I don't have the time, but I wish I had better structures in place to facilitate leveraging my time wisely.
	The lack of a graduate assistant dedicated to supporting research and scholarship in my office has been a hindrance.
	My experiences thus far have been different at a research institution versus a teaching institution. At the research institution, I had ample resources (e.g., library staff support, software, and faculty to assist with building my research design) to conduct research, but little support (e.g., time to gather data and write) from my supervisors and college because I was a practitioner. At the teaching institution, I have more support, but haven't found as many resources (e.g., faculty have large teaching loads so their time is limited for research which means fewer coauthoring opportunities, and the software access is not as strong).

In light of the challenge of carving out time for scholarship within a position that is focused on other duties, survey respondents advocated for sharing writing responsibilities and developing accountability mechanisms through writing partners or groups as well as creating external deadlines.

They spoke to the benefits of coauthoring to share the load and spread responsibilities; shared accountability to get data collected, analyzed, and written up; and responsiveness to deadlines such as calls for papers or presentations. Respondents also enjoyed partnering for scholarship, with one person indicating, "Having writing group space carved out is a blessing."

Others noted that using partnership strategies in ways that facilitate one's growth and development provides a bonus. One respondent noted, "Since my scholarship is emerging, it's helpful to work with more experienced staff and faculty who are familiar with writing and publishing processes and norms."

Another perspective focused on the importance of creating alignment between scholarly endeavors and S-LCE professional practice, as illustrated by one commenter: "I have also framed research projects on issues I have been struggling with so that through the process of research I can figure out what I need to know to professionally advance my own work."

Other supports, supplied by academic institutions or by national professional societies, were noted as important for several respondents. These included access to institutional data; completion of research methods courses and similar professional development activities; support of colleagues met through meetings such as ESC, IARSLCE, and Campus Compact; and the value of peer feedback. When an institution has established research as a priority, there is more respect for time spent away from the office for research activities and conferences, which is an important observation related to building knowledge and enhancing one's confidence to do research and scholarship.

Aligning Scholarship With the S-LCE Professional's Role

A robust theme that emerged from the surveys relates to strategies for structuring the S-LCE professional's job to support scholarship. Many respondents noted that scholarship has not been an expectation of their job and, therefore, they must engage in active strategies to make it happen and to be recognized for it. "Scholarly work technically does not fit into my responsibilities, so anything I do is on my own."

Two strong themes emerged that provide sound advice for the S-LCE professional—requesting that scholarship be made a formal part of one's job description and making the case to superiors for the value of scholarship to the S-LCE program's effectiveness:

> Scholarly work is addressed explicitly in two areas in my formal performance review template form. By having it explicitly stated there it remains a central piece of my position and my responsibilities.

> The best support for my scholarly work is having it in my job description. It prevents me from putting all my other administrative responsibilities before scholarship. This simply makes it part of my role.

> It isn't technically carved out as part of my role, but things like advancing the program and supporting faculty scholarship are, so I basically utilize how it relates to and supports my position and responsibilities as justification for my engagement in those activities.

One respondent noted the downside of having scholarship explicitly stated as an expectation of the job:

> The challenge with this expectation (for scholarly productivity) is that our unit's appointments (at least mine) do not reflect this expectation, so that I am producing scholarship in addition to fulfilling my other work roles, which continue to increase over time. Staff in similar positions to mine in other units across the institution do not have the same expectations/pressures to produce scholarship that I face. I often feel as if I am being asked to collaborate across the institution on programs, develop and manage new and existing programs, AND produce scholarship based on original research—which is quite a bit.

Some respondents offered specific strategies that have helped them conceptually and logistically align scholarship with their roles as S-LCE professionals. One noted the importance of integrating scholarship into one's professional identity, stating, "It is not directly tied to my professional position or my reviews; it is tied to my identity as a scholar-practitioner."

Another has scheduled time over the course of a year to engage in scholarship:

> I have also very intentionally timed research phases and writing phases of my scholarship to dovetail (not compete with) the hectic times in my schedule for my other professional responsibilities. So, I focus on my own scholarship over Christmas break, over spring break, in the early part of summer, but everything has to be wrapped up by mid-August because my staff responsibilities really pick up from mid-August to mid-October. I can then return to my own scholarship around Thanksgiving.

These comments suggest that, although *scholarship* is not necessarily defined as a core element of the S-LCE professional's position description, there are many opportunities and reasons to develop scholarship, independently or collaboratively. This is not to suggest that CES become a core requirement for all S-LCE professionals, as there may be some situations where scholarly work is not a priority, but it does validate and reinforce the importance of supporting S-LCE professionals when they wish to engage in CES and valuing this work as part of their role.

Conclusion

The intent of this chapter has been to encourage readers to see how faculty development work done by S-LCE professionals can lead to community-engaged scholarship. The review of relevant literature and our survey of a sample of current S-LCE professionals clearly demonstrate that there are numerous opportunities for these individuals to conduct and disseminate CES. Depending on the nature of their professional responsibilities, as well as the institutional context in which they work, there may be various motivators and barriers for CES, but it appears that there are multiple opportunities for these professionals to develop and disseminate engaged scholarship that emerges from their own work—and more opportunities are developing over time.

As one respondent to our survey stated:

> I find that through my scholarly contributions (largely peer-reviewed conference papers and presentations) I am building the time and space for practitioners to come together, to find each other, and share how many questions/problems they have in common. By creating these moments and places, I know that I am not only finding collaborators with whom to do action or applied research but also allowing them to find each other and identify questions or problems/issues that I have not had yet to contend with, and therefore, I can encourage their own research and dissemination.

Scholarship is and can be an important part of work for S-LCE professionals, helping them to share and disseminate their learning and insights while also establishing their credibility as scholars with their academic faculty, within their institutional context, and within their professional organizations and networks. As the community engagement field continues to evolve, institutions will need to acknowledge this as an important part of the professional portfolio of S-LCE professionals and foster ample time and space for S-LCE professionals to create and share their community-engaged scholarship.

References

Barker, D. (2004). The scholarship of engagement: A taxonomy of five emerging practices. *Journal of Higher Education Outreach and Engagement, 9*(2), 123–137.

Boyer, E. (1990). *Scholarship reconsidered: Priorities of the professoriate*. Princeton, NJ: Carnegie Foundation for the Advancement of Teaching.

Boyer, E. (1996). The scholarship of engagement. *Journal of Public Service and Outreach, 1*(1), 11–20.

Commission on Community-Engaged Scholarship in the Health Professions. (2005). *Linking scholarship and communities: The report of the commission on community-engaged scholarship in the health professions*. Seattle, WA: Community-Campus Partnerships for Health.

Community-Engaged Scholarship for Health. (2017). CES4Health.info. Retrieved from http://ces4health.info/

Gelmon, S. B., Holland, B. A., Seifer, S. D., Shinnamon, A., & Connors, K. (1998). Community-university partnerships for mutual learning. *Michigan Journal of Community Service Learning, 5*, 97–107.

Hutchings, P., Huber, M., & Ciccone, A. (2011). *The scholarship of teaching and learning reconsidered*. San Francisco, CA: Jossey-Bass.

Hutchings, P., & Shulman, L. E. (1999). The scholarship of teaching: New elaborations, new developments. *Change, 31*(5), 10–15.

Jordan, C. M. (2016). The Community-Engaged Scholars Program: Designing a professional development program to enhance individual capacity, community benefit and institutional support. *Journal of Community Engagement and Higher Education, 8*(3), 6–15.

Jordan, C. M., Doherty, W., Jones-Webb, R., Cook, N., Dubrow, G., & Mendenhall, T. (2012). Competency-based faculty development in community-engaged scholarship: A diffusion of innovation approach. *Journal of Higher Education Outreach and Engagement, 16*(1), 65–96.

Jordan, C. M., Gelmon, S. B., Ryan, K., & Seifer, S. D. (2012). CES4Health.info: A web-based mechanism for disseminating peer-reviewed products of community-engaged scholarship: Reflections on year one. *Journal of Higher Education Outreach and Engagement, 16*(1), 47–64.

Jordan, C., Seifer, S. D., Gelmon, S. B., Ryan, K., & McGinley, P. (2011). CES4Health.info: An online tool for peer reviewed publication and dissemination of diverse products of community-engaged scholarship. *Progress in Community Health Partnerships, 5*(2), 189–199.

MERLOT II. (2017). *Multimedia Educational Resource for Learning and Online Teaching*. Retrieved from www.merlot.org

New England Resource Center for Higher Education (NERCHE). (n.d.). *Definition of engaged scholarship*. Retrieved from http://www.nerche.org/index.php?option=com_content&view=article&id=265&catid=28

Welch, M., & Plaxton-Moore, S. (2017). Faculty development for advancing community engagement in higher education: Current trends and future directions. *Journal of Higher Education Outreach and Engagement, 21*(2), 131–166.

12

INNOVATIVE CONSIDERATIONS IN FACULTY DEVELOPMENT AND SERVICE-LEARNING AND COMMUNITY ENGAGEMENT

New Perspectives for the Future

Richard Kiely and Kathleen Sexsmith

In chapter 1, Welch and Plaxton-Moore present a new professional development framework for faculty in service-learning and community engagement (S-LCE), suggesting the field has evolved beyond the traditional approach. Serving as a bookend, the purpose of this chapter is to consider innovative approaches while providing concrete guidance to S-LCE professionals, faculty, and higher education administrators seeking to ensure that their faculty development activities promote high-quality S-LCE. To address this need, we articulate an integrative and transformative model for faculty development in S-LCE. Represented by four lenses (refer to Figure 12.1), this transformative S-LCE model (Kiely, 2017) draws on reflective practice traditions (Brookfield, 1995; Kiely, 2015; Rice, 2010; Schön, 1987). The model is intended to assist faculty and S-LCE professionals with critical reflection on their own assumptions about what constitutes robust S-LCE theory and practice in (a) teaching and learning, (b) institutional support and change, (c) knowledge generation and application, and (d) community partnerships and capacity building.

Figure 12.1. A transformative S-LCE model.

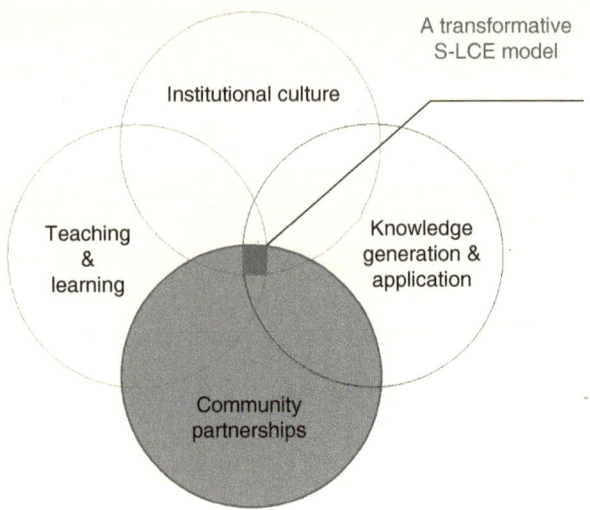

The transformative S-LCE model builds on research and theory in the fields of faculty development (Barr & Tagg, 1995; Fink, 2003; Kezar, 2011; Van Note Chism, Holley, & Harris, 2012), adult learning (Kiely, 2005; Knowles, 1980; Merriam & Bierema, 2014; Mezirow & Associates, 2000), and S-LCE (Clayton, Bringle, & Hatcher, 2013; Dostilio, 2017; Dolgon, Mitchell, & Eatman, 2017; Post, Ward, Longo, & Saltmarsh, 2016). Although we have generated empirical evidence in S-LCE of what does and does not work in each of the four lenses (Clayton, Bringle, & Hatcher, 2013), our field of vision tends to focus discretely within one or two lenses, thus neglecting interdependencies between lenses. This chapter explores how, when considered holistically, the lenses add value to each other, creating a fifth, metacognitive lens that forms an overall faculty development strategy.

Focusing on each lens as a discrete dimension of S-LCE rather than taking a holistic approach can have repercussions for how faculty development programs are designed and, in turn, how practitioners develop, implement, evaluate, and maintain quality S-LCE. For example, S-LCE course design workshops often do not ask faculty to consider how aspects of course design will influence access to institutional support, nor do they usually consider models or theories of institutional change and community development. Moreover, the workshop facilitators might not have sufficient capacity on how to assist faculty with navigating institutional culture, policies, and/or obstacles. The latter factors should be included in faculty development seminars because they will influence a faculty member's ability to develop S-LCE resources, teaching techniques, learning outcomes, and assessment strategies (Dostilio, 2017).

This chapter suggests that the integration of these core components constitutes a fifth, metacognitive lens that can help S-LCE professionals and faculty become aware of the limitations of approaching their work as if each lens works in isolation from the others. The metacognitive lens also highlights the need to consider each lens as an essential component of a more robust, transformative conceptual framework guiding S-LCE faculty development. This framework, along with the chapters in this book, supports more recent calls for the next generation of engagement and publicly engaged scholars in S-LCE (Post et al., 2016) and is consistent with the need to advance the skills and knowledge of S-LCE professionals and faculty (Dostilio, 2017).

This chapter is intended primarily as a theoretical contribution to faculty development and S-LCE. However, we draw from our research with global service-learning (GSL) faculty instructors, selected using a strategic, heterogeneity sampling method that captures diversity across postsecondary institution type, stage of progress toward or beyond tenure, and academic discipline. To complement the results of semistructured interviews, we also conducted a document analysis of participants' publications on GSL, course syllabi, and course proposals. In the sections that follow, we use our findings to highlight the transformative potential of S-LCE through the creative, innovative approaches already adopted by faculty leaders.

The chapter continues with a description of the framework as transformative and integrative, segueing to an overview of foundational faculty learning outcomes (FLOs) and threshold concepts. Then we explicate each lens of the framework in the context of the FLOs, threshold concepts, activities, and outcomes that should be included in faculty development efforts. The section that follows describes faculty development activities that introduce dissonance and foster critical reflection. We conclude by promoting a metacognitive process. Our goal is to build toward a theoretically grounded, holistic, and integrative faculty development model suggested by Welch and Plaxton-Moore in chapter 1—one that fosters enduring shifts in teaching and learning, organizational culture, epistemology and scholarship, and community partnerships.

Moving S-LCE Toward a Transformative Integrative Approach

Faculty adoption of and innovation in S-LCE, with support from community engagement professionals (CEPs), are key to the development, assessment, and institutionalization of high-quality S-LCE practices (Dostilio, 2017). Faculty often face significant challenges when integrating S-LCE due to its counternormative nature (Clayton & Ash, 2004; Howard, 1998), resource constraints, and perceived risks, especially for tenure-track faculty in research universities (Harrison & Clayton, 2012; O'Meara, 2013). However, as Eatman points out in chapter 2, faculty—as central actors within higher education—can be well positioned to challenge and transform existing social and cultural norms, beliefs, and practices in teaching and research (O'Meara, 2013; Van Note Chism, Palmer, & Price, 2013). It is essential, then, that we have an explicit theory of change aimed not only at how faculty development programs in S-LCE foster faculty learning and growth (Welch & Plaxton-Moore, 2017) but also at how to develop programs that transform faculty into agents of change in their institutions, their disciplines, and the communities where S-LCE occurs.

As a transformative approach that answers this call, the S-LCE framework described in this chapter is not only integrative but also dissonant. The model (a) disrupts the notion that faculty and CEPs focus only on course-based pedagogy (Bass, 2012; Sandmann, Kiely, & Grenier, 2009; Sexsmith & Kiely, 2014; Stoecker, 2016) and (b) questions the existing norms, practices, policies, and deeply held traditions that perpetuate a more rigid course-based teaching paradigm (Barr & Tagg, 1995) and that hinder learning-centric, "post-course" (Bass, 2012, p. 24) movement-building in S-LCE (Swords & Kiely, 2010). As described in chapter 1, the next generation of publicly engaged scholars, which includes faculty and S-LCE professionals, must be able to take on a number of roles, such as boundary spanner, organizer, networker, teacher, and scholar (Dostilio, 2017; Post et al., 2016; Sandmann et al., 2009). Articulating each of these roles is informed by well-developed theories and practices that have evolved in response to current challenges and opportunities in higher education.

The current stage of the S-LCE movement calls for a perspective shift, from a focus on pedagogy to an appreciation of the need for broader transformation of organizational culture, epistemology, research, and community partnerships (Dostilio, 2017; Post et al., 2016; Stoecker, 2016; Sexsmith & Kiely, 2014; Swords & Kiely, 2010). The transformative S-LCE model is meant to assist faculty in challenging the dominant theories, norms, assumptions, and expectations in each of the domains represented by the four lenses. In each of the lenses described, we offer a bulleted list of "disruptive questions" that provoke the reflection faculty must undertake to achieve core FLOs and to navigate the dissonant nature of threshold concepts for each lens. In what follows, FLOs, threshold concepts, and their respective roles in the transformative approach to S-LCE are explained in turn.

FLOs are the foundational knowledge, skills, attitudes, and behaviors (KSABs) that guide faculty development in S-LCE. Drawing from Sandmann and colleagues' (2009) *relational approach* to program planning in service-learning, FLOs push faculty beyond course design and content mastery in their discipline and focus KSABs on assisting faculty in learning how to serve as the primary bridge-builders among multiple stakeholder groups (students, faculty, community members, the institution, etc.). Notably, each group brings different belief systems, experiences, knowledge, languages, needs, interests, skills, assets, and resources.

Sandmann and colleagues' (2009) research suggests that S-LCE faculty need to become responsible program planners who serve in multiple roles (i.e., content experts, reflective facilitators, deliberative practitioners, power brokers, and nurturers), helping to cultivate dialogue and maintain quality relationships in the face of difference and unequal power relations among stakeholders. The authors contend that

> the strong relationships necessary for effective program planning in a service-learning context rest on effective intercultural communication, which requires a unique set of social, emotional, and technical skills to engage in listening, dialogue, critical reflection, empathy, and support. When the appropriate skills, support structures, and processes are absent, relationships break down, and the resulting communication difficulties could negatively impact the development of a robust and sustainable service-learning partnership. (p. 29)

Hence, faculty development that fosters FLOs around partnership and relationship-building in each lens is crucial for creating a more robust and sustainable approach to S-LCE. However, given the pressures tenure-track faculty face—especially related to promotion and tenure—it is a tall order to expect them to develop the KSABs to successfully challenge deeply entrenched institutional rituals and requirements. The counternormative attempt to navigate and integrate all four S-LCE lenses thus implies a transformative approach to the ways institutions approach S-LCE.

Evolving Toward Transformative Approaches With Threshold Concepts

Moving toward a transformative approach to S-LCE requires identifying and critically reflecting on the threshold concepts (Harrison & Clayton, 2012) that faculty must surmount to develop an understanding of S-LCE as a robust counternormative approach to teaching and learning, knowledge generation and application, institutional culture, and community partnerships. Figure 12.2 illustrates the transformative model, foregrounding the

Figure 12.2. A transformative S-LCE model for faculty development.

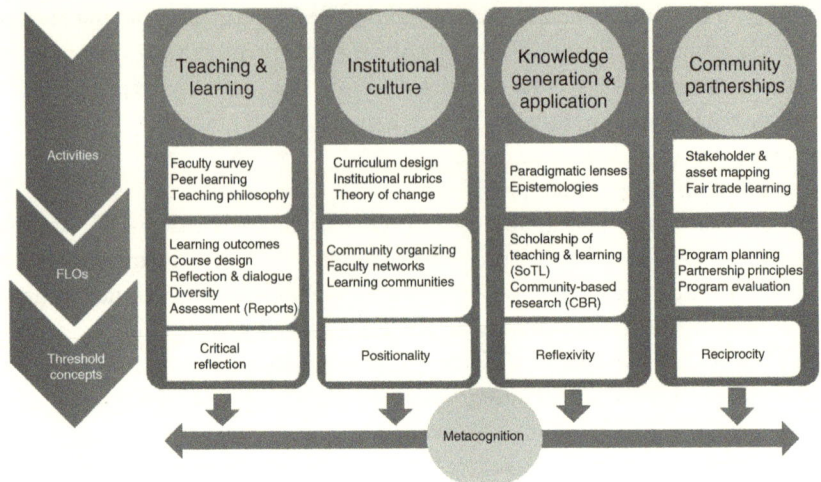

threshold concepts that will help faculty achieve a critically reflective and counternormative approach to S-LCE.

What are threshold concepts? Meyer and Land's (2006) pioneering research on threshold concepts, grounded in transformational learning theory (Kiely, 2005; Mezirow & Associates, 2000), shows significant promise as a framework for discovering, advancing, and transforming knowledge of the key concepts and practices that have fostered success in S-LCE (Harrison & Clayton, 2012; Harrison, Clayton, & Lilly-Tubbs, 2014; Kezar, 2015). According to Meyer and Land (2006), a threshold concept, like a portal, "represents a transformed way of understanding, or interpreting, or viewing something without which the learner cannot progress" (p. 1). This research, abetted by recent studies (Barradell, 2012; Zepke, 2013), identified threshold concepts as (a) troublesome, (b) transformative, (c) integrative, (d) irreversible, (e) discursive, (f) bounded, (g) reconstitutive, and (h) liminal. Learning of new threshold concepts is an important area for faculty development; because these moments are rarer for faculty, they imply greater dissonance and resultant metacognitive shifts.

Challenges associated with the "troublesome" nature of threshold concepts can cause learners to become stuck in a condition of "liminality" (i.e., cognitive limbo), in which they are unable to cross a conceptual threshold of knowledge (Meyer & Land, 2006). Knowledge gleaned from moving across a conceptual threshold can be both disruptive and exciting, prompting a considerable shift in knowledge and practice (Meyer & Land, 2006). Researchers have begun to examine the challenges faculty face in learning threshold concepts related to high-impact pedagogies (e.g., Bunnell & Bernstein, 2012; Cousin, 2010; King & Felten, 2012; Harrison et al., 2014). According to Harrison and colleagues (2014), "Examining faculty learning through the lens of threshold concepts and threshold experiences can help us understand, address, and embrace dissonance-related challenges and opportunities involved in learning the why's and how's of service-learning pedagogy" (p. 5). Harrison and colleagues' (2014) exploration of how faculty learn threshold concepts in service-learning indicates that faculty may learn threshold concepts such as "reciprocity" or "critical reflection" in S-LCE through "threshold experiences—reflective encounters with dissonance that give rise to deeper understanding of threshold concepts" (p. 6). It may very well be that faculty learning in S-LCE is similar to those processes and factors that influence students' transformational learning in S-LCE (Kiely, 2005; Kiely & Hartman, 2011).

The S-LCE framework in Figure 12.2 builds on emerging theory on threshold concepts in S-LCE (Harrison & Clayton, 2012; Harrison et al., 2014) and aims to stimulate critically reflective practice and dialogue so that faculty learning in S-LCE is both informative and transformative (Kegan, 2000). As Figure 12.2 illustrates, FLOs and threshold concepts are constitutive elements of each of the four lenses. FLOs are the aspects of S-LCE that theorists, practitioners, and institutions have internalized as essential considerations for high-quality programming (Dostilio, Janke, Miller, Post, & Ward, 2016; Welch, 2016), such as creating faculty learning communities (institutional lens), preparing student learning outcomes (teaching and learning lens), or working through reciprocal partnership models (community lens). Instrumental as milestones, FLOs require that "administrators and the staff for campus centers for community engagement must be knowledgeable of the basic tenets and strategies to advance this work as well as skilled at facilitating adult learning" (Welch, 2016, p. 164).

Therefore, the threshold concepts are the crux of the framework, requiring CEPs to be well-versed in adult learning (Kiely, Sandmann, & Truluck, 2004; Merriam & Bierema, 2014) as well as transformational learning theory in adult education and S-LCE (Kiely, 2005, Kiely & Hartman, 2011; Mezirow, 1991; Mezirow & Associates, 2000). They represent not only concepts (means of organizing knowledge and ways of knowing) that faculty must learn but also, in this case, the specific mental, discursive, and material practices that those concepts promote (critical reflection, positionality, reflexivity, and reciprocity). The activities provide concrete examples and tools that faculty and other practitioners can use to assist faculty in addressing dissonance and critically reflecting on their assumptions about best approaches to each lens, as a means of ascertaining a full comprehension of the threshold concept for that lens. Finally, the outcomes are examples of the products derived from critically reflecting on one's assumptions, as undertaken through the activities. An aspirational goal of this framework is to build toward the theoretically grounded, holistic, and integrative faculty development model suggested by Welch and Plaxton-Moore (see chapter 1 of this text)—one that fosters enduring and beneficial shifts in teaching and learning, organizational culture, epistemology and scholarship, and capacity-building through community partnerships.

Lens 1: S-LCE as a Transformative Approach to Teaching and Learning

In higher education, we often use the language of pedagogy. As adult and community development educators drawn to service-learning's progressive, humanist, and radical philosophical underpinnings, we question the use of *pedagogy*, defined by prominent adult education theorist Malcolm Knowles (1970, 1980) as primarily a teacher-dependent, subject-centric approach to teaching children, as the most appropriate language to convey the meaning of S-LCE's counternormative, experiential critique of traditional classroom-based pedagogy (Clayton & Ash, 2004; Rhoads & Howard, 1998).Grounding our work in learning theories based on research with adults rather than children can have beneficial outcomes for CEPs who work with faculty in higher education and, in turn, for faculty who are teaching young adults (Steocker, 2016). This is because pedagogy is grounded in the assumption of student dependence on teachers for information, identity formation, experience, and the motivation to learn, whereas andragogy assumes and promotes the autonomy of learners through a student self-directed approach (see Table 12.1). In this way, the theory and practice of S-LCE is already counternormative to dominant, classroom approaches to pedagogy, and therefore the language, meaning, theory, and practice of teaching and learning in S-LCE should reflect that through a clear and close connection to the methods and theories around educating adults.

A good point of departure for developing a new, adult-centered language for teaching and learning in S-LCE is the work of Malcolm Knowles. A prominent adult educator in the 1970s and 1980s, Knowles introduced the term *andragogy*—the art and science of teaching adults—to his field, proposing a theory and/or a set of assumptions about how adults learn differently than children (Merriam & Bierema, 2014). The six assumptions underpinning Knowles's (1980) work have significant implications for approaches to teaching and learning in S-LCE and for faculty development in S-LCE, and they align well with its counternormative idea of teaching and learning.

TABLE 12.1
From Pedagogy to Andragogy to S-LCE

Theme	Pedagogy	Andragogy	Implications for Faculty Development in S-LCE
The Learner	Children tend to be dependent on adults for learning. Formal schooling with lecturing, textbooks, and teacher-centered, subject-driven instruction, reaffirms dependency and passive approaches to learning.	In terms of their self-concept, adults tend to see themselves as more responsible, self-directed, and independent learners. Educators are facilitators promoting student-centered, active approaches to learning.	Faculty see themselves as independent, autonomous, and responsible for the content, format, and focus of teaching and research. Using a lecture format may cause resistance. Faculty development should view faculty as colearners and promote (inter) active learning. Faculty development should focus on surfacing faculty members' philosophical assumptions on teaching.
Learner's Experience	Children have limited experience outside of school and self-concept and identity are often influenced by parents, family members, school, church, sports, and so on. The experience of the teacher, counselor, coach, or mentor shapes learning.	Adults have a larger, more diverse stock of knowledge and experience to draw from and to shape their identities (i.e., work, parenting, travel, and stages in life). Adult experience and knowledge is a resource for learning.	CEPs should draw from, invite, and use faculty life experiences and knowledge of learning, teaching, work, service-learning, and research as a key point of departure in workshops and consultation. Surfacing knowledge and critically reflecting on the validity of their assumptions on the purpose of education, teaching, learning, roles of teacher and learner, knowledge, the discipline, community, and the institution are essential to development.

(*Continues*)

TABLE 12.1 (Continued)

Theme	Pedagogy	Andragogy	Implications for Faculty Development in S-LCE
Readiness to Learn	Learning for children is geared toward moving on to the next grade in school and sequenced proficiency in subject matter.	Adults' readiness to learn is based on their social roles, developmental life stages, and real-life responsibilities.	Faculty development in S-LCE should consider organizing format, content, and activities to teach good practices in S-LCE as well as address the multiple roles, tasks, and responsibilities that faculty engage in on a daily basis.
Orientation to Learning	Children primarily learn in school, where a subject-centered, set curriculum is delivered in a sequenced format.	Adults' orientation to learning is most often problem-centered and relevant to their social/professional roles and/or current life situation.	Faculty development in S-LCE should create a menu of flexible learning opportunities that focus on more immediate needs, problems, issues, and challenges that faculty experience in S-LCE (i.e., observations, meetings, consultations, workshops).
Motivation for Learning	Children tend to be externally motivated to learn (i.e., grades, tests, peer pressure).	Adults tend to be more internally motivated and make choices about whether to participate in learning opportunities.	Faculty development in S-LCE is often not required so it is important to survey faculty to understand their motivations for engaging in S-LCE activities (i.e., personal, professional, philosophical, political, civic) and explore effective ways to align with their interests.
Need to Know	Children are required to learn specific subjects in order to get a good grade, pass a test, and advance/graduate to the next level.	Adults have a stronger need to know the reasons for learning something, based on responding to a personal or professional need.	CEPs need to provide a compelling rationale for S-LCE training; otherwise, faculty may not see the relevance of S-LCE as an effective approach to professional development.

Source: Adapted from Knowles, 1970, 1973, 1980; Knowles, Holton, & Swanson, 1998; Merriam & Bierema, 2014.

As indicated in Table 12.1, moving from pedagogy to andragogy to faculty development for S-LCE would entail starting with faculty members' experience in and knowledge of teaching. With this in mind, CEPs should consider some key disruptive questions when working with faculty:

- What is unique about faculty as adult learners?
- Are there patterns or common sets of experiences, knowledge, skills, and interests that define faculty as adult learners or set faculty apart from other adult learners?
- What learning theory informs faculty teaching practices?
- How do faculty define *reflection*?
- What conceptual frameworks are used to assist students with reflection?

To better understand the experiences of faculty as adult learners in higher education, a useful starting point for any development activity is to survey faculty in order to gain a better sense of their knowledge of and experience in S-LCE, as well as their self-assessment of key competencies and motivations to learn about or engage in S-LCE (O'Meara, 2013).

Drawing from andragogy (Merriam, 2001), the CEP has an opportunity to create an interactive learning environment, acting as a facilitator of peer-based teaching and learning, wherein participants share and colearn and coconstruct knowledge about approaches to S-LCE (Harrison et al., 2014). Importantly, andragogy offers a model of the counternormative way in which teaching and learning in service-learning occurs both inside the classroom with students and outside it with community members—who also bring knowledge and experience to the S-LCE relationship (Clayton & Ash, 2004; Howard, 1998). Andragogy helps reinforce Eatman's discussion in chapter 2 as well as other SLCE scholars (Harrison et al., 2014; Welch, 2016)—namely, that in S-LCE contexts, faculty are colearners along with peers, students, and community members.

Not all faculty have had an opportunity to critically examine their experience, knowledge, and approach to teaching and learning, let alone S-LCE. However, we found evidence with several of our research participants that involvement in S-LCE creates dissonance and incites a critical assessment and eventual revision of approaches to teaching and learning, replacing traditional pedagogy with a transformative approach that puts students in a more central and active role (Sexsmith & Kiely, 2014). Once faculty experience this transformative impact of S-LCE, it comes to influence their approach in the conventional classroom setting as well. As one research participant from a private college shared:

> I think global service-learning pedagogy adds to my teaching. It was a humbling experience the first time around and it really made me think about my pedagogy across the board. I followed the idea of learning being reciprocal, and being a give and take between professor and student. And that you're learning from your students.

S-LCE may trigger *critical reflection* on one's teaching, a threshold concept that faculty come to internalize through direct experience in the field (summarized in Table 12.2). Situated under the auspices of andragogy, faculty development activities present an opportunity for faculty to critically reflect on their knowledge and experience with key FLOs in teaching and learning (i.e., student learning outcomes, backward course design, reflection and assessment). Critical reflection can be encouraged in workshops by inviting faculty to examine their routinized teaching practice, often informed by taken-for-granted or uncritically accepted assumptions and beliefs. Elias and Merriam's (1980) framework for the five philosophical traditions in adult education theory and practice (i.e., behavioral, liberal arts, humanist, progressive, and radical approaches) is a helpful tool for examining and reflecting on one's teaching philosophy (Brookfield, 1995). More specifically, the tool provides a way for faculty to surface and examine assumptions held by each tradition, including the purpose of education, the educator's role, the learner's role, key theories, theorists and concepts, and educational practices. A useful complement is Zinn's (1990, 1994) Philosophy of Adult Education Inventory (PAEI), which results in a representation of a faculty member's orientation to teaching and learning within the five philosophical traditions.

After engaging in this critically reflective exercise and completing the PAEI, faculty often experience "aha" moments, having become, perhaps for the first time, more aware of their assumptions, and more reflective about why and how they teach, how and what students learn, and the relative value of their current approach. They also learn other philosophical approaches that help maximize student learning. Argyris and Schön's (1974) notion of the distinction (or disconnect) between what faculty think they teach in terms of both theory and practice (i.e., espoused theory) and what they actually do teach (i.e., theory in use) is useful here. When exposed to the five different philosophies of education, faculty may come to see that there are many ways to think about the purpose of education and that there are different merits to each tradition, especially in terms of the purpose of education, their role, impacts on student learning, explanatory theories, and the contribution of education to society. Because the exercise exposes faculty to unfamiliar territory, they may experience dissonance. The exercise becomes a "teachable moment" or potentially transformative experience—an opportunity to

TABLE 12.2
First Lens: Teaching and Learning

Threshold Concept: Critical Reflection		
Faculty Learning Outcomes	*Activities*	*Outputs*
• Teaching philosophy • Learning outcomes • Course design and reflection • Diversity • Assessment (reports)	• Faculty survey • Peer-based/ Colearning • PAEI • Disruptive	• S-LCE philosophy • Andragogy

introduce and reflect on S-LCE as a particular philosophical approach to teaching and learning that draws from humanist, progressive, and radical traditions in adult education.

The learning described herein draws from key processes in transformational learning theory (Mezirow & Associates, 2000). That is, the exercise creates dissonance in the way faculty understand teaching and learning, triggering critical reflection, which is a reexamination or reinterpretation of one's assumptions about teaching and learning. In addition, the exercise fosters dialogue among peers on the philosophical assumptions guiding S-LCE, as well as on the relative strengths and limitations of service-learning as an approach to teaching and learning. As an aspirational goal in the spirit of the adult learning theories previously described, these critically reflective exercises provide faculty with the tools, confidence, and independence to experiment with and transform their teaching practice from traditional classroom pedagogy to S-LCE andragogy.

Lens 2: S-LCE as a Transformative Approach to Institutional Culture

S-LCE can be a transformative approach to organizational culture (Argyris & Schön, 1996; Kezar, 2011; Latta, 2009) and to scaling institutional change that supports robust S-LCE (Bringle, Games, & Malloy, 1999; Bringle & Hatcher, 2000; Furco & Holland, 2004; Rothman, 1998). Although it is not unusual to observe a number of discrete service-learning courses offered each semester, it is rare to find participants in service-learning courses collaborating across departments and disciplines, communicating results, and/or connecting the knowledge generated to their department faculty, college administrators, and institutional leaders (Kecskes, 2006; Welch, 2016). Even more infrequent are faculty and students who transfer knowledge, skills, values, attitudes, and aspirations generated from service-learning courses to the wider audience inside their institution and outside the service setting—including the service-learning field, policymakers, and business leaders (Stoecker, 2016). Communicating the impact of S-LCE helps raise awareness of the social contribution students and community partners have made, while fostering appreciation for the value of S-LCE as an approach to andragogy, knowledge transfer, policy change, and community development (refer to case studies in chapter 4; also see Dolgon et al., 2017; Stoecker, 2016).

There are a number of strategies that promote faculty involvement and leadership in institutionalizing S-LCE (refer to case studies in chapter 5). For example, CEPs must engage with faculty in a critical examination of how curricula, majors, minors, and departments are designed; how resources are allocated; and whether the goals of S-LCE and values of the public good were taken into consideration (Kecskes, 2006). In this vein, there are a number of useful strategies for scaling up community-engaged learning and high-impact teaching practices (see Figure 12.3).

In addition to the preceding strategies, as well as initiatives featured in the case studies in chapters 4, 5, and 6, CEPs might use toolkits and rubrics to assist faculty in assessing the level and quality of engagement in their department, college, or institution, and in generating dialogue on how to improve efforts to incorporate S-LCE more broadly within the curriculum (Furco, 2002; Holland, 1999). CEPs can partner with faculty to identify the

Figure 12.3. Scaling up S-LCE.

- Strategies for Scaling Up S-LCE
  - Creating forums for deliberation to help people understand the need for a change
  - Cultivating social networks or learning communities to customize an innovation to a campus, connecting people with similar ideas
  - Creating moral support to sustain people over time
  - Offering incentives (funding or awards) to provide recognition or motivation
  - Supporting longer-term faculty and staff development interactions, such as ongoing consultation and feedback for instructors trying out S-LCE
  - Becoming familiar with the literature on organizational change
  - Aligning the change initiative with a strategic plan and other related campus priorities, using existing infrastructure (e.g., committees) rather than something new
  - Working with faculty who champion S-LCE
  - Using multiple approaches—workshops, online resources, annual big events, brown bag lunches—to promote S-LCE

Source: Adapted from Bass, Holloway, Kiely, Kusano, & Wright, 2017. See also Chamberlin & Phelps-Hillen, 2017; Henderson, Beach, & Finkelstein, 2011; Kezar, 2011, 2015; Van Note Chism, 2011.

appropriate rubric and assist with the design, implementation, and analysis of the results (Chamberlin & Phelps-Hillen, 2017).

Although these strategies can point to factors that may impact institutional change in support of more robust approaches to S-LCE, it may be that faculty have not thought about their identities beyond traditional roles related to teaching, research, and service. Indeed, many of the participants in our research described "falling into" their GSL work, implying that deliberate reflection on one's role as a prospective agent of change in the institution through the promotion of S-LCE work is rare (Sexsmith & Kiely, 2014).

Moreover, CEPs and faculty members may not be willing or prepared to become change-makers because of the perceived and real risks of asking administrators difficult questions about institutional norms, policies, and practices that hinder more robust approaches to S-LCE. For example, the faculty members participating in our research tended to describe a lack of institutional support for conducting research on S-LCE. Faculty generally expressed the inability to change these institutional structures. However, faculty also identified support for engagement from administrators, which could imply a gradual "top-down" change in support of S-LCE (Post et al., 2016; Sexsmith & Kiely, 2014).

The threshold concept for this second lens is *positionality* (e.g., identity as a teacher, researcher, global citizen, institutional change agent)—more specifically, critical reflection on one's positionality and ability to become a change agent at one's institution. Often, positionality entails a profound shift not only in one's view of self-identity but also of the identity of one's institution and one's role beyond traditional norms related to teaching, research, and service (Ward & Miller, 2016). Disruptive questions such as the following can help unpack one's positionality, agency, and/or potential leadership role as an institutional change-maker on campus:

- Did you take a faculty position at this institution to change it?
- Did you come into your department to change the curriculum or create a new publicly engaged major or minor?
- Have you thought of your role as a faculty member as an organizer or change agent and in what ways?
- What are the opportunities and obstacles for you to change your department's curriculum or create a new publicly engaged major or minor?
- What would it look like to create curricula that are community-centric, interdisciplinary, and problem-driven, as opposed to subject-centric and unidisciplinary?

- What would it look like to build a coalition or network to support an institutional culture supportive of S-LCE?

Not surprisingly, there are few faculty who come to academe to consciously challenge or change existing structures, policies, and norms. If we are committed to S-LCE approaches that maximize student and community impact, then larger questions about one's positionality—and one's role in shaping the curriculum, the department, and the institution to include support for quality S-LCE—are necessary elements of a transformative approach to S-LCE (Bringle et al., 1999; Butin, 2010; Dostilio, 2017; O'Meara & Terosky, 2010). Therefore, faculty development is about developing KSABs not only in teaching and learning S-LCE but also in how CEPs and faculty function as organizers, boundary spanners, coalition-builders, networkers, and agents of change willing to work together, to challenge existing cultural norms, structures, and policies (Gelmon & Agre-Kippenhan, 2002; Ward & Miller, 2016).

The "positionality pie chart exercise" (Merriam & Bierema, 2014, pp. 255–257) is a useful exercise for engaging faculty in reflection on how they relate to and intersect with others based on their position, faculty, rank, race, gender, class, culture, nationality, language, religion, and so on (see Table 12.3). In a group, community or classroom setting, participants construct a positionality pie chart by identifying group affiliations (i.e., gender, race, culture, nationality, religion, etc.) that help give meaning to their concept of self or identity. Once created, participants describe and share the meanings they attribute to dimensions of their identity described in their positionality pie. Importantly, participants should examine the ways in which their identities and group affiliations are positioned in terms of how they are privileged or marginalized in specific contexts. Participants then engaged in dialogue on how they might support each other (i.e., become authentic allies) in navigating their positionality in specific contexts or situations

TABLE 12.3
Second Lens: Institutional Culture

Threshold Concept: Positionality		
Faculty Learning Outcomes	*Activities*	*Outputs*
- S-LCE program models and curriculum design - Institutional policies, norms, and structures that support quality SLCE faculty learning	- Institutional rubrics - Positionality pie - Disruptive questions	- Positionality pie - S-LCE program model - Curriculum map

especially in supporting those participants whose identities are marginalized and oppressed. In general, it is likely that faculty have not had an opportunity to reflect on these multiple facets of identity, particularly on how institutional power dynamics structure and shape different aspects of identity as well as obstacles or opportunities to build coalitions and networks to affect change at the institution. This exercise allows for reflection about what it means to be a transformative leader, to address unequal relations of power, and to advocate for social justice education priorities supporting more robust S-LCE (Dostilio, 2017).

Lens 3: S-LCE as a Transformative Approach to Knowledge Generation and Application

For CEPs and faculty who have taught service-learning courses over time, there is a realization that faculty-driven, course-based S-LCE may serve as a high-impact approach to teaching and learning. Rarely does an individual course result in a long-term commitment or provide significant benefits to community partners unless there are sufficient, sustained resources and good succession planning leading to continuity (Hartley & Saltmarsh, 2016; Kiely, 2007; Stoecker, 2016). To preempt the potential harm caused to communities by the largely unsustainable, individual faculty–driven approach to S-LCE, CEPs should introduce faculty to diverse S-LCE program models and facilitate critical reflection on the limits of unsustainable S-LCE models (Kecskes, Gelmon, & Spring, 2006). Further, a transformative approach to S-LCE often means that CEPs work with more advanced faculty to critically examine their approach to scholarship, particularly whether the knowledge generated through their research contributes to the public good.

In terms of FLOs, a useful point of departure for CEPs working with faculty is to consider at least three approaches to knowledge generation and application in S-LCE:

1. Offer students community-based research (CBR) opportunities as part of the S-LCE course or program
2. Conduct research on the impact of S-LCE teaching on student learning outcomes (SLOs)
3. Conduct CBR with community partners as part of their scholarship (Kiely & Hartman, 2011; Strand, Marullo, Cutforth, Stoecker, & Donohue, 2003; Williams, 2015)

Considering the first approach, although undergraduate research has emerged as a significant form of high-impact learning, it is most commonly rooted in disciplinary frameworks. Undergraduate students have fewer opportunities than their graduate counterparts to conduct research that addresses a community problem or informs a wider audience outside the academy. Further, most undergraduates have little understanding of how to generate knowledge using a specific methodological approach in collaboration with community stakeholders to address an ongoing problem. Although this might discourage educators from experimenting with service-learning as a research approach, S-LCE coursework provides excellent opportunities for students to engage in single, mixed methods, and/or community-based research (CBR) in a variety of ways—exploratory, directed at a specific problem or issues, and/or in collaboration with specific stakeholders (Kiely & Hartman, 2011; Strand, 2003).

The second approach to knowledge generation and application in S-LCE is for faculty to engage in the scholarship of teaching and learning (SoTL),[1] whereby they conduct research on the impact of S-LCE on student learning and/or community partners (Williams, 2015). A SoTL approach to S-LCE also gives CEPs and faculty an opportunity to partner on a research project, because most faculty have not conducted research on their teaching and, in many cases, they appreciate the time and expertise CEPs can contribute (Richlin, 2006). As discussed in this volume's case study chapters and detailed in chapter 7 especially, CEPs in centers that support S-LCE might collaborate with colleagues in other units on campus (i.e., Center for Teaching and Learning) to leverage resources and incentivize faculty to conduct research on the impact of their S-LCE coursework on student learning. Having an award, fellowship, or grant opportunity to conduct research on the impact of their S-LCE teaching, ideally with the support of teaching or CEP staff, would create multiple benefits, such as alleviating faculty workload, providing SoTL expertise, and adding value to a faculty member's tenure package.[2] In conjunction with institutional change efforts, promotion and tenure guidelines might be rewritten to support both SoTL and S-LCE research.

In the third approach, CEPs might also assist faculty in collaborating with community partners in the design, implementation, and reporting dimensions of the CBR process. There are a number of CBR resources for faculty and CEPs to engage in CBR with community partners (see Beckman & Long, 2016; Greenwood & Levin, 1998; Strand et al., 2003). It should be noted that each of the three approaches described offers opportunities for faculty and CEPs to work together to generate useful knowledge with community partners.

In addition to the preceding FLOs, S-LCE can be a transformative means of engaging in dialogue with faculty on the role of knowledge in higher education, how it is constructed, and for whose benefit (Deshler & Gruden-Schuck, 2000; Greenwood & Levin, 1998; Strand et al., 2003). Most researchers are socialized into a particular epistemological stance that continues to be reinforced by mentors and peers from within their discipline; thus, it can be difficult to conceptualize the research process—including rules, norms, and criteria—in any way different from that which dominates their research stream within their field (Kiely & Hartman, 2011). Indeed, our study participants from outside the field of education often described a significant epistemological gap between their primary discipline and S-LCE, in terms of what constitutes valid knowledge and research processes (Sexsmith & Kiely, 2014).

However, finding a way to bridge this gap can allow faculty to make theoretical innovations both in their fields and in S-LCE. In our study (Sexsmith & Kiely, 2014), for example, a medical anthropology professor opted for a study "about experiential learning, about what happened to the students, about these ethical dilemmas and engagements and controversies that happened in the course of our collaboration with these institutions," rather than a "traditional anthropological approach" to the public health challenges the student project focused on. His approach challenged assumptions about what constituted real anthropological knowledge as well as about who can validly produce that knowledge. Thus, introducing faculty to the threshold concept of *reflexivity*, a dynamic process whereby we critically reflect on the ways in which our paradigmatic assumptions influence our research processes and their outcomes (Etherington, 2004; Kiely & Hartman, 2015; Morrison, 2015), may disrupt faculty members' understanding of the purpose and public value of research in a way that benefits students and communities, an idea which is emphasized in chapter 11 of this text as well.

Morrison (2015) describes the following key elements that faculty can practice to better incorporate reflexivity into their research: (a) mindfulness, (b) self-awareness, (c) learning, (d) interpretations, (e) relationships, and (f) ethical action. Engaging in these elements of reflexivity may prompt faculty to examine assumptions about who participates in and who benefits from the knowledge generated from research, and to consider as well how knowledge can be applied beyond the production of academic journal articles (Morrison, 2015; Strand et al., 2003). Morrison (2015) argues:

> Without understanding what and how our thinking is shaped by the paradigms and assumptions we make as we conduct research and analyze data, there is no way to truly evaluate the quality of our research. Worse yet, we may unknowingly perpetuate inequities or harm the communities we are researching. (p. 56)

There are a number of resources (Creswell, 1998; Greenwood & Levin; 1999; Lincoln & Guba, 2000; Strand et al., 2003) useful in assisting faculty in critically reflecting on the ontological, epistemological, axiological, and methodological assumptions embedded in distinct research paradigms (positivist, postpositivist, constructivist, critical, and participatory). Based on the insights these resources provide, we suggest CEPs might ask the following disruptive questions:

- What criteria do you use for evaluating quality knowledge generated through research?
- Where did these criteria come from?
- What are the implications of these criteria for community impacts?

Such questions about the criteria used to evaluate the quality of knowledge often trigger an in-depth reflection on the assumptions underpinning the validity of traditional quality criteria, such as causality, replicability, reliability, and generalization. Depending on the faculty members' research background, these questions may cause some dissonance for those who conduct research but have not critically evaluated their assumptions on quality criteria or on the role of knowledge in contributing to the public good (Kiely & Hartmann, 2011; see also Table 12.4). Additional follow-up questions might include the following:

- Who benefits from research when it is done well?
- How is quality knowledge constructed?
- Who participates in the design, implementation, and communication of the results of research?
- How might students, staff, and community partners participate in the different elements of the research design?
- What implications does stakeholder participation in research have for the quality and usefulness of knowledge generated? (Deshler & Gruden-Schuck, 2000; Greenwood & Levin, 1999; Reardon, 1994; Strand et al., 2003).

TABLE 12.4
Third Lens: Knowledge Generation and Application

Threshold Concept: Reflexivity		
Faculty Learning Outcomes	*Activities*	*Outputs*
• SoTL • CBR methods and principles	• Lincoln & Guba (2000) paradigmatic lenses • Surfacing assumptions on disciplinary epistemology(ies) (e.g., Boyer, 1990; Strand et al., 2003)	• Reflective statement on epistemology

These and other questions provoking epistemological reflexivity will assist faculty in surfacing and critically examining their assumptions regarding the role of knowledge and how S-LCE might be used to generate knowledge with community partners to benefit local, regional, national, and international communities (Kiely & Hartman, 2011, 2015).

Lens 4: S-LCE as a Transformative Approach to Community Partnerships

Finally, S-LCE can be a transformative approach to community partnerships and to capacity-building in communities (Hamerlinck & Plaut, 2014). As mentioned, it is rare for a semester-long service-learning course to make a substantial contribution to the alleviation of long-standing, complex community problems (Stoecker, 2016). Using S-LCE as a transformative approach to community partnerships means demonstrating a willingness to commit to long-term community capacity-building through relationship-building with stakeholders, coursework, research, resources, technology, and ongoing networking (Green & Haines, 2002; Stoecker & Tryon, 2009). There is much to be learned from a growing body of research on the impact of higher education institutions as "anchors" providing a solid foundation from which other key community stakeholders can collectively leverage their assets to build a more sustainable, equitable approach to community health and well-being (Harkavy & Hartley, 2009; Hodges & Dubb, 2012; Pease, 2017).

Drawing from this volume's cases studies, key practices described in chapter 10, and the scholarship of community-campus partnerships, FLOs in this lens should focus on guiding frameworks, principles, and good practices for developing, maintaining, and sustaining reciprocal partnerships (Jacoby, 2015; Strand et al., 2003). Fortunately, field-based organizations supporting S-LCE, such as Campus Compact and Community-Campus Partnership for Health, have developed a number of web-based resources and tools (see Table 12.5). In addition to serving as knowledge hubs, these and other S-LCE organizations, practitioners, and scholars have come together to generate a set of guidelines and principles of good practice in partnership development, such as the fair trade learning (FTL) principles (Hartman, Morris-Paris, & Blache-Cohen, 2014) described later in this section.

Key FLOs in Lens 4 include the following capacities:

- Describe diverse program and community partnership models
- Conduct site visits
- Design a plan for risk management

- Explain the history and meaning of community from multiple perspectives
- Identify key elements to nurturing a healthy and sustainable community-campus relationships (Jacoby, 2015)

It can be a meaningful faculty development exercise to generate a list of key principles and guiding questions for engaging in dialogue with potential community partners on what constitutes a quality community-campus partnership from the initial development of the relationship (Gelmon, Holland, Driscoll, Spring, & Kerrigan, 2001; Jacoby, 2015; Strand et al., 2003) through goal attainment. CEPs can assist faculty in unpacking what it means to develop a quality community partnership focused on building capacity and drawing from existing principles that have been generated over time. FTL principles (Hartman et al., 2014) were developed initially through a global service-learning, third-party provider, Amizade, and then through extensive dialogues with stakeholders in the field of global service-learning. FTL offers a useful set of guiding principles for developing sustainable and reciprocal community-campus partnerships and ensuring that both campus and community stakeholders benefit from S-LCE. CEPs might also engage faculty in a stakeholder mapping exercise, ideally with community members, to identify the community needs and assets that should inform S-LCE planning participation, decision-making, and project goals and objectives (Green & Haines, 2002; Hartman et al., 2014; Jacoby, 2015; Kretzmann & McKnight, 1993).

Harrison and Clayton (2012) suggest that *reciprocity* in S-LCE partnerships is a threshold concept that, once understood, transforms the assumptions about building community partnerships that faculty members take for granted. Our research illuminated faculty difficulty in striking a balance

TABLE 12.5
Fourth Lens: Community Partnership

Threshold Concept: Reciprocity		
Faculty Learning Outcomes	*Activities*	*Outputs*
• Models, principles, and practices for campus-community partnerships • Community asset-mapping • Community development approaches, theories, and models	• Stakeholder and asset-mapping template • Principles of good practice • Fair trade learning rubric	• Stakeholder asset map • Community partnership principles

between accountability to their institutions and the communities where the projects are carried out. They sometimes tend to structure their research and teaching to address community needs rather than building reciprocal relationships based on both needs and assets (Kretzman & McKnight, 1993; Stoecker & Tryon, 2009). Alternatively, their S-LCE courses may overfocus on meeting conventional student learning outcomes, at the expense of sufficient reciprocity with communities, who hold expectations regarding investments of student time and support (Hartman et al., 2014; Stoecker & Tryon, 2009). For all of these reasons, it is not unusual for faculty to maintain a "deficit" approach to S-LCE in communities (Hamerlinck & Plaut, 2014).

A participant in our study (Sexsmith & Kiely, 2014) from a research university resolves this dilemma by aiming to strike a balance between institutional needs and community needs by using a language of "mutual reward." She said that before engaging in a new international service-learning initiative, "I need to be really clear. . . . These are the rewards for me. What are the rewards for you?" This approach helps builds sustainable partnerships by ensuring that university stakeholders see a benefit in the initiative, while also ensuring that community partners have engaged in proactively shaping the terms of the relationship. In this vein, CEPs and faculty might draw from Enos and Morton's (2003) useful model and a set of criteria (i.e., purpose, roles, commitment, etc.) for distinguishing between a transactional and transformational partnership.

To get at this distinction, as well as other elements that constitute a campus-community partnership, one might ask disruptive questions:

- What is an asset (in the context of campus-community partnerships)?
- How are assets identified and incorporated into the partnership?
- What does a reciprocal community-campus partnership mean?
- What constitutes a healthy campus-community relationship?
- How is benefit (to all parties) understood and evaluated?
- What are appropriate guiding principles for campus-community partnerships?

CEPs are advised to assist faculty in understanding how to design an asset-based approach to building partnerships in S-LCE, such as learning how to develop a stakeholder map, assess relations of power, listen eloquently, embrace humility, encourage voice, and develop relationships with community members based on trust, fairness, inclusion, voice, and mutual benefit of both service and learning (Sandmann et al., 2009; Welch, 2016).

There is consensus in the field that community partnership development and capacity-building is the area in S-LCE that requires the greatest amount of attention (Hartman et al., 2014; Post et al., 2016; Stoecker & Tryon, 2009). Specifically, the S-LCE field is searching for more robust approaches to including partners in the decision-making process; appreciating the knowledge and experience that partners bring; ensuring that resources, roles, and responsibilities are equitable; and measuring the learning outcomes and impact of the community-campus partnerships (Hartman et al., 2014; Reardon & Forester, 2016; Stoecker & Tryon, 2009). A transformative approach to partnership development in S-LCE is a positive and hopeful step in the right direction.

Lens 5: Metacognition—A Transformative Approach to Faculty Development in S-LCE

Faculty and CEPs are key to developing and implementing a robust theory of change for high-quality S-LCE programs, curricula, research, and institutional structures that sustain community partnerships and build capacity in communities (Welch & Plaxton-Moore, 2017). Eatman's compelling reminder in chapter 2 that "faculty are central to the traditions, character, and ethos of an institution over time" (p. 59, this volume) affirms not only the role that faculty have played in shaping the evolution of higher education but also their potential for transforming colleges and universities into highly engaged, socially responsible learning organizations.

This chapter suggests a theory of change in which CEPs and faculty developers embrace a multifaceted, potentially transformative approach to S-LCE by supporting faculty development in teaching and learning, knowledge generation and application, institutional change, and community partnerships (see Figure 12.2). The model suggests that in order to achieve high-quality S-LCE, faculty development programs should foster faculty learning that is instrumental (i.e., FLOs) and transformational (i.e., threshold concepts). Learning within each lens is powerful, yet learning that integrates all four lenses is *metacognitive*—a fifth lens whereby faculty develop a critical awareness of the potential of S-LCE as a transformative approach. Faculty who develop this lens would have an awareness of key learning outcomes in S-LCE related to each of the four lenses and, through engaging with the key threshold concepts of critical reflection, positionality, reflexivity, and reciprocity, would be able to clearly articulate the sets of assumptions underpinning their approach to teaching and learning in S-LCE; their role as change-makers in their department, college, and/or institution; their epistemological understanding of the knowledge generation process; and the principles informing their approach to community partnerships.

Faculty who have developed metacognition will have likely experienced some level of dissonance, leading to difficulties navigating cultural norms and expectations in the classroom, department, or institution. They may feel that they risk social capital. Therefore, it is crucial for CEPs and faculty to develop learning communities to provide support for each other as they engage in counternormative, movement-building S-LCE work (Clayton & Ash, 2004; Kiely, 2007; Kiely & Nielsen, 2003; Swords & Kiely, 2010).

Conclusion

The transformative S-LCE model described in this chapter provides faculty and faculty development professionals a number of different pathways to critically examine their assumptions through four key lenses. It centralizes the threshold concepts of critical reflection, positionality, reflexivity, and reciprocity, which, once mastered through critical reflection and dialogue, provide CEPs and faculty with the tools to engage in transformative S-LCE. A further reflection on these threshold concepts reveals that they differ from traditional threshold concepts in that they are processes and mental exercises that provoke undetermined outcomes. We pose the fifth metacognitive lens as a paradox to the S-LCE field, as a further, higher-level challenge regarding the critical importance of surfacing assumptions about what, and whose, knowledge counts; who participates in the knowledge generation-learning process; and who ultimately benefits from these key processes (Chambers, 1998; Deshler & Gruden-Schuck, 2000; Strand et al., 2003). Here, we wholeheartedly agree with Mezirow (1991) that to predetermine the outcome of transformational learning is "tantamount to indoctrination" (Mezirow, 1995, p. 59). Hence, the chapters in this book represent our "best tentative judgment" (Mezirow, 2000, p. 11) on what constitutes high-quality faculty development in S-LCE. Taken together, they provide faculty development professionals an opportunity to undertake a more meaningful and robust dialogue on current and future forms of S-LCE that maximize faculty and student learning and, ultimately, have a positive impact on communities.

Notes

1. The scholarship of teaching and learning (SoTL) encourages faculty and teachers from any discipline to view curriculum, teaching, and student learning as an opportunity for inquiry and research. Importantly, SoTL means disseminating and publishing the results of one's research on teaching and learning beyond one's classroom so that what was learned from that inquiry can be reviewed and critiqued

so that other faculty and teachers can build on it, advance theory, and accumulate knowledge in the area of teaching and learning (Hutchins, Huber, & Ciccone, 2011; Williams, 2015).

2. See for example, the University of Michigan's Third Century Initiative (http://thirdcentury.umich.edu), which offers funding for faculty who would like to conduct research on their engaged learning projects. Engaged Cornell also offers engaged research grants to faculty to, among other areas, assess the impact of community engagement on student learning outcomes (http://engaged.cornell.edu/grant/engaged-research-grants-for-faculty), and IUPUI offers writing institutes for faculty and staff to publish engaged scholarship (http://csl.iupui.edu/about/conferences/academy.shtml).

References

Argyris, C., & Schön, D. (1974). *Theory in practice. Increasing professional effectiveness.* San Francisco, CA: Jossey-Bass.

Argyris, C., & Schön, D. A. (1996). *Organizational learning II: Theory, method, and practice.* Reading, MA: Addison-Wesley.

Barr, R. B., & Tagg, J. (1995). From teaching to learning: A new paradigm for undergraduate education. *Change, 27*(6), 12–25.

Barradell, S. (2012). The identification of threshold concepts: A review of theoretical complexities and methodological challenges. *Journal of Higher Education, 65,* 265–276.

Bass, R. (2012, March/April). Disrupting ourselves: The problem of learning in higher education. *EDUCAUSE Review, 47*(2). Retrieved from https://er.educause.edu/articles/2012/3/disrupting-ourselves-the-problem-of-learning-in-higher-education

Bass, R., Holloway, J., Kiely, R., Kusano, S., & Wright, M. (2017, January). *Engaged learning at scale: Scaling up high-impact practices for all students.* Paper presented at AAC&U Annual Conference, San Francisco, CA.

Beckman, M., & Long, J. F. (2016). *Community-based research: Teaching for community impact.* Sterling, VA: Stylus.

Bringle, R., Games, R., & Malloy E. (1999). *Colleges and universities as citizens.* Needham Heights, MA: Allyn & Bacon.

Bringle, R., & Hatcher, J. (2000). Institutionalization of service-learning in higher education. *Journal of Higher Education, 71*(3), 273–290.

Brookfield, S. D. (1995). *Becoming a critically reflective teacher.* San Francisco, CA: Jossey-Bass.

Bunnell, S. L., & Bernstein, D. J. (2012). Overcoming some threshold concepts in scholarly teaching. *Journal of Faculty Development, 26*(3), 14–18.

Butin, D. (2010). *Service-learning in theory and practice: The future of community engagement in higher education.* New York, NY: Palgrave Macmillan.

Chamberlin, J., & Phelps-Hillen, J. (2017). Competencies community engagement professionals need for faculty development. In L. Dostilio (Ed.), *The community* engagement professional in higher education: A competency model for an emerging field* (pp. 179–200). Boston, MA: Campus Compact.

Chambers, R. (1998). Beyond "Whose reality counts?" New methods we now need? *Studies in Cultures, Organizations and Societies, 4*(2), 297–301.

Clayton, P., & Ash, S. (2004). Shifts in Perspective: Capitalizing on the counternormative nature of service-learning. *Michigan Journal of Community Service Learning, 11*(1), 59–70.

Clayton, P., Bringle, R., & Hatcher, J. (2013). *Research on service learning: Conceptual frameworks and assessment,* (Vol. 2A: Students and Faculty), Sterling, VA: Stylus.

Cousin, G. (2010). Neither teacher-centred nor student-centered: Threshold concepts and research partnerships. *Journal of Learning Development in Higher Education, 2*, 1–9.

Creswell, J. W. (1998). *Qualitative inquiry and research design: Choosing among five traditions.* Thousand Oaks, CA: Sage Publications.

Deshler, D., & Gruden-Schuck, N. (2000). The politics of knowledge construction. In A. L. Wilson and E. Hayes (Eds.), *Handbook of adult and continuing education.* San Francisco, CA: Jossey-Bass.

Dostilio, L., Janke, E., Miller, A., Post, M., & Ward, E. (2016). Disrupting role dichotomies. In M. Post, E. Ward, N. Longo, & J. Saltmarsh (Eds.), *Publicly engaged scholars: Next-generation engagement and the future of higher education* (pp. 117–129). Sterling, VA: Stylus.

Dostilio, L. (2017). *The community engagement professional in higher education: A competency mode for an emerging field.* Boston, MA: Campus Compact.

Dolgon, C., Mitchell, T., & Eatman, T. (2017). *Cambridge handbook of service-learning and community engagement.* Cambridge, UK: Cambridge University Press.

Elias, J. L., & Merriam, S. (1980). *Philosophical foundations of adult education.* Huntington, NY: Krieger.

Enos, S., & Morton, K. (2003). Developing a theory and practice of campus-community partnerships. In B. Jacoby and Associates (Eds.), Building partnerships for service-learning. (pp. 20–41). San Francisco, CA: Jossey-Bass.

Etherington, K. (2004). *Becoming a reflexive researcher: Using ourselves in research.* London, England: Jessica Kingsley.

Fink, L. D. (2003). *Creating significant learning experiences.* San Francisco, CA: Jossey-Bass.

Furco, A. (2002). *Self-assessment rubric for the institutionalization of service-learning.* Berkeley, CA: UC Service-Learning Research & Development Center.

Furco, A., & Holland, B. (2004). Institutionalizing service-learning in higher education: Issues and strategies for chief academic officers. In M. Langseth and W. Plater, *Public work and the academy: An academic administrator's guide to civic engagement and service-learning* (pp. 23–30). Bolton, MA: Anker.

Gelmon, C., Holland, B., Driscoll, A., Spring, A., & Kerrigan, S. (2001). *Assessing service-learning and civic engagement: Principles and techniques.* Providence, RI: Campus Compact.

Gelmon, S. B., & Agre-Kippenhan, S. (2002). A developmental framework for supporting evolving faculty roles for community engagement. *Journal of Public Affairs, 6*(1), 161–182.

Green, G., & Haines, A. (2002). *Asset building and community development.* Thousand Oaks, CA: Sage.

Greenwood, D., & Levin, M. (1998). *Introduction to action research: Social research for social change.* Thousand Oaks, CA; Sage.

Hamerlinck, J., & Plaut, J. (Eds.). (2014). *Asset-based community engagement in higher education.* Minneapolis, MN: Minnesota Campus Compact.

Harkavy, I., & Hartley, M. (Eds.). (2009). *Universities in partnership: Strategies for education, youth development, and community renewal* (New Directions for Youth Development No. 122). Hoboken, NJ: Wiley Periodicals.

Harrison, B., & Clayton, P. (2012). Reciprocity as a threshold concept for faculty who are learning to teach with service-learning. *Journal of Faculty Development, 26*(3), 29–33.

Harrison, B., Clayton, P., & Lilly-Tubbs, G. (2014). Troublesome knowledge, troubling experience: An inquiry into faculty learning in service-learning. *Michigan Journal of Community Service Learning, 20*(2), 5–18.

Hartley, M., & Saltmarsh, J. (2016). A brief history of a movement: Civic engagement and higher education. In M. Post, E. Ward, N. Longo, & J. Saltmarsh (Eds), *Publicly engaged scholars: Next-generation engagement and the future of higher education* (pp. 34–60). Sterling, VA: Stylus.

Hartman, E., Morris-Paris, C., & Blache-Cohen, B. (2014). Fair trade learning: Ethical standards for international volunteer tourism. *Tourism and Hospitality Research, 14*(1–2), 108–116.

Henderson, C., Beach, A., & Finklestein, N. (2011). Facilitating change in undergraduate STEM instructional practices: An analytic review of the literature. *Journal of Research in Science Teaching, 48*(8), 952–984.

Hodges, R., & Dubb, S. (2012). *The road half traveled: University engagement at a crossroads.* Lansing, MI: Michigan State University Press.

Holland, B. A. (1999). Factors and strategies that influence faculty involvement in public service. *Journal of Public Service and Outreach, 4*(1), 37–43.

Howard, J. P. F. (1998). Academic service-learning: A counternormative pedagogy. *New Directions for Teaching and Learning, 1998*(73), 21–29.

Hutchins, P., Huber, M. T., & Ciccone, A. (2011). *The scholarship of teaching and learning reconsidered. Institutional integration and impact.* San Francisco, CA: Jossey-Bass.

Jacoby, B. (2015). Taking campus-community partnerships to the next level through border crossing and democratic engagement. *Michigan Journal of Community Service Learning, 22*(1), 140–157.

Kegan, R. (2000). What form transforms? A constructive-developmental approach to transformative learning. In J. Mezirow (Ed.), *Learning as transformation: Critical perspectives on a theory in progress* (pp. 35–69). San Francisco, CA: Jossey-Bass.

Kecskes, K. (Ed). (2006). *Engaging departments: Moving faculty culture from private to public, individual to collective for the common good*. Bolton, MA: Anker.

Kecskes, K., Gelmon, S.B., and Spring, A. (2006). Creating engaged departments: a program for organizational and faculty development. *To Improve the Academy*, 24, 147–165.

Kezar, A. (2011). What is the best way to achieve broader reach of improved practices in higher education? *Innovative Higher Education, 36*, 235–247.

Kezar, A. (2015). *Scaling and sustaining change and innovation: Lessons learned from the Teagle Foundation's "Faculty Work and Student Learning" initiative* [Teagle Foundation Report]. Retrieved from http://www.teaglefoundation.org/getmedia/f5560934-c4db-42e3-8e52-439bd7aa82f6/Kezar-Sustaining-Change

Kiely, R. (2005). A transformative service-learning model: A longitudinal case study. *Michigan Journal of Community Service Learning, 12*(1), 5–22.

Kiely, R. (2007). Service learning as reflective practice: A four-lens model. In P. Horrigan (Ed.), *Extending our reach: Voices of service-learning* (pp. 64–71). Ithaca, NY: Cornell University.

Kiely, R. (2015). *Considering critical reflection*. Retrieved from http://globalsl.org/criticalreflection/

Kiely, R. (2017, April). A transformative approach to community engaged scholarship [keynote address]. *Transforming twenty-first-century higher education through community-engaged scholarship*. Northwestern University, Evanston, IL.

Kiely, R., & Hartman, E. (2011). Qualitative research in ISL. In R. Bringle, J. Hatcher, & S. Jones, (Eds.), *International Service Learning: Conceptual Frameworks and Research*. Sterling, VA: Stylus.

Kiely, R., & Hartman, E. (2015). Reflexivity in research: Reflecting on the borders and boundaries of the GSL field. *Michigan Journal of Community Service Learning, 22*(1), 48–52.

Kiely, R., & Nielsen, D. (2003). International service-learning: The importance of partnerships. *Community College Journal, 3*, 39–41.

Kiely, R., Sandmann, L. R., & Truluck, J. E. (2004). Adult learning theory and the pursuit of adult degrees. In J. Pappas & J. Jerman (Eds.), *Developing and delivering adult degree programs* (New Directions in Adult and Continuing Education No. 103, pp. 17–30). San Francisco, CA: Jossey-Bass.

King, C., & Felten, P. (2012). Threshold concepts in educational development: An introduction. *Journal of Faculty Development, 26*(3), 5–7.

Knowles, M. (1970). *Modern practice of adult education: Andragogy versus pedagogy*. Englewood Cliffs, NJ: Cambridge Adult Education.

Knowles, M. (1973). *The adult learner: A neglected species*. Houston, TX: Gulf Publishing.

Knowles, M. (1980). *Modern practice of adult education: From pedagogy to andragogy* (2nd ed.). Englewood Cliffs, NJ: Cambridge Adult Education.

Knowles, M. S., Holton, E. F. III, & Swanson, R. A. (1998). A theory of adult learning: Andragogy. In M. S. Knowles, E. F. Holton III, & R. A. Swanson, *The adult learner: The definitive classic in adult education and human resource development* (5th ed., pp. 35–95). Houston, TX: Gulf Publishing.

Kretzmann, J., & McKnight, J. (1993). *Building communities from the inside out: A path toward mobilizing a community's assets*. Evanston, IL: Institute for Policy Research.

Latta, G. (2009). Maturation of organizational development in higher education: Using cultural analysis to facilitate change. In L. Nilson & J. Miller (Eds.), *To improve the academy* (pp. 32–71). San Francisco, CA: Jossey-Bass.

Lincoln, Y. S., & Guba, E. (2000). The only generalization is: There is no generalization. In R. Gromm (Ed.), *Case study method* (pp. 27–44). London: Sage Publications.

Merriam, S. B. (2001). Andragogy and self-directed learning: Pillars of adult learning theory. In S. B. Merriam (Ed.), *The new update on adult learning theory* (New Directions for Adult and Continuing Education No. 89, pp. 3–14). San Francisco, CA: Jossey-Bass.

Merriam, S., & Bierema, L. (2014). *Adult learning: Linking theory and practice*. San Francisco, CA: Jossey-Bass.

Meyer, J., & Land, R. (2006) (Eds.). *Overcoming barriers to student understanding: Threshold concepts and troublesome knowledge*. New York, NY: Routledge.

Mezirow, J. (1991). *Transformative dimensions of adult learning*. San Francisco, CA: Jossey-Bass.

Mezirow, J. (1995). Transformation theory in adult education. In M. R. Welton (Ed.), *In defense of the lifeworld: Critical perspectives on adult learning* (pp. 39–70). Albany, NY: SUNY.

Mezirow, J., & Associates. (2000). *Learning as transformation: Critical perspectives on a theory in progress*. San Francisco, CA: Jossey-Bass.

Morrison, E. (2015). How the I shapes the eye: The imperative of reflexivity in global service-learning qualitative research. *Michigan Journal of Community Service Learning, 22*(1), 52–66.

O'Meara, K. (2016). Legitimacy, Agency and Inequality: Organizational practices for full participation of community-engaged faculty. In M. Post, E. Ward, N. Longo, & J. Saltmarsh (Eds.), *Publicly engaged scholars: Next-generation engagement and the future of higher education* (pp. 96–109). Sterling, VA: Stylus.

O'Meara, K. A. (2013). Research on faculty motivations for service-learning and community engagement. In P. Clayton, R. Bringle, and J. Hatcher (Eds.), *International Service Learning: Conceptual Frameworks and Assessment* (pp. 215–243). Sterling, VA: Stylus.

O'Meara, K., & Terosky, A. L. (2010). Engendering faculty professional growth. *Change: The Magazine of Higher Learning, 42*(6), 44–51.

Pease, K. (2017). *Anchored in place: How funders are helping anchor institutions strengthen local economies*. Coral Gables, FL: Funders' Network for Smart Growth and Livable Communities.

Post, M., Ward, E., Longo, N., & Saltmarsh, J. (2016). *Publicly engaged scholars: Next-generation engagement and the future of higher education*. Sterling, VA: Stylus.

Reardon, K. (1994). Undergraduate research in distressed urban communities: An undervalued form of service-learning. *Michigan Journal of Community Service Learning, 1*(1), 44–54.

Reardon, K., & Forester, J. (2016). *Rebuilding community after Katrina: Transformative education in the New Orleans Planning Initiative.* Philadelphia, PA: Temple University Press.

Rice, K. (2010). Becoming a reflective service-learning professional. In B. Jacoby and P. Mustascio (Eds.), *Looking in, reaching out: A reflective guide for community service-learning professionals* (pp. 1–16). Boston, MA: Campus Compact.

Richlin, L. (2006). *Blueprint for learning: Constructing college courses to facilitate, assess and document learning.* Sterling, VA: Stylus.

Rhoads, R., Howard, J. (Eds). (1998). *Academic service learning: A pedagogy of action and reflection.* San Francisco, CA: Jossey-Bass.

Rothman, M. (1998). *Service matters: Engaging higher education in the renewal of America's communities and American democracy.* Providence, RI: Campus Compact.

Sandmann, L., Kiely, R., & Grenier, R. (2009, Spring). Program planning in service-learning: A neglected dimension. *Michigan Journal of Community Service Learning, 15*(2), 17–33.

Schön, D. (1987). *Educating the reflective practitioner: Toward a new design for teaching and learning in the professions.* San Francisco, CA: Jossey-Bass.

Sexsmith, K., & Kiely, R. (2014). *Faculty experiences in global service-learning: A qualitative study.* New Orleans, LA: International Association of Research on Service-Learning and Community Engagement.

Stoecker, R. (2016). *Liberating service learning and the rest of higher education civic engagement.* Philadelphia, PA: Temple University Press.

Stoecker, R., & Tryon, E. A. (2009). *The unheard voices: Community organizations and service learning.* Philadelphia, PA: Temple University Press.

Strand, K. (2003). Principles of best practice for community-based research. *Michigan Journal of Community Service Learning, 9*(3), 5–15.

Strand, K., Marullo, S., Cutforth, N., Stoecker, R., & Donohue, P. (2003). *Community-based research in higher education.* San Francisco, CA: Jossey-Bass.

Swords, A., & Kiely, R. (2010, Fall). Beyond pedagogy: Service learning as movement building in higher education. *Journal of Community Practice, 18*(2), 148–170.

Van Note Chism (2011). Ready or not: An international study of the preparation of educational developers. In J. Miller & J. Groccia (Eds). *Into the Academy. Resources for Faculty, Instructional and Organizational Development, 29*(1), 260–273.

Van Note Chism, N., Holley, M., & Harris, C. J. (2012). Researching the impact of educational development: Basis for informed practice. *To improve the academy, 31*, 129–145.

Van Note Chism, N., Palmer, M., & Price, M. (2013). Investigating faculty development for service-learning. In P. Clayton, R. Bringle, and J. Hatcher (Eds.), *International service learning: Conceptual frameworks and assessment* (pp. 187–214). Sterling, VA: Stylus.

Ward, E., & Miller A. (2016). Next generation engaged scholars: Stewards of change. In M. Post, E. Ward, N. Longo, & J. Saltmarsh (Eds.), *Publicly engaged scholars: Next-generation engagement and the future of higher education* (pp. 184–194). Sterling, VA: Stylus.

Welch, M. (2016). *Engaging higher education. Purpose, platforms, and programs for community engagement.* Sterling, VA: Stylus.

Welch, M., & Plaxton-Moore, S. (2017). Faculty development for advancing community engagement in higher education: Current trends and future directions. *Journal of Higher Education Outreach and Engagement, 21*(2), 131–165.

Williams, K. (2015). *Doing research to improve teaching and learning: A guide for college and university faculty.* New York, NY: Routledge.

Zepke, N. (2013). Student engagement: A complex business supporting the first year experience in tertiary education. *The International Journal of the First Year in Higher Education, 4*(2), 1–14.

Zinn, L. M. (1990). Identifying your philosophical orientation. In M. W. Galbraith (Ed.), *Adult learning methods: A guide for effective instruction* (pp. 39–56). Malabar, FL: Krieger.

Zinn, L. (1994). *Philosophy of adult education inventory.* Boulder, CO: Lifelong Learning Options.

EDITORS AND CONTRIBUTORS

Editors

Becca Berkey is the director of service-learning for the Center of Community Service at Northeastern University. She holds a BS in biology from Butler University, an MS in college student personnel from Miami University, and a PhD in environmental studies from Antioch University. In addition to her academic work around service-learning and community engagement, she conducts research at the intersection of leadership, change, and environmental justice with a specific interest in the justice issues facing farmworkers. She has multiple publications in both areas, including her book *Environmental Justice and Farm Labor* (Routledge, 2017), which came out in March 2017. Berkey is active in several professional associations and farmworker advocacy groups, and serves on the board of directors for the International Association for Research on Service-Learning and Community Engagement (IARSLCE).

Emily A. Eddins is the founding service-learning practitioner-scholar at Old Dominion University in Norfolk, Virginia; is the assistant director of leadership and student involvement; and supervises the wonderful staff of the Center for Service & Civic Engagement. Eddins received her PhD and MS in human dimensions of natural resources from Colorado State University and a BA in geography from Miami University (Ohio). With a fellowship from the Center for Collaborative Conservation, she completed her doctoral research on international service-learning in rural Panama. She's received two major grants to develop service-learning projects that address sea level rise, climate change, and conservation at Old Dominion University, and serves as treasurer of the WHRO/WHRV Public Radio Emerging Leaders Board. She chooses to work in service-learning because of its complexity, global-local significance, and the belief that collaborative processes between universities and surrounding communities can enact real social and environmental change.

Patrick M. Green is the founding director of the Center for Experiential Learning at Loyola University Chicago and a clinical instructor of experiential learning. Green received his PhD in education from Roosevelt University (Chicago, IL), and his research interests include intersections in experiential education. He is coeditor of *Crossing Boundaries: Tension and Transformation in International Service-Learning* (Stylus, 2014). Green serves as an Engaged Scholar with National Campus Compact and served on the board of directors of the International Association for Research on Service-Learning and Community Engagement (IARSCLE).

Cara Meixner is the executive director of the Center for Faculty Innovation and an associate professor of psychology at James Madison University, where she also received her BS. Meixner also holds an MA from the University of Maryland and a PhD from Antioch University. While her primary professional love is teaching, Meixner coleads a community-based research agenda to enhance access to crisis intervention services for survivors of traumatic brain injury. She has served as coprincipal investigator of several sponsored projects, with a vast array of presentations and publications (e.g., *Rehabilitation Psychology, Journal of Head Trauma Rehabilitation, NeuroRehabilitation*). Most critically, this body of inquiry has contributed to the development of noteworthy policy changes and advocacy initiatives, including the coauthored *Access to Neurobehavioral Services in Virginia* (DARS, 2015).

Contributors

Anna Bailey is the coordinator for faculty and community partnerships in service-learning and an adjunct instructor in foundational studies at Boise State University. Bailey received her PhD in history from the University of Washington in Seattle.

Gabriel Ignacio Barreneche is a professor of Spanish and the associate dean for advising at Rollins College. In 2003, he received his PhD in Hispanic languages and literatures from the University of California, Los Angeles. He has authored peer-reviewed journal articles on the intersections of foreign language pedagogy and service-learning, as well as on film and literature from Latin America and the U.S.-Latino community. His coedited volume *Educational Technology for the Global Village: Worldwide Innovation and Best Practices* (Information Today, 2014) outlines projects and case studies that explore how the use of technology can impact student learning and enhance our students' global perspectives.

Carey Borkoski is an assistant professor at the Johns Hopkins University School of Education. She holds an EdD from Johns Hopkins and a PhD from the University of Maryland-Baltimore County. Her research interests include online teaching and learning, improving support and development for teaching faculty at research universities, and the role of communities and social learning as a means to provide training, knowledge, and support to faculty in different geographical locations but part of the same university and program. Current research projects include an investigation of the role of sync sessions and text-based discussions in doctoral student learning and preparation for important educational milestones, an exploration of the role of online communities of practice in faculty development around teaching, and the potential role of online communities in supporting and building closer connections with adjunct faculty and full-time faculty at a distance.

Melody Bowdon is associate dean of undergraduate studies, executive director of the Karen L. Smith Faculty Center for Teaching and Learning, and professor of writing and rhetoric at the University of Central Florida. She received her PhD in English from the University of Arizona, and her research interests include technical and professional communication, innovative teaching strategies, and community-based learning and research. Bowdon has served as senior research fellow for Florida Campus Compact since 2005.

Kara Brascia is the director of the service-learning program at Boise State University. Brascia received her MA in communication from the University of Utah, and her research interests include strategic communication to recruit and retain volunteer participation. In addition to her university position, Brascia is a commissioner on the Governor's Commission for Service and Volunteerism (Serve Idaho).

Andreas Broscheid is an assistant director for career planning programs in the Center for Faculty Innovation at James Madison University. Broscheid received a PhD in political science at Stony Brook University. His disciplinary work focuses on decision-making in the U.S. Courts of Appeals and the scholarship of teaching and learning. Since 2006, Broscheid has been a faculty member at James Madison University, where he is also a professor of political science. His current focus is on developing programs to support comprehensive faculty career planning through mentoring and performance documentation at various career stages.

Timothy K. Eatman, inaugural dean of the Honors Living-Learning Community and associate professor at Rutgers University-Newark, is an educational sociologist and publicly engaged scholar who received his PhD from the University of Illinois at Urbana-Champaign. Eatman is active within the community of higher education researchers taking up questions of equity and policy in academe and society. He is coeditor of *The Cambridge Handbook of Service Learning and Community Engagement* (Cambridge University Press, 2017), serves as national cochair of the Urban Research Action Network (URBAN), and is on the board of directors of the

International Association for Research on Service-Learning and Community Engagement (IARSLCE).

Kristin English is an associate professor of strategic communication in the Department of Communication at Georgia College & State University. English received her PhD in mass communication research from the University of Georgia Grady College of Journalism and Mass Communication. Her research interests are in the areas of political communication, service-learning, community engagement, and social and digital media. Her previous experience includes serving as an interim director of the Georgia College Engage Program, an Engage Fellow, and a Governor's Teaching Fellow.

Sherril B. Gelmon is professor and director of the Health Systems and Policy PhD program in the Oregon Health & Science University & Portland State University School of Public Health in Portland, Oregon. She received her PhD in public health and health policy from the University of Michigan. Her research addresses community-engaged scholarship, community health improvement, and community/university partnerships. She is a senior scholar with CES4Health, and was an Engaged Scholar with Campus Compact. She was founding chair of IARSCLE. She is a recipient of both the IARSLCE Distinguished Research Award and the Thomas Ehrlich Civically Engaged Faculty Award from Campus Compact.

Sandra Godwin is professor of sociology at Georgia College & State University. Godwin received her PhD in sociology from North Carolina State University. She recently designed a community-based course, Sociology of Food and Agriculture, that includes three different farm tours for students and community gardeners. She and a community partner, drawing on their experience in this course, have a chapter forthcoming in *Handbook of Service-Learning for Social Justice* (Darren Lund, editor): "Participatory Assessment: Enlisting Community Partners to Facilitate Boundary Spanning, Reflexive Student Activism, and Institutional Change." Her recent research interest is exploring barriers to critical reflection in community-based learning.

Emily O. Gravett is an assistant director in the Center for Faculty Innovation and an assistant professor in the philosophy and religion department at James Madison University. She received her PhD in religious studies from the University of Virginia, and her research interests include educational development and the scholarship of teaching and learning. In addition to publishing broadly, Gravett serves on the editorial board of *To Improve the Academy*.

Ann E. Green is a professor of English at Saint Joseph's University. She is the recipient of the 2017 Outstanding Leader in Experiential Education Award from the National Society of Experiential Education, and she teaches writing and service-learning courses in narrative medicine; environmental justice; and race, class, and gender. She has published in *College Composition and Communication, The Michigan Journal of Community Service Learning*, and a number of edited collections. She has taught immersion courses in Ireland and China, as well as Dimensions of Freedom, a course in the Inside/Out Prison Exchange Program, for both incarcerated and traditional students.

Scott Gross is the associate vice president of community engagement at California State University San Marcos (CSUSM). Gross earned his PhD in educational leadership from the Joint Doctoral Program at the University of California San Diego (UCSD) and CSUSM, and his research interests include leadership and social networks, particularly as they relate to civic engagement. Gross serves on the board of directors of SIATech, a network of charter schools designed to reengage and motivate out-of-school youth to earn their diplomas.

Julie Hatcher is associate professor in the Lilly Family School of Philanthropy and serves as executive director of the Center for Service and Learning at Indiana University–Purdue University Indianapolis (IUPUI). Hatcher holds a PhD in philanthropic studies and an MS in college student personnel from Indiana University. Hatcher's research focus is on the public purposes of higher education with a focus on civic learning outcomes. She developed the Civic-Minded Professional Scale (2008) and collaborated with colleagues on the Civic-Minded Graduate Scale and other tools. She is coeditor of the IUPUI Series on Service Learning Research (Stylus, 2011, 2013, 2015). In 2016, she was awarded the International Association for Research on Service-Learning and Community Engagement (IARSLCE) Distinguished Career Award for research. She serves on the national advisory board for the Carnegie Elective Classification for Community Engagement.

Kim Jensen Bohat is the director of the Center for Teaching and Learning, Service Learning Program at Marquette University in Milwaukee. She also teaches service-learning courses in the Department of Social and Cultural Sciences and Biomedical Sciences. Jensen Bohat received her MS in educational leadership and policy from Marquette. She is currently serving as the chair of the American Jesuits Colleges and Universities (AJCU) Service Learning Professionals Conference, and she was the founder of the Midwest Service Learning Leaders Conference. She has worked as a consultant and presenter both regionally and nationally on a variety of topics, including critical reflection, student leadership, faculty development, program development, and community impact assessment.

Vanya Jones, PhD, MPH, is an assistant professor at the Johns Hopkins Bloomberg School of Public Health in the Department of Health, Behavior and Society. She is also a core faculty member of the Johns Hopkins Center for Injury Research and Policy, where she works to reduce the burden of injuries. Jones is a Robert Wood Johnson Foundation Interdisciplinary Research Fellow and a Senior Faculty Service-Learning Fellow for SOURCE (Student Outreach Resource Center) at Johns Hopkins University.

Catherine M. Jordan is associate professor of pediatrics and extension at the University of Minnesota. Jordan received her PhD in clinical psychology from Wayne State University (Detroit, MI). Her scholarship and teaching and training activities focus on partnership development, innovative approaches to peer review and publication, and navigating promotion and tenure as a community-engaged scholar. She is the founding and executive editor of CES4Health. Jordan is the recipient of the University of Minnesota President's Outstanding Community Service Award and an inaugural inductee of the Academy of Community Engagement Scholarship as well as a member of its board of directors.

Ann Marie Jursca Keffer is the director of the Faith-Justice Institute at Saint Joseph's University in Philadelphia. She earned a BS in psychology with minors in Spanish and theology from the University of Scranton, an MSW from the Catholic University of America and a certificate from the University of Pennsylvania's Robert A. Fox Leadership Program. Jursca Keffer is a licensed social worker in the states of New Jersey and Pennsylvania, and her work in higher education reflects her interests in and commitment to educating for social justice and community engagement.

Kevin Kecskes, PhD, is associate professor of public administration at Portland State University (PSU) where he teaches on global and community leadership, ethics, nongovernmental organizations, and civic engagement. For over a decade, Kecskes provided university-wide leadership at PSU as associate vice provost for engagement and director for community-university partnerships. He actively consults with U.S. universities as well as internationally and has published multiple journal articles and book chapters along with *Engaging Departments: Moving Faculty Culture from Private to Public, Individual to Collective Focus for the Common Good* (Jossey-Bass, 2006)

Through an ongoing U.S. Department of State grant, Kecskes works with young leaders and their universities in the Middle East and North Africa region.

Richard Kiely is a senior fellow with the Office of Engagement Initiatives, Cornell University. He received his doctorate from Cornell University in 2002 and served as assistant professor at the University of Georgia from 2002 to 2006. He received national recognition as a John Glenn Scholar in Service-Learning in 2005 for his longitudinal research that led to a transformative model for service-learning. He is cofounder of globalsl.org, a multi-institutional hub supporting ethical global learning and community campus partnerships, and coauthor of *Community-Based Global Learning: The Theory and Practice of Ethical Engagement at Home and Abroad* (Stylus Publishing, 2018).

Mindi Levin, MS, CHES®, (trademark registration for The National Commission for Health Education Credentialing, Inc.) is the founder and director of SOURCE (Student Outreach Resource Center), the community engagement and service-learning center for the Johns Hopkins University Schools of Public Health, Nursing, and Medicine. She holds faculty appointments in the Johns Hopkins Bloomberg School of Public Health, Department of Health Policy and Management, and Johns Hopkins School of Nursing, Department of Community Public Health. Levin trains faculty, community, and students in service-learning pedagogy, with a focus on forming mutually beneficial partnerships in Baltimore, Maryland, to improve community health.

Devorah Lieberman is the president at the University of La Verne. Lieberman earned her PhD from the University of Florida, MA from San Diego State, and BA from Humboldt State University. Lieberman's expertise is in intercultural communication and diversity issues in higher education. She has published and coauthored dozens of books and articles relating to diversity, access to education, institutional transformation, and current issues affecting higher education.

Leslie McBride is professor of community health at the Oregon Health and Science University, Portland State University School of Public Health. Her recent publications have focused on the scholarship of teaching and learning in health promotion, faculty learning communities, academic portfolio development, curricular and faculty development for sustainability, and social sustainability. She is a founding editorial board member for *Pedagogy* *in Health Promotion: The Scholarship of Teaching and Learning*, and served five years as associate vice provost for teaching, learning, and assessment at Portland State. McBride received her PhD in education, with emphasis on community health, from Southern Illinois University.

Julia Metzker is the executive director for the Brown Center for Faculty Innovation and Excellence and professor of pedagogy at Stetson University. Metzker has a PhD in chemistry from the University of Arizona and a BS from Evergreen State College, where she learned the value of a transformative liberal education. As cofounder of the Innovative Course-building Group (IC-bG) she promotes curricular innovation through course-design institutes that use civic issues and engaged pedagogies to support transformative student learning. Her most recent project, a certificate in Course Design for Essential Learning for college-level educators, launched in January 2018.

Micki Meyer serves as Lord Family Assistant Vice President of Student Affairs & Community at Rollins College in Winter Park, Florida. Meyer received her MA in college student personnel from Bowling Green State University, and her research interests include high-impact learning and community engagement. Meyer serves as an Engaged Scholar with National Campus Compact, and a Certified Scholar with Florida Campus Compact, and she has been actively involved with NASPA's Civic Learning & Democratic Engagement Initiative. She is the recipient of honors for service-learning including the Community Engagement Educator Award and Thomas E. Gamble Service Legacy Award, both from Florida Campus Compact.

Chavonda Mills, is interim associate dean, College of Arts & Sciences, and professor of chemistry at Georgia College, Milledgeville. Mills holds a PhD in medicinal chemistry from Florida A&M University. A champion for enhancement of science curricula, Mills is the recipient of several NSF grants focused on science curriculum development and reform. She holds a patent in the development of synthetic flavonoids as methods of treatment of HIV infection and other pathologies and has published in the areas of medicinal chemistry and science education. Her most recent activities focus on addressing underrepresentation of minorities in science.

Star Plaxton-Moore is the director of community-engaged learning at the Leo T. McCarthy Center for Public Service and the Common Good at the University of San Francisco (USF). Plaxton-Moore holds an MEd from George Washington University and is currently completing course work for an EdD in international and multicultural education at USF. Plaxton-Moore directs institutional support for community-engaged courses and oversees public service programs for undergraduates, including the public service and community engagement minor. Her scholarship focuses on faculty development for community-engaged teaching and scholarship, student preparation, assessment of civic learning outcomes, and community engagement in institutional culture and practice.

Mary Price is the director of faculty development at the Indiana University–Purdue University Indianapolis Center for Service and Learning and adjunct faculty in the Department of Anthropology. Price holds a PhD in anthropology from Binghamton University, SUNY. Her current scholarly interests include community-campus partnerships as craft, faculty socialization and identity as community engaged scholars, improving institutional climates for the practices of engaged scholarship, and global service-learning. She is a cochair of Imagining America's Assessing the Practices of Public Scholarship research group. The group has recently published in the *Michigan Journal of Community Service Learning* on values-engagement in service-learning/community engagement assessment.

Kathleen Sexsmith is assistant professor of rural sociology at Pennsylvania State University. Sexsmith received her PhD in developmental sociology from Cornell University. Her research interests include gender, agriculture, migration, and international rural development. Her work has been published in several edited volumes and journals including *Citizenship Studies*, *Globalizations*, and *Oxford Development Studies*.

Caile Spear teaches in and administers the Health Education and Promotion program at Boise State University. Spear received her PhD in health science from University of Arkansas (Fayetteville), and her research interests include service-learning and health education and promotion programming. The Boise State Service-Learning Office views Spear as a service-learning Jedi. She has used service-learning pedagogy since 1997, served on the service-learning Advisory Board, and mentors faculty newly engaging in the wonderful world of service-learning.

Amy Spring is the community research and partnership director at the Portland State University Office of Strategic Partnerships. Spring holds degrees in sociology, urban studies, and planning and an MA in public administration from Portland State University. Spring has worked on several curriculum development efforts and managed the Student Leaders for Service program for 10 years. She has served on several leadership committees working to advance community-university partnerships, coauthored several publications focused on assessment of community partnerships and student learning, and coedited a special issue of *Metropolitan Universities*, a journal of the Coalition for Urban and Metropolitan Universities.

Mike Stefancic is the assistant director of the service-learning program at Boise State University. Stefancic received his MA in education from the University of Washington and his work is focused on leveraging critical reflection as a tool for creating meaningful learning experiences for students. Stefancic serves his community on various committees and boards to create a better, more connected city.

Stephanie T. Stokamer is the director of the Center for Civic Engagement and a faculty member at Pacific University. Stokamer received her PhD in educational leadership and MA in postsecondary education and social science, all from Portland State University. She has taught and administered community-engaged courses in both undergraduate and graduate programs since 2005. Stokamer's scholarship focuses on service-learning and civic engagement, particularly with respect to pedagogical practices, institutional structures, community collaboration, and faculty development to advance civic learning.

Chirag Variawa is director, first-year curriculum, and assistant professor, teaching-stream, at the Faculty of Applied Science and Engineering, University of Toronto, Canada. He received his PhD in industrial engineering from the University of Toronto, where his work investigates the language of engineering education in the context of universal instructional design and artificial intelligence. Variawa works across the engineering curriculum and coordinates/teaches computer programming to over 500 students. His research team aims to understand and mitigate barriers to inclusive learning for first-year student populations via many diverse collaborations and partnerships.

Marshall Welch has been a research-practitioner in the field of service-learning and community engagement for over 20 years. He served as the assistant vice provost for community engagement at Saint Mary's College of California and the director of the Lowell Bennion Community Service Center at the University of Utah. He is the author of *Engaging Higher Education: Purpose, Platforms, and Programs* (Stylus Publishing, 2016) and the coauthor of the National Inventory of Institutional Infrastructure for Community Engagement (NIIICE). In addition to teaching service-learning courses,

Welch has numerous articles, book chapters, and presentations on topics related to service-learning and community engagement focusing on faculty development, reflection, and infrastructure for campus centers advancing community engagement. At the time of this publication, he served as chair of the International Association for Research on Service-Learning and Community Engagement (IARSLCE). He is now an independent scholar living in the Portland, Oregon, area.

Amy Zeh joined the University of Central Florida team as program director of service-learning and assistant director of experiential learning in 2006. From 2004 through 2006, she served as program coordinator with the Center for the City at the University of Missouri-Kansas City. Zeh has worked closely with the nonprofit sector since 1986. She received her MA in English from the University of Missouri, Kansas City, and BFA from the University of Illinois at Urbana-Champaign.

INDEX

AAC&U. *See* Association of American Colleges & Universities
academic development, 181, 184, 192
academic integration principle, 224, 226, 227, 233
academic legitimacy, 233
academic success centers, 91
Ackerman, R. L., 233
Adam, B. E., 69
ADDIE. *See* analyze, design, develop, implement, and evaluate
adult-centered language, 290
adult-learning, 292, 293
　FLOs facilitating, 289
　framework for, 34
　theories, 37–38, 271, 274, 284, 295
advocacy culture in ED, 186, 188
Age of the Developer (1980s), 181, 182
Age of the Learner (1990s), 181, 182, 188
Age of the Network (2000s), 181, 182, 188–89
Age of the Scholar (mid-1950s-1960s), 181, 182
Age of the Teacher (late 1960s-1970s), 181, 182
Agre-Kippenhan, S. B., 33
aha moments, 294
Amey, M. J., 252
Amizade, 304
analyze, design, develop, implement, and evaluate (ADDIE), 209–10, 218

andragogy, 296
　CEPs and, 293
　introduction of, 290
　moving from pedagogy to S-LCE, 291–92
Anzaldúa, Gloria, 2, 15, 17
appropriate assessment principle, 224, 227
ARCS. *See* attention, relevance, confidence, satisfaction
Argyris, C., 294
assessment
　appropriate assessment principle, 224, 227
　assessment and feedback principle, 245
　in Georgia College & State University case study, 120
　in Marquette University case study, 168–70
　syllabus, 168–70
asset-based approach, 15, 243, 305
Association of American Colleges & Universities (AAC&U), 73, 87, 148, 168
　conferences for organizational development, 197
　support in Pacific University case study, 231–32
assumptive world, 62
attention, relevance, confidence, satisfaction (ARCS), 211–12, 218
Auburn University, 73
Austin, A. E., 85, 179

INDEX

authenticity, 8, 11, 12, 13, 16
   balancing, 205
   motivation from, 211
   of S-LCE, 217
awareness of positionality, 18, 19
Axtel, S., 39, 53

backward design approach, 85–88, 210–11, 294
Barker, D., 267
Bass, R., 197–99
Beach, A. L., 85, 179
Bellarmine University, 73
Benson, M., 52
Bergquist, W. H., 181, 183, 184, 185, 186, 189
Beyond the University: Why Liberal Education Matters (Roth), 62
Big Brothers Big Sisters programs, 87
blame-gaming, 71
Blanchard, L. W., 33, 39–40, 53
blogs, 82, 89, 93, 121, 171
Boise State University case study, xviii, 189
   context for, 108, 110, 114
   CPs in, 114, 116
   faculty development phase models, 110–14
   lessons learned and advice from, 117
   methods, 114–16
   results, 116
   SL in, 108, 110, 114–16
   timeline of, 109
borderlands, 15
   exploring, 2–4
   scholarly personal narrative, collaborative inquiry, collaborative ethnography and, 4–5
Borderlands/La Frontera: New Mestiza (Anzaldúa), 2

boundary crossing, 7, 8, 15, 16, 17, 19, 20
Bowen, H. R., 61
Boyer, Ernest, 62–63, 108, 235, 247, 266
Boyte, Harry, 27, 71
Brookfield, S. D., 121
Brown, Malcolm, 64, 65
brown bag lunches, 50, 112, 296

Calhoun, C. J., 68
California State University San Marcos (CSUSM), 245–46, 250–51
   Faculty Director initiative, 257
   SL designation for courses, 254
   tenure system at, 256
   workshops at, 257
Campus Compact, 28, 73, 91, 128, 129, 236–37, 248
   guidance and resources from, 256, 303
   meetings, 279
Cantor, Nancy, 69, 70, 74
career services, 91
Carnegie Classification for Community Engagement, 52, 148, 228, 229
Carnegie Foundation, 146
Carruthers, C. P., 233
case studies
   Boise State University, xviii, 108–17, 189
   challenges and strengths, 153–54
   conclusion, 133–34
   faculty development, xviii
   Georgia College & State University, xviii, 117–24, 189
   implications of FLCs for practice and research, 152, 154
   Indiana University-Purdue University Indianapolis, 140, 145–48, 153

INDEX *329*

Johns Hopkins University, 140,
 149–52, 153–54
Marquette University, 165–73
overview, 107–8, 139–40
Pacific University, 221–38
Portland State University, xviii,
 125–33, 189
RFP for, 6–7
Saint Joseph University, 160–65
S-LCE design, 214–18
University of Central Florida,
 173–77
University of San Francisco, 140–45,
 153
C-bEL. *See* community-based engaged
 learning
CBL. *See* community-based learning
CBR. *See* community-based research
CCPH. *See* Community Campus
 Partnerships for Health
CCREC. *See* Center for Collaborative
 Research for an Equitable
 California
CE. *See* civic engagement
CEL. *See* community-engaged learning
Center for Collaborative Research for
 an Equitable California (CCREC),
 73
Center for Courage and Renewal, 10
Center for Teaching and Learning
 (CTL), 170, 183
Center for Teaching Excellence (CTE),
 141, 153
centrality of engagement in higher
 education, 60
CEPs. *See* community engagement
 professionals
CES. *See* community-engaged
 scholarship
CES4Health.info, 277
Checkoway, B., 69
civic action, 188
civic engagement (CE), xvi, 18, 91,
 126. *See also* Principles of Quality

Academic Civic Engagement at
 Pacific University
Civic Engagement Breakfast series,
 129
developing opportunities for, 187
in Indiana University-Purdue
 University Indianapolis case study,
 146
Institute for Civic Engagement and
 Democracy, Miami-Dade College,
 246
in Pacific University case study,
 222–24, 229, 232–33, 235
Civic Engagement VALUE Rubric, 87
civic ethos, 188
civic inquiry, 188
civic literacy, 188, 267
civic professionals, 20, 27, 98
civic scholarship, xvi
class discussions, 54, 170, 171, 234
class size, 208–9, 212–14
Clayton, P., 304
clients, xvi, 45, 89, 161, 216–17, 246
coaching, 51, 96, 98, 164, 183, 208,
 291
cocurricular programs, 28, 176, 187,
 193, 233, 236, 265
coeducators, 249, 255
cohort models, 37, 120
colearners, 48
 faculty as, 60, 68–69, 291
collaboration
 CCREC, 73
 collaborative ethnography, 4–5
 collaborative inquiry, xvii, 4–5
 faculty development and, 71–74
 opportunities in CES, 275
 P3 Collaboratory, Rutgers University,
  73–74
 reciprocity and, 65–67
 respectful collaboration principle,
  224, 226
 S-LCE professionals developing, 198
 teamwork and, 205

330   INDEX

collaborative engagement paradigm
  for faculty as colearners, 60, 63–65
  faculty development and, 71–74
  PES and, 65
collective impact, 190
collegial culture in ED, 185
common good, 12, 38, 223
  community engagement for, 247–48
  Leo T. McCarthy Center for Public Service and the Common Good, 141, 246
communication
  intercultural, 287
  open communication principle, 245
  plan of S-LCE scholar-practitioner, 259
community, 12, 13, 71
  defined, 243
  presence, 48, 204
  S-LCE professionals and, 53
  as source of knowledge, 15, 16
community-based engaged learning (C-bEL), 117, 120, 122–24
community-based learning (CBL), 14–15, 159, 224, 232
  institutionalizing, 247–48
  in Marquette University case study, 166
  in Portland State University case study, 125–30, 132
  recognizing, 235
  in Saint Joseph University case study, 160, 166
  scholarship from, 267
  standardizing, 253
community-based organizations, 186, 196
  at community colleges, 258
  higher education and, 61
  in partnerships and reciprocity, 241, 242, 249, 252, 259
  at Rollins College, 244
community-based research (CBR), 128, 299, 300

Community Campus Partnerships for Health (CCPH), 34, 39–40, 147, 277, 303
community colleges, 228–29
community-engaged learning (CEL), xvi
  career development and, 228
  defining faculty development for, 30, 33
  focus in University of San Francisco case study, 141–45
  publications for, 276–77
  with SL, 137
  strategies for scaling up, 296
community-engaged research, 144, 146, 229, 268, 270–71
community-engaged scholarship (CES), 54, 236
  aligning with S-LCE professional's role, 279–81
  applying principles of, 39
  campus culture and, 139
  CEPs and, 268–71
  collaboration opportunities in, 275
  competencies for, 27, 40
  conclusion, 281
  definitions, 265–68
  discussion and recommendations, 271–81
  disseminating, 130, 275–76
  examples of, 271
  in job descriptions, 279–80
  material for, 273–74
  as mutually beneficial, 266
  partnership potential, 274–75
  pitfalls to avoid, 277–78
  role in SL, 268–71
  scheduling for, 280
  S-LCE professionals and, 272–73
  S-LCE stakeholders and, 42
  tips for, 277–79
  value of, 137
  workshops on, 265
community engagement

Center for Leadership and
    Community Engagement, Rollins
    College, 257
collective impact of, 190
for common good, 247–48
conclusion, 56
continuum framework for, 250
developing ethos of, 247–49
discussion of meta model for
    professional development, 54–56
evolution of, 281
faculty development and, 28, 30–40
faculty development trends for
    advancing, 33–38
framework for, 30, 42–49
higher education and, 59–60
*International Journal of Research on
    Service-Learning and Community
    Engagement*, 276
learning, xvi, xix
meta model for professional
    development, 40–54
overview, 27–30
reflections on, 248–49
Rollins College courses in, 253–54
community engagement professionals
    (CEPs), xvi, 6, 19–21, 265, 290
alignment with faculty development,
    231
andragogy and, 293
asset-based approach and, 305
CBR and, 300
CES and, 268–71
disruptive questions of, 302
examining curricula and
    departments, 296
intersections with service-learning
    literature, 184–95
knowledge, skills, abilities,
    dispositions of, 188
as organizers, boundary spanners,
    coalition builders, agents of
    change, 298
promoting S-LCE, 285

rationale for S-LCE, 292
roles and responsibilities of, 40
SL experiences and, 271
theory of change for, 306
transformative model and, 285–86
in workshops, 291
community-faculty roundtables, 166
community-focused nature
    boundary crossing subtheme, 15, 16
    community as source of knowledge
        subtheme, 15, 16
    engagement in multiple spaces
        subtheme, 15, 16, 17
    from narrative inquiry, 7–8, 14–17
community of practice (CoP), 137–39
community partners (CPs),
    xvi–xvii, xix
    in Boise State University case study,
        114, 116
    concerns of, 242–43
    in course design, 253
    identifying and cultivating, 249
    lens 4 transformative approach to,
        253
    relationships with S-LCE
        professionals, 275
    role at Rollins College, 253–54
    S-LCE stakeholders and, 44–45
    workshops and, 51, 98, 246
*The Community Engagement Professional
    in Higher Education* (Dostilio and
    Perry), 20
compassion, 12, 160, 248
competency
    for CES, 27, 40
    faculty, 53–54
    intercultural, 166
    model, 38–40, 188, 189
    in SL, 138
Connors, K., 92
consciousness of identity
    awareness of positionality subtheme,
        17, 18
    hybrid roles subtheme, 18, 19

intersection of identities as agents of change subtheme, 18, 19
multiple roles subtheme, 17, 18, 19
from narrative inquiry, 7–8, 17–20
constructivist paradigm, 16, 302
consultations, 296
  empathy in, 98
  instructional, 85
  one-on-one, 37, 56, 166, 168
  in Portland State University case study, 130
  promoting S-LCE, 51
  short-term programs, 90, 98–99
continuum of scholarship paradigm, 67–68
CoP. *See* community of practice
Corella and Bertram F. Bonner Foundation, 252
counselors, 29, 31, 291
course design, 127, 138, 287–88. *See also* S-LCE design
  backward, 294
  challenges in, 121
  class size and, 212–14
  CPs in, 253
  institutes, 100
  integrated, 166–67, 172
  literature, 204, 212
  workshops, 284
CPs. *See* community partners
craft development, 65
Creating Significant Learning Experiences: An Integrated Approach to Designing College Courses (Fink), 167
Creating Strategic Partnerships: A Guide for Educational Institutes and Their Partners (Eddy and Amey), 252
Creating the Future of Faculty Development (Sorcinelli, Austin, Eddy, Beach), 179
creative practices
  conclusion, 177–78

Marquette University case study, 165–73
overview, 159
Saint Joseph University case study, 160–65
SL and, 177–78
University of Central Florida case study, 173–77
critical consciousness, 17
critical paradigm, 302
critical race theory, 234
critical reflection, 288, 294, 307
cross-cultural interaction, 251
A Crucible Moment: College Learning and Democracy's Future, 187–88
CSUSM. *See* California State University San Marcos
CTE. *See* Center for Teaching Excellence
CTL. *See* Center for Teaching and Learning
culture, 71
  advocacy in ED, 186, 188
  campus, 139
  collegial in ED, 185
  developmental in ED, 185, 188
  of ED developers, 185–86
  faculty, 234–36
  institutional, xviii, 233–37
  student, 236
  tangible in ED, 186, 189
  virtual in ED, 186, 188
curiosity, 11, 12
curriculum
  changing, 297
  faculty development topics, 37
  subject-centered, 292

decision making, 6, 47, 65, 304, 306
deficit approach, 305
De Laat, M., 151
Demb, A., 39, 53
Democracy Commitment, 236–37

depth of experience principle, 224, 225–26
design thinking approaches, 147
developmental culture in ED, 185, 188
Dewey, John, 63
Diamond, R. M., 69
Dick and Carey model, 211
diffusion of innovation model, 34
Dillon, S., 236
disability services centers, 91
disciplinary guildism, 52
Donahoe Higher Education Act, 61
Dostilio, Lina, 19–20, 40, 50, 188–89
Dreyfus skill acquisition, 71
Du Bois, W.E.B., 63
Duke University, 246

Eatman, Tim, 148
ED. *See* educational development
Eddy, P. L., 179, 252
education. *See also* higher education
　as learning mechanism, 13
　as values subtheme, 13
educational development (ED), xvi
　advocacy culture in, 186, 188
　Age of the Learner (1990s), 181, 182, 188
　Age of the Network (2000s), 181, 182, 188–89
　Age of the Scholar (mid-1950s-1960s), 181, 182
　Age of the Teacher (late 1960s-1970s), 181, 182
　Age the of Developer (1980s), 181, 182
　approaching from different directions, 189–90
　backing into, 184, 187–89, 195
　collegial culture in, 185
　conclusion, 197–99
　critical reflection called for, 196
　cultures of developers, 185–86
　developers as migrants and navigators, 183–84
　developmental culture in, 185, 188
　history, role, evolution of, 180–84
　impact of service-learning and community engagement in, 190
　intersections with service-learning literature and community engagement professionals, 184–95
　managerial culture in, 185
　in margins, 183–84
　organizational development and, 180–81
　overview, 179–80
　partnerships in, 190–91, 195–97
　shared pathways in, 195–97
　S-LCE fostered with, xv, xvii
　S-LCE professionals and, 179–80
　student learning emphasized in, 188
　tangible culture in, 186, 189
　vignettes illustrating complexities in, 191, 194, 195
　virtual culture in, 186, 188
e-learning, 170
electronic mailing lists, 93
Elias, J. L., 294
empathy, 185, 255, 287
　building, 248
　in consultations, 98
　in faculty development, 41
　student learning and, 86
empowerment, 49
　faculty, 235
　in partnerships and reciprocity, 248–49
Engaged Campus initiative, 34, 40
engagement in multiple spaces, 16, 17
Engagement Scholarship Consortium (ESC), 277, 279
ENGAGE program, 117, 118–24
Engineering Strategies and Practice (ESP) case study
　anecdotes from, 217
　background for, 214–15
　design of, 215–16

reflection component of, 217–18
reports generated in, 217
UID approach in, 218
Enos, S., 256, 305
entrepreneurship, 20, 91, 138, 245
equal distribution of teaching and learning principle, 245
ESC. *See* Engagement Scholarship Consortium
ESP. *See* Engineering Strategies and Practice
ethics
  ethical action, 301
  ethical decisions, 160
  ethical perspective, 88
  ethical problems, 266
  ethical responsibility, 27
  ethics boards, 256
Evaluating Service-Learning activities and Programs (Payne), 92
Executive Report on the Current Status of Community-Engaged Learning at USF and Recommended Future Directions, 143
experiential learning, 34, 91, 114, 119, 193, 301
  activities, 176
  approach in faculty development, 155
  expanding, 108
  model for, 170
  outside classroom, 223–24
Experiential Learning: Experience as the Source of Learning and Development (Kolb), 92
experiential learning model, 34, 91, 92, 170
extended programs, 100–103
Eyler, J., 86–87, 92

Facebook, 93
faculty
  75% shuffle, 59
  in changing higher education landscape, 61–62
  collaborative engagement and faculty development and, 71–74
  collaborative engagement paradigm and, 60, 63–65
  compensation in University of Central Florida case study, 175
  concerns over partnerships, 241–43
  considerations in partnerships and reciprocity, 252–58
  CSUSM Faculty Director initiative, 257
  culture, 234–36
  empowerment, 235
  engaged scholarship across roles of, 62–63
  expectations, in Saint Joseph University case, 160–61
  faculty-driven programming, 174–75
  faculty-student partnerships, 101–2
  norms, 70
  as organizers, boundary spanners, coalition builders, agents of change, 298
  paradigms for scholarship, 254–56
  peer-to-peer relationships, 257
  PES key elements and, 65–68
  PES politics and, 67–71
  power of story and, 74–75
  preparation, xv
  as sages on the stage, 254
  S-LCE professionals working with, 50
  S-LCE stakeholders and, 42, 50
  student learning and, 60
faculty as colearners, 291
  changing landscape with, 61–62
  cocreation of knowledge and public scholarship, 68–69
  collaborative engagement and faculty development, 71–74
  collaborative engagement paradigm for, 60, 63–65

conclusion, 74–75
elements of PES and, 65–68, 75
goals and, 60–61
overview, 59–60
politics of PES in academe, 69–71
scholarship across faculty roles, 62–63
faculty development
alignment with CEPs, 231
approaches for, 5
Boise State University case study models, 110–14
case studies, xviii
coining of, 181
collaboration and, 71–74
community-engagement and, 28, 30–40
curriculum topics, 37
defined, 30
defining for CEL, 30, 33
empathy in, 41
experiential learning approach in, 155
flexible learning opportunities in, 292
Journal of Faculty Development, 276
knowledge, skills, dispositions for facilitating, 41
lens 5 to transformative approach to, 306–7
literature review, 33–36
models of, xviii
modifying definition of, 29
questions for evaluation of, 274
role of, 60
scope of, 30, 32
for sustainable partnerships and reciprocity, 257–58
terminology for, xvi
tiered, xviii
transformative model building on, 284
trends for advancing community-engagement, 33–38
workshops, 28, 37, 50, 236, 257

faculty development models
backward design approach in, 85–88
conclusion, 103–4
extended and immersive programs, 100–103
faculty-student partnerships, 101–2
fellowship programs, 103
FLCs, 101
grants, stipends, awards for, 94–96
informational resources for, 91–94
institutes and, 100–101
mentoring programs, 102
overview, 85
short-term programs for, 96–100
student learning outcomes and, 86–87
summary of types, 89–90
support, incentive, recognition programs for, 94–96
supporting S-LCE, 88–103
faculty learning communities (FLCs), 1, 101, 128
case studies challenges and strengths, 154
case studies overview, 139–40
challenges and strengths of case studies, 153–54
conclusion, 154–55
CoP and, 137–39
defined, 137–38
implication of case studies for practice and research, 152, 154
in Indiana University-Purdue University Indianapolis case study, 140, 145–48, 153
in Johns Hopkins University case study, 140, 149–52, 153–54
literature review, 138–39
in Marquette University case study, 166–68
overview, 137–38
S-LCE in, 139
in University of San Francisco case study, 140–45, 153

faculty learning outcomes (FLOs), 91, 95, 97, 285
   defined, 286
   facilitating adult learning, 289
   internal conferences and symposia and, 99
   positionality and, 298
   reciprocity and, 304
   reflexivity and, 302
   student learning and, 86
   for teaching and learning, 295
Faculty Toolkit for Service-Learning in Higher Education (Seifer and Connors), 92
Fairfield University, 73
fair trade learning (FTL), 288, 303, 304
fellowship programs, 103
Fink, L. Dee, 167–68
FLCs. *See* faculty learning communities
FLOs. *See* faculty learning outcomes
flow problem, 212
forums, 296
Freire, P., 17
Fretz, E., 27
FTL. *See* fair trade learning
Full Participation initiative, 72
Furco, A., 231

Gaff, J. G., 181, 183
Georgia College & State University case study, xviii, 73, 189
   assessment toolbox for, 120
   C-bEL in, 117, 119, 122–24
   challenges of and lessons learned from, 123–25
   context for, 117, 118
   ENGAGE program in, 117, 118–24
   practitioner participation in, 122–23
   practitioner retention in, 123
   program model for, 118–21
   QEP for, 117, 118
   results, 122–23
   student participation in, 122
   timeline for, 119
   workshops in, 120–21
Gibson, C. M., 63
Gilbert, Kesler, 252
Giles, D. E., 86–87, 92
Glassick, C. E., 69, 70
global service-learning (GSL), 285, 294, 297, 304
Google Communities, 149–51
grants and stipends, 94–95
Green, D. A., 183
GSL. *See* global service-learning

Haamer, A., 138
Hanleybrown, F., 190
Hans-Kolvenbach, Peter, 160
Harkavy, I., 52
Hartley, M., 52
high-control dynamic, 205–6
higher education, 20, 63–64, 92
   centrality of engagement in, 60
   civic mission of, 187
   community-based organizations and, 61
   community engagement and, 59–60
   Donahoe Higher Education Act, 61
   faculty in changing landscape, 61–62
   Journal of Service-Learning in Higher Education, 276
   NERCHE, 36
   North Central Accreditation Higher Learning Commission, 146
   S-LCE professionals and, 52
   value of S-LCE in, 270
Hitt, John C., 173
HLLC. *See* Honors Living-Learning Community
Holland, Barbara A., 70, 231
Honors Living-Learning Community (HLLC), 64
hooks, bell, 13
Howard, Jeffrey, 142
Huber, M. T., 69
Hurney, C. A., 86
Hutchings, P., 266

hybrid roles, 18, 19

IA. *See* Imagining America
IARSLCE. *See* International Association for Research on Service-Learning and Community Engagement
Imagining America: Artists and Scholars in Public Life (IA), 61, 65, 69, 71, 147, 148
   cultural organizing and, 72–73
immersive programs, 100–103
Indiana University-Purdue University Indianapolis case study, 73
   CE in, 146
   challenges and strengths of, 153
   context and goals of, 146
   design of, 146–47
   outcomes of, 147–48
   overview, 140, 145
   workshops in, 147–48
individualized approach to student learning, 208–9
informational resources
   blogs, 82, 89, 93, 121, 171
   electronic mailing lists, 93
   for faculty development models, 91–94
   libraries, 50, 89, 91, 92, 94, 149
   social media, 93–94
   websites, 92
inner landscape, 10
inquiry approach, 4
institutes. *See also* Imagining America: Artists and Scholars in Public Life
   course design, 100
   faculty development models and, 100–101
   Institute for Civic Engagement and Democracy, Miami-Dade College, 246
   institutional characteristics, 223–31
   institutional culture, xviii, 233–37
   institutional priorities, 222–23, 231–33

   as learning communities, 104
   national and international, 197
   roundtables as, 100
   from workshops, 99, 100
instruction
   instructional design, 212–15
   instructional development, 181
   instructional improvement, 181
   instructional pathway, 138
integrative strategy, 231
intellectual property rights, 256
intercultural communication, 287
intercultural competency, 166
internal conferences and symposia, 90
   FLOs and, 99
   short-term programs, 99–100
International Association for Research on Service-Learning and Community Engagement (IARSLCE), 13, 197, 256, 268, 277, 279
International Journal of Research on Service-Learning and Community Engagement, 276
internships, 28, 88, 91, 252
intersection of identities as agents of change, 18, 19
ivory tower, 59, 61, 65, 70

Jacoby, B., 92
James Madison University, 192, 194
Jeandron, C., 228–29
job descriptions, 234, 278, 279–80
Johns Hopkins University case study
   challenges and strengths, 153–54
   context and goals of, 149
   design of, 149–50
   implementation, 150–51
   outcomes of, 151–52
   overview, 140, 149
   SL in, 149–50
   social learning framework, 151
   ZPD and, 151–52
Johnson, M., 252

Journal of Faculty Development, 276
Journal of Higher Education Outreach and Engagement, 34
Journal of Service-Learning in Higher Education, 276
Journal on Centers for Teaching and Learning, 276
justice, 8, 11, 12, 13–14, 229. *See also* social justice

Kania, J., 190
Kansas State University, 73
Karm, M., 138
Keller, J. M., 211
Kerr, Clark, 61
Kezar, A. J., 55, 59
knowledge, skills, attitudes, and behaviors (KSABs), 286, 287, 298
knowledge generation-learning process, 307
knowledge-making, 62, 65–67, 74
knowledge transfer, 296
Knowles, Malcolm, 290
Kolb, David, 34, 92
  What? So What? Now What? reflection model, 170
Kramer, M., 190
KSABs. *See* knowledge, skills, attitudes, and behaviors
Kuh, G. D., 232

Land, R., 288
Langseth, M., 236
Lassiter, L. E., 4–5
Lave, J., 138
learning. *See also* student learning
  community-engagement, xvi, xix
  CTL, 170, 183
  education as mechanism for, 13
  e-learning, 170
  experiential, 170
  FLOs for, 295
  FTL, 288, 303, 304

initiatives, in Marquette University case study, 175–76
Journal on Centers for Teaching and Learning, 276
lens 1 transformative approach to, 290
MERLOT, 277
metacognitive, 306–7
theories, 37–38
learning environment design, xv, xviii
  engineering of, 206–7
  instructional design and, 212–15
  situational awareness in, 212
  S-LCE design and, 204–6
  teamwork in, 211
learning process, 43, 64
  approaches to modeling, 208–12
  broader society in, 219
  democratizing of, 255
  knowledge generation, 307
  mapping, 218
lens 1 transformative approach to teaching and learning, 290, 293–95
lens 2 transformative approach to institutional culture, 295–99
lens 3 transformative approach to knowledge generation and application, 299–303
lens 4 transformative approach to community partnerships, 303–6
lens 5 to transformative approach to faculty development, 306–7
Leo T. McCarthy Center for Public Service and the Common Good, 141, 246
Lepp, L., 138
Levine, S. D., 69, 70
libraries, 50, 89, 91, 92, 94, 149
LinkedIn, 93
literature
  course design, 204, 212
  faculty development, 33–36
  FLCs, 138–39

intersections with service-learning, 184–95
  within SoTL, 209
Little, D., 183
logic-mapping, 212
Longo, N. V., 63
low-control dynamic, 205–6
Loyola University, 73, 193

Maeroff, G. I., 69
managerial culture in ED, 185
Marquette University case study
  CBL in, 166
  challenges in, 170–73
  design and implementation of, 166–70
  finances and, 171
  Fink's taxonomy for, 167–68
  FLCs in, 166–68
  impact on student learning, 172
  overview, 165–66
  postservice discussion board in, 171–72
  SL in, 166, 168, 170, 172
  syllabus assessment in, 168–70
  workshops in, 166
Maurrasse, D. J., 61, 70
Maxey, D., 59
McCarthy, Charles, 61
McKee, C. W., 29
meaningful learning opportunities principle, 224, 225
mentoring programs, xviii, 213, 291, 301
  challenges in, 164–65
  class visits in, 162
  faculty development models for, 102
  finances for, 165
  identifying mentors, 161–62
  impact of, 163
  reciprocity in, 162
  at Rollins College, 257–58
  in Saint Joseph University case study, 161–65

  shared pedagogy in, 164
  social capital from, 163–64
MERLOT. *See* Multimedia Educational Resource for Learning and Online Teaching
Merriam, S., 294
metacognitive learning, 306–7
Meyer, J., 288
Mezirow, J., 8, 34, 307
Miami-Dade College, 246
Michigan Journal of Community Service Learning, 34, 92, 142, 276
mindfulness, 301
Modern Language Association, 70
Moore, T. L., 228
moral support, 296
Morris, A. D., 63
Morrison, E., 301
Morton, K., 256, 305
Multimedia Educational Resource for Learning and Online Teaching (MERLOT), 277
multimodal instruction, 213–14
multiple roles, 18, 19
mutual benefit principle, 245

narrative inquiry, 4–5
  community-focused nature from, 7–8, 14–17
  consciousness of identity from, 7–8, 17–20
  themes from, 7–8
  transformative experiences from, 7–10
  values from, 7–8, 10–13
Nash, R. J., 7, 11
National Forum on Higher Education for the Public Good, 296
National Service-Learning Clearinghouse, 248
National Society for Internships and Experiential Education, 187
National Task Force on Civic Learning and Democratic Engagement, 187

National Youth Leadership Council, 93
NERCHE. *See* New England Resource Center for Higher Education
Netter Center for Community Partnerships, University of Pennsylvania, 233
New American College, 62
New England Resource Center for Higher Education (NERCHE), 36
New Professionals Study Group, 74
Nicolle, P. S., 138
North Central Accreditation Higher Learning Commission, 146
Northeastern University, 193, 194

O'Meara, K., 235
one-on-one consultations, 37, 56, 166, 168
online resources, 296
open communication principle, 245
Oregon State University, 73
organizational development. *See also* Professional Organizational Development
  AAC&U conferences for, 197
  ED and, 180–81
Our Stories Matter: Liberating the Voices of Marginalized Students Through Scholarly Personal Narrative Writing (Nash and Viray), 7

P3 Collaboratory, Rutgers University, 73–74
Pacific University case study
  AAC&U support in, 231–32
  CE in, 222–24, 229, 232–33, 235
  cocurricular programs in, 233
  conclusion, 238
  context for, 222
  implications for S-LCE professionals, 237
  institutional characteristics and, 223–31
  institutional culture and, 233–37
  institutional priorities in, 222–23, 231–33
  morale in, 235
  overview, 221
  PQACE in, 224–29, 233, 238
  workshops in, 227, 229
PAEI. *See* Philosophy of Adult Education Inventory
Palmer, Parker, 10
paradigms. *See also* collaborative engagement paradigm
  constructivist, 16, 302
  continuum of scholarship, 67–68
  critical, 302
  for faculty scholarship, 254–56
  participatory, 302
  positivist, 302
  postpositivist, 302
  for student learning, 254–56
  for teaching, 254–56
participatory paradigm, 302
partnerships. *See also* collaboration; collaborative engagement paradigm; community partners
  CCPH, 34, 39–40, 147
  cross-cultural interaction in, 251
  in ED, 190–91, 195–97
  faculty-student, 101–2
  listening in, 251
  Netter Center for Community Partnerships, University of Pennsylvania, 233
  potential in CES, 274–75
  purpose in, 251
  among S-LCE professionals, 180, 198
partnerships, reciprocity and
  assessment and feedback principle, 245
  challenges and pitfalls in, 258–59
  community-based organizations in, 241, 242, 248, 249, 252, 259
  conclusion, 259–60

developing ethos community engagement, 247–49
empowerment in, 248–49
equal distribution of teaching and learning principle, 245
evaluation of, 259
faculty concerns over, 241–43
faculty considerations in, 252–58
faculty development for sustainable, 257–58
framework for, 249–52
mutual benefit principle, 245
open communication principle, 245
overview, 241–43
practices and principles for, 244–46
role of S-LCE scholar-practitioner in, 251–52
shared goals and outcomes principle, 245
standardized S-LCE practices in, 253–54
steps for cultivating effective partnerships, 251–52
strategic partnership models for, 252
Pawlak, K., 184, 185, 186, 189
Payne, David, 92
pedagogy, 4, 7, 13
defined, 290
in mentoring programs, 164
moving to andragogy to S-LCE, 291–92
pedagogical training, xv, xviii
peer-reviewed journals and papers, 275, 276, 281
peer-to-peer relationships, 257
Perry, Lane, 20
PES. *See* publicly engaged scholarship
Peters, Scott, 72, 148
philanthropy, 249, 252
Phillips, S. R., 181, 183
Philosophy of Adult Education Inventory (PAEI), 294
Plater, W. M., 55, 236
Plaut, J., 252

POD. *See* Professional Organizational Development
policy change, 139, 296
Portland State University case study, xviii, 73, 229–30, 289
budgeting in, 132
CBL in, 125–30, 132
CBR in, 128
consultations in, 130
context for, 125, 127
credibility, 133
FLCs in, 128
implications of and recommendations from, 131–33
location of, 131
organizational and staffing structure for, 132
organizational demands and, 133
organizational evolution from, 133
program methods and models, 127–29
reporting structure, 131
success and faculty engagement, 129–31
sustainability, 133
timeline for, 126–27
positionality, 28, 288, 297, 306, 307
awareness of, 17, 18
FLOs and, 298
in institutions, 191
pie chart and, 298
positivist paradigm, 302
Post, M. A., 60
postpositivist paradigm, 302
postservice discussion board, 171–72
PQACE. *See* Principles of Quality Academic Civic Engagement at Pacific University
Practitioner Scholar Forum, 296
President's Honor Roll for Community Service, 52
Principles of Quality Academic Civic Engagement at Pacific University (PQACE)

academic integration principle, 224, 226
appropriate assessment principle, 224, 227
depth of experience principle, 224, 225–26
meaningful learning opportunities principle, 224, 225
in Pacific University case study, 224–29, 233, 238
public citizenship principle, 224, 227
public interest principle, 224, 225
reciprocity principle, 224, 226
reflection on experience principle, 224, 226–27
relevant problem solving principle, 224, 225
respectful collaboration principle, 224, 226
Prins, E. S., 228
professional development, 181
professional educational development, 29
competency-based models of, 38–40
meta model for, 40–50
Professional Organizational Development (POD), xvi, 29, 93, 168, 197, 277
Profiles in Community-Engaged Learning, 142–44
publications
for CEL, 276–77
ESP reports, 217
Executive Report on the Current Status of Community-Engaged Learning at USF and Recommended Future Directions, 143
Journal of Faculty Development, 276
Journal of Higher Education Outreach and Engagement, 34
Journal of Service-Learning in Higher Education, 276
Journal on Centers for Teaching and Learning, 276

Michigan Journal of Community Service Learning, 34, 92, 142, 276
peer-reviewed journals and papers, 275, 276, 281
Portland State University case study reports, 131
Purdue Journal of Service-Learning, 92
of University of San Francisco case study, 142–44
public citizenship principle, 224, 227
public interest principle, 224, 225
publicly engaged scholarship (PES), xvii, 60
change and, 70–71
collaborative engagement and, 65
continuum of scholarship paradigm urged by, 67–68
key elements of, 65–68, 75
politics of, 69–71
Publicly Engaged Scholars: Next Generation Engagement and the Future of Higher Education (Longo and Gibson), 63–64
Public Scholarship at Indiana University-Purdue University Indianapolis, 148
Purdue Journal of Service-Learning, 92

quality enhancement plan (QEP), 117, 119

Ramaley, Judith A., 70
reciprocity, xix, 114, 307. *See also* partnerships, reciprocity and
building programs for, 118
collaboration and, 65–67
FLOs and, 304
in mentoring programs, 162
reciprocity principle, 224, 226
S-LCE guided by, 88
reflection on experience principle, 224, 226–27

reflexivity, 288, 301, 302, 307
relationships
    with CPs and S-LCE professionals, 275
    peer-to-peer, 257
    stress-strain, 212
relevant problem solving principle, 224, 225
Remmik, M., 138
Rendón, L. I., 4, 7
request for proposal (RFP), 6–7
research
    from case studies, 152, 154
    CBR, 128, 299, 300
    CCREC, 73
    community-engaged, 144, 146, 229, 268, 270–71
    IARSLCE, 13, 197, 256, 268
    transpersonal, 4
resource availability, xviii
respectful collaboration principle, 224, 226
RFP. *See* request for proposal
Rivard, J. K., 85
Robinson, G., 228–29
Rochester Institute of Technology, 73
Rogers, E. M., 34, 40
Rollins College, 251–52
    Center for Leadership and Community Engagement, 257
    community-based organizations at, 244–45
    community engagement designation for courses and role of CPs, 253–54
    mentoring programs at, 257–58
Roth, Michael, 62
roundtables
    community-faculty, 166
    as part of institutes, 100
    short-term programs, 90, 97–99
    teaching, 228
    as workshops, 104
Rutgers University-Newark (RU-N), 73–74

Rychen, D. S., 38

sabbaticals, 181
sages on the stage, 254
Saint Joseph University case study
    CBL in, 160, 166
    design and implementation of, 160–64
    faculty expectations in, 160–61
    mentoring program, 161–65
    overview, 160
    SL in, 160–65
Salganik, L. H., 38
Saltmarsh, J., 52, 107, 187
Sandmann, L. R., 286–87
scholarly personal narrative, 4–5
scholarly talks, 90, 98
scholarship. *See also* community-engaged scholarship; publicly engaged scholarship
    attitudes toward public, 70
    from CBL, 267
    civic, xvi
    continuum of scholarship paradigm, 67–68
    of discovery, 95
    ESC, 277
    across faculty roles, 62–63
    paradigms for, 254–56
    S-LCE and, xvii
    S-LCE professionals and, 266, 269–70
    Tenure Team Initiative on Public Scholarship, 72
scholarship of engagement (SoE), 266–77
scholarship of teaching and learning (SoTL), xvii, 168, 300
    contributions to, 5
    defined, 266
    literature within, 209
    publishing, 307n2
    in University of Central Florida case study, 175–76

Scholarship Reconsidered (Boyer), 62
"The Scholarship of Engagement" (Boyer), 62, 235
Schön, D., 294
Scobey, David, 148
Seifer, S., 92, 231
self-awareness, 301
self-concept, 291
self-directed approach, 290
Senge, P. M., 138
Sentipensante (Sensing/Thinking) Pedagogy (Rendón), 4, 7
service-learning (SL)
  in Boise State University case study, 108, 110, 114–16
  CEL with, 137
  collective impact of, 190
  competencies, 138
  creative practices and, 177–78
  designation for CSUSM courses, 254
  emergence of, 187
  experiences and CEPs, 271
  as integrative strategy, 231
  International Journal of Research on Service-Learning and Community Engagement, 276
  intersections with literature and community engagement professionals, 184–95
  in Johns Hopkins University case study, 149–50
  Journal of Service-Learning in Higher Education, 276
  in Marquette University case study, 166, 168, 170, 172
  National Service-Learning Clearinghouse, 248
  role of CES for, 268–71
  in Saint Joseph University case study, 160–65
  strategic planning and, 231
  in University of Central Florida case study, 173–74, 176
  in University of San Francisco case study, 141
  value of, 137
service-learning and community engagement (S-LCE)
  authenticity of, 217
  best practices, 255
  CEPs supporting, 285
  conceptual matrix for, 38–39
  consultations promoting, 51
  deficit approach to, 305
  educational development fostering, xv, xvii
  evidence-based practices, 178
  faculty development models supporting, 88–103
  FLCs in, 139
  fulfilling aspirations of, 53–54
  institutionalizing and improving, 6
  language for, xvi
  moving toward transformative approach for, 285–87
  from pedagogy to andragogy, 291–92
  rationale for CEPs, 292
  reciprocity guiding, 88
  scholarship and, xvii
  standardized practices in, 253–54
  strategies for scaling up, 296
  student learning outcomes in, 86–87
  traditions transformed by, 242
  transformative model for, 283–87
  value in higher education, 270
  workshops promoting, 296
Service-Learning in Higher Education: Concepts and Practices (Jacoby), 92
75% faculty shuffle, 59
shared goals and outcomes principle, 245
Shinnar, R. S., 233
short-term programs
  consultations, 90, 98–99
  for faculty development models, 96–100

internal conferences and symposia, 99–100
roundtables, 90, 97–99
scholarly talks, 90, 98
workshops, 90, 96–97
Shulman, L. E., 266
single-standing workshops, 75
skill sets, 33, 38, 55, 177, 275, 277, 278
SL. *See* service-learning
S-LCE. *See* service-learning and community engagement
S-LCE design, 284
ADDIE in, 209–10, 218
approaches to modeling learning processes, 208–12
ARCS model in, 211–12, 218
backward design, 210–11
case study, 214–18
class size and, 208–9
conclusion, 218
course design and class size framework, 212–14
Dick and Carey model, 211
engineering learning environment design, 206–7
learning environment design and, 204–6
multimodal instruction and, 213–14
overview, 203–4
UID and, 213–14
S-LCE professionals, xvi, 1, 27
accounting for push and pull factors, 55
aligning role with CES, 279–81
analysis approaches for, 5
as change-oriented leaders, 20
community and, 53
developing collaborations and partnerships, 180, 198
discipline development and, 51–52
dissemination and, 276

educational development and, 179–80
experience with CES, 272–73
higher education changes and, 52
influence in classroom, 51
institutions impacted by, 52
involving CPs, 51
metacognitive lens for, 285
Pacific University case study implications and, 237
relationships with CPs, 275
roles and responsibilities of, 28–32
scholarship and, 266, 269–70
serving students, 50–51
survey of, 36–38
working with administrators, 51
working with faculty, 50
as workshop facilitators, 187
S-LCE scholar-practitioner, xvi, 1, 52
analysis approaches for, 5
communication plan of, 259
identities of, 3
reader reflections for, 3
role in partnerships and reciprocity, 251–52
S-LCE stakeholders, 40
administrators and, 44
CES and, 42
contexts for, 41, 45–49, 50
CPs and, 44–45
expectations of, 207
factors to consider, 53
faculty and, 42, 50
faculty competencies and, 53–54
students and, 43, 50–51
SLOs. *See* student learning outcomes
social capital, 163–64
social justice, xvi, 17, 48, 160, 165, 170, 234
social learning framework, 151
social media, 93–94
social networks, 296
SoE. *See* scholarship of engagement

Sorcinelli, M. D., 85, 179, 181, 183, 188
SoTL. *See* scholarship of teaching and learning
staffing, xviii, 132
stakeholders. *See* S-LCE stakeholders
Stoecker, Randy, 14
storytelling, 71
strategic partnership models, 252
strategic planning, 60, 74, 173, 222, 231–32, 296
strengths, weaknesses, opportunities, and threats (SWOT), 88
stress-strain relationship, 212
student learning, xv
 barriers to, 208
 class size and, 208–9
 ED emphasizing, 188
 empathy and, 86
 faculty and, 60
 faculty development models and, 86–87
 faculty-student partnerships, 101–2
 FLOs and, 86
 in Georgia College & State University case study, 122
 impact of Marquette University case study, 172
 individualized and systematic approaches to, 208–9
 lifelong, 255
 paradigms for, 254–56
 self-directed approach, 290
 S-LCE stakeholders, professionals and, 43, 50–51
 student culture and, 236
 support centers, 91
student learning outcomes (SLOs), 86–87, 299
study abroad programs, 91
subject-centered curriculum, 292
SWOT. *See* strengths, weaknesses, opportunities, and threats
syllabus assessment, 168–70

systematic approach to student learning, 208–9

talent and development centers, 91
tangible culture in ED, 186, 189
teaching, 13. *See also* scholarship of teaching and learning
 CTE, 141, 153
 CTL, 170, 183
 FLOs for, 295
 Journal on Centers for Teaching and Learning, 276
 lens 1 transformative approach to, 290, 293–95
 MERLOT, 277
 paradigms for, 254–56
 roundtables, 228
 teachable moments, 294–95
Teaching Community: A Pedagogy of Hope (hooks), 13
teamwork, 204–5, 214–15, 218
 in learning environment design, 211
technology transfer, 256
tenure, 28, 69, 70, 103, 235
 coeducator model and, 255
 at CSUSM, 256
 Tenure Team Initiative on Public Scholarship, 72
 University of Central Florida case study and, 177
Tew, W. M., 29
Third Century Initiative, 308n2
third-space professionals, 9
Thomas Ehrlich Civically Engaged Faculty Award, 96
threshold concepts
 evolving to transformative approach with, 287–307
 nature of, 288
tiered faculty development, xviii
top down change, 101, 235, 297
transformational leadership theory, 55
transformative approach

building on faculty development, 284
CEPs and, 285–86
conclusion, 307
evolving toward with threshold concepts, 287–307
lens 1 to teaching and learning, 290, 293–95
lens 2 to institutional culture, 295–99
lens 3 to knowledge generation and application, 299–303
lens 4 to community partnerships, 303–6
lens 5 to faculty development, 306–7
moving S-LCE toward, 285–87
for S-LCE, 283–87
transformative experiences
articulating, 9
as catalysts, 9–10
from narrative inquiry, 7–10
transformative learning theory, 8, 34
transpersonal research, 4
Trayner, B., 151
Tryon, Elizabeth A., 14
Twitter, 93
Tyler, J. A., 2

The Unheard Voices: Community Organizations and Service Learning (Stoecker and Tryon), 14
universal instructional design (UID)
in ESP case study, 218
principles of, 215
S-LCE design and, 213–14
University of Central Florida case study, 246
challenges in, 176–77
competitive application process in, 175
design and implementation of, 173–76
faculty compensation in, 175

faculty-driven programming in, 174–75
overview, 173
SL in, 173–74, 176
SoTL in, 175–76
sustainability through connections with initiatives and values, 176
tenure and, 177
workshops in, 174–75, 177
University of Florida, 73
University of Massachusetts, 232
University of New Mexico, 73
University of North Carolina-Greensboro, 73
University of Northern Colorado, 73
University of Northern Florida, 73
University of Northern Iowa, 73
University of San Francisco case study
CEL focus, 141–45
challenges and strengths of, 153
context and goals of, 141
CTE in, 141, 153
design of, 141–42
implementation, 142–43
Leo T. McCarthy Center for Public Service and the Common Good, 141, 246
outcomes of, 143–45
overview, 140
publications of, 142–44
SL in, 141
workshops in, 141–42, 144
University of South Africa, 73
University of the Free State, 73

values
authenticity as subtheme, 11, 12
community as subtheme, 12, 13
constituting inner landscape, 10
curiosity as subtheme, 11, 12
education as subtheme, 11, 12, 13
justice as subtheme, 12, 13
from narrative inquiry, 7–8, 10–13
qualities or arenas of, 11

Vanderbilt University, 73
Van Hise, Charles, 61
Viray, S., 7
Virginia Commonwealth University, 94
virtual culture in ED, 186, 188
Vogel, A. L., 231, 233–34
volunteerism, 91, 126, 187, 246, 252
Vygotsky, L. S., 151

Wade, A., 39, 53
Ward, K., 228
websites, 92
Wenger, E., 151
What? So What? Now What? reflection model, 170
Where's the Learning in Service-Learning? (Eyler and Giles), 92
Whitchurch, C., 2, 9
White savior complex, 123
Widener University, 73
The Wisconsin Idea (McCarthy), 61
workshops, 1, 195
   CEPs in, 291
   on CES, 265
   course design, 284
   CPs and, 51, 98, 246
   critical reflection in, 294
   at CSUSM, 257
   developing and delivering, 55
   facilitators, 29, 187, 233, 284

faculty development, 28, 37, 50, 236, 257
   in Georgia College & State University case study, 120–21
   in Indiana University-Purdue University Indianapolis case study, 147–48
   institutes from, 99, 100
   instructional, 85
   in Marquette University case study, 166
   in Pacific University case study, 227, 229
   promoting S-LCE, 296
   roundtables as, 104
   short-term programs, 90, 96–97
   single-standing, 75
   in University of Central Florida case study, 174–75, 177
   in University of San Francisco case study, 141–42, 144
Wright, M., 138

Young, C. A., 233
Young, D. A., 233

ZDP. *See* zone of proximal development
Zinn, L. M., 294
Zlotkowski, E., 36, 38–39
zone of proximal development (ZDP), 151–52

to locate the right individuals on campus; and addresses issues of mission, expectations for roles, tasks, training, supervision, and evaluation that can be fraught with miscommunication and misunderstanding. Most importantly it provides a model for achieving full reciprocity in what can be an unbalanced relationship between community and campus partners so that all stakeholders can derive the maximum benefit from their collaboration.

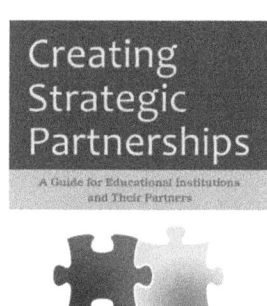

Creating Strategic Partnerships

A Guide for Educational Institutions and Their Partners

Pamela L. Eddy and Marilyn J. Amey

Foreword by Debra D. Bragg

"Partnerships are essential for the advancement of higher education in the twenty-first century. This book is a solid resource for institutional leaders seeking to develop and sustain partnerships, especially those designed to enhance student success."—**Michelle Asha Cooper**, *Institute for Higher Education Policy*

This book serves as a guide to the successful implementation of partnerships. It provides the context and tools for readers who are responding to the increasing demands of policymakers, funders, and institutional leaders to use partnerships to address local, state, and federal issues; achieve external mandates; meet public or internal agendas; or pursue international collaborations.

22883 Quicksilver Drive
Sterling, VA 20166-2019

Subscribe to our e-mail alerts: www.Styluspub.com

Also available from Stylus

Publicly Engaged Scholars

Next Generation Engagement and the Future of Higher Education

Edited by Margaret A. Post, Elaine Ward, Nicholas V. Longo, and John Saltmarsh

Foreword by Timothy K. Eatman

Afterword by Peter Levine

"*Publicly Engaged Scholars* is a much-needed look at the future of higher education as more of the public, increasingly diverse in every way, pushes for more of the academy to engage in high-impact scholarship, collaborate broadly, and be a locus of democratic practice and educator of democratic citizens. . . . This is an exciting time, and this volume pulls us enthusiastically into that future." —*Nancy Cantor*, *Chancellor, Rutgers University-Newark*

The scholars featured in this book make the case for public scholarship and argue that, in order to strengthen the democratic purposes of higher education for a viable future that is relevant to the needs of a changing society, we must recognize and support new models of teaching and research and the need for fundamental changes in the core practices, policies, and cultures of the academy.

Community Partner Guide to Campus Collaborations

Enhance Your Community by Becoming a Co-Educator With Colleges and Universities

Christine M. Cress, Stephanie T. Stokamer, and Joyce P. Kaufman

This guide offers insights and strategies to leverage student learning and community empowerment for the benefit of both parties. Recognizing both the possibilities and the pitfalls of community-campus collaborations, it demystifies the often confusing terminology of education; explains how

(Continues on preceding page)